10ᵗʰ International Architecture Exhibition
Cities. Architecture and Society

Cities
Architecture and Society

la Biennale di Venezia

10. Mostra Internazionale di Architettura

Fondazione
La Biennale di Venezia

Friends of La Biennale
Friends of La Biennale is an independent,
international, non-party initiative, aimed at
public or private companies and associations.
The funds collected will be used to support
the activities and programmes of La Biennale.
Companies and bodies (in the person of their
presidents and managing directors) can
join the initiative. The invitation is also for
individuals, on the bases of their competence
in the areas in which La Biennale works and
their specific cultural, academic and political
interests in Italy and abroad.

Founding members

Assicurazioni Generali
Antoine Bernheim, *president*

Edizione Holding
Gilberto Benetton, *president*

Participating members

Colussi
Angelo Colussi, *president*

Gruppo Coin
Stefano Beraldo, *managing director*

Porsche Italia
Loris Casadei, *general manager*

RaiCinema
Giancarlo Leone, *managing director*

Thanks to Friends of La Biennale
for the support to the activities.

10th International Architecture Exhibition
Cities. Architecture and Society

Director
Richard Burdett

Manager
Renato Quaglia

Administrative secretariat
Stefania Guerra
Maria Bruschi

Organizing coordination
Rita Bertoni
Paolo Cimarosti

Participating countries Responsible exhibition venues
Roberto Rosolen

Collateral events, jury and workshop organization
Paolo Scibelli

with Chiara Costa

Public promotion and didactics activity
Martina Flaborea

Arabella Adamo
Fabiana Causin
Lucia De Manincor

Relations with Partner
Micol Saleri

Workshop curator
Guido Martinotti

Coordinator Learning from Cities project
Francesco Garofalo

Exhibition content development
Sarah Ichioka
(coordination)

Spatial data research (London School of Economics/Urban Age)
Bruno Moser
(coordination)

Miguel Kanai
Adegbola Ojo
Andres Tacsir
Jorge Vera-Garcia
Megan Worthington

Film/video project manager
Cassim Shepard
(editing and supervision)

Michael Ichioka
(sound assistant)
Paul Bercovitch
(sound editor)

Installation concept
Cibic & Partners
Project by
Aldo Cibic
Luigi Marchetti

Project managers
Gian Luca Poggi
Roberta Sartori
Luigi Fumagalli

Art direction and exhibition graphic design
FRAGILE
Mario Trimarchi
Andrea Plenter
Pamela Visconti
Alessandro Boscarino
Marco Miglio
Elena Riva
Julia Maquieira
Luisa Vozza
Chiara Poletti
Chiara Banchini

Art direction and communication graphic design
Dario and Fabio Zannier

Rescape
Neutral

Christian Grou
Tapio Snellman
Cristina Liao
Michael Castellana

Mobility studies
Systematica

Fabio Casiroli
Davide Boazzi

Picture research
Mika Burdett
Ji Yoon Moon
Emily Smith
Valentina Vecchio

Film archive
John Smith, BBC Worldwide
Alan Yentob, BBC
Claire Gould and Kate
  Warner, BBC Motion
  Gallery
Stella Waltemade and Lluis
  Ruscalleda, Footage Farm
Daisy Njoku, Human
  Studies Film Archive—
  Smithsonian Institution
  Museum Support Center,
  Washington D.C.
James Kearney, Film
  Images, London

Exhibition texts translation
Manuela Crea
Floriana Pagano

Cities of Stone
Section of the
10th International
Architecture Exhbition
promoted by the project
Sensi Contemporanei

Curator
Claudio D'Amato Guerrieri

Organizing coordination
Matteo De Vittor

Franco Defilippis
Giuseppe Fallacara
Michele Montemurro

Installation concept
Cerardo Cejas
La Biennale di Venezia Servizi SpA
Enzo Magris
La Biennale di Venezia Servizi SpA

Website editor
Dario Daddabbo
Marco Orsini

Photographic campaign
Guido Petriccioli

Graphic design
Nunzio Perrone

City-Port
Section of the
10th International
Architecture Exhbition
promoted by the project
Sensi Contemporanei

Curator
Rinio Bruttomesso

Organizing coordination
Francesca Montorio

General coordination
Marta Moretti

Portus Prize coordination
Paola Pierotti

Installation coordination
Nicola Tonutti

International relations
Maria Giulia da Sacco
Mara Vittori

International section consultant
Alessandra Badami

Relations with italian cities
Oriana Giovinazzi

Portus Prize secretariat
Paola Vitiello

Curator secretariat
Federica Marafante

Secretariat
Cinzia Mauri
Antonella Ruggiero

Installation concept
Davide Testi
La Biennale di Venezia Servizi SpA

**Palazzo Forcella De Seta
City-Port. Maps for New
Urban Routes**
Studio Italo Rota & Partners

**Sant' Erasmo
City-Port. Great South
City-Port. Palermo,
Mediterraneo**
Alessandra Raso,
Luca Poncellini,
Matteo Raso,
Stefano Testa / CLIOSTRAAT

**EXPA Galleria di
Architettura
City-Port. Portus
Architecture Prize**
Tiziano Di Cara
and Giuseppe Romano

Portus Prize Website
Mario Caruso
AgoràMed

Italian Pavilion
Commissioner
Pio Baldi

Curator
Franco Purini
with Nicola Marzot
Margherita Petranzan
Livio Sacchi

Installation project
Franco Purini
with Massimiliano De Meo
Carlo Meo Colombo
Franco Puccetti
Valter Tronchin

Organizing coordination
Renato Quaglia

Installation management
Angelo Boscolo

Structures and security management
Enzo Magris

Film
Marta Francocci

Direction
Giorgio De Finis

Scientific advisor
Franco Purini
Livio Sacchi

Le Città Nuove
Franco Purini
Livio Sacchi
Laboratorio di Disegno della
  Facoltà di Architettura di
  Pescara
Emiliano Auriemma
Giovanni Caffio
Alessandro Luigini
Massimiliano Mazzetta
Verusca Collicchio
Fabrizio De Rosa
Tatiana Mariani
Francesco Martelli
Roberto Potenza
Fabrizio Susi

Webcam
Marco Brizzi
Furio Barzon

Vema
Masterplan
Franco Purini
with
Francesco Menegatti

Model
DIAPREM, Facoltà di
  Architettura di Ferrara

Logistic technical services
Cristiano Frizzele

Nicola Bon
Lucio Ramelli
Pino Simeoni
Maurizio Urso

Insurance and transport of works
Alessandra Durand de la Penne
Sandra Montagner

Matteo Liguigli

Angela Bianco
Luana Lovisetto
Elena Seghetti

Purchasing
Fabio Pacifico
Marianna Ferrazzuto

La Biennale di Venezia Servizi SpA

Exhibition concept
Manuela Lucà Dazio

Massimiliano Bigarello
Nicola Ragazzini
Silvia Catami

Logistic, facilities and security
Piero Novello
Mascia Pavon

Organizing services
Angelo Boscolo
Maurizio Celoni
Elisabetta Parmesan
Jessica Giassi
Alessandro Mezzalira
Cristiana Scavone

Technology and information sistems
Andrea Bonaldo
Michele Schiavon
Leonardo Viale

Vernissage press room installation concept
Elena Lingeri

Communications
Giovanna Usvardi

Assistant to Communications
Veronica Mozzetti-Monterumici

Communications administrative secretariat
Cristina Lion

Head of press office Architecture
Alessandra Santerini

Assistants to press office and accreditation
Elena Casadoro
Lucia Veronesi

with Sara Chiotto and Giovanni Sgrignuolo

Biennale press office coordination
Paolo Lughi

International press accreditation
Michela Lazzarin

Italian press accreditation
Fiorella Tagliapietra

Website
Giovanni Alberti

Publicity and graphic design office coordination
Eugenia Fiorin

Michela Mason

Lucia Toso

Maddalena Pietragnoli

Graphic realization
Alberta de Grenet
Nicola Monaco

Photographer
Giorgio Zucchiatti

Catalogue

Catalogue content development
Sarah Ichioka

Interviews
Ellis Woodman

Editorial staff
Francesca Del Puglia

Chiara Calciolari
Letizia Gullo
Stefania Ivanovich
Valentina Vecchio

Catalogue graphic design
Dario and Fabio Zannier

Fund management
Gaetano Guerci (ad interim)

Elena Croci

Francesco Di Cesare
Marzia Cervellin
with Glenda Manzetto

Events management
Gaetano Guerci (ad interim)

Elena Croci

Events management administrative secretariat
Cristina Graziussi

Protocol office and events organization
Elisa Ceri

Cristina Cinti
Daniele Maruca
Eleonora Mayerle

Daniela Dagnino Donà dalle Rose

Hospitality
Enrica Zanchetta

Laura Aimone
Zeudi Fiorasi

President and General manager's secretarial office
Daniela Barcaro
Roberta Savoldello

Valentina Baldessari

General manager staff
Sandro Vettor

Legal services
Debora Rossi

Cinzia Bernardi
Alberto Bogoni
Federica Marchiori

Human resources
Debora Rossi

Silvia Bruni
Graziano Carrer
Giovanni Drudi
Cristina Innocenti
Antonella Sfriso
Alessia Viviani

Chief Financial Office
Valentina Borsato

Martina Fiori
Bruna Gabbiato
Manuela Pelliccciolli
Cristiano Tanduo
Giorgio Vergombello
Sara Vianello
Leandro Zennaro

Special projects
Pina Maugeri

Jörn Brandmeyer
Davide Ferrante
Arianna Laurenzi

Archivio Storico delle Arti Contemporanee
Giorgio Busetto

Angelo Bacci
Maria Elena Cazzaro
Valentina Da Tos
Erica De Luigi
Lia Durante
Roberta Fontanin
Giuliana Fusco
Michele Mangione
Giovanna Pasini
Antonia Possamai
Adriana Scalise
Michela Stancescu

Catalogue production
Marsilio Editori

Editing and layout
in.pagina srl
Mestre-Venezia

Copy editing and translations
David Graham

Photolithography
Fotolito Veneta
San Martino Buonalbergo, Verona

Press
Offset Print Veneta
Verona

Binding
Legatoria Barizza
Loreggia, Padova

© 2006 Fondazione
La Biennale
Ca' Giustianian,
San Marco 1364/a
30124 Venezia
www.labiennale.org

First published in the United States of America in 2006 by Rizzoli International Publications, Inc.
300 Park Avenue South
New York, NY 10010
www.rizzoliusa.com

ISBN-10: 0-8478-2879-4
ISBN-13: 978-0-8478-2879-1
Library of Congress
Control Number:
2006925129

First edition: September 2006
2006 2007 2008 2009 /
10 9 8 7 6 5 4 3 2 1

10th International Architecture Exhibition
Cities

The 2006 edition of the International Architecture Exhibition – the tenth – proposes rather than an exhibition of (models and examples of) architecture, a discourse on the consequences and possibilities of architecture applied to urban and meta-urban systems: the world-city. A discourse on architecture offering interpretations of themes closely related to questions of civil coexistence, the obligation to plan the future and its proposals for changing the way of living in the present.

The Exhibition directed by Richard Burdett is entitled *Cities. Architecture and Society*, and focuses on the key themes currently faced by urban and meta-urban agglomerations with a population of over three or four million (the new global cities). The Exhibition analyses aspects that have become critical today: the interaction between city, architecture and inhabitants; the role of architects and architecture in the creation of democratic and sustainable urban contexts; the politics of intervention, and the actions of governing and developing.

At the Corderie dell'Arsenale the urban experiences of some of the most emblematic cities on four continents are represented: Shanghai, Mumbai and Tokyo in Asia; Caracas, Mexico City, Bogotá, São Paulo, Los Angeles and New York in the Americas; Johannesburg, Cairo and Istanbul in Africa and the Mediterranean area; London, Barcelona, Berlin and Milan-Turin in Europe. In the Padiglione Italia at the Giardini, some international research institutes present models and projects on an urban and meta-urban scale. Some specialized publishers present projects and points of view on contemporary and historical architectural planning. The traditional collateral events will this year be flanked by three partners' initiatives. The historic presence of over 50 countries with their own national pavilions will be accompanied by a workshop with some of the Mayors of major Italian and international cities, providing an opportunity for dialogue and direct contact which La Biennale, together with its partners, intends offering on the level of experiences, models and policies for growth.

The Exhibition will, once it closes, present a "manifesto for twenty-first century cities" to be proposed to those governing or participating in the government of cities and the complex systems regulating their rhythms and development.

With a new project that saw the involvement not only of the Biennale, but also of the Ministero dell'Economia (Dipartimento delle Politiche di Sviluppo e Coesione) and the Ministero dei Beni e delle Attività Culturali - DARC, many contemporary art exhibitions and training, study and promotional activities in 2003 and 2004 were held in seven regions of the South of Italy and their main cities. Following the renewed presentation of the 9th International Architecture Exhibition, "Metamorph" in Reggio Calabria in December 2005, the discussion on architectural consequences and possibilities finds concrete (and often urgent) application opportunities in Italy's southern regions, in redefining urban trading centres (within the relation *City-Port*, the same of the exhibitions curated by Rinio Bruttomesso), as also in the projects for restoring the Italian and Mediterranean coastal landscape (in the *Cities of Stone* exhibitions curated by Claudio d'Amato Guerrieri).

The inauguration of a section of the 10th International Architecture Exhibition in Palermo (the *City-Port* exhibition), assumes a further value tied to the function that La Biennale di Venezia has wished and succeeded in taking on, in recent years, offering all of its own skills and cultural energies to the Country and its strategies for development.

With the new Italian Pavilion (which will be inaugurated this year at the Arsenale in Venice by the Biennale and DARC), and the exhibition project that Franco Purini is dedicating to a future city (possibly to be founded between Verona and Mantua), the presence of an exhibition that is explicitly representative of the Italian architectural culture (this year and in 2008; in 2007 for art) allows to respond to the expectations of the entire national system, now at last on the same level as the opportunities available in other Countries.

Moreover, it makes it possible to complete, with a further and different approach, the subject of the city that this 10th International Architecture Exhibition brings into focus on various levels and scales, and to be able to declare, once more and as in the case of other events in the disciplines covered by the Biennale, that only various viewpoints enable us to start understanding the present.

10. Mostra
Internazionale
di Architettura

Cities. Architecture and Society

Director
Richard Burdett
Venice
10 September – 19 November 2006

Cities of Stone

Curator
Claudio D'Amato Guerrieri
Venice
10 September – 19 November 2006
Section of the 10th International
Architecture Exhibition promoted by

with

REGIONE PUGLIA
Assessorato Sviluppo Economico

City-Port

Curator
Rinio Bruttomesso
Palermo
15 October 2006 – 14 January 2007
Section of the 10th International
Architecture Exhibition promoted by

with

Regione Siciliana
Assessorato dei Beni Culturali,
Ambientali e della Pubblica Istruzione

and with

Città di Palermo

Autorità
Portuale
di Palermo

Italian Pavilion

Curator
Franco Purini
Commissioner
Pio Baldi
Venice
10 September – 19 November 2006

For the support of 10th International Architecture Exhibition Fondazione La Biennale di Venezia thanks

Main Partner

Partner

TARGETTI  Automobile Club d'Italia

Sponsor

GENERALI Deutsche Bank

TELESPAZIO DIGITALGLOBE MOROSO fantoni
A Finmeccanica / Alcatel Company

ARUP

Technical sponsors

UNITED COLORS OF BENETTON. flex ART IN EUROPE
DISPLAYING YOUR IDEAS GUIDING YOUR WAY

Sponsors **Cities of Stone**

riviplast
PROTOTYPING SERVICES

Sponsors **City-Port**

ANCE Palermo
Associazione Costruttori
Edili ed Affini di
Palermo e Provincia
한국토지공사
KOREA LAND CORPORATION
MINISTERIO DE FOMENTO Puertos del Estado FORMICA

Sponsors **Italian Pavilion**

Collegio Costruttori Edili
ANCE Mantova
CONFINDUSTRIA Mantova
BAM Banca Agricola
Mantovana
GRUPPOMPS
Ceramic Tiles of Italy

Introduction

Davide Croff
President of La Biennale di Venezia

Now, in 2006, the third year of activity for the Fondazione that directs the Biennale di Venezia, we can claim that the Architecture Section is the main organizational change, and symbol of the new aims of the Fondazione itself.

The main features of this new Biennale are the responsibility and centrality of its thematic choices, the opening of the Italian Pavilion in the Tese delle Vergini, the two epoch-making exhibition events on the South of Italy, for the first time presented simultaneously in Venice and Palermo, the intense programme of international conferences and workshops and the propositional presence of important private partners. It is a Biennale that intends spending its second century taking new roads, intensifying and radicalising the initiatives undertaken both in and out of Venice rather than simply resting on its past.

It is no mere chance that the emblem of this new direction is the Architecture Section. Despite it concerning one of the oldest artistic disciplines, it is a very young part of the more than a century old Biennale: this is the 10th International Architecture Exhibition in a quarter of a century. But it has mainly been distinguished by its successful provocation, its courageous ability to find new exhibition spaces and new organizational formulas, as is widely the case again this year, gradually earning the international acclaim both of the critics and the public (whose numbers at the last two presentations exceeded the respectable figure of 100,000 over its two month season).

We briefly recall that it was the fundamental exhibition La presenza del passato (The presence of the past), directed by Paolo Portoghesi, that in 1980 inaugurated the new section on contemporary architecture.

Organized at the Arsenale, the exhibition also had the merit of reopening one of the oldest and most interesting spaces of the Serenissima, an architectural heritage

subsequently further restored by the Biennale and gradually returned to Venice and the world. Other pioneering initiatives were taken in the '70s along the way, such as the A proposito del Mulino Stucky (About the Mulino Stucky) conference on the possible ways to use this space, which is now finally being restored, and the celebrated and much quoted Teatro del Mondo (World Theatre) presented in winter 1979-1980 by Aldo Rossi at the Punta della Dogana, another place still at the centre of ongoing debates on its possible use.

These are just some of the more significant examples of our history that it is right to recall in presenting this year's news, because it is precisely with the open, innovative spirit of those initiatives and their function as a stimulus that we want to reconnect.

We firstly emphasize the reason for the theme chosen by the Biennale for this 10th Exhibition: *Cities. Architecture and Society*.

The theme is intended to confirm the Biennale's wish to aim for a highly legible, international formula, to study a critical aspect in contemporary society that now directly affects most of the planet's population and that for a decade has engaged town planners: the changes going on in the physical and social morphology of the land and of urban agglomerates.

The Biennale invited one of the leading urbanism experts in the world, the Englishman Richard Burdett, to direct the 10th Exhibition around this theme. We sincerely thank him for the enthusiasm and commitment with which he has directed the exhibition, presenting the urban experiences of 16 major cities on four continents. It will stay in the memory of specialists and the public for its scientific rigour, its great expository clarity and its concrete approach to the new urban centres' problems of governance.

On the logistical innovation and cultural front, the Biennale is for the first time opening an Italian Pavilion. It will this year be devoted to highlighting contemporary

Italian architecture, curated by Franco Purini. The pavilion will then be used for contemporary Italian art during the editions of the International Art Exhibition. This 1000-square-metre space in the first Tesa delle Vergini at the Arsenale, in the extraordinary multipurpose buildings that will house the Biennale of the future, is the result of collaboration between the Biennale and the Ministero per i Beni e le Attività Culturali – DARC. Building on the Biennale's great tradition of research and of finding new talent, it will make a decisive contribution to the international circulation and growth of our architects and artists. The Italian Pavilion thus completes the picture of national participation: 50 at this 10th International Architecture Exhibition, all of whom we want to thank, because since the origins of the Biennale they have represented its absolute originality and an incalculable exhibition and organisational strength.

The other important news is the structure of the exhibition itself. It is being organised in several sections and venues that are intended to be distinct but complementary.

The changes in architecture and town planning in the regions of South Italy are the focus of two exhibition events: one in Venice, at the Artiglierie dell'Arsenale, *Città di Pietra* (*Cities of Stone*), curated by Claudio D'Amato Guerrieri; the other in Palermo, *Città–Porto* (*City-Port*), curated by Rinio Bruttomesso, which will open in October and close in January 2007, thus extending the normal timing and locations of the Architecture Biennale.

These two events reflect the constituent form and aims of Sensi contemporanei, the project promoted since 2003 by the Biennale, the Ministero per i Beni e le Attività Culturali – DARC, and the Ministero dell'Economia e delle Finanze – DPS, for the development of contemporary art and architecture in the Italian South.

Why have the Biennale and the two ministries again joined forces this year to organise two initiatives on the South at the same time as the 10th International Architecture Exhibition?

Firstly as a matter of principle, to find new ways of meeting the Biennale's moral obligation to disseminate its knowledge and initiatives.

We think that with two complex events of original quality arising from the Biennale's experience in the South over these years we can suggest the advisability of new and interesting programming.

Secondly, but this is perhaps a corollary of the first consideration, we show how the cities and regions of Italy can even more unite to achieve common aims, also in terms of cultural development.

The Biennale is trying to go beyond a traditional condition with these initiatives, to take on new roles. In particular, we are sure of the interest that will be aroused by the main exhibition. But having noted the enthusiasm for previous Sensi contemporanei activities, which saw a solid increase in numbers, we trust in the innovation and success of the two exhibitions on the architecture of the South, together illuminated by the Mediterranean light of Venice and Palermo, and therefore ideally drawn together.

This is also because, as Le Corbusier said, architecture must above all be 'forms assembled in light'.

Introduction

Richard Burdett
Director
10th International Architecture Exhibition

The 10th International Architecture Exhibition, *Cities. Architecture and Society* celebrates cities the very year that half the world's population has become urban. A century ago only 10% of the people of the planet lived in cities, and, according to the United Nations, this number is set to rise to 75% by 2050. Understanding the impacts of this growth on people and on the environment has become a necessity, as the links between architecture and society become both more complex and more fragile. How we chose to shape our cities, buildings and public spaces – as architects, urbanists and city makers – will determine how we respond to the challenges of climate change as well as addressing human rights, justice and dignity for the billions of people who move to cities in search of work and opportunity. Addressing this question is the purpose of the 10th International Architecture Exhibition of La Biennale di Venezia.

With contributions from over 50 countries exhibited in the national pavilions – including the new Italian Pavilion featuring an exhibition curated by Franco Purini - and the Padiglione Italia in the Giardini della Biennale, the core exhibitions at the Arsenale and collateral events throughout Venice, this International Architecture Exhibition provides a truly global perspective of the interactions between urban form and urban society across the world today. Volume I of the catalogue describes the contents the main exhibition in the Corderie in the Arsenale, focussing on world cities and city-regions as well as the urban research projects by invited academic and professional institutions displayed in the Padiglione Italia. Volume II contains details of the *Cities of Stone* exhibition at the Artiglierie as well as the *City-Port* exhibition which for the first time ever brings La Biennale to Palermo – both sections of the 10th International Architecture Exhibition promoted by the 'Sensi Contemporanei' project.

Within the Corderie, *Cities. Architecture and Society* focuses on 16 cities and urbanized areas, a group selected to ensure a degree of consistency in size, broad geographical distribution, and demonstration of different types of urban change. Accounts of these cities form the central content of this volume with essays and detailed analysis of their social, political and spatial attributes, developed by the LSE Urban Age team. In addition, an extended essay by Saskia Sassen on why cities matter in a globalizing economy is complemented by interviews with leading architects, commentators, artists and urbanists exploring the connections between the making of architecture and the making of cities. The final section *Architectures for Cities* addresses the question of whether good architecture makes good cities. It features selected projects by established and emerging architects that respond to the social changes occurring in these cities. As such, the projects provide a partial but global cross-section of architecture's potential as a social condenser that can transform people's lives.

In addition to my personal acknowledgements, I would like to recognize the enormous energy and commitment of all the commissioners, curators and collaborators who have worked so hard to respond to the theme of *Cities. Architecture and Society*. I offer my thanks to the many sponsors who have contributed to the special partners' projects and other initiatives which have made this exhibition possible.

Director's acknowledgements

Richard Burdett
September 2006

The *Cities. Architecture and Society* exhibition would not have happened without the involvement of over one hundred people listed overleaf – self-motivated teams in each city who worked incessantly to produce material for the Biennale, driven by a collective passion for cities which we celebrate in Venice. In particular, though, I want to thank three colleagues based at the London School of Economics without whose personal commitment nothing at all would have ever happened at my end: Sarah Ichioka, who tirelessly travelled across the world and helped me every inch of the way to shape the intellectual content and structure of the exhibition and publications, including this catalogue which she co-edited; Bruno Moser, who reinvented himself as a specialist on every possible source of data on cities and generator of sublime images; and Cassim Shepard, whose thoughtful eye has translated human experiences of sixteen cities on screen. I have relied on a 'tribe of urbanists' - Richard Sennett, Saskia Sassen, Richard Rogers, Jerry Frug, Deyan Sudjic, Josep Acebillo, Jacques Herzog, Guido Martinotti, Andy Altman and Norman Foster, amongst others – for their insights on cities. The strong elements of the exhibition come from them, the weaknesses are all mine. The approach of an interdisciplinary analysis of cities, which links urban form to urban society, comes from the pioneering work carried out at the Urban Age project, organised by the LSE with Deutsche Bank's Alfred Herrhausen Society, a programme of conferences and investigations on of six of the cities included in the Venice Biennale. Without Wolfgang Nowak and the AHS support of this ongoing project, much of the material gathered in this exhibition simply would not exist. Guido Martinotti took on the task of exposing the architectural community to profound social thinking by curating the workshops for the Biennale. Other colleagues at the LSE have provided input and support, including Philip Rode and Miguel Kanai (who doubled as co-author and Hispanic-Japanese interpreter) together with a team of researchers led by Bruno Moser. Mika Burdett lived the intensity of the one year journey and contributed in many more ways than advising on the selection of images, supported by researchers Emily Smith and Ji Yoon Moon. Aldo Cibic and Luigi Marchetti and their colleagues at Cibic & Partners held my hand throughout in conceiving the experience of the show, and Mario Trimarchi with his team at Fragile and the Neutral team made me rethink how to communicate to the Biennale's diverse public. John Smith and Alan Yentob allowed us to use archive footage from the BBC archives. Ultimately, I would have been unable to achieve anything without the generous financial contributions from all the sponsors and wish to single out Luigi and Stefania Zunino and the Gruppo Risanamento for their patronage. The large and multi-talented Venice Biennale team, led by Renato Quaglia, with special input from Rita Bertoni and Manuela Lucà Dazio, have been all-too tolerant of my delays and indecisions, and helped steer this large urban tanker to its home in Venice. I am indebted to them all.

Acknowledgments

For the collaboration to the realization of the 10th International Architecture Exhibition
La Fondazione La Biennale di Venezia with Richard Burdett thank

Ministero della Difesa,
Marina Militare di Venezia
Ammiraglio Div. Ernesto
Muliere, Comandante
Istituto Studi Militari e
Presidio Marina Militare
Comandante di Vascello
Francesco Carlo Bottoni,
Istituto Studi Militari e
Presidio Marina Militare
Comandante di Vascello
Cristiano Patrese,
Istituto Studi Militari e
Presidio Marina Militare

Ministero delle Finanze,
Agenzia del Demanio,
sede di Venezia

Ministero delle Finanze,
Circoscrizione Doganale
Venezia II, Venezia Salute
e Venezia Marittima

Soprintendenza per
i Beni Ambientali e
Architettonici di Venezia

Regione Veneto

Autorità Portuale di
Venezia

Capitaneria di Porto

Barcelona
Barcelona Regional
Josep Acebillo
Eva Serra
Joana Llinas

Iñigo Bujedo Aguirre
Gabriele Basilico
Beth Galí
Roger Gual
Manuel Huerga
Jordi Todó/Tavisa

Berlin
Barbara Hoidn
Wilfried Wang

Senatsverwaltung für
Stadtentwicklung,
Berlin

Jens Bisky
Robert Fenz
Philipp Meuser
Lena Mueller
Markus Rosenthal
Paolo Rosselli
Anja Schlamann
Wendy Taylor
Judith Utz

Bogotá
Por el Pais que Queremos
Foundation
Oscar Edmundo Diaz
Enrique Penalosa
Eduardo Plata
Juan Camilo Macias
Carolina Rogelio

Grupo Esperienze Urbane
Simone Grobberio
Guido Robazza

Diana Barco
Claudia Bermudez
Lorenzo Castro
Adriana Cobo Corey
Alvaro Duran
Jose Roberto de Andrade
Filho
Felipe González
Alicia Naranjo
José Camilo Santamaría
Armando Silva
Giovanna Silva

Cairo
Seif El Rashidi
Maria Golia
Centre d'Etudes et
de Documentation
Economiques,
Juridiques et Sociales
(CEDEJ)
Halla Bayoumi

Contemporary Image
Collective
Christian Grou
Magdi Habachi
Linx Productions for the
Aga Khan Development
Network
Gary Otte
Mohamed El Sawy
Heiner Schmitt
Randa Shaath
Yahia Shawkat
Tapio Snellman
Nick Warner
Dario Zannier

Caracas
Urban Think Tank
Alfredo Brillembourg
Hubert Klumpner
Marcelo Elola
Karolina Stahl

Alcaldía del Distrito
Metropolitano de
Caracas
Hector Sanchez

Axel Capriles
Sara Muzio
Carlos Armando
Planchart
Luisa Ramírez
Art Rothfuss

Istanbul
Bilgi University
Murat Guvenç
Serhan Ada
Ayca Ince
Sevin Yildiz

Human Settlements
Association
Korhan Gumus
Elsa Mekki-Berrada

Instanbul Metropolitan
Planning and Urban
Design Center
Huseyin Kaptan
M. Sinan Özden

Emre Akay
Elif Akcali
Gabriele Basilico
Metin Cavus

Istanbul Metropolitan
Municipality
Emrah Engindeniz

Francesco Jodice
Margarete von Lupin
Andy Rice
David Rosenthal
Paolo Rosselli

Johannesburg
Lindsay Bremner

Hlakanaphila Analytics
(s21)
Michael O'Donovan

Statistics South Africa
Kevin Parry

Adam Broomberg
Oliver Chanarin
Ismail Farouk
Loanna Hoffmann
Mpethi Morojele
Mabet Van Rensburg
Ilana Ron

London
GLA Architecture &
Urbanism Unit
Eleanor Fawcett
Ben Burley
Emily Greeves
Mark Brearley
Richard Rogers
Deborah Mathieson
Alex Bax
Jamie Dean
Paul Harper
Toby Goevert

Transport for London
Isabel Dedring

Matteo Cainer
James Goggin
Jo Murtagh
Luca Paci
Deyan Sudjic
Alexander Weil

Architecture Foundation
Elias Redstone

Newbetter
Cityscape
Hayes Davidson
Richard Bryant
Paolo Rosselli

Los Angeles
University of California,
Los Angeles
Ed Soja
Ava Bromberg
Jacqueline Leavitt
Luca Martinazzoli

Jeffrey Inaba

Helen Kolikow Garber
Lars Jan
Young Sun Kim
Richard Koshalek
Thom Mayne
Nicholas Olsberg
Paul Preissner
Bas Princen
Paolo Rosselli
Michael Speaks
Jean Paul Travers
Donald J Waldie
Peter Zellner

Mexico City
Pamela Puchalski
Alejandro Hernandez

Pablo Benlliure
Dante Busquets
José Castillo
Gareth Jones
Francisco (Cisco)
Laresgoiti
Armin Linke
Enrique Martin-Moreno
Maria Moreno
Enrique Norten
Iliana Ortega-Alcazar
Scott Peterman
Juan Villoro

Milan and Turin
Stefano Boeri

Università degli Studi di
Milano-Bicocca
Guido Martinotti
Marxiano Melotti
Giovanni Oggioni

Gaia Caramellino
Filippo De Pieri

Bruna Biamino
Mario Boffi
Vincenzo Castella
Matteo Cibic
Piero Derossi
dot dot dot productions
Michele d'Ottavio
Marianna Dovidio
Davide Ferrario
Lorenzo Pallotta
Renzo Piano
Fabio Terragni

Mumbai
Urban Design Research
Institute
Rahul Mehrotra
Benita Menezes
Pankaj Joshi
Kapil Gupta

Biond Software
Milind Dalvi
Amit Dutta

Shai Heredia
Suketu Mehta
Gagan Palrecha
Sadia Shepard
Vineet Shroff
Dhiren Shukla
Jehangir Sorabjee
Rajesh Vora
Dario Zannier

New York City
Pamela Puchalski

NYC Department of City
Planning
Amanda Burden
Jennifer Posner

Princeton University
Guy Nordenson

Andy Altman

Gabriele Basilico
Richard Berenholtz
Purcell Carson
Majora Carter
Susan Fainstein
Hope Hall
Leah Meyerhoff
Alexander Weil

São Paulo
Prefeitura Municipal
de São Paulo
Helena Maria Gasparian
Adriana Telles Ribeiro

Raul Juste Lores

Universidade
de São Paulo
Regina Meyer

Carlos Calil
Rose Carmona
Giuliano Cedroni
Gustavo Cedroni
Otavio Cury
Roque Fernandes
Armin Linke
Regina Monteiro
Luiz Arthur Leirão Vieira
Milu Villela
Jacopo Crivelli Visconti

Shanghai
Qingyun Ma
Stephan Jentsch
Zheng Shiling

Olivo Barbieri
Peter Bialobrzeski
Bizart Center
Brancolini Grimaldi Arte
Contemporanea
Andrea Cavazzuti
Yung Ho Chang
Yang Fudong
Tomasz Gubernat
Sze Tsung Leong
Ann Mu
Ryan Pyle
Davide Quadrio
Paolo Rosselli
StART
Caterina Tognon Pimpini
Paola Tognon
Alexander Weil
Lu Yue

Tokyo
Atelier Bow-Wow
Momoyo Kaijima
Yoshiharu Tsukamoto

Tokyo University of
Science
Kaori Ito

Rumiko Ito

Hiroshi Ota

Mark Dytham
Tenrunobu Fujimori
Shigeru Itoh
Francesco Jodice
Miguel Kanai
Masahiro Katsuno
Marieke Kums
Naomichi Kurata
Takashi Machimura
Ryue Nishizawa
Takeo Obayashi
Miki Okabe
Akio Okamoto
John Parbury

Research Institute of
Economy, Trade and
Industry (RIETI)
Masato Hisatake
Masahiro Katsuno

Saskia Sassen
Norbert Schoerner
Kazuyo Sejima
Kimihiro Sonoda
Tomoaki Tanaka

Tokyo Metropolitan
Government
Kenichiro Kawabe

Contents

AcoruñaAdelaideAlbaceteAlcobaçaAlmadaAlmeríaAmsterdamArcipelagoEgeoAscoliPicenoAscona
BadajozBallarat**Barcelona**BaselBe'erShevaBèglesBegurBeijingBelgradeBellinzona**Berlin**Bilbao**Bogotá**
BolognaBostonBragaBraunschweigBremenBrisbaneBrnoBrusselsBucurestiBudapestBuenosAires
CádizCaenCagliari**Cairo**CalaisCambridgeCapeTown**Caracas**ChiassoChiosChongqingChonlaDoCiudad
RealClaroCoimbraCologneCórdobaDarmstadtDetroitDresdenDubayyDubrovnikDunkirkDurbanDüsseldor
EmeraldIsleFerraraFrankfurtFukuokaGandGattonGenovaGerraGambarognoGiurgiuGondolaGuadalajara
GuangzhouHakodateHaifaHalleHamburgHangzhouHellínHelsinkiHongKongIcheonIoannina**Istanbu**
IvanovoJerusalemJinHua**Johannesburg**KaiserslauternKanagawaKelerberrinKirunaKowloonKumamoto
KyotoL'HospitaletdeLlobregatLagosLasPalmasdeGranCanariaLefkosiaLeipzigLeiriaLinzLisboaLiverpool

LjubljanaLocarno**LondonLosAngeles**LouvainLaNeuveLuganoLugoLuxembourgMacau**Madrid**Manchester
MarseilleMelbourneMendrisio**MéxicoCityMilano**MinusioMontevideoMoscow**Mumbai**MunichNagano
NamurNanjingNant'ouNantesNapoliNeuchâtelNewOrleans**NewYork**NiigataNíjarNingboNovisadOita
OlotOuluPalencia**Paris**PatraPerthPescaraPoitiersPoitouCharentesPorthElizabethPorto**Praha**P'yongyang
RabatRainbowRavnaGoraReykjavíkRigaRijeka**Roma**RoncasopraAsconaRosariodelTalaRotterdam
RoubaixSanSebastiánSantaDomingoSantanderSantiago**SãoPaulo**Sevilla**Shanghai**SheffieldShizuokaSibiu
SingaporeSiracusaSkopje**Seoul**SplitStuttgart**Sydney**T'ainanT'aipeiT'bilisiTallinTarifaTartuTegnaTelAviv
ThessalonikiTirana**Tokyo**TongLi**Torino**TromsøTübingenValaeValencia**Vancouver**VeneziaVeniceVeronaVianado
CasteloVigoVilladoCondeVranceaWaggawagga**Warszawa**Wien**Xi'an**YerevanYilanYinanZaragoza**Zürich**

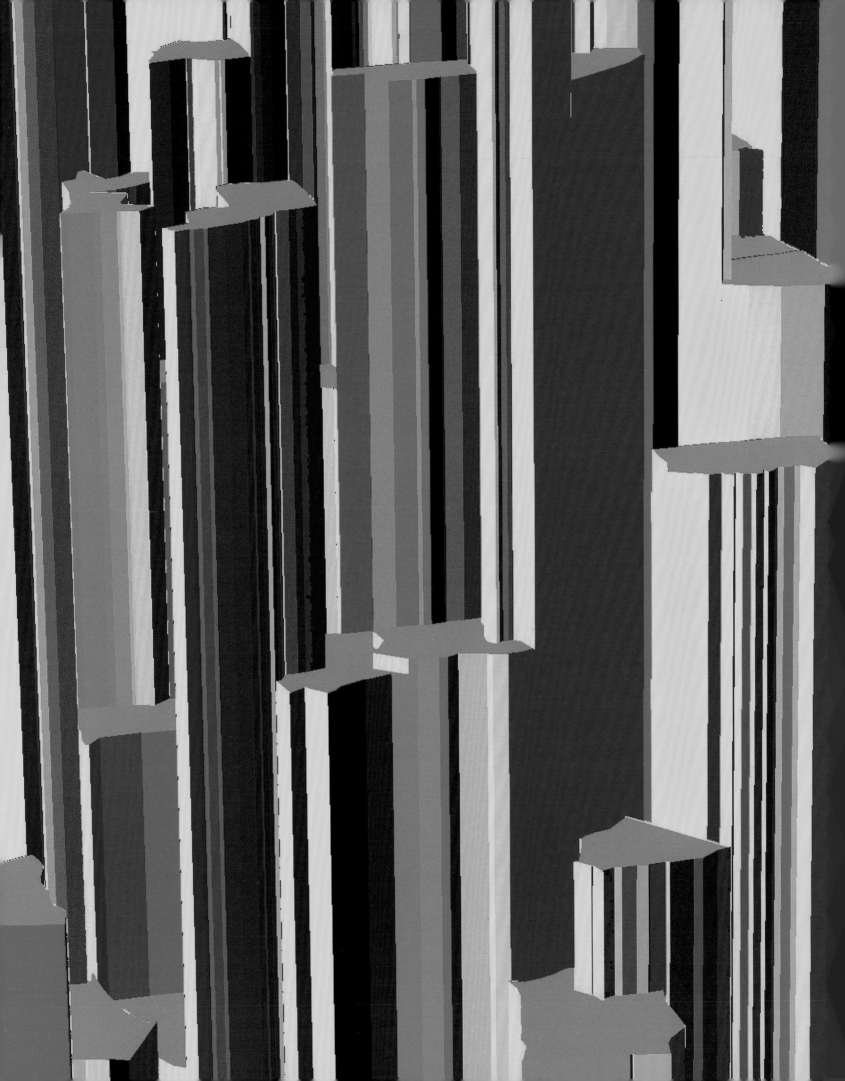

City-building in
an age of global urban
transformation

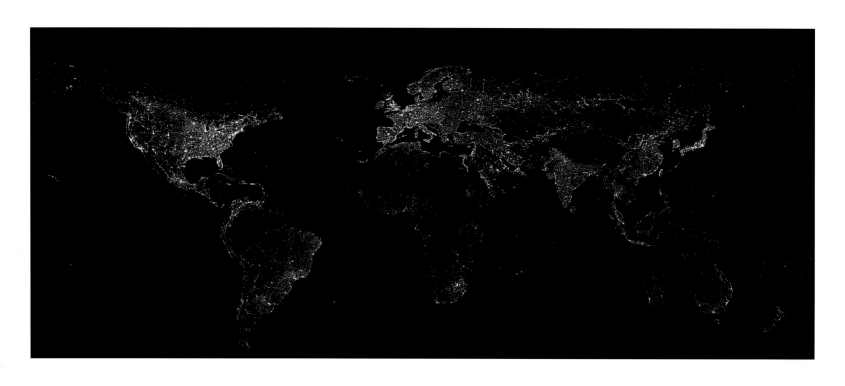

The world at night.

COURTESY MARC IMHOFF OF NASA
GSFC AND CHRISTOPHER ELVIDGE
OF NOAA NGDC. IMAGE BY CRAIG
MAYHEW AND ROBERT SIMMON,
NASA GSFC.

City-building in an age of global urban transformation

Richard Burdett with Miguel Kanai

A few decades have passed since we first became aware that the world is a single system, integrated and synergetic but also small and fragile. We now know that, for the first time in human history, the majority of people in the planet are living urban lives. Projections tell us that this trend will continue: 75% of the global population is expected to concentrate in cities by 2050 – mostly in mega cities of several million people each and massively urbanized regions stretching across countries and continents.

What does this vastness mean for both those who inhabit and those who build the city? How can the model of urbanity that has supported human existence for centuries serve us to comprehend the emerging form of 'cityness' that the new century of massive global urbanization is delivering? What is the complex relationship between urban form and city life; how to intervene and bring about positive change? These are some of the questions we seek to address in the 10th International Architecture Exhibition at La Biennale di Venezia, which features architecture from over 100 cities from across the world.

The quintessential urban paradox comprising confrontation and promise, tension and release, social cohesion and exclusion, urban wealth and intense squalor, is a profoundly spatial equation with enormous democratic potential. Ultimately, the shape we give society affects the daily lives of those who live and work in cities across the world. The creation of a small gymnasium, a cultural centre or a landscaped open space at the heart of a slum dignifies the existence of disenfranchized communities, and can fundamentally transform people's lives. As architects, planners and city-makers we engage every day in creating the very infrastructure that can either enable social interaction or become a source of exclusion and domination. By focusing on how cities of the world are changing at global and local levels, by investigating how new forms of transport and urban design can promote social justice and equity, by exploring the links between city form and sustainability and by understanding the cohesive potential of public spaces, this exhibition provides an international perspective on the social value of architecture in cities.

Imagine that we could see the entire earth from space at night time. The enormous patches and cordons of light closely mirror the world maps of urban extents and the wider human footprints associated to them. Therefore, this simulated yet powerful visualization spurs a reflection on the contemporary state of global urbanization. If we think of the concentrations of consumption of electricity as representations of human settlements, then large-scale patterns of urban development begin to take shape before our eyes. From this we see that most of Europe is criss-crossed by urban development and that a dense band of urbanization is consolidating at the core of this continent, stretching from southern England to northern Italy. In North America, vast parts of the United States, except perhaps its deserts, are covered by an almost geometric grid that also links sections of Canada and Mexico. These spatial continuities illustrate the high degree of integration that has developed between cities and their respective regions.

However, there are many other interdependencies and continuities – a theme elaborated by Saskia Sassen in her essay – both within and across continents that are not evidenced by these images. Take for instance the yearly flow of passengers between London and New York, which now constitutes the single busiest air route in the world. It is the tip of the iceberg of a set of economic, social and cultural interactions between these urban centres –a unified transnational space dubbed 'NYLON' – (New York – London) by academics and the popular media. It is in the context of this newfound, stretched-out urbanity that the resurgence of these two cities must be understood – both growing after years of decline, with rich and varied populations of migrants adding to the vibrancy of their local cultures and economies. London, for example, has had to reinvent itself as a city that accepts increased density, with taller buildings and new housing stock to accommodate more than 800,000 new residents over the next 15 years. For its part, New York City has once again started to build affordable public housing – the first design competition for this in nearly 4 decades was announced this year – and is rediscovering its waterfront as a resource for its diverse communities.

Looking beyond North America and Europe, we identify

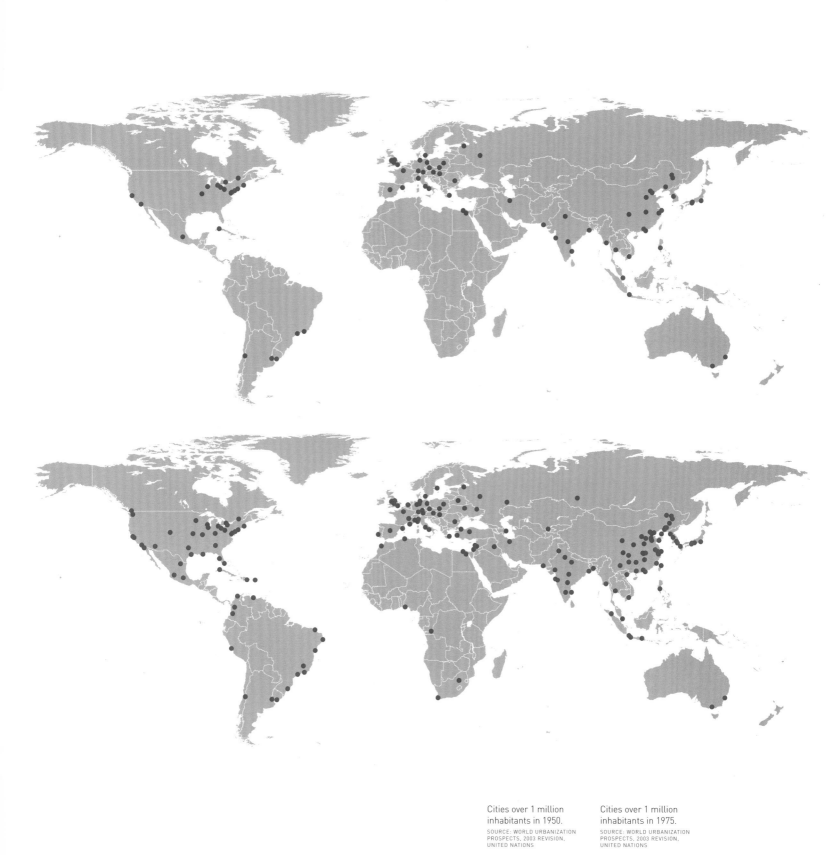

Cities over 1 million
inhabitants in 1950.
SOURCE: WORLD URBANIZATION
PROSPECTS, 2003 REVISION,
UNITED NATIONS

Cities over 1 million
inhabitants in 1975.
SOURCE: WORLD URBANIZATION
PROSPECTS, 2003 REVISION,
UNITED NATIONS

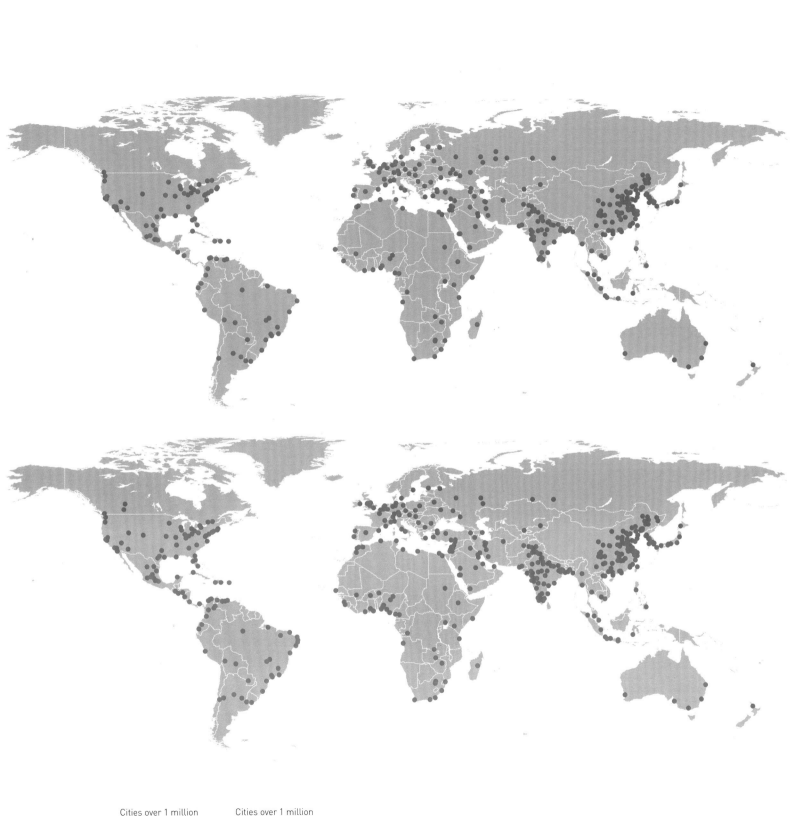

Cities over 1 million
inhabitants in 2000.
SOURCE: WORLD URBANISATION
PROSPECTS, 2003 REVISION,
UNITED NATIONS

Cities over 1 million
inhabitants in 2015.
SOURCE: WORLD URBANISATION
PROSPECTS, 2003 REVISION,
UNITED NATIONS

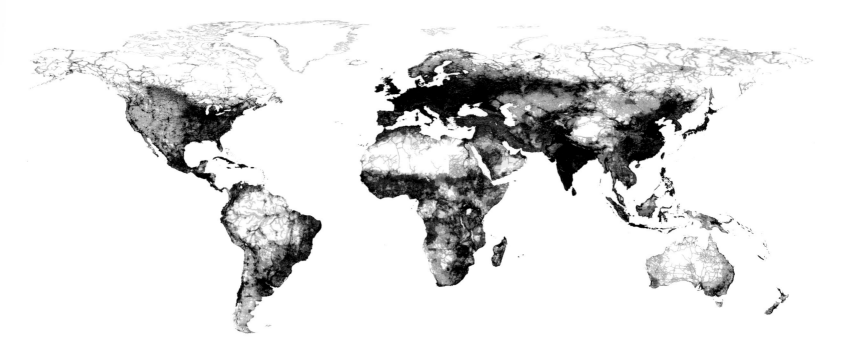

other areas of intense urban dynamism. From the sky, the entire Japanese archipelago - a relatively older urban system that shares many commonalities with North America and Europe - looks almost like an urban continuum. This can be seen as a reflection of the fact that Tokyo's capital region can be accessed from anywhere in the country in a few hours' time via a sophisticated high-speed rail network. In Tokyo, nearly 80% of the population use public transport to get to work (in Los Angeles, by contrast, 80% use private cars), which provides a model for efficient growth for what is today the world's largest metropolitan area with over 30 million people. After a period of relative economic stagnation, Tokyo is beginning to once again explore its unique characteristics; its architects and planners are engaging with issues of public space and particularly the relationship to water within this dense and fragmented mega-city.

The world map clearly indicates the extensive city-regions that are rapidly forming in southern Asia and coastal China, areas expected to concentrate close to half of the world's urban population within a couple of decades. According to the United Nations, Mumbai – India's dynamic powerhouse – is set to overtake Tokyo as the world's largest city by 2050,

but nowhere is the dizzying velocity of this transformation as tangible as in the largest Chinese conurbations. Shanghai is now one of the world's fastest growing cities while Beijing is hurriedly transforming itself in anticipation of the 2008 Olympic Games. As Shanghai grapples with the social challenges of integrating a 'floating population' of rural in-migrants numbering perhaps five million people – the population of greater Milan – it continues to grow at a breathtaking rate in both height and breadth, with nearly 3,000 buildings over ten storeys high in a city that had fewer than 300 only ten years ago. The city is planning to build 280 new underground stations and a new eco-city the size of Manhattan on Dongtan Island as a response to the fewer coordinated development of recent years exemplified by the shining towers of the Pu Dong business district. Fuelling this growth is not only in-migration but the desire for existing residents to increase the amount of personal space they inhabit. The average amount of space per person has tripled in just over a decade, from less than four metres per person to over 12 square metres, still a modest figure compared to the averages of most western countries. Beyond Shanghai and Beijing, Shenzhen is the most well-known of the many instant million-plus cities of China, each with their

Human footprint.
SOURCE: GLOBAL HUMAN FOOTPRINT DATASTE (GEOGRAPHIC). WILDLIFE CONSERVATION (WCS) AND CENTER FOR INTERNATIONAL EARTH SCIENCE INFORMATION NETWORK (CIESIN), COLUMBIA UNIVERSITY.

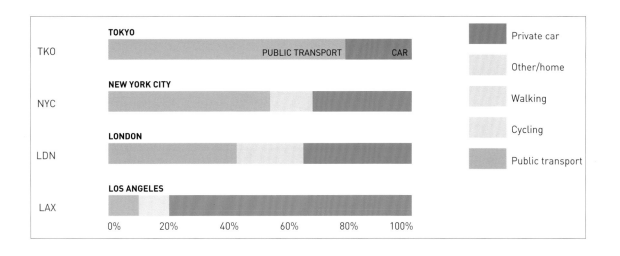

TKO	**TOKYO**					
			PUBLIC TRANSPORT		CAR	
NYC	**NEW YORK CITY**					
LDN	**LONDON**					
LAX	**LOS ANGELES**					
	0%	20%	40%	60%	80%	100%

- Private car
- Other/home
- Walking
- Cycling
- Public transport

City East Development
Scenario, London.
PROJECT COURTESY
ARCHITECTURE + URBANISM UNIT,
GREATER LONDON AUTHORITY

Transport mode
comparison Los Angeles
and Tokyo.
LONDON SCHOOL OF ECONOMICS
RESEARCH.

View of the East River
Waterfront Esplanade
looking toward the
Brooklyn Bridge from
South Street Seaport,
New York City.
COURTESY SHOP ARCHITECTS.

Dongtan Eco City,
Shanghai
PROJECT COURTESY ARUP URBAN
DESIGN, SHANGHAI. IMAGE
ELABORATED BY OAKER.

Pu Dong, Shanghai.
© PAOLO ROSSELLI.

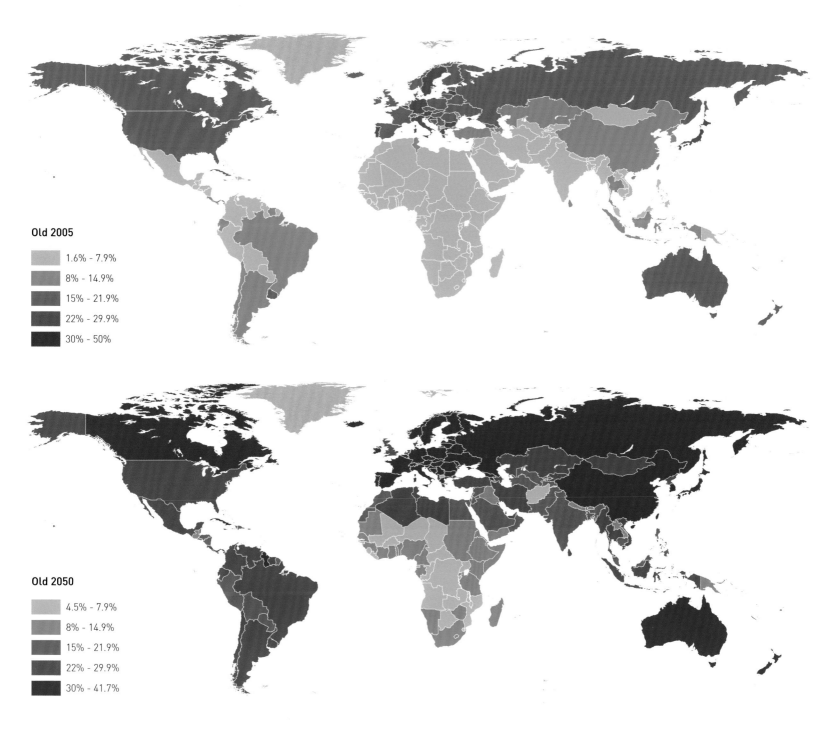

Old 2005

- 1.6% – 7.9%
- 8% – 14.9%
- 15% – 21.9%
- 22% – 29.9%
- 30% – 50%

Old 2050

- 4.5% – 7.9%
- 8% – 14.9%
- 15% – 21.9%
- 22% – 29.9%
- 30% – 41.7%

Old people, 2005.
WORLD URBANIZATION
PROSPECTS, 2003 REVISION,
UNITED NATIONS

Old people, 2050
(projection).
WORLD URBANIZATION
PROSPECTS, 2003 REVISION,
UNITED NATIONS

own airport or opera house, that have emerged out of the largest rural to urban migration movement in the history of humanity – again only in the short span of a few decades.

But rapid urbanization is not always paralleled by the exponential economic growth and comprehensive infrastructure investments of the Asia Pacific region. In central and coastal Africa, what may appear as dim clusters of light during the night are actually massive urban agglomerations sheltering millions of residents with, as indicated by the scanty reach of their electrical grids, only the most basic and deficient infrastructure. Demographic

pressures are bound to continue – by 2015 with each passing hour, Lagos will add 67 new residents, Kinshasa 34 – leading to a disproportionate concentration of young people in the southern hemisphere that coincides with a global imbalance of social indicators such as literacy and income levels.

In Egypt, one child is born every 20 seconds and many people move to Cairo within the space of one generation. In this city, over 60% of the population lives in informal settlements with buildings up to 14 storeys high in a city with only one square metre of open space per person (each

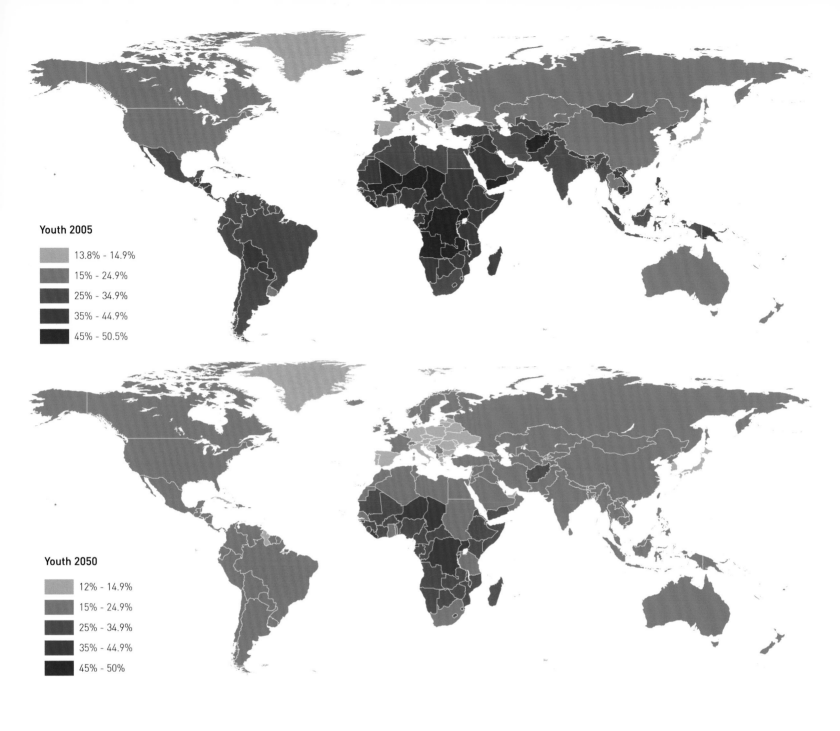

Youth 2005

- 13.8% - 14.9%
- 15% - 24.9%
- 25% - 34.9%
- 35% - 44.9%
- 45% - 50.5%

Youth 2050

- 12% - 14.9%
- 15% - 24.9%
- 25% - 34.9%
- 35% - 44.9%
- 45% - 50%

Londoner, by contrast, has access to 50 times that amount). Thus, an intervention like the Al Azhar Park, a green lung at the centre of Cairo's old city, offers a social value that transcends its aesthetic merits.

Even Johannesburg, that economic and cultural engine of southern Africa, is challenged to maintain its current levels of infrastructure provision in the face of a growth scenario whereby its population may double in a matter of decades. In this post-apartheid city that is struggling with crime, fear, segregation and AIDS, there are attempts to bring people back to the abandoned downtown, from which in the last decade many businesses fled to anonymous corporate areas on the urban fringes, with small-scale projects around transport hubs (or 'taxi ranks') that are designed to re-humanize the public realm of the city otherwise hidden behind security fences and inside gated communities. Given the social risks associated with exponential growth, the global urgency of an urban agenda for Africa cannot be over-stressed, in a continent that is expected to have a slightly larger share of the world's urban population than Europe by the year 2030.

There is a growing awareness that the urban agenda is

Young people, 2005.
SOURCE: WORLD URBANIZATION PROSPECTS, 2003 REVISION, UNITED NATIONS.

Young people, 2050 (projection).
SOURCE: WORLD URBANIZATION PROSPECTS, 2003 REVISION, UNITED NATIONS.

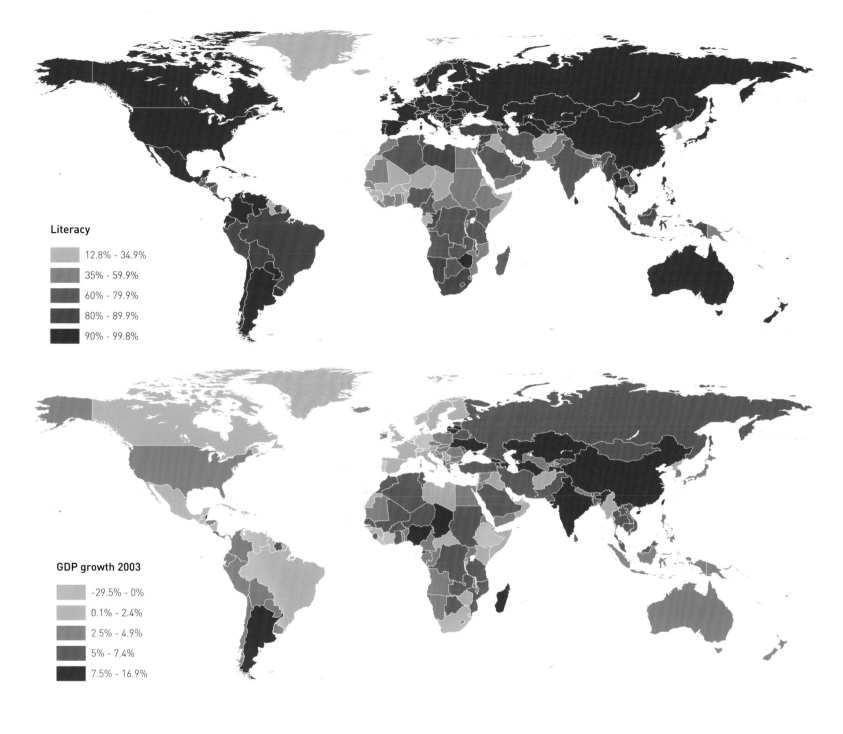

Literacy

- 12.8% - 34.9%
- 35% - 59.9%
- 60% - 79.9%
- 80% - 89.9%
- 90% - 99.8%

GDP growth 2003

- -29.5% - 0%
- 0.1% - 2.4%
- 2.5% - 4.9%
- 5% - 7.4%
- 7.5% - 16.9%

Literacy.
SOURCE: UNITED NATIONS
EDUCATIONAL, SCIENTIFIC
AND CULTURAL ORGANIZATION
(UNESCO) INSTITUTE FOR
STATISTICS AND OWN
ELABORATIONS.

Gross Domestic Product
annual growth, 2003.
SOURCE: DEVELOPMENT DATA
GROUP, THE WORLD BANK.

a global agenda. The environmental impacts of cities are enormous, due both to their increasing demographic weight and to the amount of natural resources that they consume. Every aspect of urban living has significant implications for the planet – from the billions of people driving cars along metropolitan highways to the energy required to either heat or cool buildings and to bring in food, often from the opposite corner of the world. In the developed economies, it is estimated that over 50% of energy is consumed by buildings and 25% by transport. Thus, a slight change to this energy equation in cities will have a massive impact on the global

stage. It has been argued that the degree of dispersion of urban forms can be related to consumption of non-renewable resources and emissions. On this front, the cities of more developed countries bear a particular responsibility towards the global commons – the per capita levels of energy consumption and global warming emissions in these countries are the highest in the world.

London, following the lead of Singapore, has addressed one aspect of this issue by introducing a Congestion Charge for private vehicles entering the city centre. This initiative has

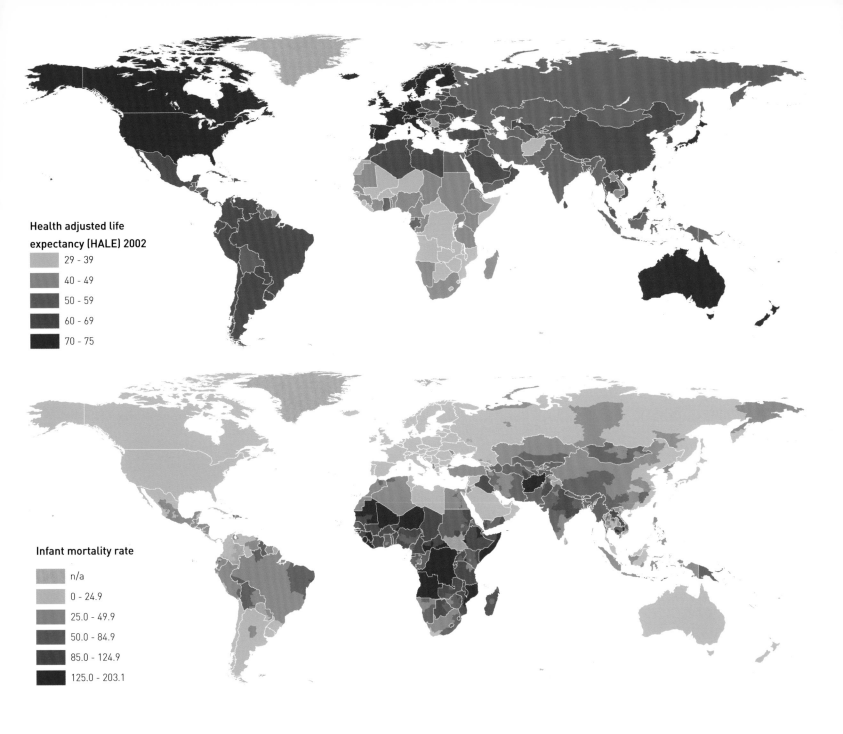

Health adjusted life expectancy (HALE) 2002

- 29 – 39
- 40 – 49
- 50 – 59
- 60 – 69
- 70 – 75

Infant mortality rate

- n/a
- 0 – 24.9
- 25.0 – 49.9
- 50.0 – 84.9
- 85.0 – 124.9
- 125.0 – 203.1

not only noticeably reduced traffic volumes and air pollution but has also been linked with increased investment in and use of public transport infrastructure (bus use has doubled in the last five years) and the creation or refurbishment of high quality public spaces. This policy has been carefully scrutinized by other cities around the world, with Stockholm set to be the next European capital to introduce a similar mechanism.

In the United States, cities such as Portland have attempted to stop the American appetite for horizontal sprawl by introducing urban growth boundaries in a bid to concentrate activity and investment within their city centres. In the past decade, Chicago has set new standards of urban liveability by investing in parks, tree-planting and inner city housing, establishing a model of civic leadership and urban interventionism that parallels the successes of Barcelona in the 1990s.

A generation of urban leaders is rising to meet these challenges. In Europe, for example, many big-city mayors are implementing important urban reforms that will enable

Health adjusted life expectancy (HALE), 2002.
SOURCE: WORLD HEALTH ORGANIZATION (WHO).

Infant mortality rate.
SOURCE: CENTER FOR INTERNATIONAL EARTH SCIENCE INFORMATION NETWORK (CIESIN), COLUMBIA UNIVERSITY.

Al Azhar Park, Cairo.

Faraday Market and
Transport Interchange,
Johannesburg.
PROJECT AUTHORS: ALBONICO
SACK MZUMARA ARCHITECTS AND
URBAN DESIGNS IN ASSOCIATION
WITH MMA ARCHITECTS. PHOTO
CREDIT: AADILL BHAM AND
NKULULEKO BHENGU.

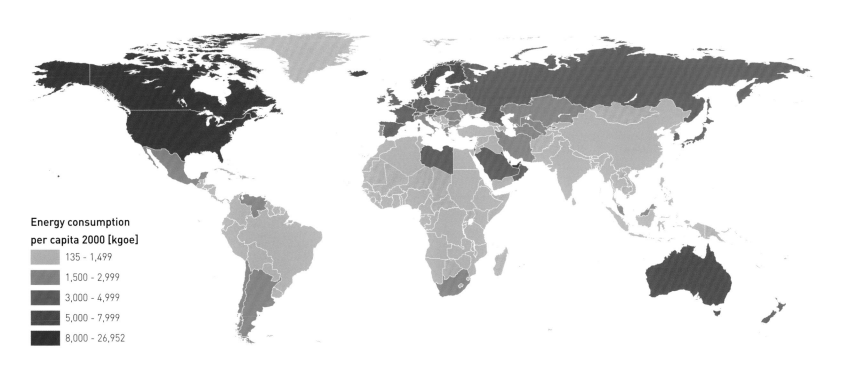

**Energy consumption
per capita 2000 [kgoe]**

- 135 - 1,499
- 1,500 - 2,999
- 3,000 - 4,999
- 5,000 - 7,999
- 8,000 - 26,952

their cities to be more competitive in the global economy and smarter producers of knowledge and culture. These cities are responding to contemporary social challenges, in some cases accommodating the large-scale influx of new residents and in others managing demographic decline without imploding irreversibly. Turin's shrewd policy of encouraging new technology industries will do much to sustain its social and economic profile as its car industry declines. This initiative is paralleled by an exemplary programme of investment in public spaces and public art as well as the transformative projects associated with the 2006 Winter Olympics.

Barcelona's own well-documented history of visionary urban projects –undertaken over 20 years by three successive mayors – has had a lasting impact on its economy. The city's annual GDP has increased by 38% since the 1992 Olympic Games and the number of visitors tripled to reach ten million a year.

These are just a few instances of the growing momentum that urban leadership is acquiring around the world, from metropolitan coalitions for smart growth and growth with equity in the United States, to the big-city governments in China whose social reforms may allow for less segregated

Kilograms of oil
equivalent (kgoe) per
person per year, 2000.
SOURCE: INTERNATIONAL ENERGY
AGENCY (IEA), 2004.

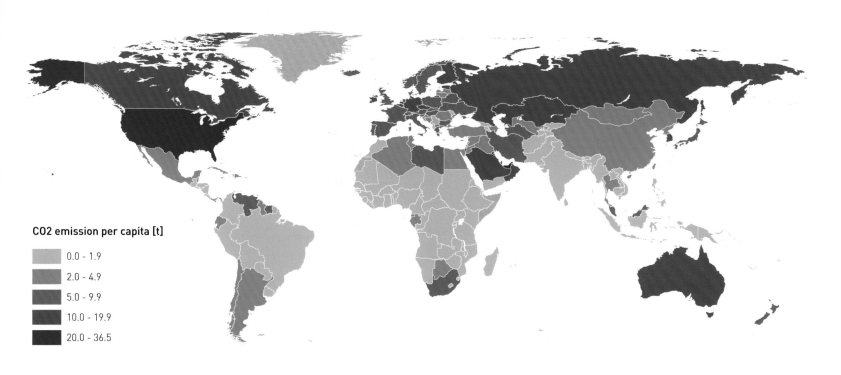

CO2 emission per capita [t]

- 0.0 - 1.9
- 2.0 - 4.9
- 5.0 - 9.9
- 10.0 - 19.9
- 20.0 - 36.5

urban settlements and more integrated labour markets.

Some of the most innovative urban interventions of the past 20 years have in fact come from Latin America, a region otherwise mired in macroeconomic problems and widening social inequalities. Following the exemplary case of Curitiba in Brazil, Bogotá today stands out as a perhaps unexpected best-practice case of egalitarian urban transformation. The effect of a series of coordinated actions by successive mayors has turned a once violent, car-dominated city facing dramatic levels of in-migration from its rural hinterlands, into a calm and well-managed city that still exudes the passions and experiences of its syncretic Latin American culture. Here, in the space of only a few years,

the city administration introduced the effective and efficient Transmilenio rapid transit bus system (partly replacing a polluting and chaotic system of informal microbuses) and built a network of cycleways, public parks and urban plazas that have changed the way the majority of the over six million inhabitants come to and move around the city, with a measurable impact on quality of life and reduction in crime. The United Nations recently singled out São Paulo – a city with 16 million inhabitants and six million cars – as a positive exemplar of urban management with its mixed programme of investment in public schools, community facilities and public transport designed to relieve the lives of the residents of the city's poorest *barrios*. Caracas - a city which claims

CO_2 Emissions per capita. Units: metric tons of carbon dioxide per person, 2002.
SOURCE: CLIMATE ANALYSIS INDICATORS TOOL (CAIT) VERSION 3.0.

Congestion Charge
scheme, London.

Cicloruta.

GIMNASIO VERTICAL™ is a prefabricated sport system that can be placed on existing inner city basketball courts. Registered by Urban-Think Tank Architects and Urbanists /Alfredo Brillembourg & Hubert Klumpner (Semi-Finalsit INOVEX ideas 2005 Award) www. ccstt.org Basketball in the Barrio La Cruz / Caracas.

in Petare the largest informal settlement in Venezuela with over one million people living cheek-by-jowl in three to four storey structures, often without running water or sewage – is home to a series of notable experiments in social and spatial retrofitting designed to make these *barrios* liveable. Unpaved, steep paths rising the equivalent of a 39-storey building, which regularly turn into dangerous mudslides, are being replaced by well-designed steps, conduits for water and sewers to the inhabitants of these dense urban environments. Small medical centres, aimed principally at women, are dispersed throughout the city's poor neighbourhoods, while community kitchens provide subsidised meals. Extremely high levels of crime – which claims many untargeted teenage victims –are a key concern in a city with a young, unemployed population, insufficient schools and easy access to drugs. Yet, the construction of a new 'Vertical Gym' within one of the city's *barrios* seems to have done much to engage local youth and reduce crime. While this and other examples – the new local schools are reported to have had similar effects on crime rates in São Paulo – do not imply a one-to-one correlation between architecture and social cohesion, they do raise awareness of the fragile yet significant link between the design of buildings and their impacts on society.

From this partial and selective survey of the state of the world's cities, we see that our current urban age is problematic, and rife with urgent challenges, yet also promising, in that it offers the potential to re-think the meanings, functions, capabilities and virtues of different city forms and urban strategies. Although each city faces its own particular and complex set of challenges, there is a growing consensus on some broad issues which cities in virtually every region of the world must address if they are to become more socially-equitable and ecologically sound. We could simplify our understanding of the situation by arguing that the basic task at hand is to how to accommodate the masses of newcomers in dense conditions and with constrained resources. Yet this straightforward phrasing would mask the complex intersection of economic, social and environmental dimensions that must be tackled and the range of mutually-reinforcing interventions that need to be devised along the following lines.

Cities in the 21st century should increasingly recognize their roles as centres of tolerance and justice for people rather than sites of conflict and exclusion. They should reduce their impact on the global environment by embracing dense and compact development rather than allowing profligate sprawl. Through their physical form they should foster a landscape of greater complexity and integration between people and spaces rather construct one of difference made up ghettoes for rich and poor, new and old, black and white. They should harness the potential of public transport not only to use energy more efficiently but also to provide access to economic and social progress. They should inspire their citizens with beautiful and accessible architecture and public spaces. Through good design and governance, cities should exercise that fundamental right of the *polis* to create a fair and democratic environment for the over four billion people who will inhabit the urban landscapes of the 21st century. By identifying and embracing these challenges and opportunities, the 10th International Architecture Exhibition does not proclaim a one-size-fits-all manifesto, but is a call-to-action for architects and city builders to participate in the construction of a more equitable and sustainable world.

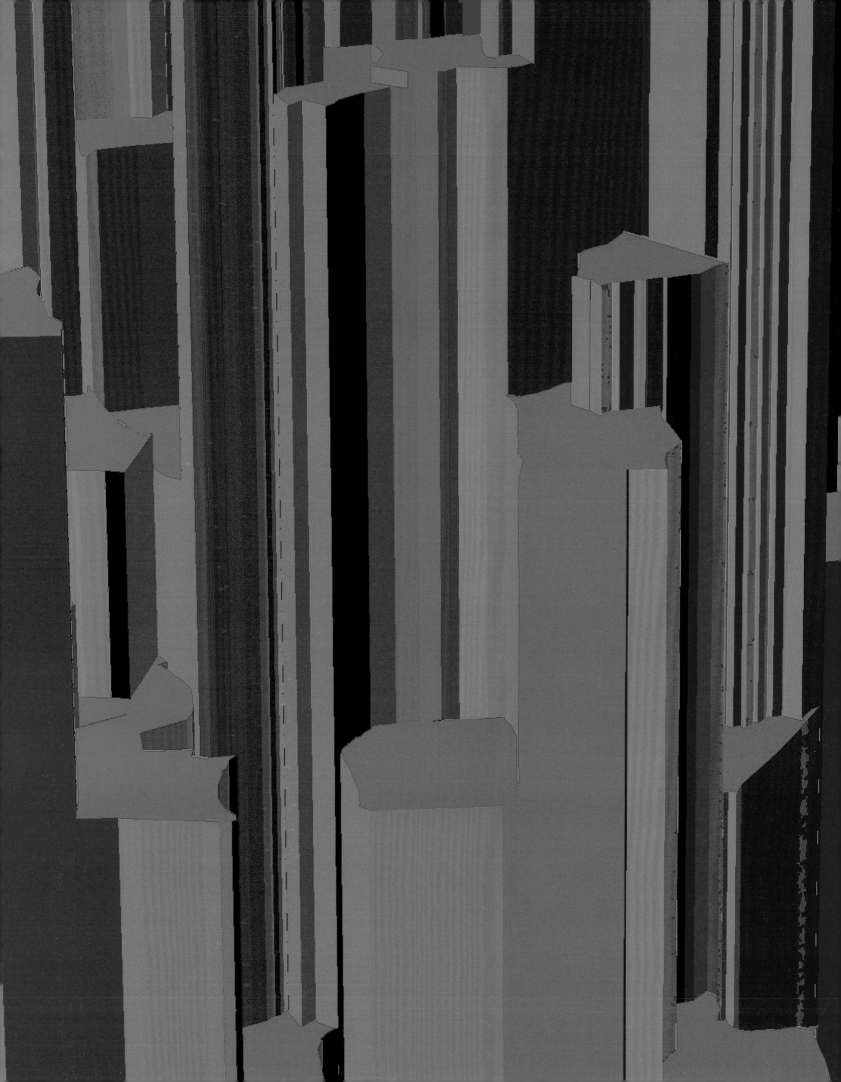

Why cities matter

1. Mumbai.

PHOTO BY RAJESH VORA.
COURTESY URBAN DESIGN
RESEARCH INSTITUTE.

Why cities matter

Saskia Sassen

Saskia Sassen
(University of Chicago
and London School
of Economics) is the
author most recently
of *Territory, Authority,
Rights: From Medieval
to Global Assemblages*
(Princeton University
Press 2006). She has
now completed for
UNESCO a five-year
project on sustainable
human settlement for
which she set up a
network of researchers
and activists in over 30
countries. Her books
are translated into
sixteen languages.
Her comments have
appeared in The
Guardian, The New
York Times, Le Monde
Diplomatique, the
International Herald
Tribune, Vanguardia,
Clarin and the Financial
Times, among others.
PHOTO BY ALAN RUSBRIDGER

By the mid-twentieth century, many of our great cities were in physical decay, losing population, losing economic activity, losing key roles in the national economy and losing their share of national wealth. As we move into the twenty-first century, cities have re-emerged as strategic places for a wide range of projects and dynamics. This essay explores the whys, the hows and the whats of this shift. It does so through the economic, architectural and political dimensions of cities. These are briefly described below before entering into the inevitable sea of details.

Critical and partly underlying all the other dimensions, is the new economic role of cities in an increasingly globalized world and the associated architectural and technical revolutions this has entailed. The formation of inter-city geographies is contributing a critical infrastructure for a new global political economy, new cultural spaces and new types of politics. Some of these inter-city geographies are thick and highly visible: the flows of professionals, tourists, artists and migrants among specific groups of cities. Others are thin and barely visible: the highly-specialized financial trading networks that connect particular cities depending on the type of instrument involved, or the global commodity chains for diverse products that run from exporting hubs to importing hubs.

These circuits are multi-directional and criss-cross the world, feeding into inter-city geographies with both expected and unexpected strategic nodes. For instance, New York is the leading global market to trade financial instruments on coffee even though it does not grow a single bean. But a far less powerful financial centre, Buenos Aires, is the leading global market to trade financial instruments on sunflower seeds. Cities located on global circuits, whether few or many, become part of distinct, often highly-specialized intercity geographies. Thus if I were to track the global circuits of gold as a financial instrument, it is London, New York, Chicago and Zurich that dominate. But if I track the direct trading in the metal industry, Johannesburg, Mumbai, Dubai and Sydney all appear on the map (picture 4). Looking at globalization through the lens of these specificities allows us to recover the particular and diverse roles of cities in the global economy. Each of the cities profiled in this Biennale is part of particular global circuits. Many others not profiled are on such circuits as well, as is indicated, for instance, by the fact that the top 100 global service firms together have affiliates in 315 cities worldwide.

While many of these global circuits have long existed, what has begun to change since the 1980s is their proliferation and their increasingly complex organizational and financial framings. It is the new challenge of coordinating, managing and servicing these increasingly complex, specialized and vast economic circuits that has made cities strategic. It is perhaps one of the great ironies of our global digital age that it has produced not only massive dispersal, but also extreme concentrations of top level resources in a limited number of places. Indeed, the organizational side of today's global economy is located and continuously reinvented, in what has become a network of about 40 major and not-so-major global cities; this network includes most of our 16 Biennale cities. These global cities must be distinguished from the hundreds of cities that are located on often just a few global circuits; while these cities are articulated with the global economy, they lack the mix of resources to manage and service the global operations of firms and markets.

The more globalized a firm's operations and the more digitised its product, the more complex its central headquarter functions become and hence the more their execution benefits from dense, resource-rich urban environments. In global cities, then, the interaction of centrality and density takes on a whole new strategic meaning: physical density is the urban form, housing an increasingly complex set of activities for the management, service, design, implementation and coordination of the global operations of firms and markets.

Architecture and civil engineering have played a critical role in building the new and expanded urban settings for the organizational side of the global economy. This is architecture as inhabited infrastructure. Let me explain. The much talked about homogenization of the urban landscape

2. The 16 cities profiled in the Corderie at the 10th International Architecture Exhibition.

in these cities responds to two different conditions. One is the consumer world, with homogenizing tropes that help in expanding and standardizing markets to the point that they can become global. But this is to be distinguished from the homogenization involved in the organizational side of the global economy: state-of-the-art office districts, airports, hotels, services and residential complexes for strategic workforces. Architecture and engineering have invented and produced these state-of-the-art environments and provided the key visual vocabularies for the reshaping of significant portions of these cities. This reshaping responds to the needs associated with housing these new economies and the cultures and politics they entail. I would say that this homogenized environment for the most complex and globalized functions is more akin to an infrastructure, even though not in the conventional sense of the term. Nor is it simply a visual code that aims at signalling a high stage of development, as is so often posited in much of the commentary on the matter and is the belief of many developers.

We must go beyond the visual tropes and the homogenizing effect, no matter how distinguished the architecture. The key becomes understanding what inhabits this homogenized state-of-the-art urban landscape that recurs in city after city. We will find far more diversity and distinct specializations across these cities than the newly-built urban landscapes suggest. The global economy requires a standardized global infrastructure, with global cities the most complex of these infrastructures. But the actual economic operations, especially on the organizational side, thrive on specialized differentiation. Thus as the global economy expands and includes a growing diversity of national economies, it is largely in the global cities of each of these that the work of capturing the specialized advantage of a national economy gets done. To do this work requires state-of-the-art office districts, infrastructures and all the requirements of luxury living. In that sense then, much of this architectural environment is closer to inhabited infrastructure, inhabited by specialized functions and actors.

But these conditions themselves have produced a variety of responses, from renewed passions for aestheticising the city, preserving the city and ensuring the public-space aspect of cities. The massive scale of today's urban systems has brought with it a revaluing of 'terrains vagues' and of modest spaces, where the practices of people can contribute to the making of public space, beyond the monumentalized public spaces of state and crown. Micro-architectural interventions can build complexity into standardized spaces. This type of built complexity can in turn engage the temporary publics that take shape in cities in particular spaces at specific times of the day or night.

The city is one moment in often complex processes that are partly electronic, such as electronic markets, or part of hidden infrastructures, such as fibre optic cables. Embedded software for handling mass systems, such as public transport and public surveillance, is an often-invisible layer in a growing number of cities. Such embedded software is guided by logics that are not necessarily part of the social repertory through which we understand those systems. As the use of embedded software expands to more and more infrastructures for daily life, we will be interacting increasingly with the artefacts of technology. Technical artefacts gradually become actors in the networks through which we move. Buildings today are dense sites for these types of interactions. These acute concentrations of embedded software, and of connectivity infrastructures for digitised space, make the city less penetrable for the ordinary citizen.

Yet at the same time, the city is also potentially the site where all these systems can become visible, a potential further strengthened by the multiple globalities—from economic to cultural to subjective—that localize partly in cities. This in turn brings up political challenges; at various points in history cities have functioned as spaces that politicized society. This is, again, one of those periods. Today's cities constitute the terrain where people from all over the world intersect in ways they do not anywhere else. In these complex cities, diversity can be experienced through the routines of daily life, workplaces, public transport and urban events such as demonstrations or festivals. Furthermore, insofar as powerful global actors are making increasing demands on urban space and thereby displacing less-powerful users, urban space becomes politicized in the process of rebuilding itself. This is politics embedded in the physicality of the city. The emergent global movement for the rights to the city is one emblematic instance of this struggle. In urbanizing rights it makes them concrete: the right to public space, to public transport, to good neighbourhoods.

One question is whether a new type of politics is being shaped through these conflicts; a politics that might also make the variety of inter-city networks into platforms for global governance. Most of today's major social, political and economic challenges are present in cities, often in both their most acute and their most promising forms: the sharpest juxtapositions of the rich and the poor, but also struggles for housing; anti-immigrant politics, but also multiple forms of integration and mixing; the most powerful and globalized economies, but also a proliferation of informal economies; the most powerful real estate developers, but also the largest group of builders in the world today: people making shanty dwellings. How can we not ask whether networks of cities can become platforms for new types of global governance?

Cities in the world: then and now

Cities have long been at the intersection of cross-border processes; flows of capital, labour, goods, raw materials, merchants, travellers. Asia and Africa have seen some of the oldest and vastest of these flows, Europe some of the densest. Cities were strategic spaces for the economies and cultures that arose out of these flows and for the housing of power: economic, political and symbolic. The widespread formation of nation-states that took off about a hundred years ago brought with it a move away from these older patterns; the project became one of national territorial integration. From the perspective of this new political economy, cities were mostly routine administrative centres. If anything, the strategic spaces had become the suburbs and the mass manufacturing districts, with the state the critical actor, whether the Keynesian state or the centralized planning state.

It is this last condition, the state as the critical actor, that began to change in the 1980s, accelerated in the 1990s and continues today. Diverse dynamics contributed to the shift: economic, technological, cultural and political. In the economy, it was a result of the privatization of public sector operations, deregulation of the economy, the emergence of new information technologies, the opening of national economies to foreign firms and foreign professionals and the growing participation of national firms and professionals in global markets. States continue to matter and wherever there is war, they play key roles.

Commodity exchanges

3. Commodity exchanges (within 24-city sample). LONDON SCHOOL OF ECONOMICS RESEARCH.

4. Commodity gold. LONDON SCHOOL OF ECONOMICS RESEARCH.

RANK	ALL SERVICE SECTORS	COMMODITY	EXCHANGE
1	LONDON	LME	London Metal Exchange
		LIFFE	London International Financial Futures Exchange
2	NEW YORK	NYCE	New York Futures Exchange (Division of NYBOT)
		NYMEX	New York Mercantile Exchange (Division of NYBOT)
3	TOKYO	TCE	Tokyo Commodity Exchange (formerly TOCOM)
		TGE	Tokyo Grain Commodity Exchange
4	MILAN	SIA	Italian Stock Exchange/Milan Domestic Futures Exchange
5	SÃO PAULO	BM&F	Bolsa de Mercadorias & Futuros (São Paulo)
6	BUENOS AIRES	MTBA	Mercado Termino Buenos Aires
7	MUMBAI	BOOE	Bombay Oilseeds and Oils Exchange
8	SHANGHAI	SHFE	Shanghai Futures Exchange
9	MOSCOW	IRUCE	Inter-republican Universal Commodity Exchange
		MNFME	Moscow Non-Ferrous Metal Exchange
10	ISTANBUL (IST)	ITB	Istanbul Commodity Exchange
		IAB	Istanbul Gold Exchange

3

Commodity Gold

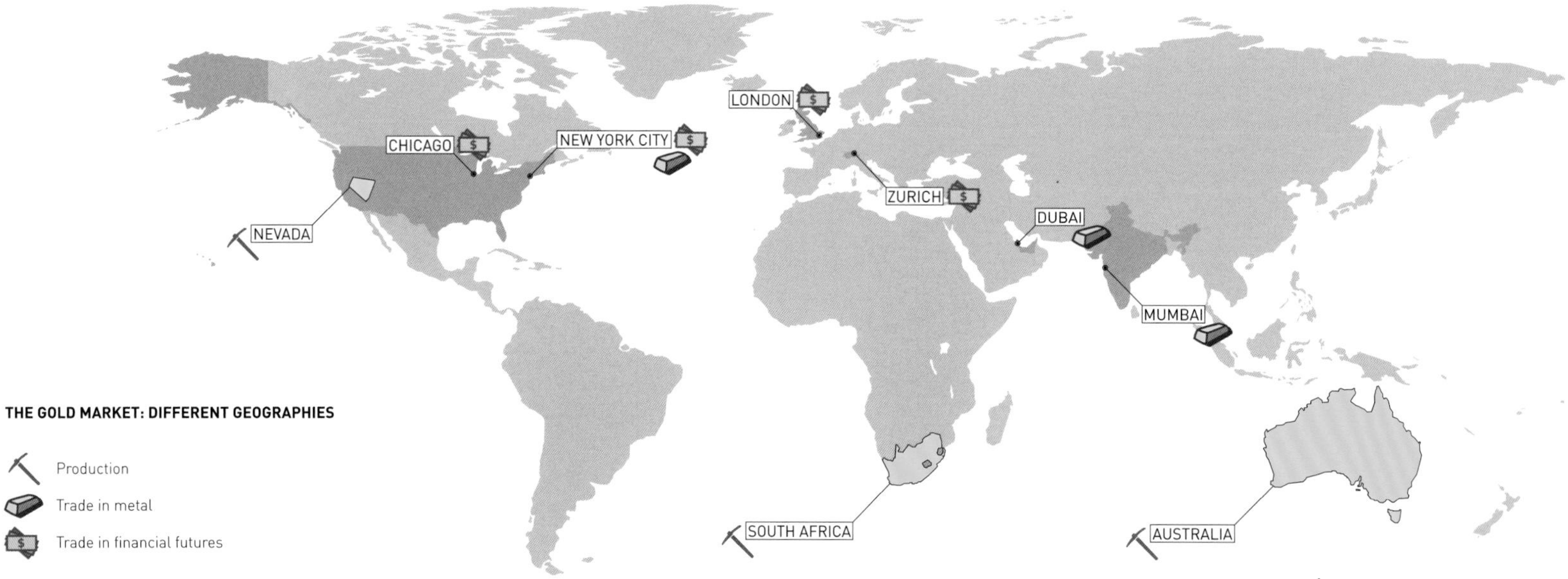

THE GOLD MARKET: DIFFERENT GEOGRAPHIES

- Production
- Trade in metal
- Trade in financial futures

4

While states are still the main global actors, they have lost at least some economic, political and symbolic ground to other actors: global firms and global cities. Global firms have taken over functions and governance capabilities from national states and the 100 richest firms are richer than most except the 20 richest states. The major international flows of people that may have dominated an era (crusaders, armies, colonial functionaries) were once coordinated by states. Today's major international flows of people are more likely to be immigrants, transnational professionals and tourists. In many parts of the world and among many population groups, urban culture is today a far more compelling image than national culture and is becoming increasingly experienced as part of a transnational urbanity. As more and more people live in small towns and suburbs, the large, complex city becomes a tourist destination not just for its museums and monuments, but for its urban surprises, urban dwellers as exotica.

But why do cities matter for today's global economy?
Much is known about the wealth and power of today's global firms. Their ascendance in a globalizing world is no longer surprising. And the new information and communication technologies are typically seen as the handmaidens of economic globalization, both as tools and as infrastructure.

Less clear is why cities should matter more today in a globalized world than they did in the Keynesian world of the mid-1900s. Today we see a growing number of cities emerging as strategic territories that contribute to articulate a new global political economy. Architecture, urban design and urban planning have each played critical roles in the partial rebuilding of cities as platforms for a rapidly-growing range of globalized activities and flows, from economic to cultural and political.

One way of thinking about the global economy is in terms of the many highly-specialized circuits that constitute it. Different circuits contain different groups of countries and cities. Viewed this way, the global economy becomes concrete and specific, with a well-defined geography. Globally traded commodities like gold, butter, coffee, oil or sunflower seeds are redistributed to a vast number of destinations, no matter how few the points of origin are in some cases. With globalization, of course, this capacity to redistribute globally has grown sharply. The planet is crisscrossed by these trading circuits.

This networked system also feeds unnecessary mobilities, because the intermediary economy of specialized services thrives on mobilities. Thus in the case of the UK economy, a study by the New Economics Foundation and the Open University of London found that in 2004, the UK exported 1,500 tonnes of fresh potatoes to Germany, and imported 1,500 tonnes of the same product from the same country; it also imported 465 tonnes of gingerbread, but exported 460 tonnes of the same product; and it sent 10,200 tonnes of milk and cream to France, yet imported 9,900 tonnes of the same dairy goods from France.

The global map tightens when what is getting traded is not the butter or coffee as such, but rather financial instruments based on those commodities. The map of commodity futures (picture 3) shows us that most financial trading happens in 20 financial futures exchanges, most of which are included in the 16 cities profiled in this Architecture Biennale. These 20 include the usual suspects, New York and London, but in perhaps less familiar roles as well. Thus, New York City, the famous coffee producer, accounts for half of the world's trading in coffee futures. London, not necessarily famous for its mining, is the largest futures trader in the metal palladium. But besides these two major financial centres, these 20 also include Tokyo as the largest trader in platinum, São Paulo as one of the major traders in both coffee and gold, and Shanghai in copper. Finally, some of these centres are highly-specialized in unexpected ways: for example, we have London in control of potatoes.

The map tightens even further when we aggregate the 73 commodities thus traded into three major groups. Five major global futures exchanges (NYME, LME, CBOT, TCOM and ICE Futures) located respectively in New York, London, Chicago, Tokyo and Atlanta concentrate 76% of trading in these 73 commodities futures traded globally. Aggregated into three major groups, one single market clearly dominates in each. For agricultural commodities futures, the CBOT (Chicago) controls most global trading; for energy it is the NYME (New York); and for metals, the LME (London).

This escalation in the capacity to control points to the multiple global economic spaces that are being generated. Thus the commodities themselves come from well over 80 countries and are sold in all countries of the world, although only about 20 financial exchanges control the global commodities futures trading. This tighter map of commodities futures trading begins to show us something about the role of cities in today's globalizing and increasingly electronic economy.

Global service connectivity

GENERAL		ADVERTISING		LAW		MANAGEMENT CONSULTING	
	CONNECTIVITY		CONNECTIVITY		CONNECTIVITY		CONNECTIVITY
LONDON	1,00	NEW YORK CITY	1,22	LONDON	1,00	NEW YORK CITY	1,06
NEW YORK CITY	0,97	LONDON	1,00	NEW YORK CITY	0,90	LONDON	1,00
HONG KONG	0,73	HONG KONG	0,77	FRANKFURT	0,70	PARIS	0,84
TOKYO	0,70	AMSTERDAM	0,72	HONG KONG	0,69	MADRID	0,79
PARIS	0,69	SYDNEY	0,70	WASHINGTON	0,66	STOCKHOLM	0,78
SINGAPORE	0,67	SINGAPORE	0,69	BRUSSELS	0,62	MILAN	0,78
CHICAGO	0,63	TORONTO	0,69	PARIS	0,56	TORONTO	0,74
LOS ANGELES	0,59	TOKYO	0,66	SINGAPORE	0,55	SINGAPORE	0,74
MILAN	0,59	MIAMI	0,65	TOKYO	0,51	CHICAGO	0,74
FRANKFURT	0,58	FRANKFURT	0,65	MOSCOW	0,44	WASHINGTON	0,71
SYDNEY	0,58	MILAN	0,64	AMSTERDAM	0,40	SYDNEY	0,68
MADRID	0,57	PARIS	0,64	BERLIN	0,39	HONG KONG	0,68
BRUSSELS	0,56	MADRID	0,64	PRAGUE	0,38	ZURICH	0,66
AMSTERDAM	0,56	MELBOURNE	0,61	BUDAPEST	0,38	BOSTON	0,66
TORONTO	0,55	TAIPEI	0,58	LOS ANGELES	0,35	BRUSSELS	0,64
SÃO PAULO	0,53	LISBON	0,58	CHICAGO	0,34	TOKYO	0,63
SAN FRANCISCO	0,50	MUMBAI	0,58	MUNICH	0,33	SÃO PAULO	0,62
ZURICH	0,48	BRUSSELS	0,58	DUSSELDORF	0,32	AMSTERDAM	0,61
MEXICO CITY	0,46	COPENHAGEN	0,56	MILAN	0,31	BUENOS AIRES	0,60
BUENOS AIRES	0,46	SÃO PAULO	0,54	BANGKOK	0,29	KUALA LUMPUR	0,53

5

It is here that global cities enter the picture. They are not the places where commodities are produced, but they are the places where commodity futures are invented so as to facilitate the global trading of these commodities and partly manage some of the associated risks. They are the places where these futures are traded. It brings to the fore the distinction between the sites and networks for producing the actual good and the sites and networks for managing and coordinating the trading of the actual good and the financial instruments they support. It makes concrete what is one of the main counterintuitive trends we see in today's global economy: that the more globalized and non-material the activity, the more concentrated the global map of those activities. This is a puzzle, especially since location in major cities brings added costs to the operations of firms and exchanges. Cities contain the clues to the answer. But before developing that answer, an examination of other such global maps, beyond commodities and commodities futures. An examination of the global networks of global service firms, migration flows and flight patterns shows us a far more distributed global map.

The global connectivity of Biennale cities
Here we examine the same types of questions, but with a focus on the top 100 specialized corporate services firms in law, advertising, management consulting, accounting and insurance. These firms operate in 315 cities worldwide, each firm with offices (either headquarters or branches) in at least 15 countries. Each of the sixteen cities profiled in the international exhibition of the 10th Venice Architecture Biennale has some of these offices.

These global firms produce and deliver critical inputs for firms, markets and even governments around the world. They service the types of firms involved in the commodity trading and futures markets and the financial services firms described later. And they service architectural and engineering firms, major international art exhibitions, Biennales and avant-garde circuses. In brief, they are in the business of specialized servicing and ready to service the latest inventions not only in the world of firms, but in any world.

Mapping their global operations shows almost the opposite of the sharp concentration of the financial futures exchanges. The servicing operations of these firms are in demand everywhere. When countries open up to foreign firms and investors and allow their markets to become

integrated into global markets, it is often foreign service firms that take over the most specialized servicing. This is, clearly, one particular mapping of interconnectivities among a group of very diverse cities

What follows is confined to the inter-city connections among 24 selected cities, including our 16 Biennale cities, rather than the 315 cities in the original data-set generated by Peter Taylor and his colleagues at the GaWC project, who have generously put the data in the public domain. What the numbers capture is the extent to which these 24 cities are connected through the office networks of these 100 firms. This information is one microcosm of a pattern that repeats itself over and over with a variety of other types of transactions, such as the almost meaningless measure of a city with McDonald's outlets or the extreme concentration of the commodities futures discussed earlier. Against this background, the connectivity measures of such office networks are a middle ground, very much a part of the infrastructure for the new inter-city geographies (picture 7).

Except for Turin and Lagos, all the cities in our sample are in the top third of the 315 cities where these firms either have headquarters or branches. Five of our 24 cities (picture 5) are among the top ten of the worldwide total for the 315 cities where these firms have operations. London and New York stand out in our sample, as they do in the world generally, with vastly higher levels of connectivity than any other city. A second, rather diverse grouping for the 24 cities includes Tokyo, Milan, Los Angeles and São Paulo. A third grouping includes Mexico City, Jakarta, Buenos Aires, Mumbai, Shanghai and Seoul; a fourth grouping Moscow, Johannesburg, Istanbul, Manila and Barcelona; and a fifth group Caracas, Bogotá, Berlin, Dubai and Cairo. Turin and Lagos are at a considerably lower level of connectivity. Yet we should clarify that Turin, with the lowest connectivity of our selected cities, nonetheless houses offices of 14 of these global firms, pointing to the extent to which these firms network the world, albeit on their specialized and partial terms.

Some of these outcomes reflect key patterns in the remaking of space economies. Thus Berlin and Turin rank low because the major international financial and business centres in their respective countries, Frankfurt and Milan, are extremely powerful in the global network and concentrate a growing share of the global components in their national economies. This is a pattern that recurs in all countries; I return to it in the next section. In banking and finance, Jakarta's connectivity is high because it is a major and long established banking centre for the Muslim world in Indonesia's geopolitical region and hence is of great interest to Western firms but is also in need of these firms to bridge into the West. Shanghai's connectivity is high because it is one of the major financial centres for its region and has become the leading national stock market in China –with Hong Kong having regained its position as China's leading international financial centre. South Korea is the tenth largest economy in the world and has undergone significant deregulation after the 1997 Asian financial crisis. It has made Seoul an attractive site for Western financial firms as foreign investors have been buying up a range of holdings in both South Korea and Thailand since the 1997 financial crisis.

Dubai is an interesting case that points to the making of a whole new region, one not centred in the operational map of our top 100 global service firms. Only in the last few years has Dubai become an important financial and business centre at the heart of a new emergent region that stretches from the Middle East to the Indian Ocean; its financial global connectivity is not principally derived from Western financial firms but increasingly its own and its region's firms. Its specific financial connectivity is not picked up when we focus on the interactions among the 24 cities, but its accounting connectivity is extremely high for the very simple reason that Western style accounting rules the world.

When we disaggregate these global connectivity measures by specialized sectors, there is considerable reshuffling because of the high level of specialization that marks the global economy. In accountancy, Mexico City and perhaps most dramatically, Dubai and Cairo, move to the top. These cities are becoming deeply connected with global economic circuits, they mediate between the larger global economy and their regions and hence they offer the top global accounting firms plenty of business. In contrast Shanghai moves sharply down; the global accounting firms have set up their operations in Beijing because going through the Chinese government remains critical.

The other sectors evince similar reshufflings. The often sharp changes in the degree of connectivity for different sectors in a given city is generally due to misalignments between global standards for legal and accounting services and the specifics of the national systems. Global insurance firms have clearly decided that locating in Johannesburg

and Shanghai makes sense, as these move to the top ten among our selected cities. It signals that the domestic insurance sector is either insufficiently developed or is too 'unwestern' to satisfy firms and investors and hence foreign insurance firms can gain a strong foothold. The low connectivity of Seoul and Mumbai tells us that the domestic insurance sector is taking care of business. The high connectivity for legal services in the case of Moscow, São Paulo and Shanghai, which all move into the top 10, signals the need for Western style legal services in a context of growing numbers of foreign investors and firms. São Paulo, for instance, hosts about 70 financial services firms from Japan alone. In management and consultancy, Buenos Aires, São Paulo, Seoul and Jakarta move into the top ten of the 24 cities, in good part due to the dynamic opening up of their national economies in the 1990s and the resulting opportunities for foreign and national firms and investors. Barcelona, Mumbai and Cairo have drawn far fewer of our global 100 service firms because either the domestic sector could provide the services, as is the case in Mumbai and Cairo, or the opportunities lie elsewhere, as is suggested by Spain's massive investments throughout Latin America and now even including banking in the UK. For the top 100 global advertising firms, Mumbai and Buenos Aires, both with rich cultural sectors and industries, were a strong draw. Again, the weaker presence of global advertising firms in Cairo and Dubai is due to these cities' sharper orientation to their emergent region. London has the strongest presence of these global firms in accounting, banking/finance and insurance, and New York is strongest in advertising and management consulting. It should be noted that this dominance is due mostly to the sharp concentration of headquarters, as well as branches.

The global map produced by the operations of the top 100 service firms is dramatically different from that produced by the financial trading of commodity futures, which is in turn different from that of the trading in the actual commodities. The extreme concentration evident in finance would stand out even more if we drew a map of goods trading and the innumerable criss-crossing circuits connecting points of origin and destination.

Similarly, the global maps of immigration flows and airplane travellers are also far broader and involve hundreds and hundreds of cities. Many of the selected cities receive immigrants. The highest share is, not unexpectedly, in Dubai, with 82% of its population foreign born, followed by

Los Angeles and New York with well over 30%, London just under 30%, to under ten percent in most of our cities and about 1 % in Jakarta, Cairo and Mexico City.

We looked at flights among the group of 24 cities to get a measure of each city's percentage of the total of flights among them. This information was derived from a far larger sample produced by Ben Derudder at the University of Ghent, who kindly has put this in the public domain. To avoid the distortion of hubs, we used the full trip. Not unexpectedly New York, London and Los Angeles have the largest number of connections within the group of 24 and with the world. NY dominates traffic with Latin America, Los Angeles with Asia and London dominates global routes. Links among these three top hubs are strong. Further, there are strong connections between particular sets of cities: Dubai and Cairo, Mumbai and Johannesburg; Johannesburg and London; Lagos and London, New York and Johannesburg. One of the strongest links is Shanghai and Tokyo and also Shanghai and Taipei. Six of our cities are among the top 20 of the 315 cities as measured by airline passenger traffic. In actual numbers of arrivals and departures, several of the 24 selected cities are among the top of the 150 cities with the largest numbers: London between 30 and 32 million, New York between 28-30 million, Paris 18-20 million, Los Angeles 16-18 million, Milan 8-10 million, Madrid and Tokyo between 6 to 8 million. The numbers for Mexico, Dubai, São Paulo, Berlin, Mumbai, Johannesburg and Seoul, each range from 4 to 6 million. Buenos Aires, Cairo, Istanbul, Shanghai, Jakarta and Moscow handle from 2 to 4 million and the remaining cities below 2 million.

The most strategic and tightest inter-city geography

Finance is probably the most extreme case for examining the question as to why the thick places that are cities should matter for global and largely electronic economic sectors. And we know that they do matter. Global finance today moves between electronic space and a network of about 40 very material financial centres worldwide. The question we actually need to ask is why does a global electronic market for the trading of digital instruments need financial centres at all, let alone a network of them? If anything, we might argue that one super financial centre should do. Examining the utility of the network of financial centres provides the most extreme answer to the general question as to why cities matter.

The geography of global finance evinces three major patterns. One is that the number of globally-articulated

financial centres began to grow sharply in the 1990s with the deregulation of their respective economies, a trend that continues today but at a slower rate. Mexico City, Buenos Aires, Istanbul, Mumbai, Shanghai and numerous other financial centres joined the global network in the 1990s. Such integration does not mean that all financial centres are located on the same financial circuits. Global finance is made up of multiple specialized circuits, well beyond those briefly discussed for commodity futures. Each of these specialized circuits involves specific groups of cities. Thus although London and New York are the largest financial centres in the world, when we disaggregate global finance into these specialized circuits, several other cities dominate in some of these circuits, notably Chicago in commodity futures trading.

A second major pattern is that notwithstanding the growth in the number of centres and in the overall volume of global finance, there is sharp concentration in the major centres. The commodities futures made this clear already. It is also evident in stock markets (picture 6).

A third major pattern is the growing concentration of global finance in a single financial centre within each country, even when that country has multiple financial centres. Further, this consolidation of one leading financial centre in each country is due to rapid financial growth and not because the other centres are declining. There are exceptions, but they are rare. In France, Paris today concentrates larger shares of most financial sectors than it did 10 years ago and once important stock markets like Lyon have become 'provincial' even though Lyon is today the hub of a thriving economic region. Milan privatized its exchange in September 1997 and electronically merged Italy's 10 regional markets. Frankfurt now concentrates a larger share of the financial market in Germany than it did in the early 1980s and so does Zurich, which once had Basel and Geneva as significant competitors.

We might think that this concentration inside countries is due to the relatively small size of these countries. But that is not the case. In the U.S. for instance, the aggregate global financial sector in New York dwarfs all other financial centres, including Chicago. The fact that Chicago concentrates far more of the global commodity futures than New York, does not significantly override New York's aggregate financial concentration. The question then becomes why such enormous concentration in one financial centre in this vast country with a multi-polar urban system? Sydney and Toronto have equally gained

Stock market capitalisation

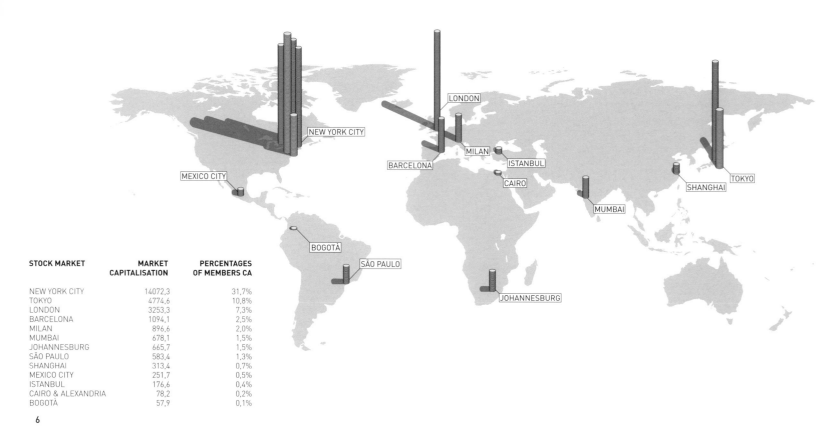

STOCK MARKET	MARKET CAPITALISATION	PERCENTAGES OF MEMBERS CA
NEW YORK CITY	14072,3	31,7%
TOKYO	4774,6	10,8%
LONDON	3253,3	7,3%
BARCELONA	1094,1	2,5%
MILAN	896,6	2,0%
MUMBAI	678,1	1,5%
JOHANNESBURG	665,7	1,5%
SÃO PAULO	583,4	1,3%
SHANGHAI	313,4	0,7%
MEXICO CITY	251,7	0,5%
ISTANBUL	176,6	0,4%
CAIRO & ALEXANDRIA	78,2	0,2%
BOGOTÀ	57,9	0,1%

6

7

6. Stock market
capitalisation.
LONDON SCHOOL OF ECONOMICS
RESEARCH.

7. Intercity geographies.
PHOTO HILARY KOOB SASSEN.

power in continental-sized countries and have taken over functions and market share from what were once the major commercial centres, respectively Melbourne and Montreal. So have São Paulo and Mumbai, which have gained share and functions from respectively Rio de Janeiro in Brazil and New Delhi and Calcutta in India. These are all huge countries with several major cities; one might have thought that they could sustain several similarly weighty financial centres.

Why is it that at a time of rapid growth in the network of financial centres, in overall volumes and in placeless electronic transactions, we have such sharp trends towards concentration both at the global level and within each country? Both globalization and electronic trading are about expansion and dispersal beyond what had been the confined realm of national economies and floor trading. Geographic dispersal would seem to be a good option given the high cost of operating in major financial centres. Further, the geographic mobility of financial experts and financial services firms has risen sharply. In brief, the weight of major centres inside each country is, in a way nonsensical, especially given multiple cities in each of these countries. But so is, for that matter, the existence of an expanding network of financial centres. Indeed, one might well ask why financial centres matter at all.

The ongoing weight of centrality and density: the other side of global dispersal

Cities have historically provided national economies, polities and societies with something we can think of as centrality. The usual urban form for centrality has been density, specifically the dense downtown. The economic functions delivered through urban density in cities have varied across time. But they are always a variety of agglomeration economies, no matter how much their content might vary depending on the sector involved. While the financial sector is quite different from the cultural sector, both benefit from agglomeration, but the content of these benefits can vary sharply. One of the advantages of central urban density is that it has historically helped defray the risk of insufficient variety. It brings with it diverse labour markets, diverse networks of firms and colleagues, concentrations of diverse types of information on the latest developments and diverse marketplaces.

The new information and communication technologies (ICTs) should have neutralized the advantages of centrality

and density. No matter where a firm or professional is located, they should have access to many of the needed resources. In fact, the new ICTs have not quite eliminated centrality and density and hence the role of cities as economic and physical entities. Even as much economic activity has dispersed, the centres of a growing number of cities have expanded physically, at times simply spreading and at times in a multi-nodal fashion. The outcome is a new type of space of centrality in these cities: it has physically expanded over the last two decades, a fact we can measure it and it can assume more varied formats, including physical and electronic formats. The geographic terrain for these new centralities is not always simply that of the downtown; it can be metropolitan and regional. In this process, the geographic space in a city or metro area that becomes centralized often grows denser than it was in the 1960s and 1970s. This holds for cities as different as Zurich and Sydney, São Paulo and London, Shanghai and Buenos Aires.

The global trend of expanded newly-built and rebuilt centralized space suggests an ironic turn of events for the impact of ICTs on urban centrality. Clearly, the spatial dispersal of economic activities and workers at the metropolitan, national and global level that began to accelerate in the 1980s represents only half of what is happening. New forms of territorial centralization of top-level management and control operations have appeared alongside these well-documented spatial dispersals. National and global markets as well as globally-integrated operations require central places where the work of globalization gets done, as shown by the case of financial centres.

Centrality remains a key feature of today's global economy. But today there is no longer a simple, straightforward relation between centrality and such geographic entities as the downtown, or the central business district (CBD). In the past and up to quite recently, the centre was synonymous with the downtown or the CBD. Today, partly as a result of the new ICTs, the spatial correlates of the centre can assume several geographic forms, ranging from the CBD to the new global grid comprising the 40 global cities discussed earlier.

There are several logics that explain why cities matter to the most globalized and digitized sectors in a way they did not as recently as the 1970s. Here I briefly focus on three of these logics.

The first one concerns technology and its many misunderstandings. When the new ICTs began to be widely used in the 1980s, many experts forecast the end of cities as strategic spaces for firms in advanced sectors. But it was the routine sectors that left cities while advanced sectors kept expanding their operations in more and more cities. Today's multinationals have over one million affiliates worldwide. But they also have expanded their central headquarter functions and fed the growth of a separate specialized services sector from which they are increasingly buying what they once produced in-house. Why were those experts so wrong? They overlooked a key factor: when firms and markets use these new technologies they do so with financial or economic objectives in mind, not the objectives of the engineer who designed the technology. As I have explained in detail in some of my other work, the logics of users may well thwart or reduce the full technical capacities of the technology. When firms and markets globalize their operations thanks to the new technologies, the intention is not to relinquish control over the worldwide operation or appropriation of the benefits of that dispersal. Insofar as central control is part of the globalizing of activities, their central operations expand as they expand their operations globally. The more powerful these new technologies are in allowing centralized control over globally dispersed operations, the more these central operations expand. The result has been expanded office operations in major cities.

Thus the more these technologies enable global geographic dispersal of corporate activities, the more they produce density and centrality at the other end; the cities where their headquarter functions get done.

A second logic explaining the ongoing advantages of spatial agglomeration has to do with the complexity and specialization level of central functions. These rise with globalization and with the added speed that the new ICTs allow. As a result global firms and global markets increasingly need to buy the most specialized legal, accounting, consulting and other such services. These service firms get to do some of the most difficult and speculative work. To do this work they benefit from being in complex environments that function as knowledge centres because they contain multiple other specialized firms and high level professionals with worldwide experience. Cities are such environments, with the 40 plus global cities in the world the most significant of these environments, but a growing number of other cities developing one or another element of such environments.

A third logic concerns the meaning of information in an information economy. There are two types of information. One is the datum, which may be complex yet is standard knowledge: the level at which a stock market closes, a privatization of a public utility, the bankruptcy of a bank. But there is a far more difficult type of 'information', akin to an interpretation, evaluation or judgment. It entails negotiating a series of data and a series of interpretations of a mix of data in the hope of producing a higher order datum. Access to the first kind of information is now global and immediate from just about any place in the highly developed world and increasingly in the rest of the world thanks to the digital revolution. But it is the second type of information that requires a complicated mixture of elements (the social infrastructure for global connectivity), which gives major financial centres a leading edge. When the more complex forms of information needed to execute major international deals cannot be retrieved from existing databases no matter what one can pay, then one needs the social information loop and the associated de facto interpretations and inferences that come with bouncing off information among talented, informed people. It is the importance of this input that has given a whole new importance to credit rating agencies, for instance. Part of the rating has to do with interpreting and inferring. When this interpretation becomes 'authoritative' it becomes 'information' available to all. The process of turning inferences or interpretations into 'information' takes quite a mix of talents and resources.

In brief, the density of central places provides the social connectivity that allows a firm or market to maximize the benefits of its technological connectivity (picture 7).

Specialized urban spaces and intercity connectivities: A world apart

The network of about 40 global cities in the world today provides the organizational architecture for cross-border flows. A key feature of this organizational architecture is that it contains both the capabilities for organizing enormous geographic dispersal and mobility and the capabilities for maintaining centralized control over that dispersal. The management and servicing of much of the global economic system takes place in this growing network of global cities and regions. While this role involves only certain components of urban economies, it has contributed to a re-positioning of cities both nationally and globally.

The types of activities described above are part of a new type of urban economy that is most pronounced in global cities but also is emerging in smaller and less globalized cities. This new urban services-centred core has mostly replaced the older typically more manufacturing oriented core of service and production activities. In the case of cities that are global business centres, the scale, power and profit levels of this new core suggest that we are seeing the formation of a new urban economy. Even though these cities have long been centres for business and banking, since the early 1980s there have been dramatic changes in the structure of the business and financial sectors and a sharp ascendance of a cultural sector. The sharp increases in the overall magnitude of these sectors, their weight in the urban economy and the critical mass of high-income professional jobs they generate, all have altered the character of cities. This mix has contributed distinct economic, social and spatial patterns in cities beginning in the late 1980s and early 1990s in much of the highly developed world and in the 1990s and onward in major cities in the rest of the world.

The growth of this services core for firms is also evident in cities that are not global. Some of these cities serve regional or sub-national markets; others serve national markets and/or global markets. While regionally- and nationally-oriented firms need not negotiate the complexities of international borders and the regulations of different countries, they are still faced with a regionally-dispersed network of operations that requires centralized control and servicing and the full range of corporate business services: insurance, legal, accounting, advertising and the like. Also in these cities we see an increase in high-income professional jobs and thereby growth in sectors linked to quality of life, including the cultural sector. Thus the specific difference that globalization makes in this general trend of growing service intensity in the organization of the economy is to raise the scale and the complexity of transactions and the orders of magnitude of profits and incomes.

The implantation of global processes and markets has had massive consequences for the restructuring of large stretches of urban space. The meanings and roles of architecture and urban design are destabilised in cities marked by digital networks, acceleration, massive infrastructures for connectivity. Older meanings of architecture and urban design do not disappear, they remain crucial. But they cannot always comfortably address these newer meanings and presences in the urban landscape.

Particular urban spaces are becoming massive concentrations of new technical capabilities. Particular buildings are the sites for a multiplication of interactive technologies and distributed computing. And particular global communication infrastructures are connecting specific sets of buildings worldwide, producing a highly-specialized interactive geography, with global firms willing to pay a high premium in order to be located within it. AT&T's global business network now connects about 485,000 buildings worldwide. This is a specific inter-city geography that fragments the cities where these buildings are located. The most highly-valued areas of global cities, particularly financial centres, now contain communication infrastructures that can be separated from the rest of the city, allowing continuous upgrading without having to spread it to the rest of the city. And they contain particular technical capabilities, such as frame relays, which most of the rest of the city lacks. This specialized layer of connectivity is perhaps most visible and easiest to appreciate if we take the types of global networks that AT&T (see picture 8, 9), for instance, has set up for multi-national firms. Multiplying this case for thousands of multi-national firms begins to give us an idea of these new inter-city connectivities, largely invisible to the average citizen.

Such globally-networked spaces of centrality are in their aggregate a platform for global operations of firms and markets. One question this raises, to which I will return in the final section, is whether they can also be used for governance purposes.

The globalized sector has imposed a new valorization dynamic in the urban economy; a new set of criteria for valuing or pricing various economic activities and outcomes. The result is not simply a quantitative transformation. It can have devastating effects on large sectors of the urban economy, even as it contributes enormous dynamism. At different times different cities have been emblematic of this creative destruction: New York, Tokyo and London in the 1980s, Buenos Aires and Mumbai in the 1990s (and Mumbai again today) and Shanghai as we moved into the twenty-first century.

The Other economy in global cities
In these cities we also see a rapid proliferation of types of firms and types of economic spaces we think of as backward, as unconnected to the advanced urban economy. This is most visible and controversial in the global cities of highly developed counties. Involved are mostly familiar activities: garment manufacturing, construction, transport, packaging, catering, auto repair and so on. These are all licit activities. But they are taking place outside the regulatory

AT&T connectivity infrastructure

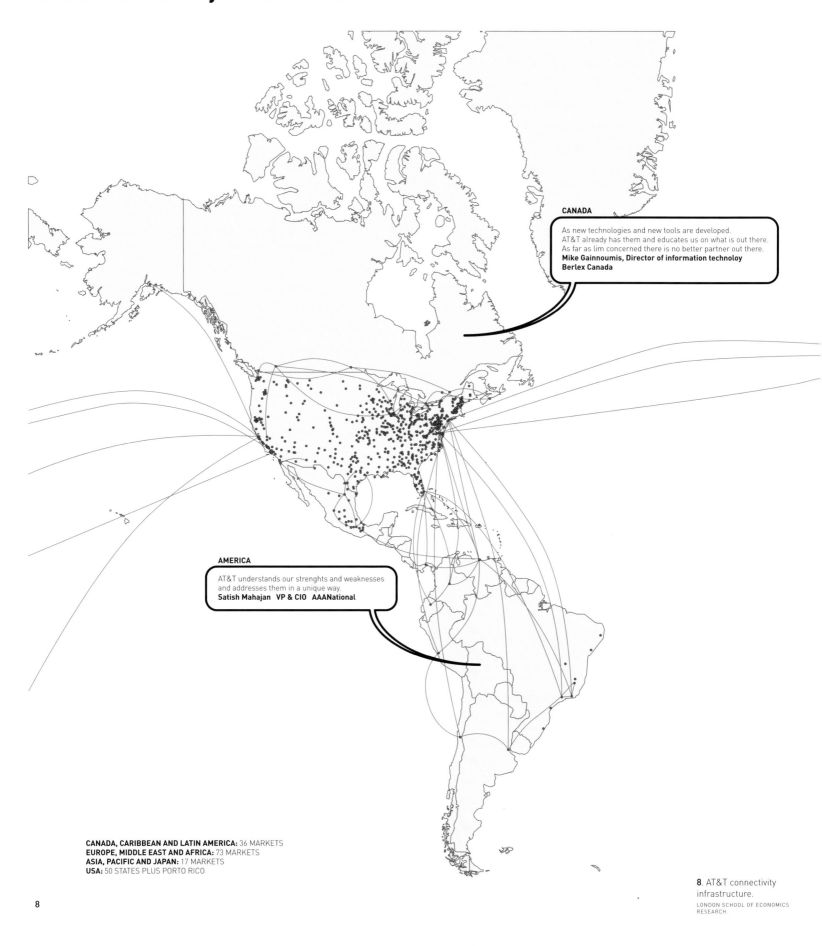

CANADA

As new technologies and new tools are developed.
AT&T already has them and educates us on what is out there.
As far as Iim concerned there is no better partner out there.
Mike Gainnoumis, Director of information technoloy
Berlex Canada

AMERICA

AT&T understands our strenghts and weaknesses
and addresses them in a unique way.
Satish Mahajan VP & CIO AAANational

CANADA, CARIBBEAN AND LATIN AMERICA: 36 MARKETS
EUROPE, MIDDLE EAST AND AFRICA: 73 MARKETS
ASIA, PACIFIC AND JAPAN: 17 MARKETS
USA: 50 STATES PLUS PORTO RICO

8. AT&T connectivity
infrastructure.
LONDON SCHOOL OF ECONOMICS
RESEARCH.

8

CHINA

We are delighted to be working with AT&T as we expand our international operations because AT&T has an unrivaled reputation globally for quality and service.
Huang jianxiong, Vice General Manager Information Technology Center Air China

Source: AT&T Pubblication

AT&T network for Olympus

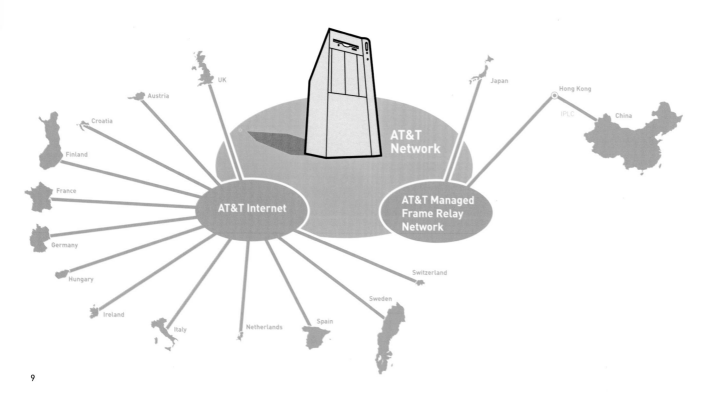

9

framework in a context where those activities are regulated. We call these informal economies and in a context of state regulation these economies can only be understood in their relation to the formal economy, that is to say, income-generating activities that adhere to existing regulations. Such informal economies have long existed in the cities of the less developed world and they include today's vast numbers of shanty dwellers, the largest group of builders in the world.

One problem in understanding the meaning of these informal economies in the global cities of the highly developed world is that analysts and policy makers often group informal and illegal activities. Both are simply classified as breaking the law. This obscures the two questions we should really be asking. Why have these licit activities gone informal? These are activities that could be done above ground, unlike illegal activities such as tax evasion or trading in banned drugs. Secondly, why have they gone informal now after a century of successful effort to regulate them in most developed countries and certainly in Europe and in Japan?

Seen in this way, the recent growth of informal economies in major global cities in North America, Western Europe and to a lesser extent, Japan, raises a number of questions about what is and what is not part of today's advanced urban economies. Typically this informality is seen as the result of a failure of government regulation and as an import from the less-developed world by immigrants replicating survival strategies typical of their home countries. Related to this view is the notion that 'backward' sectors of the economy are kept backward or even alive, because of the availability of a large supply of cheap immigrant workers. The notion of government failure and economic

9. AT&T network for Olympus.
LONDON SCHOOL OF ECONOMICS RESEARCH.

backwardness also excludes the possibility of a new type of informal economy emerging in the global cities of the less developed world; the assumption is that nothing has really changed in the longstanding informal economies of the global south.

In my reading of the evidence all of these notions are inadequate; they capture only a small part of this new reality in-the-making. Many of today's informal activities are actually new types of economies linked to key features of advanced capitalism, as I discuss in the next section. This in turn also explains the particularly strong presence of informal economies in global cities. And it contributes to explain a mostly overlooked development: the proliferation of an informal economy of creative professional work in these cities: artists, architects, designers and software developers. Finally, we are seeing similar trends towards the emergence of the new types of informal economy also in major cities in Latin America, Africa and much of Asia.

In brief, the new informal economy in global cities is part of advanced capitalism. One way of putting it, is that the new types of informalization of work are the low cost equivalent of formal deregulation in finance, telecommunications and most other economic sectors in the name of flexibility and innovation. The difference is that while formal deregulation was costly and tax revenue as well as private capital went into paying for it, informalization is low-cost and largely on the backs of the workers and firms themselves.

In the case of the new, creative professional informal economy, these negative features are mostly absent and informalization greatly expands opportunities and networking potentials. There are strong reasons why these artists and professionals operate at least partly informally. It allows them to function in the interstices of urban and organizational spaces often dominated by large corporate actors and to escape the corporatization of creative work. In this process they contribute a very specific feature of the new urban economy: its innovation and a certain type of frontier spirit. In many ways this represents a reinvention of Jane Jacobs's urban economic creativity.

Rather than assume that Third World immigration is causing informalization in the global cities of the north, we need to examine the role such immigration might or might not play in this process. Immigrants, insofar as they tend to form communities, may be in a favourable position to seize the opportunities represented by informalization. But the opportunities are not necessarily created by immigrants. They may well be a structured outcome of current trends in advanced economies. Again the case of growing informal professional creative economies in cities as varied as Berlin, New York and Buenos Aires, makes this link more transparent given the value put today on the 'creative classes'. But in fact, the immigrant informal economy is just as valuable in many of these cities to the new urban economy.

Similarly, government failure may well be involved, but governments had solved the issue of informal work by the mid-twentieth century. And for decades this was not an issue: Why now? Furthermore, if there is indeed a global infrastructure for running and servicing the global economy then it is also quite possible that the global cities of the south are undergoing a similar transformation, albeit with their own specificities. Conditions akin to those in global cities of the north may also be producing a new type of informal economy in global cities of the south, including a professional creative informal economy. Why assume these cities are not developing a new emergent informal economy that responds to the needs of their advanced economic sectors? These new informal economies need to be distinguished from the old ones that continue to operate in the global south and are still more a result of poverty and survival than of the needs of advanced economic sectors.

The same politico-economic restructuring that led to the new urban economy emerging in the late 1980s and onwards, also contributed to the formation of new informal economies. The decline of the manufacturing-dominated industrial complex that characterized most of the twentieth century and the rise of a new, service-dominated economic complex provide the general context within which we need to place informalization if we are to go beyond a mere description of instances of informal work.

Spatio-economic segmentations in the city

The ascendance of the specialized services-led economy, particularly the new finance and services complex and, to some extent, the cultural sector, brings with it the elements for a new urban economic regime, because although this sector may account for only a fraction of the economy of a city, it imposes itself on that larger economy. One of the new pressures is towards a type of spatio-economic polarization that goes well beyond the older forms of inequality that have always marked cities.

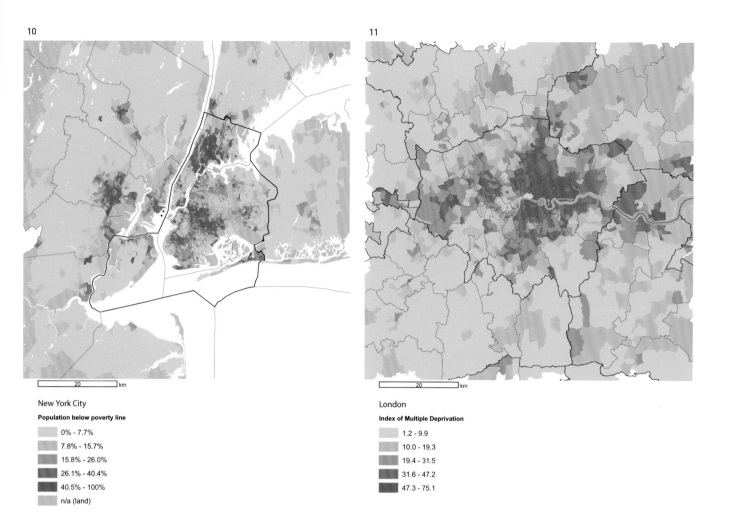

New York City

Population below poverty line

	0% - 7.7%
	7.8% - 15.7%
	15.8% - 26.0%
	26.1% - 40.4%
	40.5% - 100%
	n/a (land)

London

Index of Multiple Deprivation

	1.2 - 9.9
	10.0 - 19.3
	19.4 - 31.5
	31.6 - 47.2
	47.3 - 75.1

Critical here is the fact that the leading sectors can produce super-profits for firms and super-incomes for high level workers. The possibility for super-profits in the leading sectors contributes to devalue urban sectors that cannot generate super-profits, no matter how much the city needs their products and services. The growing demand for state-of-the-art office districts and for the spaces of luxury urban living displaces lower-profit firms and lower-income households. The more modest sectors of the middle class often leave the cities, as do firms that do not need to be in the city. Poor people easily become homeless, including significant numbers of women and children. Low-profit firms who need to be in the city struggle for survival, with many either closing down or informalizing part of their production (picture 10, 11).

High prices and profit levels in the globalized sector and its ancillary activities, such as top-of-the-line restaurants and hotels, have made it increasingly difficult for other sectors to compete for space and investments. Many of these other sectors have experienced considerable downgrading and/or displacement, as, for example, neighbourhood shops tailored to local needs are replaced by upscale boutiques and restaurants catering to new high-income urban elites. The ascendance of expertise in economic organization in turn has contributed to a whole new valuing of specialized services and professional workers. And it has contributed to mark many of the 'other' types of economic activities and workers as unnecessary or irrelevant to an advanced economy.

In this mix of conditions lie some of the key sources for informalization of both low-wage and professional creative informal work. The rapid growth of industries with strong concentrations of high and low income jobs has assumed distinct forms in the consumption structure, which in turn

10. New York City, population below poverty line.
SOURCE: U.S. CENSUS BUREAU; CENSUS 2000

11. London, index of Multiple Deprivation.
SOURCE: OFFICE OF NATIONAL STATISTICS, UK; CENSUS 2001

has a feedback effect on the organization of work and the types of jobs being created.

The expansion of the high-income work force in conjunction with the emergence of new cultural forms has led to a process of high-income gentrification that rests, in the last analysis, on the availability of a vast supply of low-wage workers. High-income gentrification is labour-intensive, in contrast to the typical middle-class suburb that represents a capital-intensive process: tract-housing, road and highway construction, dependence on private automobile or commuter trains, marked reliance on appliances and household equipment of all sorts and large shopping malls with self-service operations. High-income gentrification replaces much of this capital intensity with workers directly and indirectly. Similarly, high-income residents in cities depend to a much larger extent on hired maintenance staff than the middle-class suburban home with its concentrated input of family labour and machinery.

Behind the specialty food-shops and boutiques that have replaced many large self-service supermarkets and department stores in cities lies a very different organization of work from that prevalent in large, standardized establishments. This difference in the organization of work is evident both in the retail and in the production phase. High-income gentrification generates a demand for goods and services that are frequently not mass-produced or sold through mass outlets. Customized production, small runs, specialty items, fine food dishes are generally produced through labour-intensive methods and sold through small, full-service outlets. Subcontracting part of this production to low-cost operations and also to sweatshops or households is common. The overall outcome for the job supply and the range of firms involved in this production and delivery is rather different from that characterizing the large department stores and supermarkets where standardized production prevails. Mass production and mass distribution outlets facilitate unionising; specialty food shops and designer furniture do not.

Yet another condition driving informalization in this process of high-income gentrification is the rapid increases in the volume of building renovations, alterations and small scale new construction associated with the transformation of many areas of the city from low-income, often dilapidated neighbourhoods into higher-income commercial and residential areas. What in suburban or peripheral areas in cities might involve a massive programme of new construction, can easily be mostly rehabilitation of old structures in central urban areas that are likely to offer the highest returns on older renovated buildings. The volume of work, its small scale, its labour intensity and high skill content, the pressures of time and the short-term nature of each project all are conducive to a heavy incidence of informal work.

The expansion in the low-income population has also contributed to the proliferation of small operations and the move away from large-scale standardized factories and large chain stores for low-price goods. In good part, the consumption needs of the low-income population are met by manufacturing and retail establishments that are small, rely on family labour and often fall below minimum safety and health standards. Cheap, locally produced sweatshop garments, for example, can compete with low-cost imports. A growing range of products and services, from low-cost furniture made in basements to 'gypsy cabs' and family day-care, is available to meet the demand of the growing low-income population. The inadequate provision of services and goods by the formal sector also contributes to informal ways of securing these. This inadequacy may consist of excessively high prices, inaccessible or difficult-to-reach locations of formal providers, or actual lack of provision. It would seem that this inadequacy of formal provision involves mostly low-income individuals or areas.

The existence of a cluster of informal shops can eventually generate agglomeration economies that induce additional entrepreneurs to move in. This is illustrated by the emergence in just about all global cities of auto-repair districts, vendors' districts or clusters of both regulated and informal factories in areas not zoned for manufacturing; these areas are emerging as among the few viable locations for such activity given the increased demand for space by high bidders. The far more regulated cities in much of Europe and in Japan have kept these developments to a minimum compared with the USA and the rest of the world. Once a city has a diverse set of informal firms that use a variety of labour supplies, the entry costs for new entrepreneurs are lower and hence they can function as a factor inducing the further expansion of the informal economy.

In any large city, there also tends to be a proliferation of small, low-cost service operations made possible by the massive concentration of people in such cities and the daily inflow of commuters and of tourists. This will tend to create intense inducements to open up such operations as well as intense competition and very marginal returns. Under such conditions the cost of labour is crucial and contributes to the likelihood of a high concentration of low-wage jobs. This tendency is confirmed by a variety of data sets that show that each one percent increase in, for instance, retail jobs results in an 0.8 per cent increase in below-poverty-level jobs in large metropolitan areas of the global north.

Against this larger background we can now ask, what then is the place in an advanced urban economy of firms and sectors that appear to be backwards or lack the advanced technologies and human capital base of the leading industries? Are they superfluous? And what about the types of workers employed by such firms? The available evidence shows several sources for the expansion of informal activities.

Informality: a mode of incorporation in dualized cities
The demand for informally produced or distributed goods and services in today's global cities has several sources and characteristics. It can originate in the formal economy either from final consumers or firms. Most of the informal work in the garment, furniture, construction, packaging and electronics industries is of this type. A second source is the demand from within the communities where many, though by no means all of the informal activities take place. Immigrant communities are a leading example and probably account for much of this second type of demand. A very different type of informal economy arises out of the concentration of artists and professionals, perhaps especially urban and new-media linked professionals in the types of cities we are focusing on in the Biennale.

There are differences in the types of jobs found in the informal economy. Many of the jobs are unskilled, with no training opportunities, involving repetitive tasks. Another type of job demands skills acquisition. The growth of informalization in the construction and furniture industries can be seen as having brought about a re-skilling of the labour force, rather than the more standardized, often pre-built housing of suburban areas. Some jobs pay extremely low-wages, others pay average wages and still others pay rather well, especially in the professional creative informal economy. Across this range there seems to be a saving involved for the employers and contractors compared with what would have to be paid in the formal market.

Finally, we can identify different types of locations in the spatial organization of the informal economy. Immigrant communities are a key location for informal activities meeting both internal and external demand for goods and services. Gentrifying areas are a second important location; these areas contain a large array of informal activities in renovation, alteration and small-scale new construction. This is also the space for much of the informal creative economy. A third location can be characterized as informal manufacturing and industrial service areas serving a city-wide market.

The specific set of mediating processes ultimately promoting the new informal economies are a) increased earnings inequality and the associated restructuring of consumption in high income groups and in very low income groups; b) increased inequality in the profit-making capacities of different types of firms; and c) the inability among many of the providers of the goods and services demanded by high-income households and by high profit-making firms to continue operating in global cities where leading sectors have sharply bid up the prices of commercial space, labour, auxiliary services and other basic business costs. Informalizing part or all of these operations has turned out to be one of the ways in which they can continue to function in these cities and meet the real and often expanded demand for their goods and services. It is then the combination of growing inequalities in earnings and in the profit-making capabilities of different sectors in the urban economy that has promoted the informalization of a growing array of economic activities. These are integral conditions in the current phase of advanced capitalism as it materializes in major cities dominated by the new advanced services complex typically geared to world markets and characterized by extremely high profit-making capabilities. These are not conditions imported from less-developed countries via immigration.

Further, the new emerging creative informal economy is also caught up in these spatio-economic inequalities even as its contents and projects are radically different from those of the manufacturing and service oriented informal economies. Berlin, with its large concentration of artists, designers, new media activists and of newly emptied and unclaimed spaces, probably offers the most dramatic example of the mix of dynamics at work here.

On a more abstract level, three features stand out about informality in today's major cities. One is that informalizing production and distribution activities is a

12. Informal vendors of services, in the historic centre of Mexico City.
PHOTO BY PHILIPP RODE.

12

13. An informal street market in East London.
PHOTO BY PHILIPP RODE.

13

mode of incorporation into the advanced urban economy. Second, informalising creative work is one of the most entrepreneurial aspects of the urban economy; today's example of the much-praised economic creativity that cities make possible. Third, informalization is the low-cost equivalent of what at the top of the system we have called deregulation; but while the deregulation of finance, telecommunications and other major sectors was expensive and highly formalized, in today's informal economies the cost is absorbed by the actors themselves.

In sum, the new urban core incorporates a far larger mix of firms, workers and economic spaces than is usually recognized. Parts of the immigrant communities in the cities of the global north and parts of the shanty towns in those of the global south are also part of the new advanced urban economy. But experiencing them as such is far more difficult. The corporate complex exudes techne, precision, power and is therewith easily experienced as part of the advanced urban economy. Yet it is not alone in marking the specificity of today's global cities.

Challenges and potentials

I would like to conclude this essay with four observations that are charged with challenges and with potentials. It is, after all, this quality of being charged and slightly unruly that marks the urban condition.

A first observation concerns a critical feature of the urban condition, both in the past and today: vast scales juxtaposed with interstitial spaces. The cities we focus on and their emerging inter-city geographies are spaces of massive structures, massive markets and massive capabilities. We might wonder what options such urban spaces offer urban designers, planners and architects to express their interests and ideas. The issue here is not so much the few exceptional or lucky designers who gain a global stage in their particular field. My concern is rather a more diffuse urban landscape of opportunities for 'making' in urban spaces dominated by massive structures and powerful actors. It is not design *per se* that concerns me here, but rather the larger political economy of design in cities that are part of these new global networked geographies. What is this landscape within which design today needs to function? There are, clearly, multiple ways of positing the challenges facing architecture and planning as practice and as theory. Admittedly, in emphasising the crucial place of cities for architecture, I construct a problem that is not only positioned, but also, perhaps inevitably, partial.

One consequence of the patterns described in the first half of this essay is the ascendance, partly objective and perhaps mostly subjective, of process and flow over fixity and place. Growing velocities render a growing range of urban experiences more of flows than of things, notwithstanding the vast amount of thingness around us. One of my concerns in researching globalization and digitization is to recover the fixity and the materiality underlying much of the global and the digital and obscured by prevailing notions that everything is becoming flow. The first half of this essay showed that the globalizing of activities and flows is in good part dependent on a vast network of places, mostly global cities. These sites contain many kinds of fixed (and mobile) resources. Things and materiality are critical for digitization and globalization; and places matter for global flows.

Even as massive projects proliferate, these cities contain many under-used spaces, often characterized more by memory than current meaning. These spaces are part of the interiority of a city, yet lie outside of its organizing utility-driven logics and spatial frames. They are *terrains vagues* that allow many residents to connect to the rapidly-transforming cities in which they live and subjectively to bypass the massive infrastructures that have come to dominate more and more spaces in their cities. Jumping at these *terrains vagues* in order to maximize real estate development would be a mistake from this perspective. Keeping some of this openness might make more sense in terms of factoring future options at a time when utility logics change so quickly and often violently, excess of high-rise office buildings being one of the great examples.

This opens up a salient dilemma about the current urban condition in ways that take it beyond the more transparent notions of high-tech architecture, virtual spaces, simulacra, theme parks. All of the latter matter, but they are fragments of an incomplete puzzle. There is a type of urban condition that dwells between the reality of massive structures and the reality of semi-abandoned places. I think it is central to the experience of the urban and it makes legible transitions and unsettlements of specific spatio-temporal configurations.

The work of capturing this elusive quality that cities produce and make legible is not easily executed. Utility logics won't do. I can't help but think that artists are part of the answer; whether ephemeral public performances and installations or more lasting types of public sculpture, whether site-specific/community-based art, or nomadic sculptures that circulate among localities.

And so are architectural practices located in unforthcoming spaces. There is a diversity of such spaces. One instance is that of intersections of multiple transport and communication networks, where the naked eye or the engineer's understanding sees no shape, no possibility of a form, just pure infrastructure and its necessary uses. Another instance is a space that requires the work of detecting possible architectures where there now is merely a formal silence, a non-existence, such as a modest *terrain vague*, not a grand one that becomes magnificent through the scale of its decay, such as an old unused industrial harbour. In addition to the other forms of work they represent, architecture and urban design can also function as critical artistic practices that allow us to capture something about this elusive urban quality; going far beyond what is represented by notions such as the theme-parking of the urban.

The making and siting of public space is one lens into these types of questions. We are living through a kind of crisis in public space resulting from its growing commercialization, theme-parking and privatization. The grand monumentalized public spaces of the state and the crown, especially in former imperial capitals, dominate our experience of public space. Users do render them public through their practices. But what about the actual making of public space in these complex cities, both through architectural interventions and through users' practices? Public-access space is an enormous resource and we need more of it. But let us not confuse public-access space with public space. The latter requires making, through the practices and the subjectivities of people. Through their practices, users of the space wind up making various types of 'publicness'.

A second observation concerns the political character of these cities. The other side of the large complex city, especially if global, is that it is a sort of new frontier zone where an enormous mix of people converges. Those who lack power, those who are disadvantaged, outsiders or discriminated minorities, can gain presence in such cities, presence *vis-à-vis* power and presence *vis-à-vis* each other. This signals, for me, the possibility of a new type of politics centred in new types of political actors. It is not simply a

matter of having or not having power. There are new hybrid bases from which to act.

The space of the city is a far more concrete space for politics than that of the nation. It becomes a place where non-formal political actors can be part of the political scene in a way that is much more difficult at the national level. National politics needs to run through existing formal systems, whether the electoral political system or the judiciary. Non-formal political actors are rendered invisible in the space of national politics. Cities, in contrast, can accommodate a broad range of political activities; squatting, demonstrations against police brutality, fighting for the rights of immigrants and the homeless, the politics of culture and identity, gay and lesbian politics. Much of this becomes visible on the street. Much of urban politics is concrete, enacted by people rather than dependent on massive media technologies.

The large city of today, especially the global city, emerges as a strategic site for these new types of operations. It is a strategic site for global corporate capital. But it is also one of the sites where the formation of new claims by informal political actors materializes and assumes concrete forms.

A third observation concerns the relationship of these cities to the typical urban topographic representations we continue to use. The types of developments examined in this essay can only partly be captured through traditional topographic representations of cities. This is not a new problem, but it has become more acute under current conditions. Thus while a topographic description can make visible the global moment as it materializes in urban space, such a description obscures the underlying connections between that globalized space and the informal economies examined earlier. The immigrant communities and growing sectors of shanty towns, which are one of the sites for the new informal economies linked to the advanced globalized economy, would typically be represented as marginal to it all. Secondly, topographic descriptions do not capture the multiplication of inter-city geographies that connect specific spaces of cities, such as the networks of financial centres, or the networks of hundreds of affiliates of global firms, or the specialized infrastructures that connect a few thousand buildings worldwide. Nor can such descriptions capture the informal city as a site for transnational immigrant households and enterprises and for new types of networks of artists and new media enterprises.

More and more urban spaces are today partly embedded in global and digital systems. The emblematic case is perhaps the financial centre that is far more articulated with the global financial markets than with the economy of the city or country in which it is located. On a very different scale, but going in the same direction, it will not be long before many urban residents begin to experience the 'local' as a type of microenvironment with global span. This will include poor and even marginal actors. The outcome for urban space is that at least some of what we keep representing and experiencing as something local; a building, an urban place, a household, an activist organization in our neighbourhood is located not only in the concrete places where we can see it, but also on digital networks that span the globe. A growing number of entities located in global cities are becoming connected with other such entities in cities near and far.

What does it mean for a city to contain a proliferation of these globally-oriented yet very localized offices, households and organizations? And what is the meaning of context under these conditions? The financial centre in a global city, or the human rights activist's home are not oriented towards what surrounds them, but to a global process. In its most extreme version, the city becomes an amalgamation of multiple fragments located on diverse trans-urban circuits. As cities and urban regions are increasingly traversed by non-local, including global circuits, much of what we experience as the local because locally-sited is not necessarily local in the traditional sense of the term.

This produces a specific set of interactions in a city's relation to its urban topography. The new urban spatiality thus produced is partial in a double sense. It accounts for only part of what happens in cities and what cities are about. And it inhabits only part of what we might think of as the space of the city, whether this be understood as a city's administrative boundaries or in the sense of the multiple public imaginaries that may be present in different sectors of a city's people. If we consider urban space as productive, as enabling new configurations, then these developments signal multiple possibilities.

This brings me to the fourth and final observation. Could it be that precisely what urban topography misses is a source of a new type of inter-city potential? At a time when growing numbers of people, economic opportunities, social problems and political options concentrate in cities, we need to explore how urban governments can work internationally to further global governance.

Let me make the case that cities – more precisely, international networks of cities – can contribute to the work of global governance for at least two reasons. One of these is the fact that cities concentrate a growing share of just about all key components of our social and political architectures, including key organizational components of the global economy. A second reason is that most key global dynamics run through cities, in some cases merely momentarily and in others in more durable ways. Global corporations still need the massive concentrations of state-of-the-art specialized resources only cities can bring together; and, as we now know, organized global terrorist networks also need various resources that cities offer, including anonymity. Further, these dynamics tend to come together in cities in a way they do not in other types of places. This makes cities enormously concrete sites and in turn, makes many of these global processes concrete and more legible. These conditions can help in the work of global governance.

But there is a broader landscape within which to understand this urban potential for contributing to global governance. Cities have historically been the places for many of our best political innovations, among them civic ideals and citizenship. We are living through a time of transitions that calls for political innovation, for developing the domain of politics and citizenship. The formal political system is less and less able to address some of the key issues we face, including the power and globality of major economic actors discussed in this essay. Many of these challenges play out in cities, at least for part of their trajectories. Urban residents and leaderships should be part of the effort to address the governance challenges we face in this new global context. Much of what we think of and call 'global' actually materializes in cities and in the inter-city geographies produced by economic, cultural and political globalization. The multiple specialized circuits that constitute these inter-city geographies are *de facto* venues for inter-city politics. It is not a question of a 'United Nations of cities'. It is, rather, bringing the global down to its concrete urban moment and recognizing the extent to which one city's specific challenges might recur in a few or many other cities. These cover an increasingly broad range of economic, cultural and political issues and even types of armed violence we thought only took place in formal battlefields. The residents and leaders of cities are used to addressing concrete conditions. The recurrence of particular global conditions in a few or many cities provides a built-in platform for cross-border governing of such global conditions. Most of what cities need to address will remain domestic. But a growing number of global conditions are hitting the ground in cities. It is these that inter-city governance efforts can help address. It does not mean replacing national and supranational governance. It means capturing the specific urban conditions increasingly at play in major dynamics of our time.

BIBLIOGRAPHY

A.W. Balkema and H. Slager (ed.), *Territorial Investigations (including the Smooth Space project)*, «Lier & Boog», 14 (1999), Rodopi
J. Beckmann, *The Virtual Dimension: Architecture, Representation, and Crash Culture*, Princeton Arch, 1998
R. Bishop, J. Phillips, W.W. Yeo, *Postcolonial Urbanism: South East Asian Cities and Global Processes*, Routledge, 2003
B. Derudder, F. Witlox, *An Appraisal of the Use of Airline Data in Assessing the World City Network: A Research Note on Data*, «Urban Studies», 42 (13)
A.C. Drainville, S. Sassen, *Contesting Globalization: Space and Place in the World Economy*, Routledge, 2004
A. Graafland, *The Socius of Architecture: Amsterdam/Tokyo/NYC*, 010 Publishers, 2000
S. Hagan, *Taking Shape: A New Contract Between Architecture and Nature*, Architectural Press, 2001
L. Krause and P. Petro, New Brunswick (ed.), *Global Cities: Cinema, Architecture, and Urbanism in a Digital Age*, Rutgers University Press, 2003
R. Lloyd, *Neobohemia: Art and Commerce in the Post-Industrial City*, Routledge, 2005
M. Miles, *Art, Space and the City*, Routledge, 1997
J. Ockman (ed.), *Pragmatist Imagination: Thinking about Things in the Making*, Princeton Arch, 2000
P. Phelan and J. Lane (ed.), *The Ends of Performance*, New York University Press, 1998
M.C. Ramirez, Th. Papanikolas, G. Rangel, *Collecting Latin American Art for the 21st Century*, «International Center for the Arts of the Americas», University of Texas Press, 2002
K. Rattenbury, *This is not Architecture: Media Constructions*, Routledge, 2001
R.A. Salerno, *Landscapes of Abandonment: Capitalism, Modernity and Estrangement*, State University of New York Press, 2003
S. Sassen, *Territory, Authority, Rights: From Medieval to Global Assemblages*, 2nd ed., Princeton University Press, 2006
S. Sassen, *The Global City: New York, London, Tokyo*, Princeton University Press, 2001
I. de Sola-Morales, *Eclecticismo Y Vanguardia Y Otros Escritos*, Gustavo Gili, 2004
T. Williamson, G. Alperovitz, D.L. Imbroscio, *Making a Place for Community: Local Democracy in a Global Era*, Routledge, 2002
G. Yudice, *The Expediency of Culture: Uses of Culture in the Global Era*, Duke University Press, 2004

INTERNET

AT&T Global Network
http://www.att.com/globalnetworking/
GaWC Global cities database
http://www.lboro.ac.uk/gawc/
Kermes Urbana, Terrains Vagues in Buenos Aires
www.m7red.com.ar/m7-KUintro1.htm
World Urban Forum
http://www.unhabitat.org/wuf/2004/
see also
www.dotberlin.de/english/vision.htm
www.circleid.com/posts/city_identifiers_net_tld/

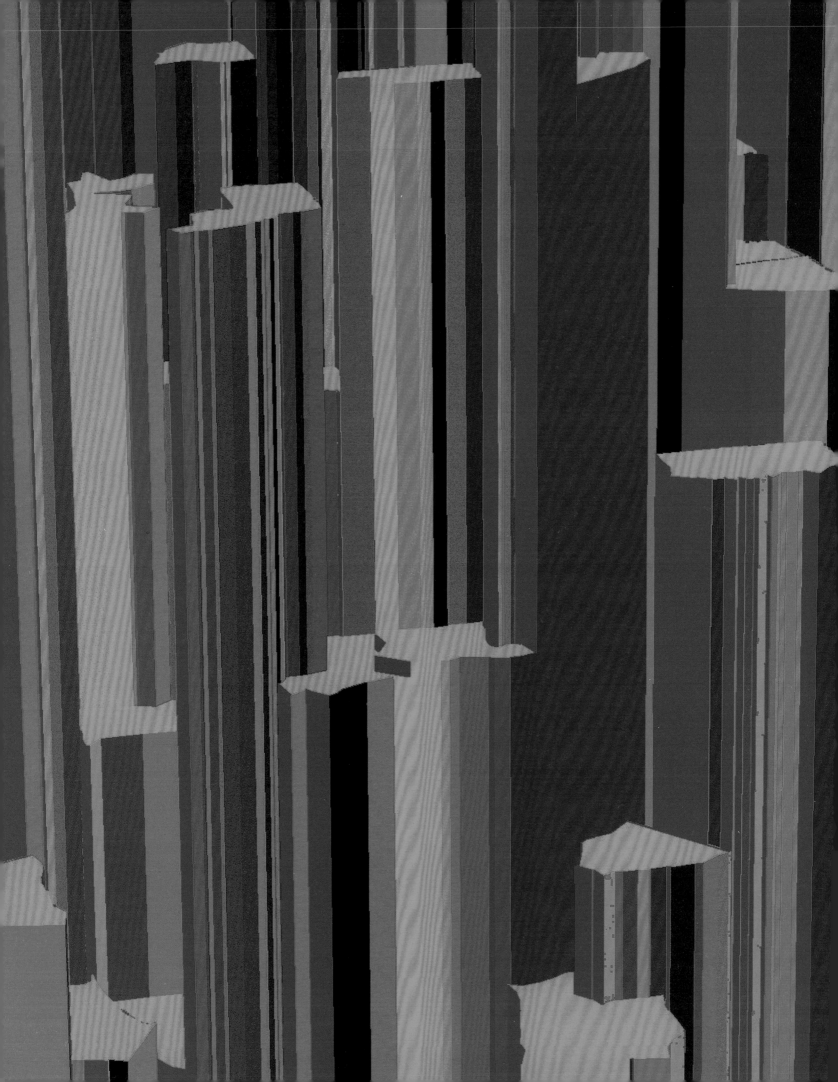

Viewpoints:
Architecture and the city

Iñaki Ábalos

I have in mind two images - a photograph of Olmstead's Central Park in New York and Le Corbusier's Ville Radieuse. If one looks at these images together, they give a strong sense of the kind of urban space we have inherited from modern times. For architects making public space today, they offer a kind of genetic code. In each one, the foreground takes the form of a natural setting from which skyscrapers emerge in the distance. The trees nourish the skyscrapers – it is a neo-picturesque idea, blurring the limits of architecture and landscape. Where historical models of public space supported narratives such as religion or justice or military might, this space doesn't represent any special kind of power. In fact, its nature is that it enables one to isolate oneself – to shun social contact. For me, the most interesting public spaces created in the past decade are always dealing with this idea of the individual isolated in the middle of a dense milieu.

The need to incorporate such places into any programme of urban reconstruction is absolutely central to their success. Once you have produced, in the middle of a dense context, a place of emptiness, a place without programme, the success of the whole area is guaranteed. I remember in San Sebastian, the impact of placing Chillida's sculpture, the Peine del Viento, at the corner of one of the most popular beaches in Spain. There is hardly anything there, but once this very romantic place had been built a lot of new buildings and ways of using the city began to appear. The need for isolation is not a question of taste. It is a quality that everyone is looking for now to a greater or lesser extent.

Once we were looking for space to meet others, but today with mobile phones, the internet and increased mobility, one is exposed to so many social contacts during the week that the need for tranquillity is pressing.

The other role that public space used to perform is as a place of political representation, but politicians completely abandoned public space once they discovered TV. The historical idea of public space has also been degenerated by the emergence of hybrids such as shopping malls and commercial atriums – spaces that are closed to certain social segments. I think it is increasingly only the more introspective spaces that can communicate a sense of truth to our society. One might say the representational role of public spaces has shifted from a collective ideal to an individual one.

However, one collective ideology that I am interested in investing in our own public space projects is that of environmental sustainability. In the course of any project we are continually asking ourselves what kind of figures, processes, materials and forms are able to represent those values. What we are searching for is an aesthetic that we term eco-monumentality. It may sound like a contradictory ambition – ecological concerns are commonly understood in opposition to monumental ones – but I am very sure of the social need to celebrate our values, and monumentality is perhaps no more than an architect's means of achieving that. *Iñaki Abalos was speaking with Ellis Woodman*

Iñaki Ábalos is Director of the Techniques & Landscapes Laboratories at the Architecture School of Madrid. His interests lie in contemporary programmes, and the relationship between technology and nature. Ábalos & Herreros's built works include Usera Library, the Valdemingómez Recycling Plant and the Luis Gordillo studio (all in Madrid). Ábalos is the co-author of *Le Corbusier. Skyscrapers, Tower and Office, Natural- Artificial*, and author of *The Good Life* and *A Picturesque Atlas Vol. I & II*.
PHOTO BY DAVID LEVENE

Josep Acebillo

Towards a new kind of urban planning

In an era of globalization, changes in urban planning culture should result from the application of new technology to infrastructure and be based upon a transition from an industrial economy to a neo-tertiary one.

FIRE parameters (Finance, Insurance, Real estate, Enterprise) are necessary but insufficient conditions for fostering change and producing urban planning policies that are both economically and socially sustainable.

All developed cities suffer from broadly similar environmental and socio-economic problems. The challenge lies in coming up with solutions that are tailored to each context rather than just trotting out generic solutions that tend to undermine each city's potential and special character.

Contemporary urban planning needs a new ideological boost that is based on: 1) *a more complex vision* of cities as open systems; 2) a review of *urban concentration* that allows "critical mass" to be attained (urban densities need to be high enough to support multiple functions); 3) a *new planning approach* capable of evaluating both material and intangible flows and exchanges.

This new urban planning needs to pay particular attention to housing, public spaces, and access. These concepts need to be re-invented and considered as key elements in any new approach.

Public housing, promoted by social-democratic societies in the first half of the 20th century, wrought great changes in the urban fabric. However, after the Second World War, housing gradually became a "good", subject to market forces, instead of a "right". This trend has weakened urban planning because it has deprived it of one of its most important pillars. It has also led to grave social imbalances – young people and immigrants now find it almost impossible to buy a place of their own.

In large cities, soaring house prices are pushing out thousands of key workers to the suburbs, which in turn threatens city centre functions. Housing is the best yarn for weaving the urban fabric and producing cities worth living in.

New morphological, typological, and technological solutions need to be sought and implemented to meet the challenges posed by longer life expectancy, smaller families, and new lifestyles (many of which have been spawned by the ICT revolution and of which tele-working and the "home office" are prime examples). In this respect, most of the housing projects undertaken over the last few years have failed to serve either the broader public interest or to take into account the wider urban context.

Massive house-building programmes, even where they produce high-quality dwellings, do not in themselves constitute a new approach to planning. What is required is urban public space that is both complex and properly planned, capable of incorporating new inter-cultural flows, and which facilitates new forms of communication and collective expression.

Public housing and public spaces are the main elements for re-structuring urban planning in today's fast-changing world. Any new approach must ensure that city-dwellers enjoy non-discriminatory access (here meaning both physical access and to opportunities in general). Failure to provide such access will undoubtedly spawn future social conflicts.

It might do some of our architecture faculties a great deal of good if they were to scrap some of their projects for contemporary art museums (and the like) and take a long, hard look at public housing. I firmly believe that the European combination of *public housing – urban spaces – accessibility* is the only way to prevent social disintegration and urban blight.

This shared, deep-seated conviction lies behind our plans to build 100,000 new houses in Barcelona. The plans are part of a series of urban schemes based on a cluster approach.

Josep Acebillo is the Chief Architect of the City of Barcelona and directs the city's regional development agency. As Director of Urban Projects for the Barcelona City Council and Director of the Institute for Urban Development, he oversaw the planning and urban design effort which preceded the Barcelona Olympics in 1992. In 1999 the RIBA awarded the annual Gold Medal to the City of Barcelona, including Acebillo.

Forum 2004, New Public Space for Barcelona.
COURTESY AJUNTAMENT DE BARCELONA, IPE.

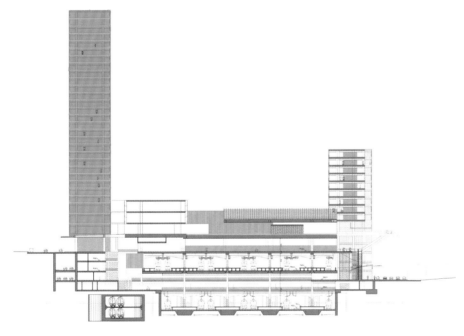

Intermodality and accessibility of the new Sagrera station, Barcelona.
COURTESY BARCELONA REGIONAL

New Housing next to Santa Caterina's Market, Barcelona.
© TAVISA/JORDI TODÓ

Robert Bruegmann

I live in a 1950s high-rise in central Chicago, which is one of the densest urban areas in the United States. My work at the university isn't far away. Nor are the libraries, museums and other institutions that I use. So my living situation suits me perfectly. But my needs are extremely unusual. I certainly don't believe I have the right or duty to impose my preferences on the population at large, the vast majority of whom have no reason to want to live in that kind of high-density situation.

For at least five hundred years the major development in affluent cities worldwide has been outward growth, typically at lower and lower densities, with affluent people pushing in one direction and poor people in the other. That characterizes ancient Rome; it has characterized London since the seventeenth century; it characterizes American cities today. In fact, almost all of what we think of as central in any city today was suburban at one point in history. For this reason I am sceptical about the field of suburban history. Done right, this history would be virtually synonymous with urban history.

To me, the notion that suddenly in the twenty-first century cities should be prevented from further expansion is highly dubious. Schemes that attempt to rein in outward growth by imposing growth boundaries, from London immediately after World War II to Portland, Oregon, today have produced many unintended consequences, most notably the way they limit the supply of land, drive up prices and have a disproportionate impact on people at the lower end of the socio-economic scale.

Historically, the reason given in support of such compaction measures has been to create better city form and protect the countryside. However, proper city form has always been a highly subjective matter. And, in fact, it appears that the architectural avant-garde is just now starting to discover the beauty in sprawl. There is certainly no reason we need to be protecting as much agricultural land as we do in North America or Europe. Almost every country in these regions produces a surplus of food. Not only is this expensive because of the subsidies involved, but these subsidies have made it possible for big food producers in the West to undercut farmers in the developing world, doing untold damage to the economies of these countries.

In the 1990s environmental groups signed onto the anti-sprawl movement in a big way. Some of the arguments presented were about the amount of surface paved over, about the run-off and about biomass but at the very top of the charge was the problem of global warming. Global warming does seem to be a significant problem, but the connection between global warming and sprawl is weak. The problem here isn't the pattern of settlement. It is the inefficient use of old technologies and the excessive reliance on fossil fuels.

Finding cleaner sources of energy is essential when we talk about the really dire problems in the urban world today. These are the problems faced primarily by the one third of the world's urban population that lives on less than a dollar a day and is subject to sanitary conditions that residents of the affluent world can barely imagine. For these people to pull themselves out of poverty is going to require access to more energy rather than less, so the solution to global warming has to involve major technological changes rather than just conservation or rearranging settlement patterns.

If one begins from that premise, there is no reason why a thinly dispersed urban form couldn't be more energy-efficient and less polluting than a densified city. If you lived in a society where each dwelling had a couple of acres of land, you could get all your energy locally through wind, solar and geothermal power. You could have much greater biomass than either the city centre, which is paved over or the cornfield, which is a monoculture. There are already a large number of people in the US and elsewhere who are living off the central power grid. Suddenly, with both low tech and high tech solutions, we are no longer talking about a fringe phenomenon but the very real possibility that large numbers of people will no longer need to rely on the 'big pipe' systems that were necessary to sustain nineteenth-century industrial cities.

In general, one of the biggest drawbacks to the whole sprawl debate is that it is predicated on the idea of the nineteenth century city as the model. What it is lacking is any curiosity about all the other possible urban models. It is strange to me that people who have called themselves progressive since the '60s – people who generally think of themselves on the political left – have stopped being interested in progress. Once they were interested in how technological innovation could shape the future. Now they seem to be absolutely paranoid about what the future will bring: about globalization, freer trade, genetic engineering and also alternative urban options. We keep talking about the car versus the train, for example, but neither of them is close to being an ideal system so let's ask what the next thing could be. There seems to be no technical reason why, in twenty years time, you couldn't go to your closet and get your pod which runs on clean fuel and which you take on very narrow guideways or up in the air. You might join up with 200 of these and go at 500 miles per hour to the nearest city. You would then unhook and drive to your destination.

If we could put aside the unproductive sprawl debate and concentrate instead on the specific and very real problems of urban life, whether in the central city, the suburbs or the very low-density exurbs beyond, we would probably be more likely to find unexpected new solutions to age-old urban challenges.
Robert Bruegmann was speaking with Ellis Woodman

Robert Bruegmann, a historian and critic of the built environment, is a Professor of Art History, Architecture and Urban Planning at the University of Illinois at Chicago. His publications include *The Architects and the City: Holabird & Roche of Chicago 1880-1918* and, most recently, *Sprawl: A Compact History*.
PHOTO BY JACK SCHAFER.

Aerial view, Phoenix.
PHOTO BY ROBERT BRUEGMANN.

David Chipperfield

Architecture without meanings

The city, historically and physically, is often the context of our work. I am always interested in finding reasons to locate or inspire each project through its contextual circumstance; moreover our attitude to the city is a fundamental part of our view of the world.

While I am frequently made aware of the limitations of a contextual approach I am still more horrified by the idea of giving up and saying that each building is an autonomous entity with no relationship to another - that in the absence of a meaningful context you should just stretch the budget, the client, the engineer and the programme in the hope of doing something extraordinary, something that might make something happen. I certainly wouldn't want to dismiss an architect like Frank Gehry, but he doesn't offer any clue as to what our cities should be like, or even what our architecture should be like. He is only concerned with what *his* architecture should be like. And yet evidently dropping a tablet like the Bilbao Guggenheim into the water generates a lot of foam – in a strange way it has created a civic condition around the building.

However, there are two concerns I have about those kinds of projects. The first is the danger that they become the focus of architects' and politicians' ambitions while we give up on any hope of engaging with our wider urban environment. The question they always raise is: does this project represent the sharp end of a more substantial urban change or is it irrelevant to the wider culture of making cities? At worst, these bon-bons can actually serve to camouflage the fact that the other 98 percent of the issues concerning our environment are no longer on the table.

My other concern is related to the impact they have on people's feelings about the cities that they live in. In a sense, these are buildings you are discouraged from having strong feelings about. They are presented like art works. We don't necessarily expect to understand them or to become endeared by them. We may over time, but that is something we are going to have to develop: these certainly aren't buildings that call on a mimetic tradition where familiarity, fondness and memory broker you into a relationship with them. We don't expect them to represent us or our values, for what values do they represent? Society has chosen to say: this is one of those special projects so suspend judgements about time, expense, even usefulness, so we can create a bubble in which a unique icon can be made. If special circumstances have to be engineered to create great architecture, what social meaning can it have? For our own part, we are asked only to recognize and accept their extraordinariness. Ultimately, that requires us to assume an attitude of indifference and I worry that it is an indifference we carry into our relationship with the wider built environment. These are buildings that tell us that society is something beyond our control. It is obeying forces that we don't have any bearing on. They are buildings that demote us to the status of voyeurs.

I feel increasingly with these major projects that possibility is swamping meaning. As more and more formal alternatives become open to the architect it surely becomes increasingly important to question the meaning of choosing one over the other. The thing I have particularly enjoyed about working on the redevelopment of the Neues Museum in Berlin is that every judgement rests on a question of meaning. There has been a movement in Berlin that opposes what we are doing – that has demanded that everything that was lost in the bombing is reinstated. I try not to be negative about that position because as soon as you get into discussions about, say, should the Schloss be rebuilt or the Palace of the Republic be knocked down, all of a sudden you realize you are cutting into a deep vein of emotion people have about their environment. It reminds you of architecture's capacity to carry meaning - to be a vehicle for people's sense of their own identity.

David Chipperfield worked for both Richard Rogers and Foster Associates before establishing his own practice in 1984. He is a founding member of the 9H gallery, London, and a trustee of the Architecture Foundation. He was short-listed for the Stirling Prize in 1999 and has won three RIBA awards. His work includes the reconstruction of the Neues Museum and the Museum Island in Berlin.
PHOTO BY NICK KNIGHT.

Computer generated
image of the Staircase,
Neues Museum,
Museum Islands, Berlin.
COURTESY DAVID CHIPPERFIELD
ARCHITECTS.

Norman Foster

Foster and Partners have been involved in a project undertaken by the 'Foresight' think-tank to envisage a range of possible urban scenarios that might come to pass by 2050. We have proceeded on the assumption that there are two key questions that will shape the future direction of urban development above all others. The first is whether mankind is going to find a low emission transport system or not. In the next 50 years are we going to have ways of moving around that do not damage the environment? The other is whether mankind is going to accept all the technology that the IT world has ready for us now. As a society, will we come to terms with the idea that everything around us contains a chip, given all the Orwellian implications that such a situation potentially entails? Let us imagine we are able to answer yes to both those questions. What kind of urban future might those conditions generate? It will be one in which we travel largely by low emission private vehicles, the controls of which are computer coordinated. We will all have digi-pads, our health will be permanently monitored, and every object around us will communicate with other objects. This *always on society* is a model where people can consume 24 hours a day. We believe it is a model that will lead to very large accumulations of people in urban centres, attracted there by all that the clean, networked city has to offer. This is one polarity.

At the opposite end of the spectrum we can imagine a society in which mankind has failed to solve the mobility problem and rejected the implications of greater technological connectivity. It is a more atomized society – one where people have moved out of the cities because being in a field and growing one's own food offers a more attractive lifestyle. It would essentially be a return to a pre-industrial way of life. In between these polarities there are myriad intermediary scenarios, but we believe it is helpful to identify the extremes so we can ask which direction we want to move in.

One of the key problems is to design the organizational framework to issue the right challenges so that society in its varying degrees of specialization and generalization can respond accordingly. If you take the quest to put a man on the moon, you not only need an organization like NASA capable of realizing the vision, but also a leader like Kennedy capable of setting out the inspirational challenge in the first place. Unless someone with that degree of power and influence can say we are going to eliminate our dependence on fossil fuels and guarantee a future for subsequent generations, then little progress will be made.

Ironically, one tends to find that kind of leadership in societies where the decision-making process is more direct than those to which we have become accustomed in Europe; societies that are less timid, and before an era of over-bureaucratization. In a sense our bureaucracy is a physical equivalent of linguistic political correctness. In our earlier era of urbanization we were able to realize in the course of months schemes that would now take years to achieve. Today in Beijing our practice is building a single airport that is the equivalent in scale to all the built and unbuilt terminals at London's Heathrow, plus 17 percent. It is being built in less time than it took to conduct the public enquiry into Heathrow's Terminal Five project. For those of us who live in the West the question of how society can reconcile that level of direct action with the democratic process is a pressing one. This is especially the case when the democratic processes of protracted public enquiries lead to foregone conclusions and in reality are closer to bureaucratic charades than any true democratic process.
Foster was speaking with Ellis Woodman

Lord Norman Foster of Thames Bank founded Foster Associates in 1967. He has won two Stirling Prizes: once for the American Hangar at the Imperial War Museum Duxford in 1998 and again for 30 St Mary Axe in 2004. He was awarded the Pritzker Architecture Prize in 1999.
PHOTO BY CAROLYN DJANOGLY.

Massimiliano Fuksas

When I think about the relationship between city and architecture, I think of democracy. Architecture can be the representation of a community. We can grasp this concept when there is an absence. When the Buddhas in Afghanistan or the Twin Towers in New York were destroyed, or the Golden Dome of Samarra in Iraq disappeared, or the synagogue in Dresden was destroyed by Nazis, there was a feeling of absence, of lack, of vacuum. Such events, after which architecture no longer exists, help us better understand its importance. Even when they are ugly, don't function or are aesthetically horrible, buildings are the representation of society.

Architecture can – or rather must – have an effect on society. Because what we architects do is try to build a set in which people are the actors. Architecture cannot be independent of people, because if we imagine a city without people, or people without architecture, there is an evident absence. Human beings are obliged to live together with their architecture. So we design a set in which the actors perform, and if this set does not allow their entrances and exits, or the culmination of the action, everything collapses.

If you say to an inhabitant of Paris's *banlieue* that the buildings should be demolished because they are ugly, he will respond that, yes, they are ugly, but he doesn't want another typology. And you think: 'How come, they're ugly, you live badly, you've burnt the stairs, the lifts don't work, the landings are a disaster, why do you want them?' And he replies: 'Because we were born here'. He has performed his human comedy in the set that was offered him, even if in the worst possible place. There is a challenge of sensitivity here, because you know you have to destroy this set so as not to perpetuate these places of desperation, but at the same time you have to find a way to enable the transition. There is no building that can be annulled in an instant.

When I do a project I speak of 'geography' and not of landscape. There are three components in geography, but we architects usually tend to ignore at least two of them. The first component is the landscape, then there

is the economy and the third is the human being. These three things are essential for proceeding toward a better understanding of what we are doing. So geography has taken on a fundamental importance. I started talking about geography 20-odd years ago without knowing what the outcomes would be. The architect is never a theorist, but rather someone who has an idea, forgets it the next day and does something else. I used 'geography' because it was more useful to me, in that I substituted it for 'morphology'. Rather than making a territorial, topological, topographical analysis of places, I used a concept, geography, which yielded greater complexity.

I also think it is necessary to talk of 'context'. There are extreme positions, the mythomaniacs of context or those who hate it. I'm not for 'fuck the context' or 'context is best'. I'm for the idea that context exists.

Another word I use a lot along with geography is 'horizon': you move the horizon, raise it, lower it, then turn it around. It's like cinema. Rossellini used to say: 'I'm never behind the camera, only in front'; he never looked through the viewfinder. Technique is useful until you understand it, after that you no longer use it.

Bruno Zevi told me that it was not enough to be a great architect. There is something more: to be a *good* architect, with interest in the greater complexity of society. I think the architect ought to resume the role of connecting those parts of society that are no longer together. We ought not to dream up visions of a future world (though no one forbids it), but rather begin to revisit the initial problem: how can the architect help many different people live together without killing one another, without insulting one another, with respect and resources for all? Of course one can't resolve everything alone, but we have to start becoming part of that process. The architect should be like Brunelleschi, who was greeted when he walked around Florence; like Masaccio, like Tintoretto, who were part of a community. As a profession, we have to go back to being part of a community.
Massimiliano Fuksas was speaking with Richard Burdett

Massimiliano Fuksas's most recent works include the Emporio Armani flagship store in Hong Kong, the Jaffa Peace Center, and the Congress Centre in EUR, Rome. He has received numerous awards including the French Grand Prix d'Architecture. Fuksas has taught at Columbia University and the Ecole Speciale d'Architecture in Paris.
©MAURIZIO MARCATO.

Shanghai
(November 1992).
© ARCHIVIO FUKSAS.

Zaha Hadid

I have always believed that a formal repertoire is critical in urbanism. I am particularly interested in shaping the ground plane by carving, imploding and exploding; not just as a formal gesture, but as a way of dealing with the complexity of the programme – the social component in architecture. Modernism ignored the ground by lifting buildings above the ground plane and leaving the open space for grazing sheep! We have to go back to the ground, study it, learn how to programme it as an event space. It is not just a formal issue but a programmatic one. I have been experimenting with placing large programme structures on the ground so they don't become a barrier since the 1960s; from my early projects at the Architectural Association and the land formation scheme in Cologne, or the Grand Buildings scheme for Trafalgar Square in London where I used the concept of carving as a way of introducing multiple events at the ground plane.

That was almost 20 years ago. It led to the idea of the ground being public and porous, so that anybody can move through it. Form and programme cannot be separated from eachother; topography brings them together. As an architect, it is significant to be engaged in the question of how form relates to programme. This is why the grid is so important. The grid allows things at different heights to exist; it is a kind of a net which can be interpreted in a variety of ways. In our recent project for Istanbul, located in a large ex-industrial urban gash off the Marmara Sea coast, we have experimented with the grid, creating mountain ranges that build up at the intersections, establishing a distorted net that changes and densifies over time. It can start as open parkland, you can occupy both the street and the land, you can either occupy the whole plot or the intersections with star-shaped towers, low-rise buildings with housing or offices. It is a fluid net that changes in time, programme and space. This gradation allows a process of 'incomplete composition', where a project grows organically over time, but looks and feels complete at any given point of its evolution. Our MAXXI project in Rome, which is composed of different buildings, works as a complete object in three, four or five segments.

I think many architects are interested in the city in an indirect way, increasingly so over the last few years. Perhaps this is a reaction against the negative impacts of zoning and planning regulations that have distorted so many city landscapes. We should move away from these two-dimensional ideas and think about layering across an entire site. Layering is an organizational system that can become complex over time. Its additive potential lends itself to a new way of reading and intervening in the contemporary city.

In the 1970s I worked on the London Project with my students. We would cross London from east to west and north to south, and draw what we saw. But then we would start again diagonally from north-east to south-west and vice-versa;

London *ad infinitum*. The students would take a section of this line, analyse its urban potential and then place buildings which they thought the city needed. Through this reading we realized how the city changes gradually in section and how unexpected things occur. For example, all the parks align along one of these axes. Through a painting technique we identified and isolated London's urban villages, which converge on the city, creating a new image of London and how it works. This process clarified to me how London could grow; that it could expand eastwards creating a new metropolis along the River Thames, more or less what is happening now nearly 30 years later.

Urban density represents to me a lifestyle condition. 20 years ago there was an anti-urban trend that favoured suburban lifestyles over metropolitan lifestyles. What makes cities interesting is the proximity of all civic programmes close to the centre; an intensity brought about by the collision of programmes that makes the city more sociable and metropolitan.

The porosity of streets is what interests me in cities. But you can't legislate for that. It happens. Many years ago I remember being overwhelmed by the darkness of Sloane Street in London, at 19.00 on a Saturday evening. There was a recession and many shops were closed; there was no light coming from shop fronts or restaurants. Now, the reverse happens. The streets are ablaze, infiltrated again by people at the ground level. This was never designed, it just happened. One of the greatest differences to the urban intensity of London in the last decade has been the replacement of corner buildings typically occupied by grand but dull banking halls by bars and restaurants which have re-programmed these spaces of great iconic presence. My point is that the debate about how to activate the ground has been around for more than 25 years, but has never been implemented through design, only programme.

I am intrigued by the urban interventions of the old guard Modernists, such as Tecton's neo-Corbusian, slab and block housing estates in London. These are large scale fragments, incomplete geometric interventions designed to replace the existing city. It is their incompleteness that interests me, because it represents the beginning of an ambition about how urban geometry can actually dictate activity on the street and building form.

It is very difficult in a historic city. It is important to intervene in a contemporary way, but you must do it in a very precise manner. That is what we have tried to do in our urban projects. In cities you need places where things can shrink and expand, but I think you need to set something out to allow for an organic kind of growth to occur.
Zaha Hadid was speaking with Richard Burdett

In 2004 Zaha Hadid, CBE became the first female recipient of the Pritzker Architecture Prize. Her winning designs include the Düsseldorf Art and Media Centre, the Cardiff Bay Opera House, Wales, the Contemporary Arts Center, Cincinnati, the Centre for Contemporary Arts, Rome, the Bergisel Ski-jump in Innsbruck, Austria, the Placa de les Artes in Barcelona and the temporary Guggenheim Museum in Tokyo. Her Aquatics Centre is one of the new venues being constructed in London for the 2012 Summer Olympics.
PHOTO BY STEVE DOUBLE

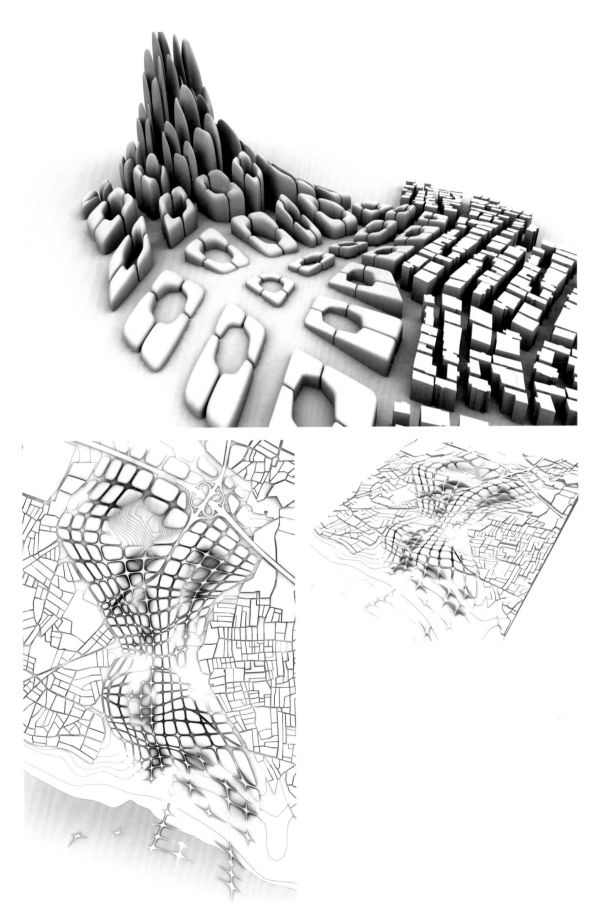

Kartal - Pendik Masterplan, 2006. Proposal for a new city centre on the east bank of Istanbul by Design Zaha Hadid with Patrik Schumacher for the Greater Istanbul Municipality.
© ZAHA HADID ARCHITECTS.

Stefan Hertmans

Generally speaking, one could argue that most European cities have on the one hand a 'historicized' (more than a historical) heart, merely a phantasmal scene of what their heritage seems to represent, according to their own fantasies of their role in history, and on the other hand, fast and unsystematically growing suburbs where modernism has been the outstanding criterion as to the division of the 'free space' outside the historic walls.

Very often, the extension of historical cities outside their own walls has hit the previously rural villages surrounding those cities quite unexpectedly. This means that the confrontation of traditional values and a modernist architectural context only 30 years ago is quite comparable to what is said to happen to Muslim communities in those suburbs today. The funny thing is that the same collision between traditional values and modernist uprootedness has been exactly the case in the Catholic villages of Flanders.

The obvious conclusion is that the clash between tradition and modernity has been the mental scene of suburbs in a far more radical way than it ever was in historical European city centres. Since those suburbs had no direct influence from the more emancipated cultural institutions such as progressive theatre, avant-garde music concerts, the latest movies etc; since the selling of more progressive press, the organization of debate evenings, the influence of university students and so on were all confined to the historical heart of those cities, the fast growing populations in the suburbs had to try to fill this vacuum. It is evident that the suburbs underwent far more direct influence from the mass media and thus became post-modern before they ever had the opportunity of becoming modern (modern meant here as

the traditional values of the Enlightenment and its historical implications in the big cities).

That is to say, the architectural void in the vaguely defined places around tall apartment buildings, which is so often cited as a cause of destroyed human relations (cf. the French *banlieues*), seems to be reflected in a cultural void. Strong individuals from the suburbs have undergone a radical initiation in estrangement from any idea of the city as shelter. This idea of the city as shelter is quite strong in the old cities, where cars are banned, ecological concerns are prioritized and whole areas are occupied by alternative-thinking people who have studied at university, who restore old houses and who take part in a politically correct discourse on the organization of housing for them and their children, founding new Steiner and Freinet schools etc. All of these sheltering activities in what Peter Sloterdijk would call spheres, have remained absent in the suburbs; there those spheres never really closed, never gave the sense of shelter. Ambitious young people who have grown up in those vulnerable contexts have been trained to stand a lot more risk and tend to redefine cultural values in quite unhistorical ways. They are more open to certain forms of 'wild' globalization, but can also easily fall prey to, for instance, populist values such as extreme right parties promising them a good, clean, fast solution. The latest disturbances in Paris have shown that there is a gap between suburban youth and the youth of the historical centre, and it is a socio-cultural one. I think this breach will cause more tensions, but also show an evolution in which suburban contexts may take advantage of their problems and even take the lead in thinking about social structures for the future.

Stefan Hertmans, a writer and poet, is professor at the Academy of Fine Arts in Ghent. His literary prizes include the Belgian State prize. His collection of essays, *Steden* (*Intercities*) was recently nominated for the Generale Bank Literature Prize.
© GEZETT.DE

A young man throws a stone towards police in Paris. Place de la Nation, March 18, 2006.
PHOTO PASCAL PAVANI
© AFP/GETTY IMAGES

Jacques Herzog

Not knowing vs. knowing.

In the early 1970s we studied under Aldo Rossi. It was a time of fading belief. Most of the architects practicing at that time did not realize that they were facing the end of modern utopian thinking and essentially the end of their influence on city planning. The arrival of two seminal books – Rossi's *Architettura della Città* and Venturi and Scott Brown's *Complexity and Contradiction in Architecture* – created a deceptive certainty about how one should perceive and plan the contemporary city. They marked the beginning of post-modern culture, which shaped the thinking of our generation. We were fascinated by them. Rossi, Venturi and Scott Brown made us believe that they *knew* what a city was, or should be. Rossi believed that cities are based on permanence and typological patterns that one should repeat. He suggested tracing historical patterns or recreating them in other locations, much like the ancient Romans did when they built their cities across the empire. Venturi and Scott Brown uncovered the informal quality of the American city, especially of 'Main Street', emphasizing the importance of iconography in architecture. They observed and described cities, and presented them as a model. This played a major role in the way we or other architects of our generation initially approached urban design.

However, while Rossi as well as Venturi and Scott Brown envisioned how the city should be, it became obvious to us that we had to live without manifestos. While they presented models of cities, we realized that we had to do without models and start with an unprecedented lack of theory. We embraced the freedom of this uncertainty as a unique opportunity. We were fascinated by the sheer fact of the city and tried to face it with as much openness as we could. Our approach was based on *not* knowing what we might rely on rather than knowing or believing; it is the same approach that we apply to our work on the design of buildings.

The term *genius loci* could hardly be a more fruitless and irrelevant means of describing a city. Cities become more specific rather than more generic under the pressure of globalization and as a consequence of ageing. In this respect they are a bit like human beings. You become more 'you' the older you get: more 'you' in the way you move, speak and look, more 'you' in your obsessions, failures and successes. Your life shapes you and conversely you shape your life. Our analysis of Switzerland has revealed the specific nature of the city, not in the sense of a romantic idea of 'locus' but rather as an inevitable fate. A kind of illness. A slow process during which patterns emerge, often unconsciously, becoming insurmountable obstacles to change and real transformation.

A comparison of two German cities and their evolution since World War II dramatically illustrates one hypothesis of the ETH Studio Basel. Both Frankfurt and Munich were practically razed to the ground. Bombed out. Frankfurt opted for a *tabula rasa* strategy in the tradition of modernism, whereas Munich decided to rebuild by imitating and simulating the old structures and reconstructing the local architecture. The Munich approach has proven to be more successful; the city has become one of the most attractive locations for younger generations. Interestingly, Munich has recreated the fake, simulated Italian Renaissance imported by King Ludwig in the nineteenth century, whereas Frankfurt has remained true to its sober, democratic and purist architecture cultivated by the local *Bürgergemeinde*. One could say that today Frankfurt has become even more Frankfurt and Munich even more Munich than ever before - despite the bombing - or because of the bombing?

Since the end of the 1960s and early 1970s, architects have been eliminated from city planning and urban design. The lack of utopia has consolidated the process of establishing technocratic city planning based on an ideology of democracy and participation. The highlights of that period are the numerous pedestrian zones, especially in German cities, and the motto of the socialists *die Stadt ist gebaut* (the city is built), which means that no major transformation should question or rethink the already-built fabric of the city. A kind of standstill.

In the late 1970s Pierre de Meuron and I started analysing Basel, the city where we live and work. We started on our own doorstep, so to speak. Later we involved Rémy Zaugg, the artist whose work is based on perception and language, and our collaboration led to an approach to cities that was certainly new and appropriate to the above-mentioned lack of utopia and models. It is based on a kind of intentional *naïveté* that rejects all *a priori* thinking and all ideological pretensions and preferences. We started by observing the artefact of the city and all of its underlying economic, social and psychological processes and transformations. We worked out a method that not only enabled us to reveal threats, but also to discover the potentials of a city and give them names that everybody could understand and act on. This has exerted significant political influence and has, for example, consolidated the *integration* of trinational metropolitan planning processes in Basel. The highly critical portrait of Switzerland, which we undertook at the ETH Studio in Basel in collaboration with Roger Diener, Marcel Meili and Christian Schmid was, in many ways, a continuation of the Basel project and has created remarkable media hype in a country that is normally rather reluctant to discuss its own urban structures.

In recent years we have witnessed an interesting new trend, which is probably independent of our urban studies on Basel and Switzerland: we (Herzog & de Meuron) have been commissioned to carry out numerous projects for large scale masterplans and even entire cities in China, Germany, Spain and the U.S. We are currently working on a masterplan for the entire city of Burgos, Spain, and for the largest piece of land ever developed in Las Vegas. In other words: not only we – the architects – cherish the city as an object of desire, but conversely the city has rediscovered the architect and architecture as the driving force for its reinvention and rejuvenation. Both developers and ambitious politicians have discovered iconic architecture designed by architects of renown to be the most attractive, the most effective and the most profitable tool to build cities.

Swiss architects Jacques Herzog and Pierre de Meuron, recipients of the 2001 Pritzker Architecture Prize, established their office in 1978. Their recent projects include the Dominus Winery (Napa Valley), the Tate Modern (London), the Prada store (Tokyo) and the de Young Museum (San Francisco). Current projects include the National Stadium for the 2008 Olympic Games in Beijing and the new Philharmonic Hall in Hamburg. Herzog and de Meuron both teach at Harvard University and at the Swiss Federal Institute of Technology Zurich. In 2002 they co-founded the ETH Studio Basel, Contemporary City Institute.
COURTESY HERZOG & DE MEURON.

We see our approach to city planning as a possible accumulation of difference, while in reality it is often reduced to a kind of accumulation of built icons and symbols, like a collection of artworks stored in a 'Schaulager'. You can visit it on demand and with special permission only.

Therefore, in recent projects, such as the Forum in Barcelona or the National Stadium for the 2008 Olympic Games in Beijing, we have tried to convince politicians to integrate new programmes and public spaces as integral parts of the buildings. We see those buildings as possible trigger points of the contemporary metropolis, comparable to acupuncture points in the human body.

Jacques Herzog was speaking with Richard Burdett

Some buildings can act as trigger points in the metropolis, comparable to acupuncture points in the human body.
© ELENA RAY

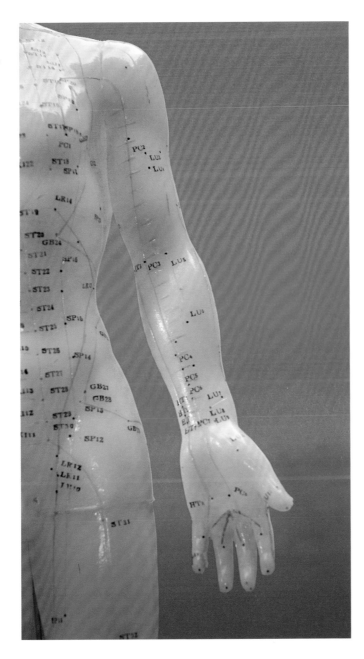

Anish Kapoor

I want to make work that engages public participation. Artists have often been reluctant to take on the idea of participation because of the risk that one ends up making work that operates as a kind of fairground experience. Thus you get Richard Serra making a work like *Tilted Arc* in New York, which embodied a hardnosed art world idea of resisting the urge to comfort public engagement. In fact it did so to such an extent that after a vehement campaign the need was felt to take it down.

I believe it is possible for artists to deal with an idea of the public and at one level it is about reinstating a sense of the symbolic. A sculpture may ostensibly have no programme – to use the word in the architectural sense - but what it needs to do before anything else is define a programme for itself: a poetic, metaphoric, symbolic programme. Unless one can return to the symbolic, making public work really continues to be an interstitial, meaningless endeavour.

There are certain obvious symbolic forms: the obelisk, the fountain and certain kinds of rites of passage such as the gate. Those are all architectural forms but as a sculptor dealing with public space what other language can one draw on? Basically, there is only the body, and contorted bodies in public space seem to me to have relatively limited potential symbolically. I am not interested in making representational sculpture but I am fascinated by the symbolic nature of objects.

My piece at Chicago's Millennium Park is conceived as a gate. It is a form that runs through architecture and has a long military and religious history. But it is perhaps older than architecture. It is a kind of proto-architecture and still seems to carry the potential to communicate a sense of wonder. In Chicago, it serves as the entry into a new vista on the city.

I am interested in the moment when public sculpture becomes something more than a jewel sitting on the lawn in front of a building. That is a model that might have had currency in the 1950s but it doesn't any longer. Yet often the expectations of the role of public sculpture are overly polite. They make it difficult for you to produce something that says: I am a thing unto myself rather than an addendum.

In Chicago, I found there was a strong understanding of the role of public sculpture – Picasso and Oldenburg's pieces are not on a polite scale. They define the city as much as the buildings do. In fact many monuments of contemporary architecture engage scale far less effectively. They may be very big things but they aren't necessarily objects of big scale. Sculpture that is nowhere near as big might have a much bigger scale. As a sculptor or an architect, the fear is that as you get bigger, what you lose is any possibility of the intimate or, ultimately, of the serious. Meaning and size usually appear to be in inverse proportion. Very rare are the circumstances when one can say: it got bigger and the meaning got bigger. But scale isn't to do with size; scale is to do with some deeper mythological function.

Anish Kapoor was speaking wuth Ellis Woodman

Born in Mumbai, Anish Kapoor currently works in London. Kapoor has produced a number of large works, including *Taratantara* and *Marsyas*, installed in the Turbine Hall of the Tate Modern. He won the Premio Duemila as Britain's representative at the 1990 Venice Biennale. The following year he won the Turner Prize. Collectors of Kapoor's work include the Museum of Modern Art in New York, the Tate Modern in London, and the 21st Century Museum of Contemporary Art in Kanazawa, Japan.
© DENNIS MORRIS, 1998.

Anish Kapoor's Cloud
Gate sculpture (stainless
steel, 2004) Millennium
Park, Chicago.
© PETER J. SCHLUZ.

Rem Koolhaas

On working cities.

Today we have a dialogue on cities which we would not have had five years ago, simply because there was neither the context nor the mechanism for that debate. We are the first generation of architects that has had a direct experience of working in so many different urban systems at any one time. Therefore, as a practitioner you have no need to privilege one system over another, but rather can enjoy all systems because you are dealing with each one of them on their own terms.

I see everything that is going on now in cities in terms of either a tension or a stand-off between two fundamental sides: the public and the private. London, where I am working on the White City redevelopment, is particularly instructive in that the public sector has found ways, in spite of its economic weakness, to influence development without investing funds. This is ingenious. However, as control is exercised only through quantity of development, the more the public sector wants, the more development they have to allow. Maximum development means maximum facilities for the public. It is a form of power dictated by this process of negotiation. In London it is a highly developed process, deeply rooted in Anglo-Saxon pragmatism and a relative absence of ideology. This equation becomes more problematic in all other conditions.

In effect the city can only have power if it tolerates an enormous amount of development. The downside is that this works best in periods where the economy is strong; it becomes very vulnerable in a period of decline or horizontality. Ironically, power can only become manifest at the moment that everyone enjoys this state of euphoria. From an architect's position, the interesting thing is that you naturally end up getting work only in situations of intense economic growth and development – always an extremely distorted condition. As a result, our thinking about the city as practitioners is often limited to those extravagant conditions.

In Beijing, the level of distortion is not primarily financial. It is fundamentally different from London because in Beijing the state pays for large scale projects like CCTV. Despite embracing the market economy, China remains unique since the government and the rules it sets are much more stable. They don't require a continuous negotiation, but are instead rather rigid. We expected to get somewhat of a free ride in terms of obtaining planning approvals for CCTV because it is a state project. However the contrary was the case; it's almost as if the state has to be excessively politically correct. We encountered very little flexibility in the face of the incredible power of the traffic and building regulations departments. The approval process delayed the entire enterprise by a year, which they are now recuperating, but that was a genuine surprise.

In that sense, working in London is much more flexible. Here the powerful are only powerful if they exercise their ambition through concessions. In China the ambition is completely explicit and up-front and is much more like what you could do traditionally as the public sector. In London, because of this game between developers and the public bodies, the public bodies are never strong enough to really impose complexity.

Today, everything works against complexity; because the state wants something from the developers, the developers will say 'yes, but then I won't have to do this'. In contrast, complexity in China is still possible. That was the unique thing about CCTV: a building housing creative, production, administrative and broadcasting facilities under one roof. In the West we would never bring all these functions together in a single moment; economic pressures would simply not allow it. In Beijing, the government was able to simply decide to put them together in the heart of the CBD, thus creating a programme for a building of genuine complexity. I have always been interested in resurrecting complexity.

In Dubai all major developers have some connection to the state or are part of it. This means there is a public dimension even to the private sector. This is a fundamentally new model: rather than being in opposition, the two sides are collapsed into a single entity. I am becoming more convinced that 9/11 has in some way made the rest of the world less dependent on the American model. Inadvertently it has led to a whole wave of new associations. In Dubai, the most surprising connections are being made between very strong axes—Dubai/Turkey, Dubai/Kazakhstan, Dubai/Libya, Dubai/Pakistan, Dubai/India—exploiting Dubai's geographical location rather than its political locus. Emaar, one of the Gulf's biggest real estate companies, is developing a linear strip of housing, commercial and entertainment projects across half the world, from North Africa to Vietnam. One begins to see a totally different, new universe, where the West is no longer a significant entity.

I don't know yet whether working in these very different contexts changes the status of the architect in a conventional sense. I don't think that either as architects or planners you can have a lot of influence here. The developer has become a virtual reality almost completely independent of architects. For example, we are working for Dubai Properties—a big company with a real sense of architectural ambition—but that ambition is very gradual. There was a rather bad master plan, which was already being executed and then our system looked at that master plan and how to develop a second version from scratch. It is a more gradual discovery process where you think of it as 'actually it could be better and actually let's change this and ...' and it's done with incredibly smart people who have thought about the urban question for months, using information from various disciplines.

I am very interested in the programme of buildings, but I think that in all these developments the key problem is that we are all supposed to generate identity and uniqueness out of generic substance. In the absence of a real public domain we are doomed to continue in this state of generalization. Since the state doesn't invest anymore, the one thing that connects all the developments in Beijing, Dubai or London is a sense that everything has become a generalized substance. Interest is created either through form or through nomenclature; where everything is a 'square' or a 'mews' or some other urbanistic term. But the real problem is that the soul—although I hesitate to use that word—of the city remains incredibly abstract.
Rem Koolhaas was speaking with Richard Burdett

Pritzker prize-winner Rem Koolhaas founded the Office for Metropolitan Architecture in 1975 and has been involved in building and urban planning projects ever since. OMA's recent projects include Casa da Musica (Porto), Seattle Public Library (Seattle), Netherlands Embassy (Berlin), and H-project (Seoul). Koolhaas is a Professor in Practice at Harvard Graduate School of Design. His publications include *SMLXL* and *Content*.
PHOTO SANNE PEPER.

Regeneration Plan for the White City Area, London (24,4 hectares site at the Western edge of the center of London is a clustered high-rise development with a link between two underground train lines, highway access, common green, office, residential, community and retail uses).
© OMA - AMO.

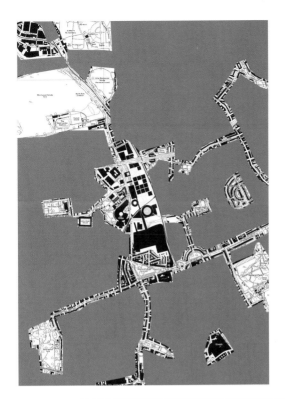

Can Dubai avoid an overcrowding of genius?
© OMA - AMO.

CCTV Television Station and Headquarters, TVCC Television Cultural Centre (20 hectares in new Central Business District), Beijing.
© OMA - AMO.

Joel Kotkin

The new suburbanism

We have known since the nineteenth century that high urban density is not an attractive scenario for most of the population. Friedrich Engels and Thomas Carlisle, H.G. Wells and Ebenezer Howard all reached that conclusion from very different perspectives.

As a rule, once people have become educated and acculturated to urban life, if they live in high density, they are not going to have children. Seoul has become one of the densest cities on the planet and has suffered one of the biggest drops in child-birth the world has ever seen. A country that was once worried about over-population will, by 2050, have caught up with Japan in its aging. The fact is that if you live in a culture where you have to wait until you are forty to buy a 500 square foot apartment in a high-rise you are not going to have children. One of the reasons Americans and Australians breed more is that they have more space. Only less-educated, first-generation immigrants will have children without space.

In the nineteenth century, suburbia was a progressive movement. Today, the message coming from people like the New Urbanists is that the enormous urban expansion we have witnessed since 1910 has been a terrible mistake. I think since 1910, suburbia has provided people with a quality of life far beyond that enjoyed by any population in the history of the world. It has offered them space, it has offered them security and now with the development of the internet, many of them are able to work from home. Engels wrote about the weaver who worked from home until he had to find work at the factories and how that tore the family structure apart. With new technology, we have the opportunity to reinvent that pre-industrial way of life. One of the key means of tackling our present level of energy consumption is for more people to become home workers. To achieve that is going to require policy change. I live in the San Fernando Valley and pay $1,000 for a business licence to work from home. Many of my neighbours do the same. We hardly ever go on the freeways but we have to pay extra even though we don't use the services.

Lewis Mumford called the suburb 'the anti-city' but the reality is that the suburb is the reinvention of the city. Compared with urbanites, suburbanites are more likely to vote, more likely to go to church and more likely to be involved in their schools and communities. The notion that they are an alienated people is simply a myth. We should also remember that the suburbs are in a very early stage of evolution. I don't believe they represent the end of urbanism but rather the triumph of urbanism at a scale and in a form that is completely new.

The ephemeral city

Today, the prosperous urban cores in the west are predominantly the abodes of the rich and the childless and the largely immigrant population that serves them. The first group will stay in the city as long as they feel they can prolong their adolescence. This 'ephemeral city' is an environment that offers little social mobility although some of the service class may eventually manage to improve their lot and also move to the suburbs. San Francisco is an extreme example of the phenomenon. It has a very high percentage of residents with inherited money and a lot of people working for non-profit organizations who are somehow being supported. Most of the economic and scientific activities have moved out and what is left is essentially a lifestyle boutique. It is the kind of place that California historian and San Francisco native Kevin Starr has called 'a theme park for restaurants'. If you are a young professional who can afford to pay $4000 a month for a two-bed apartment then a place like San Francisco might be perfect for you. But in reality, a lot of the population in these places is nomadic. If you visit the docklands area of Melbourne at 9 o'clock at night you find that three quarters of the apartments in the high rises are empty. Many of them are *pieds à terre* for overseas Chinese.

This is a model that will work for some cities, but essentially we are talking about those places that have a physical infrastructure attractive enough to appeal to such a population. Yet there are also a lot of second-tier cities staking their futures on the hope that they can establish that kind of economy. That is why Milwaukee has built a $250 million architect designed museum to house a so-so art collection while the schools are falling apart, jobs are leaving town and the sewers don't work in the city that invented sewer socialism.

A place like that would do better looking for its comparative advantage through cost, or a better business climate or the opportunity for home ownership. A lot of public money is going into these big cultural projects and the private foundations have a fixed amount that cannot be spent both on culture and the school system. In general, local government should be focusing on safety, infrastructure and economics. The market for hip and cool is a small one – perhaps 10-15% at most. In Kalamazoo, Michigan, money is being spent on scholarships so local children can go to college. I think that is a much better use of funds in a city where the arts are never going to be the basis of the economy.

Joel Kotkin was speaking with Ellis Woodman

Joel Kotkin is the author of *The New Geography: How the Digital Revolution is Reshaping the American Landscape*. His interest also lies in the connection between ethnicity and business. Kotkin has studied the future of several major cities, including New York and Los Angeles and is currently investigating the future of transportation mobility in the United States. Kotkin lectures widely and has addressed both Democratic and Republican Congressional groups.
PHOTO BY STEVE ANDERSON © THE PLANNING CENTER.

Leon Krier

The axioms of urbanism

We can safely affirm that the cities of the future will not conform to a single, unified vision. However, there are universal principles for building good cities and villages that transcend ages, climates and cultures. They are essentially anthropological principles, related to the habitual capacities of the human skeleton, body and mind:
- streets and squares;
- cities, villages and urban quarters;
- development programmes and plots;
- building methods and architecture of a certain type, size, character, aesthetic, density and functional complexity
These are the unrenounceable axioms of urbanism.

The principles of traditional architecture and urbanism are not mere historic phenomena and therefore cannot be said to be outdated. They are practical and aesthetic responses to practical problems; as timeless as the principles of musical harmony, of language, of science, of gastronomy. Modernism's philosophical fallacy lies in the infantile ambition to replace the fundamental principles of traditional architecture and urbanism in their entirety.

Modernity and modernism are distinct phenomena and can no longer be confused or amalgamated. Modernism is like so many isms, born out of an excessive, possibly a pathological desire for modernity. Like all forms of fundamentalism, it is reductive and tyrannical in its essence. Today, modernism can no longer proclaim itself against worldwide evidence to be the sole legitimate representative and embodiment of modernity. Those architects who claim today to be inventing the architecture and urbanism of the twenty-first century are even more foolish than the masters of historic modernism. If modernism wants to become a constructive part of the modern democratic world, it has to learn that democracy is based on tolerance and true plurality. Short of this change of attitude, modernism will become an outdated twentieth-century ideology.

The end of the fossil fuel age

Urban space is a void - a structural and structuring void. It has a hierarchy, it has dimensions and character; it cannot just be a leftover between haphazard building operations. Too much of it is a waste, a false luxury; too little of it is a false economy. Streets, squares and their numerous declinations are the optimum forms of collective space. Neither public nor private enterprise produce public space naturally as a mere by-product of their activities. Public space, the public realm in general, its beauty and harmony; its aesthetic quality and socializing power are never a

result of accident but of a civilizing vision and will. It is not age, but the genetic capacities of the founding principles that ensure the quality of public space. Even 1,000 years of suburban expansions will never parallel the civilizing power of urban foundations.

In all modern societies there are now public and private buildings, sacred and profane buildings, buildings for assemblies or for single individuals, buildings for rest and industry, for music and for silence, for honouring or for punishing, for hiding or for displaying, for production or consumption, for commercial and institutional purposes, for defence and for war.

Truly, the scale-less uniformity, aesthetic poverty and general vulgarity of contemporary settlements are not due to reduced social intercourse but to a global, metaphysical crisis. The exponential growth of industrial activities and power, brought about by the generalized use of fossil fuels, may indeed be the prime cause of an all-encompassing imperial hubris.

Functional zoning is the instrument of this mental and environmental catastrophe: an operation that, under the guise of planning, literally destructures our society while ensuring the maximum wastage of land, time and energies in everyday social performances.

The science and art of building cities on the one hand and the science and art of building suburbs on the other are both known to us. Opting for the one or the other is not a matter of historic fate but of cultural and political choice. There are no valid excuses of any kind, neither social, economic, political, cultural, psychological, religious, historical or simply human for building suburbs - for spoiling cities and land. Building cities is a responsible form of economic development; building suburbs is a corrupt form of economic development. Over-population, suburbanism and industrialism are epiphenomena of the fossil fuel age.

With the decline of fossil fuel availability, our notions of economic growth and hence of the planet's carrying capacity will change radically. As J.H. Kunstler demonstrates in *The Long Emergency*, we will have to return to traditional forms of settlement, agriculture, production and building whether we like it or not. Notions of sustainability will turn from being political fads to principles of existential necessity.

A common mistake of fossil fuel age 'thinking' is to distinguish between high and low technologies. Human

Leon Krier is an architect and urban planner from Luxembourg. He is known, most recently, for his development of Poundbury in Dorchester, England. Krier has taught architecture at Yale, Princeton and the University of Virginia, amongst other institutions. His publications include *Architecture: Choice or Fate*. He received the inaugural Richard Driehaus Prize for Classical Architecture in 2003.

technology will be ecological or it will have no future. Sustainable is what is ecological: it has nothing to do with progress, modernism, ideology, advanced or reactionary attitudes, creativity, industry or economy as they have been propagated for the last two centuries.

Historicity and originality

Urban centres are not called 'historic' because of their age but because of the maturity and genetic power of their organizing principles. These principles are transcendent and timeless. We can, if we so wish, build urban centres that instantly have the qualities of so-called 'historic centres'.

It is not history and age but structure, ideas and ecology that confer quality on an urban context. We are not interested in historical centres and architecture because of their age and history but because of the genetic power of the organizing principles. The fact that a building by a great architect is 500 years old or only one does not make a fundamental difference to its quality. It is its organizing structure and the sensuous quality of its materials and design that are decisive, not its historicity. The originality of a great building lies not in the age of its original material but, as J. Fest explains, in the originality of its design.
Leon Krier was speaking with Ellis Woodman

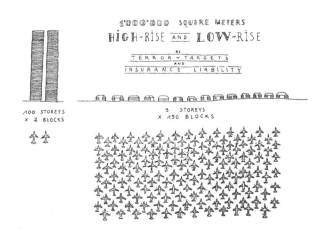

Paul Robbrecht

Creating a path amidst abundance and confusion.
Cities, and in our case European cities, reveal a history all of their own. They are increasingly the sum of an immeasurable accumulation of all that went before them. You could call this the history of innumerable half-hearted decisions, the results of which are clearly visible in the material fibre of the cities. A history that represents considerable efforts in terms of matter and which creates a deafeningly loud image

The results of this visual history are twofold: on the one hand plans have materialized, become tangible matter, which makes the history of the city more accessible, measurable and to a certain degree more useful. But at the same time, due to the multitude of events and the increasing speed at which cities grow and mutate, all coherence has been lost.

For urbanites, it is no longer possible to keep up with what is happening in cities. They are now fragmented and each of these fragments has its own character, but coherence is absent. Town planning and urbanization, although they are necessary in order to care for the environment, can do nothing to alter this.

To a certain degree this absence of coherence is experienced as a kind of collage that gives us an impression of a sort of emotional freedom. A plunge into the library of the past, the present and the future. And all of this with a bewildering simultaneity. These juxtaposed images of the city suggest different choices. Freedom that is almost endless. City dwellers head off in whichever direction they want and gaze at whatever they want. But this freedom comes over as rather relative. The city as it now appears is a mere amusement park for consumers. And it is well known that consumers are prey to the kind of manipulation that discredits the meaning of the word freedom. But we are also beyond the stage of the consumer city because urbanite consumers are bored and now they need entertainment.
On the one hand the city landscape is inundated with images and on the other hand the ever-growing building work to satisfy consumers has brought about a banalization of the city. Even the historic cities of Europe cannot escape this rotten chaos. No more do we hear about a social-historic consensus. Ring the alarm bells!

Modern architecture is wearing itself to the bone trying to attract as much attention as possible and working to create entertainment. This leads to the juxtaposition of aspects of enormous importance alongside architectural whims.

And we must not forget restoration; the unchallenged act of repairing all that is old and original. Original buildings are restored in such a way that they look exactly like the original, because there is a lack of any substantiated contemporary arguments to the contrary. This canonization of what is old as well as the demand for new 'kicks' form parts of a power struggle that is both political and economic.

What is now the role of architecture and art in the midst of all this? Apparently mutually contradictory, they are both nurtured by a lack of counterbalance in terms of content. We see examples of this in architecture and to an equal degree in art.

Both disciplines are confronted by gigantism in urban projects and in the media and both are faced with the choice of disappearing into this or of creating a precise and timely counterbalance to it. Loss can lead to innovation. Liberated from the need to create collaborative artworks, these disciplines discover that they can be natural allies. They can create a visible path through the clutter and confusion; constitute an unforgettable place. One of the missions of this partnership could be to create a public space where city dwellers are presented with a differentiation, with an awareness of time and space. Our firm has attempted this in some collaborative projects with artists, for example Rubensplein in Knokke (with artist Franz West), Leopold De Waelplaats in Antwerp (with artist Cristina Iglesias), and Barceloneta in Barcelona (with artist Juan Muñoz). If such a project succeeds, there will be a feeling of familiarity; people will be able to relate to it. It is not, in itself, dramatic if this happens sporadically. This is the very nature, in fact, of all that is exceptional.

Paul Robbrecht has practised architecture and exhibition design with partner Hilde Daem since 1975. The firm's recent major projects include the reconstruction of Leopold De Waelplaats (Antwerp), the extension and reorganization of Boijmans van Beuningen Museum (Rotterdam), a Concert Hall (Bruges) and the St-Felix Pakhuis for city archives (Antwerp). In 1994 Robbrecht & Daem received the Zerynthia Dialoghi tra Arte e Architettura Italia prize.

Robbrecht & Daem
with artist Franz West,
Rubensplein, Knokke,
Belgium.
PHOTO BY PAUL ROBBRECHT.

Robbrecht & Daem
with artist Juan Muñoz,
Barceloneta, Barcelona.
PHOTO BY PAUL ROBBRECHT.

Robbrecht & Daem with
artist Christina Iglesias
and architect MJ Van
Hee, Waterspiegel.
Leopold De Waelplaats,
Antwerp.
PHOTO BY KRISTIEN DAEM.

Richard Rogers

The Board of La Biennale di Venezia, presided by Davide Croff, has accepted the proposal by Director Richard Burdett to award the Golden Lion for Lifetime Achievement of the 10th International Architecture Exhibition to Richard Rogers. Rogers has a distinguished career as architect and is responsible for some of the most iconic buildings of the last twenty five years including the Centre Pompidou in Paris (with Renzo Piano) and Lloyd's of London. His career has been driven by a passion for cities as an architect, urbanist, advisor and author, promoting the importance of architecture in making cities more sustainable and equitable in the context of a rapidly urbanizing world.

Cities are for the face-to-face meeting of people, for the exchange of ideas and the purpose of trade. They bring a diverse number of people together in shared spaces with access to a wide range of public amenities. They are the heart of our culture and the engines that drive our economy. To maintain quality of life, cities should be socially inclusive, environmentally effective and well designed.

After decades of decline and blight, densification can bring vitality back to existing urban areas by providing compact, multi-centred and well-connected cities which support a diverse range of uses; places where people can live, work and enjoy leisure activities at close quarters in a sustainable urban environment, integrated with public transport and adaptable to change.

The industrial revolution resulted in cities which could be a living hell for the vast majority of their inhabitants. Anyone who had the means to escape them did so. The garden city movements emerged as a reaction to poor urban living conditions – Ebenezer Howard's Letchworth and Welwyn and Corbusier's 'La Ville Radieuse'. The new towns all offered an escape from James Thomson's 'City of Dreadful Night'. Previous governments have subsidized people to move out of cities, and politicians have generally been frightened of urban centres as places that encourage dissent and rioting.

Today, urban environments in the West are no longer the nightmarish environments they were in the nineteenth century. In our post-industrial, networked society, modern cities are unrivalled in their potential to provide high quality living conditions. There is a near universal feeling, whether in Amsterdam or Portland, Oregon, that the compact city – the city that doesn't sprawl – is the best response.

In the UK, the current government is the first to encourage people to move back to urban centres. Devolution has been an important part of that – UK cities and their regions are now moving towards the Italian or German concept of the 'city state'.

However, there is still much to be done. Cities that are allowed to sprawl and place a heavy reliance on the use of the car can cause considerable damage to the environment, and – in particular – failure to deal with the issue of climate change will continue to threaten our very existence. Public transport systems exist only where there is sufficient density to support them, so anyone moving out is likely to be reliant on the use of a car for the larger part of their travel needs. In contrast, in central London the combination of excellent public transport facilities and limited parking means that a significant proportion of journeys are made by bus or tube.

The exodus from cities has also created major problems for the environments that are left behind. Cities don't work without the footfall and eyes on the street needed to create a sense of security and vitality. The diminished demographic created by the middle classes moving out is another serious problem. It is a situation that breeds resentment: urban centres that have been hit by rioting in recent years are places that have suffered from a significant exodus of the middle classes.

We need to make cities much more attractive to young families as well as to older residents. For example, some 15 years ago Manchester city centre was home to 90 people. Now that figure is around 25,000. Most of those people are single, or childless couples. In Britain, as in America (though less so in continental Europe), there has been a tradition that when people have children they move out of the city. We need to build apartments that are the right size, well designed and affordable.

It is also a question of providing a hierarchy of public spaces that are well managed, including play spaces for children, areas for older people to meet and sports and leisure facilities.

Much of the potential to densify the city has emerged as a result of the fact that so much brownfield land from industrial times has been freed up. In London – where the population has increased by around one million since 1990 – the policy is that all new growth is restricted to brownfield land. To meet the demand, the mayor has now stipulated that some 50 percent of all residential development is built as affordable housing. Current estimates suggest there is a sufficient flow of brownfield land coming onto the market to meet this demand and I am confident that it can be satisfied without resorting to the use of greenfield sites.

However, a whole series of social problems have been generated by the mass movements of people out of city centres. First, as people start leaving cities, those cities become increasingly derelict and start to lose their identities. Second, there is the loss of green land. In a country like England, which has the least amount of open space per person after Bangladesh and the Netherlands, that is a particularly urgent issue. Additionally, there are tremendous economic consequences. As soon as people move out they require new homes and streets, gas and electricity supplies, town halls, schools and hospitals - while leaving behind them a large number of under-used facilities. It has been estimated that every house built outside a city framework in the UK costs taxpayers £40,000 to provide it with a basic level of infrastructure.

With half the world's population now living in cities, urban regeneration based on the principles of design excellence, social well-being and environmental responsibility is critical to improving the quality of urban life in the future.

Lord Richard Rogers is Chief Advisor on Architecture and Urbanism to the Mayor of London and Chairman of Richard Rogers Partnership. Rogers won the RIBA Gold Medal in 1985 and has since chaired the UK Government's Urban Task Force and was the first architect to give the BBC Reith Lectures. Rogers is best known for the Centre Pompidou, Lloyd's of London and the Millennium Dome.
PHOTO BY DAN STEVENS.
© RICHARD ROGERS PARTNERSHIP.

Activity in the plaza
viewed from the
principal circulation
system, Centre
Pompidou, Paris.
© RICHARD EINZIG/ARCAID.CO.UK.

Denise Scott Brown

Philadelphia

Bob [Venturi] is a very proper Philadelphian. I start out in a very different place – Johannesburg – but it is interesting that both cities are planned as grids. We have thought a lot about the Philadelphia grid, which of course Lou Kahn also analysed in his drawings of mapped traffic flows. One of the important things about the idea of a grid is that the ends are not defined. There is the possibility of going on to the frontier. It is an American metaphor and related to the idea of democracy. Also, the grid doesn't have too much hierarchy. It allows you to have a diner opposite a civic building. Philadelphia's grid has a big hierarchy in one place. Broad Street and Market Street cross and that is where we put City Hall. But there is also a hierarchy between the sizes of the major streets and the secondary service alleys that cut through the blocks. So the Philadelphia grid is really a plaid. It is an arrangement that offers much more flexibility than New York where there are no alleys and the blocks are longer. In New York, there is always the problem of what to do in the centre of a block. Philadelphia has influenced us in a number of ways. Benjamin Franklin and his philosophies are very important to us. Also, there is a quality which I call modest monumentality that is very prevalent here. A building like Independence Hall has that kind of scale and presence, which we have tried to learn from.

Las Vegas

Studying Las Vegas was really our way of studying Los Angeles and the cities of the south west – the automobile city. There are caveats about thinking of Los Angeles as purely an automobile city because the pattern was set up on a rail system. One of the reasons for going to Las Vegas, where you have the desert and then the automobile pattern, was that it offered a purer version. In Las Vegas we did a lot of pattern analysis – particularly the patterns of eye to sign co-ordination, both when driving and when walking, and we related that information to the patterns of land use. Looking at overall urban patterns, one needs to find ways of disciplining the material and not letting it overwhelm you. The important thing is to disaggregate the information and then to choose the right variables to overlay. If you choose the right variables and you can recognize a pattern emerging in their overlap, suddenly design ideas start to grow. Used in the right way, maps can really be a heuristic for design. As an architect, who thinks of herself as a functionalist, there are two reasons why I am interested in looking at that scale of information. First, because it can help me make the functional relationships in my building work better. But second, for aesthetic reasons. If you make an analysis of this kind, find relationships that are cogent, then put together a building based on those findings, you may well find it is

as ugly as all get-out. But then you might really be onto something – possibly a change of sensibility, a break from an aesthetic right into something more pertinent for the time you are facing.

Tokyo

In Tokyo we were fascinated by the whole rebuilding in ten years after the war and what that did to the medieval street pattern which, I say, is based on the span of wood. It is something Levittown and Tokyo have in common. Tokyo took this existing pattern and where it didn't consolidate land there are 'eel' or 'pencil' buildings. These might go up ten storeys with just one ten or twelve foot wide room at the front, another at the back, with a stair slotted in between. We were fascinated by the signage systems and by the exuberance of the architecture. Also we were able to reassess what the moderns told us about traditional Japanese architecture. We realized that they were viewing it with a very focused lens. When my tutors in South Africa introduced us to Japanese architecture, they had to put their hands over the thatched roof. If you look at the lower part it does look just like Mies van der Rohe but they weren't looking at it holistically. They were missing the fact that there were flowing kimonos full of colour and the landscape outside and the market just next door - all of which contrasted with the seriousness of the architecture. They were seeing what they wanted to see, which, of course, we did too.

Shanghai

For people like Bob and I who are fascinated by the intermingling of diverse cultures and what this does urbanistically, Shanghai is amazing. It has an early history of multi-culturalism from the last century. The Bund could be a bit of Edwardian London off Fleet Street. It is the major European financial street along the river. Today you can stand there and look across the river to Pudong, which is a fairyland of high-rise towers with LEDs. Into the Bund comes Nanjing Road which is a Chinese road lined with banners. They intersect at the Peace Hotel, which before the communists changed its name was called Hotel Café. It was the flagship of the Sassoons in the Far East. It is an art deco hotel and you can hear the Old Man's Jazz Band play in the Oak Lounge. It is obviously a throwback to pre-communist times when this was a really lively international city. From the same time, you can find the English and French concessions, which are full of houses that could be in Surrey, and also a housing type called 'Lilong', which is based on mews housing in London. The interesting thing is to see how it has all been acculturated by the Chinese: it is used in a Chinese way.

Denise Scott Brown was speaking with Ellis Woodman

Denise Scott Brown, an architect, planner and theorist, is a partner of Venturi, Scott Brown and Associates. The firm's recent projects include campus planning for Brown University (Providence) and Tsinghua University (Beijing). Scott Brown has written and advised on urban planning issues including the development of the World Trade Center site (New York) and Penn's Landing (Philadelphia).
COURTESY VENTURI, SCOTT BROWN AND ASSOCIATES, INC.

Classic view of the Strip,
Las Vegas.
COURTESY VENTURI, SCOTT BROWN
AND ASSOCIATES, INC.

Richard Sennet

A frequent problem with modern cities is that while they may contain an amazing collection of different people – immigrants, natives, rich and poor – when one looks at the distribution of those communities it is clear that they are rarely overlaid with one another. Each group has found its own territory, which has become very inward turned. There is still a false notion that simply by mixing up different functions or putting different people in the same place they will begin to interact. But the question of how we really get communities to recognize, accept and interact with one another is ultimately one that requires visual thinking. It is a design issue.

My understanding of the term 'public realm' is of a space where people deal with strangers - where they encounter and interact with people who are unlike themselves. One classic locus for such encounters has been the dense city centre but it is far from the only one. The edges between any two communities – whether differentiated racially, in terms of wealth or in terms of their programmatic focus – could be a site where people interact. In fact the centre may well be a space that concentrates a lot of people who are similar while the edge becomes the real zone of encounter.

Obviously, not all edge conditions offer that potential. It is worth drawing a distinction between borders and boundaries – or live and dead edges. The Périphérique around Paris is a physical implantation designed to keep one group away from another. It is an attempt to enact racial segregation: a dead edge, a boundary rather than a border. However, a living border is not simply a place where there are no obstacles to people. Like a cell membrane, it is both porous and has resistance. A cell wall is rigid but a cell membrane is a filter – it takes effort but you can pass through it. In the past that is how urban walls functioned. In wartime they were of course meant to be completely impenetrable but in peacetime that is where exiles, prostitutes, Jews, gays and illicit traders all clustered in a zone. My notion is that we again need to find ways of designing that are based on an idea of the street as somewhere where porosity and resistance coexist rather than as a valueless space of unimpeded flow.

In New York, in the 1980s, I worked on a project in New York City called La Marqueta, which was a market for the Hispanic community. It sells serapes, things to wear, it's also a community centre where hundreds of thousands of Latin American migrants meet and interact with each other. The question we faced was where to put the market. We put it at 115th and Lennox Avenue which is right at the centre of Spanish Harlem. In retrospect, what we should have done is to move it to 96th Street which is where Spanish Harlem – one of the poorest areas in New York – meets the Upper East Side, which is one of the richest areas in the world. Right now, this is a boundary between these communities but moving the market there could have transformed it into a border. It would have drawn people from this very rich area to shop, go out, get a bottle of milk, some good coffee, into a community that is a foreign territory to them. There are a lot of planning issues we could be addressing in this way. When we build schools, we should be putting them in this border condition rather than at the centre of communities.

The same dynamic works on an architectural scale. The use of plate glass at ground level establishes a non-porous relationship between inside and out. So how do we make buildings that are at once more open while still controllable in terms of security? What we want is to negotiate porosity and resistance. Very simple things become the measure of that, like having more than one door into a building.

Richard Sennett is a professor of Sociology at the London School of Economics and the Massachusetts Institute of Technology. His research interests include the relationship between urban design and urban society, the history of cities and the changing nature of work. He has served as a consultant on urban policy to the Labour party in the UK and was closely involved in the Mayors' Institute in the USA. His books include *Flesh and Stone*, and most recently *The Culture of the New Capitalism*.
PHOTO BY SIJMEN HENDRIKS.

The Périphérique, Paris.
© JACKSON LOWEN.

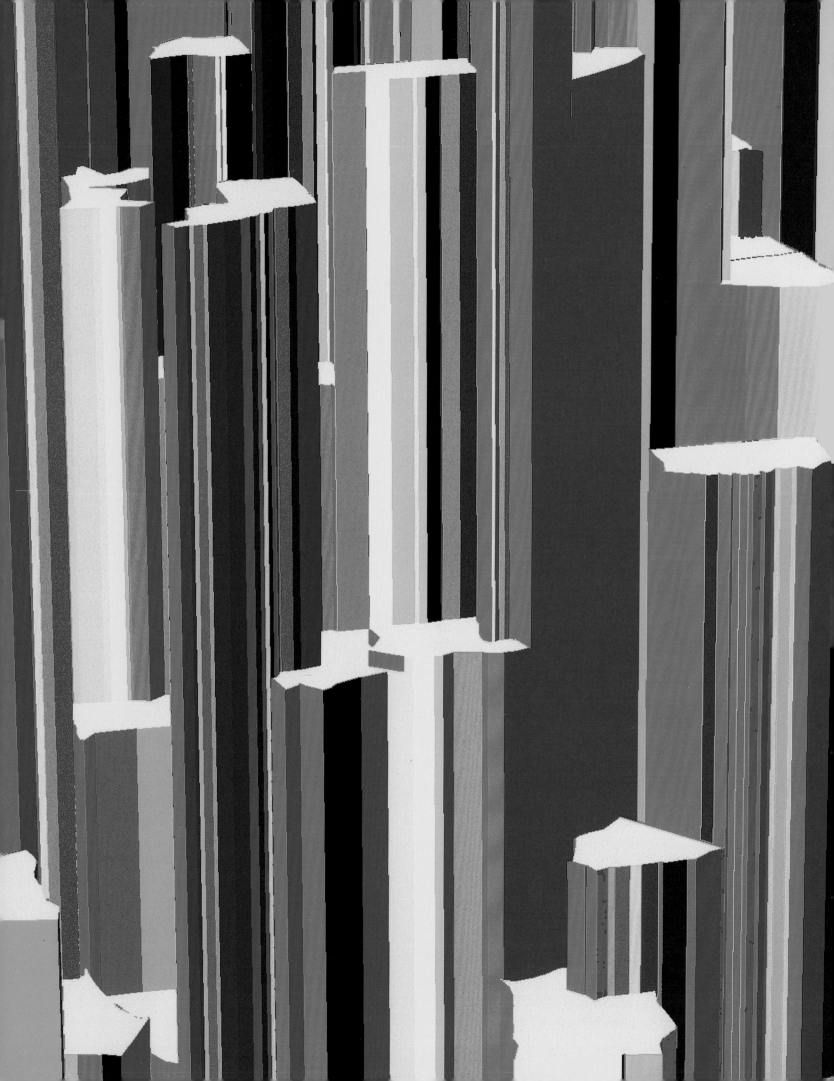

City profiles

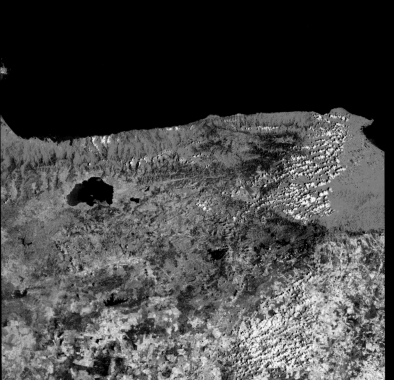

Caracas

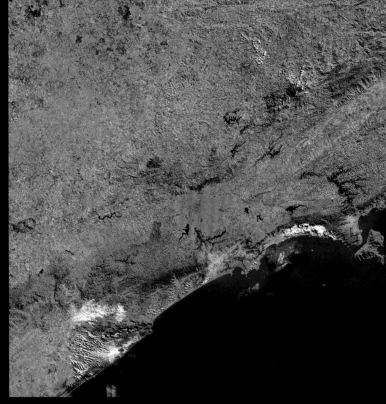

São Paulo

Bogotá

Mexico City

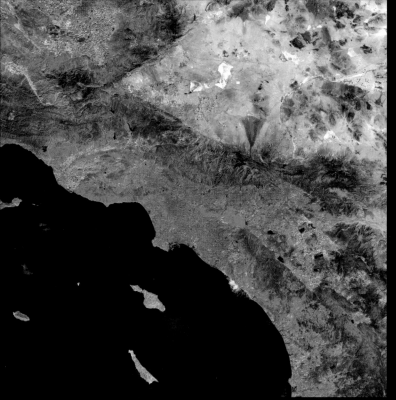

Los Angeles

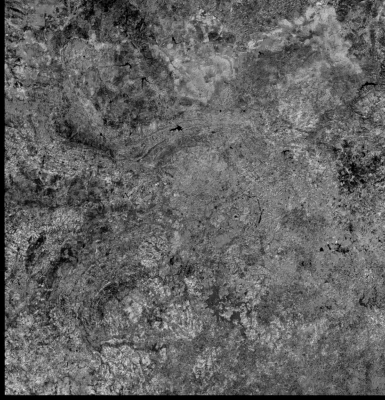

New York City

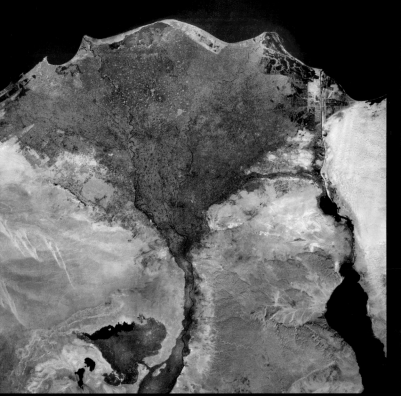

Cairo

Johannesburg

Istanbul

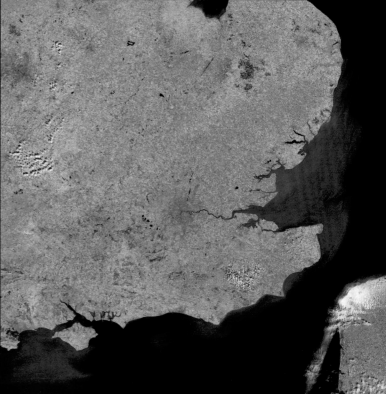

London

Barcelona

Berlin

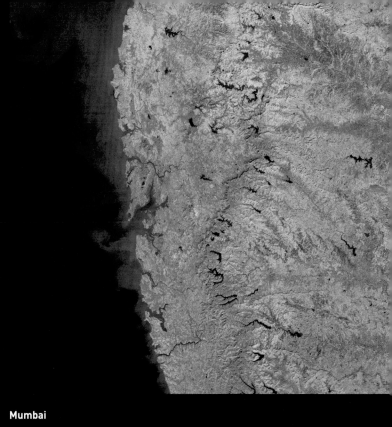

Milan/Turin

Mumbai

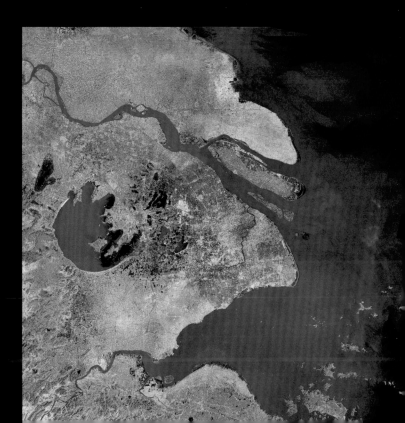

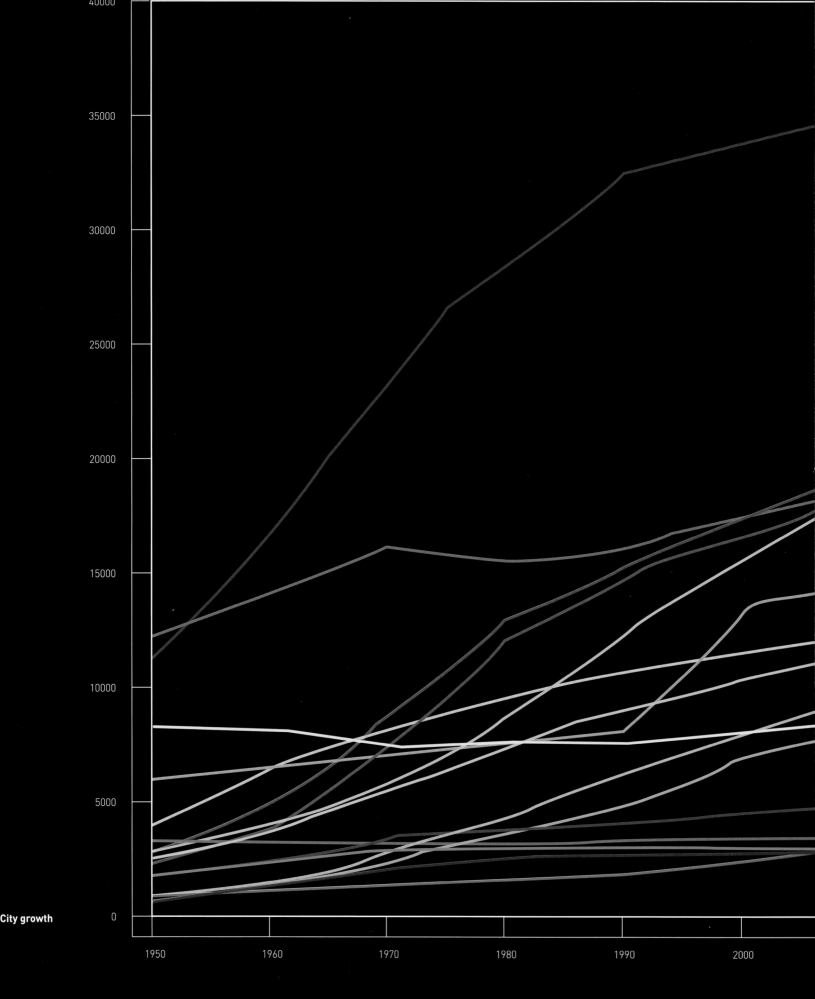

40000

35000

30000

25000

20000

15000

10000

5000

City growth   0

1950   1960   1970   1980   1990   2000

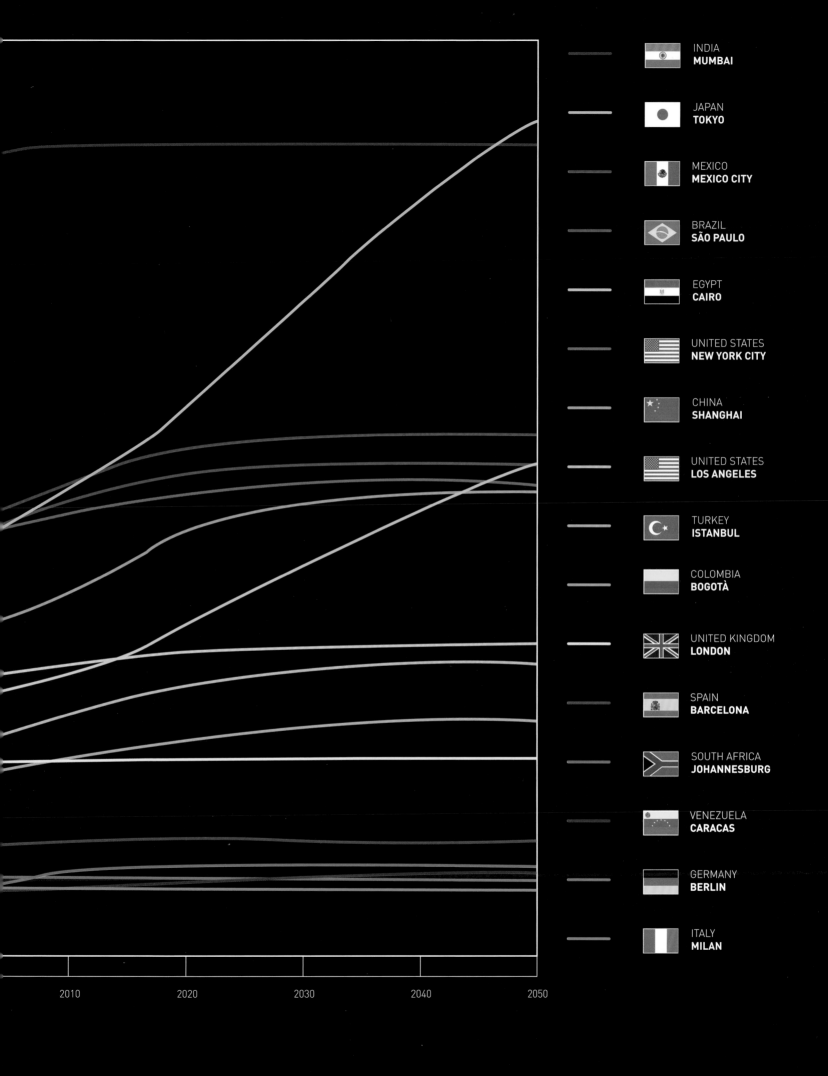

2010   2020   2030   2040   2050

INDIA
MUMBAI

JAPAN
TOKYO

MEXICO
MEXICO CITY

BRAZIL
SÃO PAULO

EGYPT
CAIRO

UNITED STATES
NEW YORK CITY

CHINA
SHANGHAI

UNITED STATES
LOS ANGELES

TURKEY
ISTANBUL

COLOMBIA
BOGOTÀ

UNITED KINGDOM
LONDON

SPAIN
BARCELONA

SOUTH AFRICA
JOHANNESBURG

VENEZUELA
CARACAS

GERMANY
BERLIN

ITALY
MILAN

São Paulo
Brazil

Raul Juste Lores

Raul Juste Lores is a
Brazilian journalist.
He writes in the World
Affairs section of Folha
de São Paulo.
In 2005 he was a special
advisor of the Secretariat
of International Affairs
of São Paulo's City
Government. From
1997 to 2003, Lores
wrote for "Veja" (weekly
magazine) holding
positions as editor of the
World Affairs section,
and correspondent in
Buenos Aires, when
he was responsible
for all Latin-America
coverage. Lores also
served as editor in chief
of Unicard-Unibanco
Brazil's Touristic Guide.
He teaches about
Argentina and Latin
America issues at the
Casa do Saber Center of
Studies.
PHOTO JULIANA SABOIA

Avenida São João
– Photo taken from
Banespa Building, one of
the tallest of the city.
PHOTO LUIZ ARTHUR LEIRÃO
VIEIRA (TUCA VIEIRA).

Pioneer of globalization, the city reflects extreme contrasts

Last May, São Paulo, the largest and richest city in Brazil, was paralysed by an informal curfew. For three days, buses didn't run, schools released their students and companies closed down in the middle of the working day. A criminal organization, the PCC (Chief Command of the Capital), had revolted against the transfer of prisoners from its clan, killing 23 policemen and spreading an atmosphere of terror throughout the metropolitan region – a region that contains 18 million people and accounts for 20% of the Brazilian GDP. The reaction of the police was not slow in coming. In clashes on the outskirts, at least 122 civilians were killed, most of whom had no criminal record. The repression did not arouse any substantial protest.

A week after the imposed curfew, the opening party for the biggest building venture in São Paulo's recent history took place. With an architectural style that is a cross between Versailles and Las Vegas, 'Parque Cidade Jardim' is a $ 700 million complex with six residential tower blocks, five more for offices and a shopping centre. The project's promoters sell the idea of living, working and spending one's leisure time (i.e. going shopping) in the same 'protected' place. 60% of the apartments, valued at between 800,000 and $ 12 million US, were already sold by the opening.

For decades, the Panorama *favela* occupied the area where Parque Cidade Jardim will stand. For the inauguration party, the entrepreneurs put up barriers to wall off Panorama. The concept of bunkers seems increasingly successful. While street commerce throughout the city suffers, 75 shopping centres prosper.

On the other side of São Paulo is Cidade Tiradentes, the largest public housing complex in the country. It was created by successive state and city administrations in an area of the *Mata Atlantica* forest and consists of hundreds of identical buildings surrounded by *favelas*. For the past 20 years most public housing complexes have tended to be built on the extreme outskirts. 280,000 people live there, 40 kilometres from the city centre. Without a decent metro or public transportation system, the average Cidade Tiradentes worker has to spend between two and three hours getting to work and the same getting home. Although it has been in existence for over 20 years, the district still has no library, cinema or bank.

São Paulo covers a surface area of 1,500 square kilometres. In 1900 it had 240,000 inhabitants. Excluding the metropolitan area, the city now has a population of almost 11 million. In 1981 there were eight million inhabitants and 1.6 million cars. Today six million cars operate on its streets and a thousand new cars are registered every day. Public transportation is growing at a much slower rate. The underground rail system, begun in 1968, extends for 60 kilometres, which is equivalent to less than a third of the system in Mexico City. There are only 26 kilometres of cycle tracks, 20 of which are in parks. However there are at least 1,000 private helicopters – the second biggest private fleet in the world.

The city centre has experienced a process of decline since the 1970s. Various campaigns to revitalize it have had very limited results. Major real estate companies and important business firms have fled the area. 18% of the houses are vacant and entire buildings have been empty for more than ten years. In the west and central parts of the city, which have the best public infrastructure, the number of inhabitants continues to decrease. Here there are three jobs per resident, while in Cidade Tiradentes, the rate is .08 per person. The disproportionate distance between residencies and places of work results in a strain on the already overwhelmed public transportation system.

The outskirts continue to expand. About 35% of the city is environmentally protected. Some of this area is occupied by two dams which provide water to the city's inhabitants. The zones around them are being increasingly invaded by informal settlements of wooden shacks. There are more than 1.6 million people living in the catchment areas of the Guarapiranga and Billings dams. Clandestine connections to water and sewers compromise the quality of the water for the rest of the city. Population growth is more concentrated in the regions least well serviced by urban, social, leisure or employment infrastructure.

São Paulo is a synthesis of the world's north-south conflicts. The best social welfare systems are in countries with low birth rates and an aging population while in countries with large young populations, there are no social welfare systems. But the richest countries build virtual or tangible barriers to keep out the poor. Being in need of cheap labour, however, they create systems that perpetuate the illegality and economic segregation of many of these people. São Paulo is already barricaded.

Anthropophagi and audacity

The city has not always been a magnet for workers. Founded in 1554 by the Jesuits, São Paulo hibernated for almost three centuries, as it was not located on the coast, nor did it have gold or precious metals. By 1822, the year of Brazil's independence, it had only 7,000 inhabitants. In 1870 the population barely reached 30,000. Thanks to the coffee plantations that developed within the state, the city attracted millions of immigrants in search of work. And thanks to its geographical location, at the source of rivers which flow towards the inlands and the end of the plateau which leads to the port of Santos, the city accumulated a vast new wealth.

São Paulo has never been the capital. A greater supply of skilled labour for Brazil's industrialization was available in the city than in other regions that had only experienced forced labour. The children of immigrants were encouraged to study and be successful in the New World. The best universities in the country were established here.

São Paulo anticipated globalization. It has mixed up Japanese, Italians, Jews, Arabs, Spaniards, Armenians, Portuguese, Blacks, Indians and Mulattoes from all over Brazil. The privileged young people who had studied overseas and discovered the European avant-gardes promoted the *Semana de Arte Moderna* in 1922. They supported 'anthropophagi': devouring foreign arts and influences like the cannibalistic indigenous groups had done with the first Portuguese; but never restricting themselves to mere imitation. Villa-Lobos combined popular rhythms with erudite music. Niemeyer added the curve to modernism. The bossa nova Brazilianized jazz and tropicalism cannibalized rock. Le Corbusier and the Bauhaus were of course tropicalized in São Paulo.

The city centre and the Higienópolis district were turned into a kindergarten for young architects, many of whom were exiles from the war in Europe. Some fine residential buildings are testimony to that period. Various adventurers turned their dreams into reality here. The immigrants and their descendents, like Giuseppe Martinelli, Pepe Tjurs and Artacho Jurado, built some of the tallest skyscrapers in the city. Assis Chateaubriand and Cicillo Matarazzo, the only great patrons of the arts in São Paulo, assembled the most impressive art collections in the country. Film and television studios, as well as the grand Bienal de Artes, were signs of vitality in São Paulo when the fourth centenary of its foundation was celebrated in 1954.

This backdrop of opportunity spurred the city's violent expansion. It would seem that excessive financial growth caused major damage, as happens to those who do not understand when to stop with the scalpel. During the military dictatorship, São Paulo allowed a viaduct, more than three kilometres long, known as the 'Minhocão' (giantearthworm), to cut through historic avenues, emptying the beautiful residential buildings alongside them. For 70 years the car has had priority in all public initiatives and private ventures; millions of dollars have been spent on tunnels, viaducts and expressways.

In recent years tunnels have been built in an attempt to ease the life of those living in the affluent residential areas of Jardins and Morumbi, but even these are now as congested as the overland routes. Major city governmental projects include the widening of expressways. Although the same approach has been taken for over 40 years and traffic continues to worsen, private transportation continues to be

São Paulo Brazil 1999.
© ARMIN LINKE. COURTESY GALLERIA MASSIMO DE CARLO

Oscar Niemeyer, Copan Tower, São Paulo Brazil 1999.
© ARMIN LINKE. COURTESY GALLERIA MASSIMO DE CARLO

Following page
Favela Paraisópolis (swimming pools). This favela on the left is ironically called Paraisópolis (Paradise city).
PHOTO LUIZ ARTHUR LEIRÃO VIEIRA (TUCA VIEIRA).

the priority of the municipal government. On Fridays the city accumulates up to 180 kilometres of traffic in a single hour.

The flight of the rich

This process has been accompanied by the internal migration of the most affluent groups towards the western regions of the city. In the last 30 years, regions like Morumbi, Berrini, Alphaville and Vila Olimpia have attracted quality residences and offices. In the name of security, walls have been heightened and extended, cars have been armoured, and thus inhospitable suburbs are born, without public squares, sidewalks or passers-by. They provide an ineffective bunker: violence in the city has exploded, ignoring the high walls and private armed guards. In 1970 there were 9.7 murders per 100,000 inhabitants. In 1999 the figure had reached 35. Currently this figure stands at 18.2 – most of which occur on the outskirts.

Excellent architecture flourished in São Paulo's golden age. The city has a legacy of buildings designed by the two Pritzker prize winners, Paulo Mendes da Rocha and Oscar Niemeyer, the latter having designed the city's most emblematic park (Ibirapuera) and building (Copan). The Italian Lina Bo Bardi, who created the celebrated MASP museum and the revolutionary Oficina theatre, has converted an old drum and fridge factory into one of the most vibrant sports, social and cultural centres in Brazil – the SESC Pompéia.

Not even all the omissions and mistakes committed have been able to contain the city's creative impulse – Brazil's power station. The country's major industries and banks, the best universities and theatre companies, some of the leading advertising agencies in the world and an emerging fashion industry are all here. More than 13,000 restaurants reflect the city's cultural diversity as well as its worldwide power of attraction. São Paulo holds the biggest Gay Pride parade in the world which, with 2.4 million people, attests that not even waves of worldwide conservatism can quench the city's spirit.

The flight of the elite continues to segregated quarters with bucolic names: Villa this, Garden that, and so forth. This elite will spend even more time snarled up in the traffic getting to their bunker refuges. They will not use their studies abroad, their resources or ideas to find solutions for a city, swamped with problems and calling out for answers. Inside their closed quarters, this elite is a long way from the best restaurants, art galleries, museums, theatres and cinemas, and as such, they are unable to relish in the chaos, energy and enjoyment that this metropolis of 18 million Brazilians has to offer.

Favela Paraisópolis, São Paulo Brazil 2001.

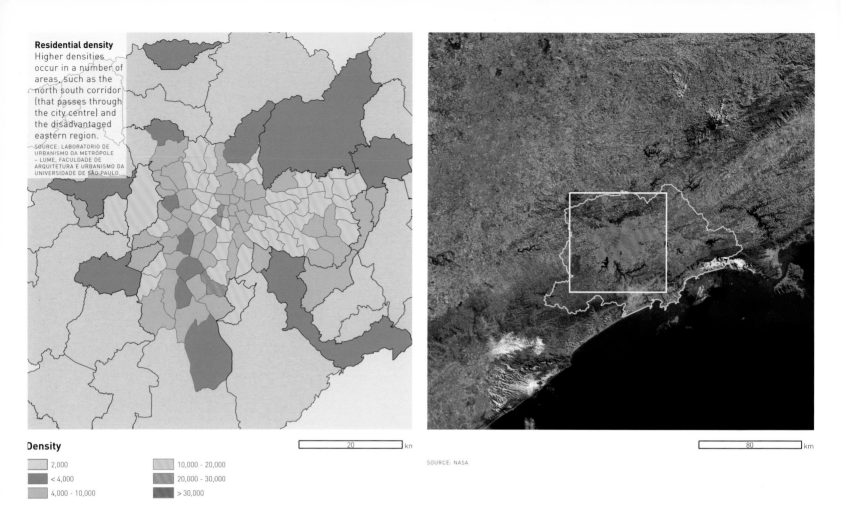

Residential density
Higher densities occur in a number of areas, such as the north south corridor (that passes through the city centre) and the disadvantaged eastern region.

SOURCE: LABORATÓRIO DE URBANISMO DA METRÓPOLE – LUME, FACULDADE DE ARQUITETURA E URBANISMO DA UNIVERSIDADE DE SÃO PAULO.

Density

- 2,000
- < 4,000
- 4,000 - 10,000
- 10,000 - 20,000
- 20,000 - 30,000
- > 30,000

20 km

SOURCE: NASA

80 km

Children
Children concentrations occur in peripheral and low income areas.

SOURCE: LABORATÓRIO DE URBANISMO DA METRÓPOLE – LUME, FACULDADE DE ARQUITETURA E URBANISMO DA UNIVERSIDADE DE SÃO PAULO.

Income
The rich and the poor sometimes live cheek by jowl. However, higher income groups tend to concentrate in the urban core and a number of suburban enclaves.

SOURCE: LABORATÓRIO DE URBANISMO DA METRÓPOLE – LUME, FACULDADE DE ARQUITETURA E URBANISMO DA UNIVERSIDADE DE SÃO PAULO

Youth (population below 14)

- 11.4% - 16.8 %
- 16.9% - 22.1%
- 22.2% - 26.9%
- 27.0% - 31.0%
- 31.1% - 35.2%

20 km

Social disadvantage (average income)

- 3,543 - 6,499
- 1,820 - 3,542
- 1,162 - 1,819
- 792 - 1,161
- 447 - 791

20 km

Images from the QuickBird Satellite of
São Paulo.
© DIGITALGLOBE EXCLUSIVE DISTRIBUITED FOR EUROPE
BY TELESPAZIO.

The population of São Paulo stands today at approximately 10.6 million. The larger metropolitan region, however, has a population approaching 20 million – making São Paulo by some counts the biggest city in the southern hemisphere. During the last 45 years its population has almost doubled and growth in the last decade stands at 9.2%. The limits of the city are in a constant state of flux as the population continues to expand. Somewhat at odds with this growth, the city centre and western areas have witnessed a steady population decline since the 1970s. Revitalization plans, coupled with relatively good public infrastructure in these areas, have failed to stop the exodus of residents and businesses. Crime and decay have eaten away at the traditional business district and almost a fifth of centrally-located houses lie vacant. The fact that the population, projected to total 11.1 million by 2015, is growing most substantially in the areas least well served by infrastructure of any kind is a critical urban issue.

The city of São Paulo spreads across the valley of the Tietê River covering roughly 1,509 square kilometres. The gross residential density of São Paulo is about 6,993 residents per square kilometre. Despite destination that over a third of the city is environmentally protected, pollution is a major problem. Two of the dams contained within this protected area host an increasing number of informal settlements, whose clandestine connections to the city's water supply and sewers threaten the viability of these services for the wider city region, and further fuel the city's pollution crisis.

Ever since São Paulo's coffee plantations enticed workers from Spain, Portugal and Japan in the 19th century, the city's population has remained multi-cultural. More recently São Paulo has experienced a further intake of migrants from Brazil's poorest north-east regions. In terms of its population's origins São Paulo is the largest Lebanese city out of Lebanon, the largest japanese city outside of Japan, and the world's third-largest Italian city. Approximately 5.1% of the current population was born outside Brazil. São Paulo's population is young – over a third of the population is under 20 years old, while a much smaller fraction are over 65.

São Paulo's Gross City Product is approximately € 4,827 per capita. The Gross City Product is substantial in terms of Brazil's national economy – it is worth over a third of the national GDP (in comparison, this is only about 4.5% of Italy's GDP).

The city of São Paulo is contained within the wider region of Greater São Paulo – a region that is subdivided into 39 municipalities and governed by a mayor. The city of São Paulo is also the capital of the state of São Paulo, which sends a representative to the Senate. The city, perhaps due to its economic standing and the fact that the mayor's constituency is the size of that of some Brazilian states, plays a key role in national politics.

São Paulo, once the industrial centre of Brazil, now struggles to hold this title against other regions; its share of national industry has dropped from 55% a decade ago, down to 40%. Industry is responsible for the employment of only 16% of the working population today; whereas well over half are employed in the service sector. At present, the city prides itself on being the financial centre of Brazil, hosting many of Brazil's banking and communications businesses. Of the 6.5 million visitors that São Paulo receives each year, three-quarters come to the city for business.

Despite this relative prosperity, poverty, unemployment and crime are still predominant features of this city. Indeed almost a fifth of the heads of São Paulo's households have an income below or equal to minimum wage. Moreover, almost 20% of the population are unemployed. In São Paulo the extremes of rich and poor are most evident in the contrast between the well-off neighbourhoods and the *favelas*. As is the case in mega-cities across the globe, the polarization between the haves and the have-nots is stronger than ever today.

Today six million cars operate on São Paulo's streets and a thousand new cars are registered every day. Just under half of daily journeys are conducted by public stet, while just over half are conducted by private car. Vehicular pollution is a worrying environmental issue, yet investment in other modes of public transport, such as the metro, has been minimal. Neglected traffic management is also responsible for lengthy commutes between home and work. In a further sign of the polarized distribution of wealth, São Paulo hosts the largest fleet of helicopters in the developing world.

Caracas
Venezuela

Axel Capriles M.

Axel Capriles M. is Professor of Economic Psychology at the Universidad Católica Andrés Bello, Caracas. He is Vice-President of the Venezuelan Society of Jungian Analysts, and Director of the Venezuelan C.G. Jung Foundation. He is also editor of a magazine on Venezuelan architecture. Capriles' books include *El Complejo del Dinero* and *Diccionario de la Corrupcion en Venezuela*.

The pleasures and misfortunes of informality

There is no better way to understand a city than to miss it from afar. It is not a question of nostalgia. Every place establishes a secret pact with its inhabitants. Hence, separation and distance force you to reconsider the contractual terms of this covenant and to read its fine print which, as it is the case with insurance policies, informs you of a hard reality only after you have been swept away by events. The organization of space, the shapes of buildings, the transport networks and the location of parks are not the objective details of an urban reality. Rather they stand as symbolic references, subjective milestones in a mental map that provides the individual with orientation and tie him emotionally to the mysterious weft of the city. The boundaries between the public – the *res publica* of the Romans – and the private domain, the massing of buildings, the quality of urban services or lack thereof, the rhythm and movement of the urban organism are all elements in a cipher that renders the inner scripts of city residents legible and allows us to perceive their innermost parochial essences. The code reveals itself more clearly, however, the farther one moves away from his own city, as the replacement of signs in his subjective map inevitably breaks down the unconscious bond between the individual and his geography. In my case, it was the imaginary presence of Caracas, my subjective framing of sharp fragments of urban memory–only emboldened by distance– that helped me rediscover chaos and informality, not just as ingenious constructions and spontaneous forms of social organization to cope with the daily struggle for survival, but rather as resources to reclaim an urban condition in which the city becomes a central place for sociability and encounter.

To orientate the reader, it is possible to draw an imaginary line that divides Caracas in two: on one side, the formal city with its modern avenues and suburbs in the flat lands – the proper *urbanizaciones* – and in the smoother slopes of the valley, and on the other the informal city with its autonomous and chaotic barrios grown mainly on the periphery and surrounding mountains. Such an image, however, would be incorrect and misleading. The whole town, in fact, is shaped by informality. Side by side with each upper and middle class *urbanización* there is a barrio, and broad areas of the formal town, main streets and avenues, are fully occupied by improvised constructions and shops hosting all type of peddlers.

Unlike the inhabitants of many other capital cities in the northern hemisphere, the people of Caracas thrive on disorder and on ever-present hazards. Imbued with a sense of reality whereby the present is all that matters, they demarcate the physical space around them as events spontaneously unfold at varying rhythms that reveal the specific opportunity of each moment. Instead of peace based on clear societal principles, we prefer excitement and daily astonishment, the feeling of potential and freedom emerges out of precariousness and chaos. If I had to describe my experience of Caracas through a single emotion, it would most likely be awe; awe in the broadest sense of the word, from the jolt in the face of the unexpected, unforeseen or absurd, through to the fear of, or fascination for, instability and change. The *genius loci* of Caracas feeds a peculiar appetite for the irregular and the intermittent; it summons the bizarre. The directions of metropolitan development follow the commands silently uttered from the *barrios*, and even the parlance of local planners reflects the informality of the place; a curt rejection of norms and strong aversion to abide by the law run through the collective soul of the people. Hence the importance of multidisciplinary research projects dedicated to the study of the informal city, one of the most significant and widespread social phenomena of our era.

Just as some of the most populous *barrios* have developed in contempt of municipal ordinances and zoning regulations, more than half of the city's population works outside the formal sector. Several studies on the informal economy point to the modes of production and exchange that emerge outside the excessive interventionism and control from the state. However, informality is far from simply being an illegal activity, an urban planning problem or an economic modality. It is, above all, a mentality. It is a liminal lifestyle, an act of placing oneself on the margins of social existence, a fondness for the events that transcend the rigid framings

Cota Wall.

imposed on our lives. If formal systems are, by definition, a set of explicit norms to regulate social life and anticipate its development, informality is a levelling system that allows for the introduction of chaos into order, an adaptive attitude that accepts the lack of foresight, surprise and randomness as unavoidable and important parts of life.

This line of argumentation may seem too sympathetic to a populist vision or a naïve interpretation that idealizes informality. Nothing is further from my intention. I know and suffer from the unavoidable problems that occur due to improvised and uncoordinated population growth: marginality, poverty, inhuman levels of subsistence, criminality and violence, environmental degradation, and the exclusion of millions of people who cannot even aspire to a livelihood that guarantees a minimum level of dignity and wellbeing. Caracas has turned into an unliveable city, oppressive and dangerous. Disorganized and anarchic, irascible and aggressive, incapable of producing public spaces that foster a civilized sociability; the city has become a provisional encampment that is hurriedly traversed by fearsome citizens in their anxious search for protection in their private abodes. And yet, the human tragedies incubated in the barrios daily are as undeniable as the power of the collective will behind their creation. We need, therefore, to

learn from them, to decode their messages. The autonomous growth of the city on the fringes of useless ordinances and regulations equates to the evolution of an organism that cannot be contained by the slow-moving forms of state bureaucracy and by legal formalisms that are unable to respond to basic human needs.

Every society sets its legitimate purposes, aspirations and goals. In other words, societies have a clear sense of what their values and culture are, and they also have prescribed rules and regulations that define the legal or accepted ways to attain such objectives. However, when contradictions between intended aims and means show evidence of splintering, deviant or anomalous behaviours emerge. But that is also the case for what we call informality: an alternative form to satisfy the needs and aspirations that conventional social structures have no response to. From this point of view, Caracas shows the failures of the elite and the inability of Venezuelan society to organize itself and creatively respond to the needs and desires of its people. Oblivious to all the alarm bells that have gone off and the incessant plea of architects, planners and civic organizations, the people of Caracas continue to witness the physical deterioration of their city and to stare at its decadence with horrified passivity. Adding to the problem,

not only have the scant public interventions proved ineffective in their tackling of the urgent problems that beset the capital but also, because of a lack of commitment and vision, the city was left to its own devises, developing directionless and with the aggravating circumstance that the political liability of populism has mortgaged its future by promoting and condoning informality over legality. No innovative solutions have emerged in response to the collapse of the *viaducto* elevated road linking the capital to the coast where its main airport and seaport are located; no concrete urban management answers to the housing crisis nor to the lack of infrastructure in a city whose population is nearing four million residents. Instead, political action has focused on allowing henhouses in balconies, and on promoting the appropriation of rental buildings and privately owned land.

Can Caracas be helped? Will we ever be able to chase away its demons? The analysis of habitats in the *barrios* of Caracas shows a particular form of atomization, an urban dismemberment that, paradoxically, provides peculiar forms of social organization that are specifically attuned to each condition and place. As much as these autonomous formations are seen as part of the problem that makes the city ungovernable, a smart urban administration could

turn them into resources to propagate more inclusive and democratic forms of governing the city – what we now call 'good governance' is the art of responding to social needs and effectively coordinating interventions from the most grassroots level of civic action. As, with the *cayapa* a collective solution to the housing predicament of an individual family where an entire neighbourhood gather to build their shelter; illegal tapping into the water and electricity grids could turn into organized forms of distributing these services to zones with difficult access; groups of *malandros* or gangs of delinquent youth could become the security forces providing protection to their local areas. In the shadow of constitutions and legal systems, at the margins of municipal ordinances and state laws, there is a world that relentlessly seeks possible expressions, systems with emergency responses for all that the logic of social power has tended to sideline. We need a certain perspective and distance to identify the internal logics of the informal city. To understand the axioms and postulates of informality and translate them into formal logic is a vital step we need to take if our cities are to contribute to a more sustainable world and a better life.

Translated from the Spanish by Miguel Kanai

PHOTOS BY ALFREDO
BRILLEMBOURG, HUBERT
KLUMPNER. COURTESY URBAN
THINK TANK CARACAS INFORMAL
CITY PROJECT.

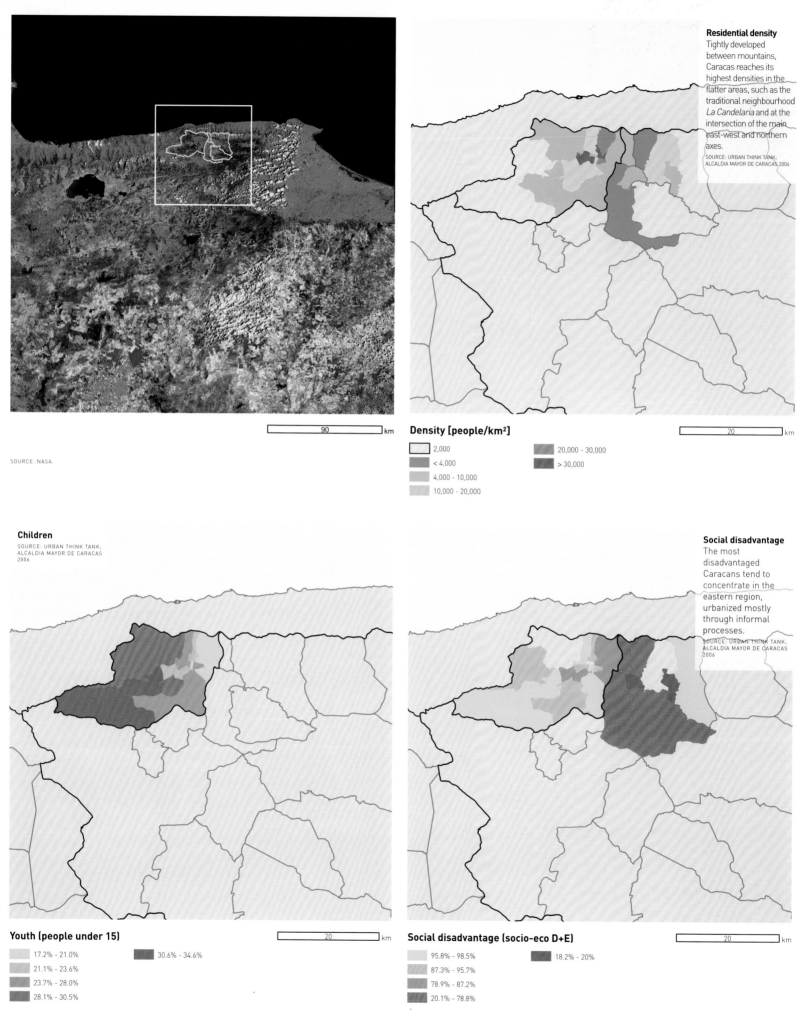

SOURCE: NASA.

90 km

Residential density
Tightly developed between mountains, Caracas reaches its highest densities in the flatter areas, such as the traditional neighbourhood *La Candelaria* and at the intersection of the main east-west and northern axes.
SOURCE: URBAN THINK TANK; ALCALDIA MAYOR DE CARACAS 2006

20 km

Density [people/km²]

2,000	20,000 - 30,000
< 4,000	> 30,000
4,000 - 10,000	
10,000 - 20,000	

Children
SOURCE: URBAN THINK TANK; ALCALDIA MAYOR DE CARACAS 2006

Social disadvantage
The most disadvantaged Caracans tend to concentrate in the eastern region, urbanized mostly through informal processes.
SOURCE: URBAN THINK TANK; ALCALDIA MAYOR DE CARACAS 2006

Youth (people under 15)

17.2% - 21.0%	30.6% - 34.6%
21.1% - 23.6%	
23.7% - 28.0%	
28.1% - 30.5%	

20 km

Social disadvantage (socio-eco D+E)

95.8% - 98.5%	18.2% - 20%
87.3% - 95.7%	
78.9% - 87.2%	
20.1% - 78.8%	

20 km

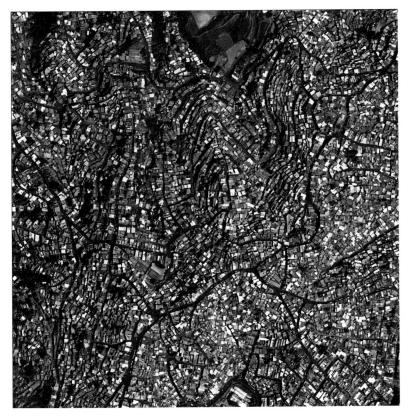

Images from the
QuickBird satellite of
Caracas.
© DIGITALGLOBE EXCLUSIVE
DISTRIBUITED FOR EUROPE BY
TELESPAZIO.

Since its foundation in the 1500s, the Caracas Metropolitan District has expanded dramatically. Today the city is home to approximately 3.8 million residents. During the last century in particular, Caracas bore witness to a substantial population growth, expanding by a massive 1900%. This expansion has slowed considerably in more recent times, and in the last decade the population has only grown by about 1%. This recent calm growth looks set to continue, with future projections suggesting only a small increase of a further 160,000 in the next ten years. Little growth is anticipated within the city's political boundaries. In contrast, it is on the city's limits, in the wider Metropolitan Region, in the satellite cities and the areas along the new expanded metro and train routes, that the population is predicted to swell. Indeed current predictions estimate that by 2015 the population will have reached 4.25 million.

Caracas's Metropolitan District follows the contours of the narrow mountain valley in Cordillera de la Costa, spanning across approximately 777 square kilometres. A seemingly substantial 37% of the city of Caracas is public open space; however in reality the city's inaccessibility and soaring crime problems rob these spaces of their appeal. The gross residential density of Caracas is about 13,980 residents per square kilometre.

Caracas is now home to immigrants from Europe, the Middle East and China, as well as from other South American countries. Indeed 6% of the city's residents were born outside of Venezuela. A tiny minority of Caracas' population is of indigenous heritage. Caracas' population is young; over a third are under 20 years old and only 6% are 65 years or older.

Over four-fifths of the population of Caracas live in extreme poverty, often on less than $ 2 a day and with no access to community housing ventures. Many of these residents also have no means with which to participate in the formal economy of the city. It is therefore not surprising that 40% of the city's population live in informal settlements, *barrios*, or that the informal sector is heavily relied upon as a source of income.

Caracas' Gross Value Added is approximately € 4,800 per capita.

Caracas' economy has continued to develop since the steady, oil-inspired growth of the first half of the 20th century. Today it maintains its position of importance within the South American economy by relying heavily on exports of oil and gas that account for 83% of the country's exports and a third of the GDP. Nationally, just under two-thirds of the population are employed in the service sector, while 23% are employed in industry and 13% in agriculture. Caracas' economy struggles, however, due to ongoing political tensions and low private investor confidence.

The informal sector is incredibly important to the livelihood of many of the city's residents, providing over half of the city's jobs. Unemployment is high at 15%. Resolution of the pressing issues of inflation and unemployment remains fundamental to the future health of the city's economy.

The city of Caracas is divided into five municipalities. It is governed by five democratically elected local mayors and an elected chamber of municipal delegates. The position of Lord Mayor has only existed since a constitutional reform in 2000.

Over half of all daily journeys in Caracas are conducted by public transport; the metro continues to be the most popular mode. Reliance on private means of transport in the city is still significant, and car journeys account for just under half of all journeys. The city has 319 private cars per 1,000 residents.

Bogotá
Colombia

Armando Silva

Armando Silva is a writer and researcher. His research and writing about 'Urban Imaginaries' looks at the contemporary studies that have affected citizens' modes of viewing urban places. He showed work at *Documenta 11* and the *São Paulo Bienal*.

Imagined Bogotá

What colour is Bogotá? It was once grey with constant rain falling 150 days of the year. Grey because, since the foundation of the city (1538), the rainwater and its melodious route had promoted the use of terracotta tiles for roofs that acted as soundboards for the rain's lullaby and its tunes which kept persuading people to stay inside their houses where they slept and dreamt. That reclusive Bogotá was celebrated in the verse of the illustrious José Asunción Silva, who at the end of the 19th century took the local literature out of its rancid rhetoric and made it into something free of superfluous epithets, something filled with beauty and mystery, something which, in sum, was modern. Later on, at the beginning of the 20th century, the local architecture, literature and the arts in general were influenced by three nations that included Bogotá in their cultural programmes: Britain, France and Italy.

As that century was drawing to a close, Bogotá began taking on reddish tone, which perhaps glows from its Spanish-Arabic inspired bricks. Brick is the noble material with which the whole city was built and that also distinguishes the work of Rogelio Salmona, Bogotá's most distinguished architect. Yet urban colour is anything but perennial – its metamorphosis both reflects and accompanies the shifting soul of the city. The sad and solemn musical rhythms of the *bambuco* or the *pasillo*, inherited from the Spaniards, may remain in the memory of the colonial grey, while the warm notes of the Caribbean Colombia, with its African influences, have also been appropriated by the city and bring it closer to the colour of the sun. So this is how, when listening and dancing to the *cumbia* or the *vallenato*, cold Bogotá warms up and gets tinged with red, giving way to the incredible mirage of an Andean city at an altitude of 2,600 metres finding its emancipation in the flare of the Caribbean.

This new urban disposition explains how the *ciclorutas*, an extensive network of cycle paths initiated two decades ago, have become one of the city's most successful initiatives to make Bogotá more sensual and more public, getting people out on to the streets to take over from architects the

main role in the urban stage. When streets are closed to vehicular traffic on Sundays, citizens have the option to stroll around on foot or on their bikes, taking in the city sights as would the most enraptured tourists. The *ciclovías* have enabled residents to regain the city's streets, almost as if, in the ardent imagination of these mountain folk, these streets were the beaches of Cartagena, the most popular holiday destination in Colombia.

But in fact, the *Bogotanos* come from all over the country. As a result of various migratory waves – the population went from 500,000 in the 1950s to the 6,500,000 of today – the city has turned into an ever-shifting blend of the country's various regions. Indeed, more than 50% of Bogotá's inhabitants were born somewhere else. The city, as a patchwork of various regions, enjoys typical dishes from each and a diversity of accents, along with a rich mix of ethnic groups. There are not only Caucasians of European origin and a multi-ethnic population derived from the mix of about 47 indigenous groups of remote origins, but the Afro-Colombians of the Pacific now also contribute to its composition, as do those who arrived breathlessly in the years of the new millennium, escaping armed and political conflict in outlying rural areas. In the end, the city takes on the multiple shades of each place that contribute to this sense of diversity, typical of the great cities of the world.

If we believe that progress in social dynamics is what gives shape to a city, then we can identify a new Bogotá of culture emerging over the past decade. This is the city that has received important international acclaim for having tripled its green areas, provided dignified libraries with good technological resources to its poorer areas, extended health services to most of its population, brought water and electricity to almost 100% coverage and conceived the *Transmilenio*, a more flexible and organized transport system that freed up hours for tormented commuters to improve their lot. This series of corrective interventions, dubbed the 'Bogotá experiment', can be interpreted as the result of contributions from different sectors: the academics who engaged in urban research beyond the mere mental games of obscure theories; the media whom with their

cameras and texts, reconstruct a different city from the viewpoint of the other; the new politicians and mayors – the most relevant arising from academia – with a vision for a new future beyond the havoc of violence in Colombia and plans to build upon the ruins left by the traditional political class and the failed planning attempts from the past.

Over the past ten years crime dropped by about 70%, and kidnappings decreased by 87% – reduced to 7 incidents a year – compared to more than 200 in some cities in Latin America. Bogotá has gone from a daytime city to one that is starting to imagine itself in night clothes – a new restaurant opens every week here. It has traded in its melancholy for an optimism that may even appear confrontational. In our

recent research on Latin American urban cultures, we found out that Bogotá is the capital city in the continent that most believes in its future. Urban experiments from Bogotá have been taken up in other cities: 'car-free day', 'women-only evening', 'hand in the car keys' (if you are planning on drinking), 'the regional day', 'cycle paths' (300 kilometres built) and the Bogotá cares (Sin Indiferencia) campaign.

The current enthusiasm that the *Bogotanos* display for their city has led to various changes and initiatives. These are manifested in the economy – the stock exchange grew by a spectacular 120% in 2005 – and in the willingness of businesses to meet the new demands of tourism, from the prompt production of maps with religious, artistic, culinary

Bogotá #5
© GIOVANNA SILVA.

Following pages.
Bogotá #2
© GIOVANNA SILVA.

and athletic circuits to the organization of daytime and evening tours of the city. This is how the city they envision is turning into a reality. Perhaps Bogotá's urban awakening could be attributed to the fact that it was one of the last big cities in the region to open up to modernity and to a metropolitan self-awareness. A few decades ago local art ignored its urban environments; cinema was poor and the almost non-existent urban literature portrayed only practices of agrarian violence; the media concerned itself exclusively with the political scene, given that Colombia is still a country where – in one vestige of our provincial times – politicians rule the publishing world. Bogotá's renaissance has important cultural and aesthetic dimensions, which explains why so many city residents have embraced the Iberian-

American Theatre Festival as their own local event. It is the biggest theatre festival in the world in terms of productions and also the most visited, with 3,000,000 people in the streets enlightening and engaging with the city.

To visualize the strengths and recent achievements – but also future challenges – of Bogotá, I propose that we think of the city as a circle with only 100 residents in it. In that hypothetical Bogotá we would find that: 54 inhabitants are women and 46 are men; 6 are over 65 and 60 are under 30; 94 belong to the poorest economic groups, 6 to the richest; the 10 poorest get 1 *peso* while the 10 richest get 54 times that sum; bank loans are held by 10 inhabitants who absorb 75% of available capital; 99 citizens are served by water and

electricity, 97 by the sewerage system; 88 have access to basic education and 40 to the internet; 58 accidents out of 100 involve pedestrians; of 100 people who travel, 3 go by foot, 4 by bike, 4 by taxi, 14 by *Transmilenio*, 15 by private vehicle, and 60 by other means of public transport; 15 own a car; 70 are satisfied with their work and 88 believe in a better future. However, this virtual Bogotá needs to be contrasted to harsh realities such as the 100 new residents who arrive daily fleeing violence in the Colombian countryside, and the dying Bogotá River buried under piles of rubbish. Only then can we begin to uncover some of the city's real problems that may have been left unanswered by the – thus far – successful vision of urbanity for Bogotá.

With all of that said, our decision to portray Bogotá as an urban and civic model may still be justifiable. With the *Bogotanos* having taken control of the urban development process, their mental maps of the city, the *croquis ciudadano*, are no longer constrained by the stiff armatures of traditional politics. They rather reflect and imprint the citizenry's wishes which brings to the fore the intimate relationship between public art and urban imaginaries. *Translated from the Spanish by Miguel Kanai*

Bogotá #8
© GIOVANNA SILVA.

Bogotá #7
© GIOVANNA SILVA.

Bogotá #9
© GIOVANNA SILVA.

Jobs

Jobs in Bogotá are concentrated in the city centre and in a job-rich corridor towards the wealthy suburbs of the north, where a number of shopping malls, entertainment centres and other new economy nodes have developed.

SOURCE: FUNDACIÓN POR EL PAÍS QUE QUEREMOS; ARCHITECT CAMILO SANTAMARÍA

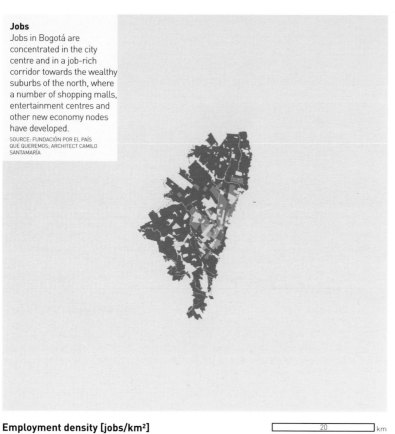

Employment density [jobs/km²]

20 km

- 4,999 or less; 5,000 - 9,999
- 10,000 - 19,999
- 20,000 - 29,999
- 30,000 - 39,999
- 40,000 - 49,999; 50,000 or more

90 km

SOURCE: NASA.

Residential density

The *Bogotá Sabana* frames the city's development and its elongated shape. Bogotá's highest densities appear in the south and in areas of the northwest. Both regions have grown through informal processes, and they present concentrations of poor people.

SOURCE: FUNDACIÓN POR EL PAÍS QUE QUEREMOS; ARCHITECT CAMILO SANTAMARÍA

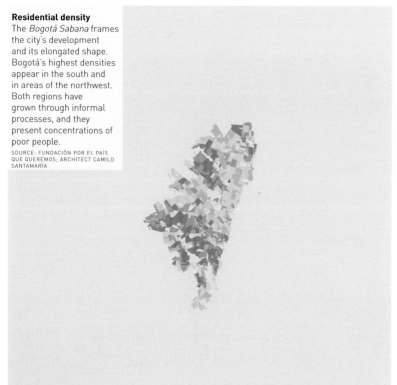

Social Groups

The highest socio-economic strata of Bogotá live in the city's northeast in neighbourhoods and suburbs on the foothills. Hillside informal developments in the south concentrate the most disadvantaged segments of the city's population.

SOURCE: FUNDACIÓN POR EL PAÍS QUE QUEREMOS; ARCHITECT CAMILO SANTAMARÍA

Density [people/km²]

20 km

- 0 - 1,999
- 2,000 - 3,999
- 4,000 - 9,999
- 10,000 - 19,999
- 20,000 - 29,999
- 30,000 - 82,666

Socio Economic Classification (estrato)

20 km

- 5 - 6
- 4
- 3
- 2
- 0 - 1

Images from the
QuickBird satellite of
Bogotá.
© DIGITALGLOBE EXCLUSIVE
DISTRIBUITED FOR EUROPE BY
TELESPAZIO.

Bogotá (Santa Fe de Bogotá) is Colombia's capital and largest city with a total population of approximately 6.8 million. The city's rate of growth has been phenomenal; today Bogotá's population represents a tenfold increase since the 1960s, and the city is about 25% larger than a decade ago. However, in recent years growth has slowed to its current annual rate of around 2%.

Bogotá is located 2,640 metres above sea level and at the geographical centre of the country, stretching across approximately 1,635 square metres. A substantial one-fifth of the city is designated as open space. Gross residential density remains fairly low at about 4,150 residents per square kilometre.

Over the last 30 years Bogotá has undergone a disorganized urbanization process that has increased the number of informal, illegal settlements in areas of risk, notably in the surrounding landslide- and flood-prone areas. To address this problem in 1999 the city created a land bank programme, which has diminished illegal settlements.

98.3% of Bogotá's population are white and approximately 0.42% of the current population were born outside Colombia. Bogotá is an extremely young city – almost 40% of the population are under the age of 20, and only 4% are over 65.

Bogotá's Gross City Product is approximately € 2,186 per capita. This is equivalent to 22% of Colombia's national economy, or about 0.9% of Italy's GDP. Bogotá is Colombia's economic capital; home to the national stock exchange, government institutions and the majority of foreign and national business headquarters. The service sector represents 75% of Bogotá's economy. Although it supports the highest concentration of industrial facilities in Colombia, only a fifth of the city's population are employed in manufacturing. The city has captured nearly 85% of the total income from direct foreign investment in the country.

Bogotá, the capital of the state of Cundinamarca, is divided into 20 districts. Neighbourhoods to the north and north-east are fairly wealthy, while those to the south and south-east are poorer, and include some 'squatter' areas. Each county is governed by a publicly-elected administrative board. Bogotá's mayor appoints the district mayors as proposed by the respective boards.

Bogotá is a much safer city than it was in the 1990s. Although its murder rate has dropped to 22.9 per 100,000 residents – lower than Mexico City, São Paulo, Caracas, Washington DC and many other cities in the Americas – it still has a long way to go to match European rates.

In the last decade the city has prioritized investments in public transport over road infrastructure. Although the number of registered cars is high at 655 vehicles per 1,000 residents (twice the proportion of Berlin, for example), private car use has dropped from 17% in 1997 to 12% today. Over three-quarters of all daily journeys in Bogotá are conducted by public transport – regular buses and *Transmilenio* (a bus rapid transit system that today covers 82 of a planned 355 kilometres). Bogotá also boasts one of the world's largest dedicated city cycle networks, *ciclorutas*, covering 330 kilometres, which is used every day by 400,000 people.

Mexico City
Mexico

Juan Villoro

Juan Villoro is author of *El testigoi*, *La casa pierde* and *Efectos personales*. Villoro has been Professor at UNAM, Mexico City, Yale and Pompeu Fabra University, Barcelona. For three years he was editor of *La Journada Semanal* and has written on arts, politics and culture for many Spanish-speaking magazines and journals. Villoro has presented at many conferences on Mexico City.
PHOTO ALEJANDRO FERNÁNDEZ.

Mexico City: the bearded lady

In Mexico City, the passing of time implies a disproportionate and relentless reproduction of the human species. When I was born, in 1956, the city had four million inhabitants; it now has 18 or 20. And even with this ballpark population figure, there are undoubtedly too many of us here. So we are now facing an odd phenomenon: we have moved to a different city without ever changing location, we live in a nomadic metropolis. By convention we continue to talk about Mexico City, but the landscape is at large, transfiguring itself over and over again.

It is a long time since nature was forced to retrench out of sight. Now the airport is part of the city centre and the only land available for agriculture is found on roof terraces. We have drained the lake that demarcated the floating city of the Aztecs; we have paved over the entire valley and shattered its blue sky. Why then are we still living here? It is not ignorance that retains us. We, the people of the capital, are well aware of ecological nightmares – we produce expert diagnoses of pollution-related skin rashes; readings of lead levels in our blood; and estimates of earthquake risks. And yet we do not seem to really believe that these hazards apply to us, all the accumulated evidence notwithstanding. Welcome to our post-Apocalyptical culture! In our peculiar perception of our environment, we see our lives as the result – never the foretelling – of a tragedy. Thus we explain the vitality of a place on the brink of collapse, whose greatest mystery is that it still works.

Numerous surprises await those who set out to cross Mexico City. Every day, five million people navigate underground on the metro. They are the denizens of another city yet to come, a Mexico where people will be born, live and die all within Aztec crypts, without ever needing to venture out onto the surface. The *metronauts* of today already enjoy the cafes, shops, exhibitions and learning courses at their disposal underground. They even count on their own patron saint to protect them: the Virgin of the Metro appeared at Hidalgo Station at the time of a water leakage in 1997.

Back on the surface, taxi cabs circulate, seemingly directionless after their surrender to macropolitan awe. Drivers confess their ignorance to the hapless passenger who merely produces a destination address: 'You please tell me how to get there'.

When Günter Grass visited Mexico in the early 1980s, he asked, with Germanic exactness, 'How many people live in the city?' The answer then deemed appropriate turned out to be mind-boggling for him: 'Between 12 and 16 million'. The discrepancy, the *margin of error*, had an equal magnitude to the population of West Berlin, where Grass lived at the time.

The monotony in our street names may well indicate the repeated attempts to glorify anew our past heroes. Open the *Guía Roji*, the well-known city map, and you will find 179 Zapatas, 215 Juarezes and 269 Hidalgos – enough streets to trace 20 new cities, all of them with a fairly patriotic flare. On our restless map not even statues are secure. The equestrian monument to Charles IV has occupied three different sites so far, jumping to new locations like the knight on a chessboard.

The Federal District has turned into a bearded lady of sorts in the freak show portrayed by the international press. The city parades its eloquent faults to fascinate them: press reports target pollution, the lack of security, earthquakes, and the manifold menaces to digestive tracks in which our traditional cooking sauces of dubious reputation play no small part. And yet we are incapacitated to sever the umbilical cord that joins us to the city – according to one etymological interpretation, the word Mexico means 'moon navel'. Lunatic and Oedipal, we resemble the libertine in the *The Rake's Progress* – just as Auden's libretto indicates for the opera by Stravinsky, we end up in love with the bearded lady.

In Mexico City there is no standard practice, there is improvisation instead. Even the earth's crust, in its erratic behaviour, makes mistakes regarding the city's age. The 1985 earthquake puzzled experts when the subsoil seemed to be ignoring the laws of physics in its movements. After six years of research dedicated to the enigma, the seismologist Cinna Lomnitz reached the following conclusion: on the

Construction continues on the dizzying Segundo Piso del Periférico, a complex webbing of elevated highways intended to ease traffic congestion in the western core of Mexico City.
© DANTE BUSQUETS, 2006.

Following pages
Mexico City, Mexico, 1999
© ARMIN LINKE. COURTESY GALLERIA MASSIMO DE CARLO.

Street vendors
throughout Mexico City
domesticate public
space in establishing
provisional take-out
or "dine in" micro-
restaurants.
© DANTE BUSQUETS, 2006.

morning of 19 September 1985, Mexico City *was a lake*; the seismic waves flowed like sea waves.

The Aztecs founded their capital on a small island and progressively reclaimed ground from the water. The Spanish conquistadors, who had fought in the Italian Wars, did not hesitate to compare Tenochtitlan to Venice. The city was drained over the centuries with river beds turned into streets. In the city centre, the colonial buildings sinking like wrecked ships are the main remainder of the lake. The memory of water creates a bond with our origins. From a seismological point of view, we still inhabit a navigable basin: our cars travel through a virtual lake.

The criss-crossing of temporalities is not surprising in a place whose underground responds to an original past, to which its surface is oblivious. It is impossible to install telephone lines in the city centre without practising an accidental archaeology. Even when technicians try to find narrow passages for their fibre-optic cables, they end up finding obsidian spearheads, messages from the pre-existing indigenous mosaic. But there is more recent evidence of the ancient peoples of the valley. According to the *Instituto Nacional Indigenista*, about two million Indians maintain their rites and customs in Tenochtitlan today.

Every metropolis may have been erected in opposition to nature, but few have had the destructive fury of Mexico City. Once water had been annulated, the destructive impulse shifted to the sky. The urban landscape is defined by these fundamental losses. Some years ago, when I was visiting an exhibition of children's drawings, I noticed that none of the children painted the sky blue; their pencils chose a different shade for reality: celestial coffee.

The dominating informal economy appropriates public space for the private, unregulated sales of vendors offering a multitude of commodities.
© PAMELA PUCHALSKI, 2005.

Informal market vendors in the Centro Historico, adjacent to the Zocalo.
© PAMELA PUCHALSKI, 2006.

Anyone landing in Mexico City at night gets the impression of arriving in a topsy-turvy galaxy. And this lively sea, which takes up the entire valley, continues to swell. Its logic demands constant expansion. What direction can it take? All the signs point downward. The metro's underground extension stands as our last frontier. Beyond any geological imperatives, these dynamics bear a powerful symbolic charge. In pre-Hispanic mythology, life begins and ends beneath the ground.

Borges summed up his tormented fervour for Buenos Aires in two lines: '*No nos une el amor sino el espanto/ será por eso que la quiero tanto*' (It is not love that unites us but fear / this is why I love it so much). The contradictory pleasures of Mexico City hold the same currency. We constantly swear to leave her and constantly give in to her embrace; she is the inalienable companionship that we deserve. Let others live in the nice towns with orderly traffic. We lay claim to the complex personality and the ambiguous beauty of the bearded lady.
Translated from the Spanish by Miguel Kanai

Mexico City Ecatepec,
Mexico 2006.
PHOTO BY SCOTT PETERMAN.
COURTESY MILLER BLOCK GALLERY
BOSTON.

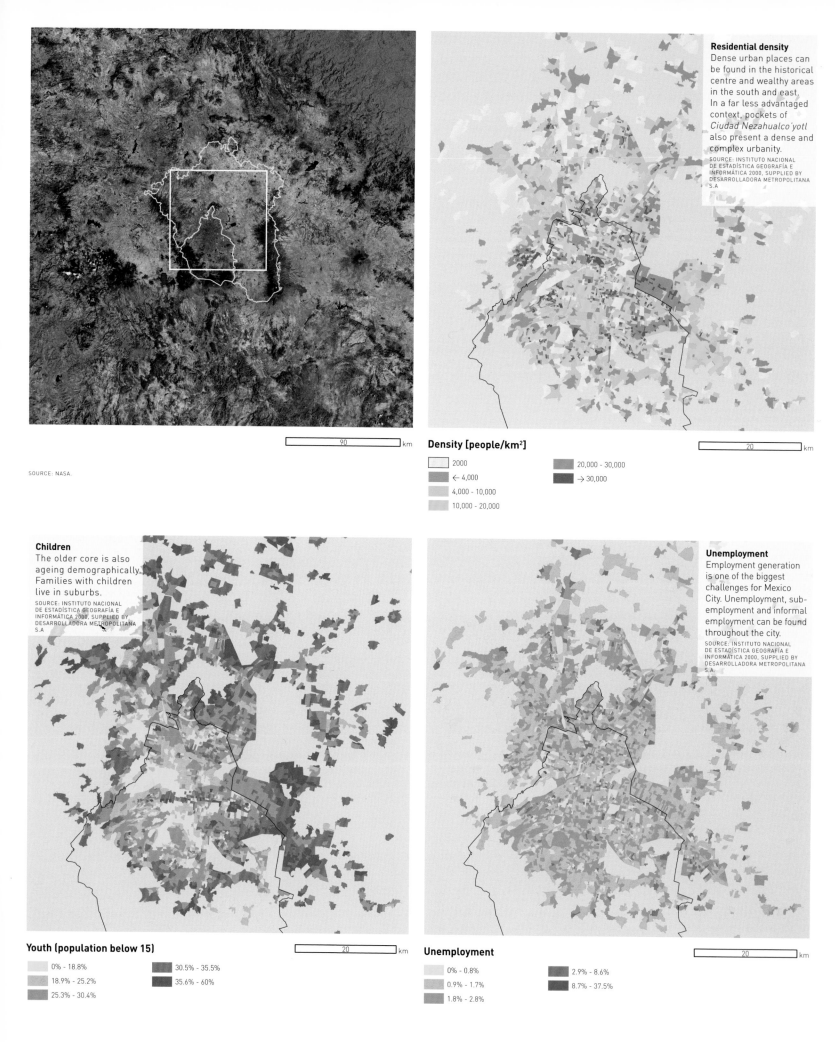

SOURCE: NASA.

Residential density

Dense urban places can be found in the historical centre and wealthy areas in the south and east. In a far less advantaged context, pockets of *Ciudad Nezahualco'yotl* also present a dense and complex urbanity.

SOURCE: INSTITUTO NACIONAL DE ESTADÍSTICA GEOGRAFÍA E INFORMÁTICA 2000, SUPPLIED BY DESARROLLADORA METROPOLITANA S.A

Density [people/km²]

- 2000
- ← 4,000
- 4,000 - 10,000
- 10,000 - 20,000
- 20,000 - 30,000
- → 30,000

Children

The older core is also ageing demographically. Families with children live in suburbs.

SOURCE: INSTITUTO NACIONAL DE ESTADÍSTICA GEOGRAFÍA E INFORMÁTICA 2000, SUPPLIED BY DESARROLLADORA METROPOLITANA S.A

Youth (population below 15)

- 0% - 18.8%
- 18.9% - 25.2%
- 25.3% - 30.4%
- 30.5% - 35.5%
- 35.6% - 60%

Unemployment

Employment generation is one of the biggest challenges for Mexico City. Unemployment, sub-employment and informal employment can be found throughout the city.

SOURCE: INSTITUTO NACIONAL DE ESTADÍSTICA GEOGRAFÍA E INFORMÁTICA 2000, SUPPLIED BY DESARROLLADORA METROPOLITANA S.A.

Unemployment

- 0% - 0.8%
- 0.9% - 1.7%
- 1.8% - 2.8%
- 2.9% - 8.6%
- 8.7% - 37.5%

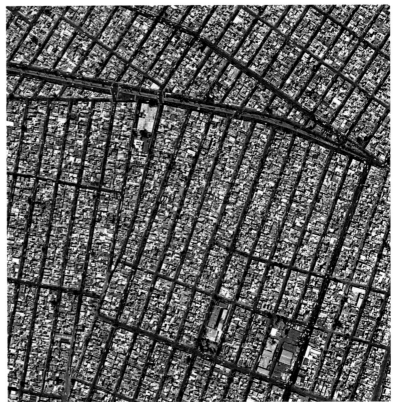

Images from the
QuickBird satellite of
Mexico City.
© DIGITALGLOBE EXCLUSIVE
DISTRIBUITED FOR EUROPE BY
TELESPAZIO.

The current population of Mexico City Metropolitan Area is estimated to stand at 18 million, of which 8.6 million live within the Federal District. Both the population and urbanized area of Mexico City Metropolitan Area have expanded dramatically since the mid 20th century. Both continue to grow in complex patterns – whereas the urban core has regained some population, suburban sprawl continues apace, fuelled by low-cost mortgages and a lax regulatory framework.

The Federal District covers approximately 1,488 square kilometres. In the urbanized northern portion, open and recreational space is scarce. The gross residential density in this part of the district is about 20,894 people per square kilometre. Expanding the amount of recreational space and the number of cultural facilities for the residents of this high-density area is considered a fundamental priority among many Mexican town planners.

Almost half of the population currently living in the Federal District was born somewhere else. Lured by its economic opportunities and city lights, people from all over Mexico have moved to the capital, bringing with them their cultures, hopes and conflicts. This urban promise has yet to materialize – it is estimated that 2 out of 3 households in the city live in poverty conditions. More than 25% of the city's population is made up of children under the age of 14.

Mexico City is of paramount importance for the Mexican national economy. Its gross city product (totalling € 105,000 million) contributes 22% of Mexico's GDP. The international relevance of this urban economy is denoted by the fact that it is equivalent to almost 10% of Italy's GDP. With a product per capita of approximately € 9,000, Mexico City can be considered a middle-income economy.

Although the metropolis has lost much of its industry, 16% of the labour force is still employed in manufacturing. The brunt of employment falls in the services; 82% of workers are in this sector, some in formal businesses and services linked to the globalizing Mexican economy, but most in low-wage occupations. Most of the employment growth in Mexico City has been registered in the informal sector, which is now is believed to employ the majority of the city's labour force.

Car-ownership is considered a highly desirable social condition in Mexico City. However, only 16% of all daily journeys are conducted by private car. The majority of the population (79%) relies on public transport, an eclectic system composed of the city's extensive yet insufficient underground network and an array of buses and minibuses.

The Federal District is divided into 19 *delegaciones* that provide a number of local services and have limited planning powers. Since the mid 1990s, city residents have the right to directly elect their mayor and this position has become one of the most visible elected offices in the country.

Los Angeles
United States of America

D. J. Waldie

D. J. Waldie is the author of *Holy Land: A Suburban Memoir*, *Real City: Downtown Los Angeles Inside/Out*, *Where We Are Now: Notes from Los Angeles*, and *Close to Home: An American Album*. Waldie is a contributing writer at *Los Angeles Magazine*. His book reviews and commentary have appeared in the *Los Angeles Times* and the *New York Times*. Waldie has been the Public Information Officer of the city of Lakewood since 1978.

PHOTO BY MARISSA ROTH.

What is Los Angeles? Colonial city. Captured city. City of edges. City of amnesiacs. City of *mestizos*. Anxious city. This city of the angels, of thoughtless belief and so faithless.

Its founding elements were air, earth, sunshine and too little water. Notice that one lack. Los Angeles was perilously close to perfection when California's Spanish governor sketched the city's outline in his notebook in September 1781. Ever since, only a little more water or more money or power or speed, we thought, would render this unlikely place adequate to our desire.

And when this city proved disappointing and the city we wanted failed to appear, our longing cast off a succession of provisional cities. Some were real, some mythic; some are cruelly near to hell. Los Angeles is an archipelago of cities... cities of desire now deemed unnecessary. They crowd the bright landscape... cities that are epitaphs for the future.

Everyone lives in Los Angeles. The world is its citizens because they have seen so many movies. In the movies, Los Angeles is the shrouded city of 'treacherous unbrightness', the city that always cheats on its lovers, that is always painted in the colours of smog, the city always seen from a height, from a freeway overpass, from a seat in a descending jetliner, the hapless observer always going under, down to a carcinogenic sea.

Los Angeles has a crooked heart. The heart of Los Angeles – there actually is one – is cocked about 36 degrees from the north-south grid that was the enlightened dream of President Thomas Jefferson for filling in the map of America. The streets of central Los Angeles have their different reveries. They do not lead to the cardinal points of the compass but to the uncertain spaces in between.

Look at a map of Los Angeles and you'll see what I mean. Within the triumphant national grid that extends across the plain of the Los Angeles River lies the grid of another city, four Spanish leagues square pointing toward other aspirations.

Or stand in front of the Biltmore Hotel on Pershing Square and look down at the brass compass rose set into the sidewalk that shows, against the evidence of your eyes, that the streets of downtown Los Angeles still resist, after more than 150 years, the city's American occupation in 1847.

Downtown's streets conform, as best they can, to the orders of Charles III, King of Spain. His ordinances in the Law of the Indies required city grids to have a 45-degree disorientation from true north and south to give, it was said, equal light to every room in every house throughout the day. Given the way Los Angeles extended along the bank of its uncertain river, only 36 degrees of compliance with the royal order were possible.

Other obligations claim those who cross the misdirected thoroughfares of central Los Angeles today. Those who pass almost never recall the original grid over which they travel except, perhaps, as they reorient themselves to President Jefferson's American scheme at the edge of downtown, passing from one imperial imagination to another. We long to forget in Los Angeles, but the streets themselves remember.

This is a ghost story. There once was a *mestiza* who was treated cruelly by her Spanish husband. He abandoned her and his two brown children for a fair woman. Mad with grief and shame, the *mestiza* flung her children in a flooded arroyo and then herself. She became a ghost. Now, she haunts dry creek beds and open drainage ditches.

The ghost of the woman lures careless children who are playing there in the rain and drowns them in the suddenly rising water. If you are unlucky, you'll see her in the muddy wave rushing at you, her grey gown curling at her feet and her white *rebozo* thrown over the weeping eye sockets in her *calavera* face.

City officials circulate a video and educational guide called *No Way Out* to explain the hazards of the Los Angeles River: the slick floor of the concrete channel, the quick hypothermia of the cold water, and the impossibility of finding a place to hold on in a current flowing as fast as a speeding car.

Los Angeles, 2000.
© PAOLO ROSSELLI.

La Llorona is the custodian of the void we've made of the Los Angeles River, a river paved with her tears. She is our image and our agent. She is still invoked to frighten the children of undocumented immigrants illegally laundering their clothes in the shallow band of processed wastewater that flows in the centre of the channel in even the driest months.

When I look into the glare of the white, empty river from a bridge on a hot August afternoon, the concrete below is a burning mirror reflecting our contempt for what we've made. And *La Llorona* stirs.

I ride the bus. The bus rider in Los Angeles is, by definition, a diminished figure. Bus riders know that life doesn't have a story unless it's narrated with a car. There's nothing on the bus equal to the primal Los Angeles experience that begins with an adolescent joyride in a car at dusk and that ends, after adventures across half the county, with an amazement of tangled bodies in the back seat.

When I tell people here that I don't drive, they express admiration, as if riding the bus had a moral purpose. Then I tell them I don't drive because an accident of genetics makes my eyesight unreliable. I tell them that the bus is a third-world city on wheels, so unlike the intimate room they've made of their car, but I'm describing a city they have no intention of visiting. They imagine a future Los Angeles

Immigration bill
demonstration.

Los Angeles, 2000.

in which they'll always be drivers. They think they'll always be in control. They tell me about the high cost of driving, the terrible traffic, and the ugly behaviour of other drivers. They tell me how lucky I am.

We who do not drive are equally removed from those who do. We're the ones at the periphery of the driver's gaze, standing at the bus stop at an intersection where a car has just turned right against the red light without even slowing.

The most anxious one among us, who had been peering into the oncoming traffic for a bus that's 20 minutes late, abruptly steps back from the curb, a bulging discount-store bag digging a red band into the flesh across the back of the hand she has thrust through the plastic handle (that red line is the pedestrian stigmata). The most resigned among us has been hanging back, his head down and hands jammed into the pockets of a drooping jacket. And all of us in silent attendance on the traffic bunching and flowing in its minute-long pulses as the traffic signals change red to green; not one of us observing with the exaltation it deserves the glowing arc of cars turning left, as lovely as the advancing line of dancers in a corps de ballet.

Los Angeles is finished. The city is finished because the sub-urban 'frontier' of Los Angeles is closed. There is nowhere else to go to build a better paradise of the ordinary. The city's suburban fringe has already dispersed to Las Vegas, Phoenix, Fresno, and Coeur d'Alene, Idaho. It took about hundred years of intense selling – from the boom of the 1880s to end of the 1990s – to make Los Angeles what it always will be: a moderately dense, multi-polar aggregation of single family homes, with a strong dependence on more densely urbanized nodes clustered along axes of transportation, around cultural institutions or in loose zones of lifestyle affiliation.

In many ways, Los Angeles isn't Los Angeles any more: it's more urban, denser, less mobile and far less white and Protestant. We often find it difficult to talk coherently about this kind of place. I think we lack a workable 'rhetoric of place' for our situation. The story of Los Angeles needs to be broadened and deepened – needs to have more actors added to it – because the stories that are commonly told about Los Angeles are tragically inadequate to resolve the consequences of the failed public policies that were based on them.

A Night View of Los Angeles. A 360 degree panorama of the entire city of Los Angeles taken from the top of the U.S. Bank Tower.
© HELEN KOLIKOW GARBER.

'Grid' La Brea and
Olympic, 2005

The future of a city is in the stories it tells. Where I live, in a small city on the edge of a vast city of edges, the stories contain a share of failure and of heroism, too. The stories also are familiar, small scale and believable. But many Los Angeles residents find nothing to believe in the disfigured story of their fractured city, because that story contains so little about them and what they yearn for. They yearn for accountability, identity and decency.

It is difficult to say if the recent rise of Latino and union political power, coupled with structural changes in the city's outdated charter (that were enacted in the late 1990s), will fulfil any of the desires of Los Angeles. It's even harder to predict if the planners, architects and builders of Los Angeles can successfully imagine into existence a city that would shelter the stories of the city's immigrant multitude. And it's still questionable if they will have the air, water, and earth... and jobs and homes... they will need.

When I walk out the door of my home and see the familiar pattern of house, street, parks, schools and stores, I see the human-scale, porous, flexible, neighbourhood-specific landscape that working people longed for in mid-20th century

Los Angeles and in which they still seek to live. A lot of Los Angeles – even in the parts some of us avoid – can be seen as a spectacle of democracy: a middling landscape where millions of working people expressed their flawed and hopeful idea of home. Flawed in the boom years of the 1950s because it had no room for people of colour, and flawed today because our suburbanized landscape isn't adequate to every demand we make of it. But hopeful then as now because dignified lives were lived there as a result of (not in spite of) the kind of place Los Angeles is.

We need Los Angeles. Los Angeles is a necessary city, if only as an object lesson. It educates through its complex ethnic and racial blending, which increasingly has transformed the old binaries of white and non-white. It educates in its struggle to be both urban and suburban, another blending that will consume much of suburbanized America in the coming decades. It will show if an essentially twentieth-century city can transition to a globalized economy without further degrading the condition of its working-class population. Los Angeles already shows the effects of a neglected infrastructure and inadequate public transit. We need what Los Angeles teaches if we're to make fit places for the globalized immigrants, commuters, business owners, landlords, homeless, working poor and homeowners for whom every city of desire is a ruined paradise and, as a result, a home.

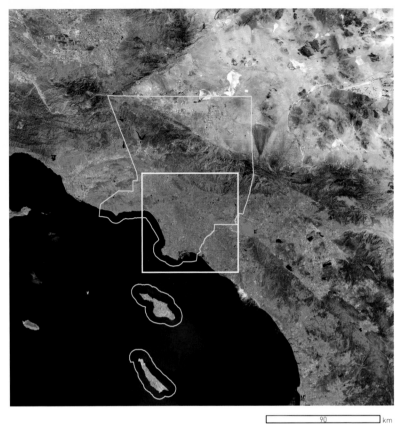

SOURCE: NASA.

90 km

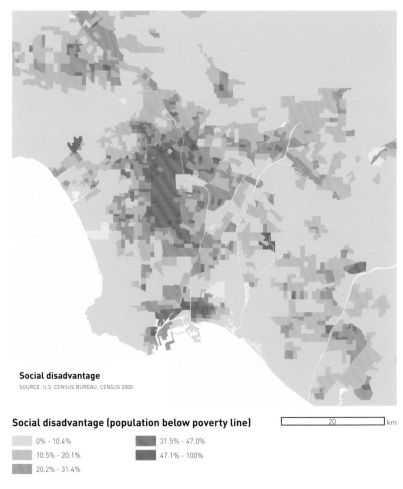

Residential density
Los Angeles has grown
horizontally, at relatively
low residential densities.
Recent immigration and
limits to metropolitan
expansion are leading to
the densification of its
core.

SOURCE: U.S. CENSUS BUREAU;
CENSUS 2000

20 km

Density [people/km²]

2,000		10,000 - 20,000	
< 4,000		20,000 - 30,000	
4,000 - 10,000		> 30,000	

**Ethnic and racial
minorities**
Angelenos trace back their
origins to places all over
the world. Ethnic groups
can be found throughout
the metropolitan area,
living in urban and
suburban neighbourhoods.

SOURCE: U.S. CENSUS BUREAU; CENSUS
2000

Ethnic minorities

0% - 19.5%	58.9% - 78.8%
19.6% - 38.5%	78.9% - 98.4%
38.6% - 58.8%	

20 km

Social disadvantage

SOURCE: U.S. CENSUS BUREAU; CENSUS 2000

Social disadvantage (population below poverty line)

0% - 10.4%	31.5% - 47.0%
10.5% - 20.1%	47.1% - 100%
20.2% - 31.4%	

20 km

Children
Children have a significant presence in most areas of Los Angeles, except those with very high land values.
SOURCE: U.S. CENSUS BUREAU; CENSUS 2000

Unemployment
Unemployment in Los Angeles tends to concentrate in formerly industrial areas, mainly along a corridor between downtown and the port.
SOURCE: U.S. CENSUS BUREAU; CENSUS 2000

Youth (people below 15)

0% – 11.3%	24.1% – 29.7%
11.4% – 18.6 %	29.8% – 46.7%
18.7% – 24.0%	

Unemployment

0% – 5.1%	12.6% – 17.7%
5.2% – 8.5%	17.8% – 34.5%
8.6% – 12.5%	34.6% – 100%

Images from the QuickBird satellite of Los Angeles.
©DIGITALGLOBE EXCLUSIVE DISTRIBUTED FOR EUROPE BY TELESPAZIO.

The current population of the City of Los Angeles is approximately 3.9 million. In the 20th century, Los Angeles grew relentlessly, multiplying its population size by a factor of ten, to become the urban core of the second largest metropolitan region in the United States. The city, that has historically seen itself as a collection of suburbs, now faces demographic pressures and the need for a structural densification of its built environment. With the largest municipal territory in the US, Los Angeles covers approximately 1,215 km^2, encompassing in its extension the Santa Monica mountains and a range of other natural features. The gross residential density of Los Angeles is about 3,041 residents per km^2. In stark contrast to the image of a green city on the California coast, many communities in South Los Angeles are highly deprived of open and green spaces.

Americans often use Los Angeles as shorthand for ethnic and racial diversity, both its promise and its predicaments. About half of the population identify themselves as *Latinos* or *Latinas*, 30% are White (Anglophones), while African Americans and Asians hold similar shares at around 10% each – however, as the presence of the latter continues to increase, the former follow the inverse path. Adding to the city's complexity, approximately 40% of its current population was born outside of the United States of America – many of them are recent immigrants. Diversity in Los Angeles runs along many other dimensions. A multitude of subcultures inhabit the city, producing a visually eclectic urban landscape and a maelstrom of cultural products, fashions and fads that often impacts the world over. In terms of age, Los Angeles is a young city: less than 10% of its residents are 65 or older and about 30% of all Angelenos are younger than 20. Socio-economically, the wide urban scope of Los Angeles assumes a *noir* tone. Home to some of the wealthiest people in the world, the city also has more than one-out-five families living in poverty and 10% of all Los Angeles families scrape by with less than $1,000 a month.

If Southern California was an independent country, this five-county metropolitan economy centred in Los Angeles would rank among the top ten largest national economies in the world; its product amounts to approximately 60% of Italy's GDP. The Los Angeles economy is also broad and complex – three-fourths of its labour force works in a gamut of business and services and almost 20% of workers are employed in industry – producing anything from rockets and high-tech equipment to furniture, garments and ethnic foods.

Private cars are the prevalent transport mode in Los Angeles. Public transport only serves 10% of all daily journeys undertaken in the city. The City of Los Angeles is divided into 15 council districts. Recently, attempts have been made to expand mayoral powers and to improve mechanisms of neighbourhood and local representation.

Railroad overpass
LA River, 2005

New York City
United States of America

Susan Fainstein

Susan Fainstein is professor of urban planning in the Graduate School of Design, Harvard University. Previously, she taught at the Graduate School of Architecture, Columbia University and Rutgers University's School of Urban and Regional Policy. Fainstein is author of *Urban Political Movements*; *Restructuring the City*; and *The City Builders*. She co-edited *Divided Cities*, and edited the forthcoming *Cities and Visitors*.

New York, New York

Long advertized as the crossroads of the world, Times Square remains true to that clichéd phrase. Newly resurrected, roundly criticized as sanitized and Disneyfied, the intensely used space encapsulates the contradictions of twenty-first-century New York. The buildings are sheathed in high-tech signage, advertising globally available beverages, underwear, and television brands; stock and commodity market statistics shoot around their cornices. A series of new high-rise office towers houses media monopolies, giant financial institutions, and corporate law firms; noisy bars and chain restaurants cater to tourists and suburbanites; the hulking Marriott Marquis Hotel represents an earlier effort to keep visitors off the streets; while the studios of MTV, with their windows allowing views of ongoing productions, attract sidewalk gawkers. The Broadway theatres are drawing more patrons than ever, who are there to see musicals accessible to anyone with sufficient funds, regardless of their English language ability. Yet, at the same time as the area acts as an epicentre for the major institutions of modern capitalism and their marketing, small businesses, many immigrant-owned, fill up the interstices, offering discounted electronics, souvenirs, salad bars and, even now, sex toys and adult videos. The tens of thousands of people crowding the sidewalks, despite the laments of the area's critics, are extraordinarily diverse. With crime down, usage is up and all classes, races and nationalities – commuters and residents, down-and-out and affluent – driven by a vast variety of reasons, pass through Times Square.

A less well-known crossroads exists at the intersection of a different Broadway, which meets Roosevelt Avenue in Jackson Heights, Queens. The subway, here elevated, rumbles overhead. One of the adjacent streets is lined with spice stores, sari shops, boutiques selling heavy gold jewellery and Indian restaurants. Roosevelt Avenue itself offers Latino bakeries, video stores, *bodegas* and restaurants, ranging from Mexican *taquerias* to Peruvian seafood purveyors and white-tablecloth establishments patronized by middle-class Ecuadorians. Throngs of people fill these sidewalks, too, representing the extraordinarily varied immigrant groups that have replenished New

York's population in the last two decades. The surrounding residential area, notable for its substantial apartment buildings that enclose large, park-like inner courtyards, have proved particularly hospitable to middle-class Indian immigrants but also shelter a mélange of other groups. Unlike Times Square, Jackson Heights does not bear the marks of government-sponsored urban redevelopment. Its revival has been a simple product of increased demand for housing and of entrepreneurship.

Contemporary New York is remarkable for its hybridity and liminality, for the mix of people in its public spaces and the paths it continues to offer for upward mobility. At the same time it remains a highly segregated and unequal city as measured by indices of class and race. To the extent that black-white segregation is lessening, it is the result of white inroads into black ghettos, as Harlem in Manhattan and Fort Greene and Bedford-Stuyvesant in Brooklyn are being pressured by New York's real estate boom. Improved levels of public safety have prompted young professionals and growing families to repopulate neighbourhoods once deemed too risky. Even though it is primarily immigration that is feeding the city's current population expansion, the pull of New York to the fashionable and the would-be fashionables, to artists, writers and musicians, and simply to cosmopolitans who savour the joys of urbanity does not diminish. Population has reached an all-time peak and, despite a residential building boom, availability of affordable housing continues to shrink. The city, with little help from the federal government, has increased its capital expenditure on low-cost housing, but the amount produced is dwarfed by the demand. Tales abound of immigrants living five to a room, recalling the days at the turn of the last century when European refugees crowded the lower East Side.

The city's planning efforts have focused on stimulating economic expansion and residential construction. City-sponsored redevelopment projects feature sports venues (a new Yankee Stadium in the Bronx, a new Shea Stadium in Queens and a Frank Gehry-designed basketball arena in central Brooklyn). Despite a widely held consensus among public policy experts that such enterprises do not contribute

New York.
© GABRIELE BASILICO.

New York.
© GABRIELE BASILICO

to economic development or improvement in the surrounding areas, public subsidies to these private ventures are justified as promoting growth. The city has rezoned waterfront areas from manufacturing to residential uses. While this has resulted in much new, primarily high-end housing, it has also stimulated speculative purchases of land, adding to the issue of price inflation. Breaking with past administrations' focus on Manhattan, the Bloomberg regime has large projects on the drawing boards in all five boroughs. Many of these will add important public amenities; however, since the policy is to capture private investment to pay for public uses, they typically involve height and density bonuses for developers and various tax subsidies as a *quid pro quo*.

The seeming belief on the part of city government that manufacturing is obsolete or an inefficient use of well-located land has resulted in shrinking space for industrial uses and the consequent displacement of viable enterprises. Even though many of New York's traditional industries – large-scale garment manufacturing, sugar refining, etc. – do not have much of a future, specialty food processing, custom printing and metalworking, high-end fashion and other niche enterprises are crucial to New York's service economy and lately can find no place to go within the five boroughs.

The main issues facing the city's planners today result from the competing demands on space and stand-offs between public officials, residents, developers, and current business occupants over proposed redevelopment schemes. Plans for rebuilding the World Trade Center site falter over security concerns and political infighting. Transportation problems continue to plague the city. A number of major projects have now been discussed for years – a Second Avenue subway in Manhattan, extension of the line connecting Queens and Grand Central Station to the far west side of Manhattan, a Long Island Railroad link to Grand Central, a new train tunnel under the Hudson River to New Jersey and a rail connection between Downtown Manhattan and Kennedy Airport top the list. No authority, however, seems able to set priorities among them, so far funding is not assured for any of them.

Competition with its suburban ring also underlies the city's planning policies. The exodus of corporate headquarters for greener areas has largely ceased, but major financial institutions find accommodation for their back-office functions across the Hudson River in New Jersey and in Westchester County to the north. The overflow has produced a central business district in Jersey City rivalling

New York.
© GABRIELE BASILICO

Downtown Manhattan in size. The out-migration of middle and working class families to the suburbs is proceeding unstaunched, precipitated by property prices, school quality and the desire for roomier surroundings. Nevertheless, New York is unique among US cities in the extent to which people who work in the city, live in the city.

Despite the enormous increase in wealth achieved by the city's elites, the middle class has been shrinking and the median income dropping. Unemployment, while low in the aggregate, is very high within parts of Brooklyn and the Bronx, and few jobs at a living wage are being generated for those without higher education and English language skills. The metaphor of duality has frequently been applied and misapplied to New York. The multiplicity of ethnic groups, interest groups and differences among those who share a similar income status belie this simple dichotomy. Yet, even as Manhattan's glitter shines ever more brightly, star architects cast their lustre on new projects there and neighbourhoods within the boroughs recapture their former vitality, millions of New Yorkers remain stuck in poverty and can find little in local or national programs to assist them out of their situation.

At the same time, New York displays characteristics that cause it continually to rebound from adversity. It has survived the deindustrialization afflicting so many American cities better than most, as its financial, business services and cultural sectors have continued to gain strength. Tourism, after its post-2001 slump, has regained its former peak. The varied character of its immigrant population, wherein no single group dominates, combined with New York's tradition of assimilation, has meant an easier absorption of new arrivals here than elsewhere in the United States. Unlike in the western part of the country, no politician runs for office on an anti-immigrant platform. The sheer diversity of the city's residents and users, the ratcheting down of divisive rhetoric under the current mayoral administration and the intensity of activity in 'the city that never sleeps' all contribute to the excitement of 21st century New York. New York resembles a few other major US cities, especially Chicago and Los Angeles, in being a Mecca for immigrants and visitors. Still, it remains the most important financial centre and cultural producer in the United States; elsewhere in the world only London, with a similar economic base, population size and demographic heterogeneity stands as a real counterpart.

Following pages
Vertigo-Avenue of Americas, New York City.
© RICHARD BERENHOLTZ

Central Park in Autumn.
© RICHARD BERENHOLTZ

SOURCE: NASA.

|————————————— 90 —————————————| km

Unemployment
The spatial distribution of unemployment overlaps with the geography of poverty, but unemployment is less concentrated.
SOURCE: U.S. CENSUS BUREAU; CENSUS 2000

|————————————— 20 —————————————| km

Unemployed

	0% – 6.4%		22.2% – 46.1%
	6.5% – 12.8%		46.2% – 100%
	12.9% – 22.1%		n/a (land)

The urban poor
Concentrated poverty in the South Bronx, northern Brooklyn and parts of Manhattan are still one of the most pressing social issues.
SOURCE: U.S. CENSUS BUREAU; CENSUS 2000

|————————————— 20 —————————————| km

Ethnic and racial minorities
Ethnic and racial minorities live all over the city. They make up the overwhelming majority in many neighbourhoods.
SOURCE: U.S. CENSUS BUREAU; CENSUS 2000

|————————————— 20 —————————————| km

Population below poverty line

	0% – 7.7%		26.1% – 40.4%
	7.8% – 15.7%		40.5% – 100%
	15.8% – 26.0%		n/a (land)

Ethnic minorities

	0.9% – 21.8%		63.2% – 85.3%
	21.9% – 40.9%		85.4% – 100%
	41.0% – 63.1%		n/a (land)

Images from the
QuickBird satellite of
Los Angeles.
©DIGITALGLOBE EXCLUSIVE
DISTRIBUTED FOR EUROPE BY
TELESPAZIO.

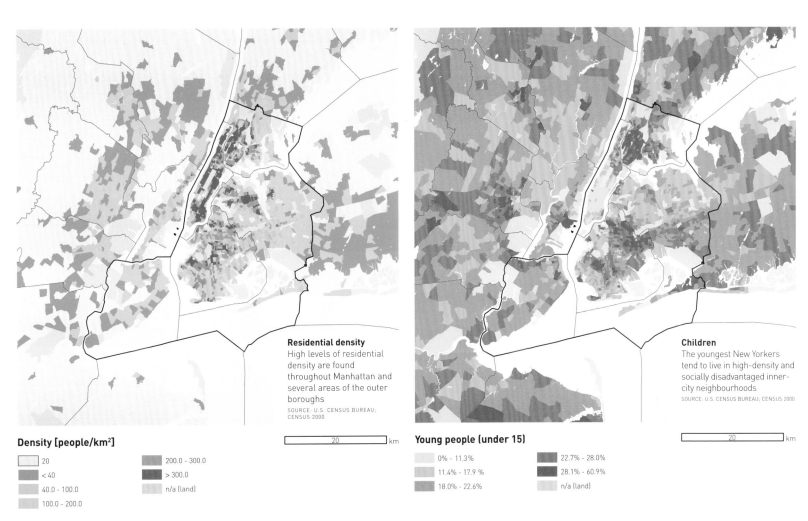

Residential density
High levels of residential
density are found
throughout Manhattan and
several areas of the outer
boroughs
SOURCE: U.S. CENSUS BUREAU;
CENSUS 2000

Children
The youngest New Yorkers
tend to live in high-density and
socially disadvantaged inner-
city neighbourhoods
SOURCE: U.S. CENSUS BUREAU; CENSUS 2000

Density [people/km²]

20	200.0 - 300.0
< 40	> 300.0
40.0 - 100.0	n/a (land)
100.0 - 200.0	

20 km

Young people (under 15)

0% - 11.3%	22.7% - 28.0%
11.4% - 17.9 %	28.1% - 60.9%
18.0% - 22.6%	n/a (land)

20 km

For the first time in its history, New York City's population passed the 8 million mark in the year 2000 after a decade of strong growth. Since then, the city has continued to add residents and this trend is expected to continue over the next ten years.

New York City covers approximately 830 square kilometres, of which 25% is dedicated to open and recreational space. The gross residential density of New York City is about 8,400 residents per square kilometre, by far the highest in the United States. However, residential densities within the city are unevenly distributed and vary widely from peaks in parts of Manhattan to the relative low densities of areas in the outer boroughs with a notably suburban character.

New York is an extremely diverse city, Whites of non-Hispanic ancestry make up only 35% of the population, Latinos 27%, Blacks 25% and Asians 10%. Because of this demographic composition New York is usually referred to as a 'majority-minority' city. Additionally, New York is a city of immigrants. Approximately 36% of its current population was born outside the United States of America. Together with their children, these residents constitute the majority of New Yorkers.

New York is not a city where many seniors choose to live; only 12% of its population has reached the age of 65. On the other hand, children and young people under 20 years old represent 27% of the city's population – many of them growing up in poverty or disadvantaged living conditions. Overall, more than 20% of New York City's residents depend on some form of income support.

Persistent poverty perplexes those familiar with the enormous wealth that the city generates. With a Gross City Product of approximately € 39,500 per capita, New York is one of the world's richest cities. This juggernaut urban economy generates up to 4% of the vast US product or the equivalent of 28% of Italy's GDP.

The city's employment profile is thoroughly post-industrial. More than 90% of active New Yorkers have a job or work free-lance in the services and business sector. Although urban manufacturing employs less than 5% of the labour force, it has been argued that this small figure obscures the wider economic and social importance of this sector in the city.

New York City has an extensive public transport system that provides for more than half of all daily journeys conducted in the city everyday. The fiscal resources needed to keep this service up-to-date are massive and the task of running the system as a safe, efficient and appealing transport option is ever-challenging.

New York City is divided into five boroughs and run by a mayor with large discretionary powers. The combined city budget is approximately € 5,287 per capita.

Hudson Yards is one of the last frontiers available for development in Manhattan. The area is bounded by West 42nd Street and West 30th Street, Eighth Avenue to the Hudson River.
COURTESY CITY OF NEW YORK.

Pedestrian traffic at Herald Square, a busy transportation and retail hub in the middle of Midtown Manhattan.
© ADAM WISEMAN, 1998.

Cairo
Egypt

Maria Golia

Long-time resident of Egypt, Maria Golia writes fiction and non-fiction. She is the author of *Cairo: City of Sand*, opinion columnist for the Beirut Daily Star, speechwriter for Egyptian potentates and reviewer for the Times Literary Supplement. Golia is also a fellow of the London-based Institute of Ecotechnics.

Unseen city

If cities are the legacy humanity leaves to itself, then to examine them is to look ourselves in the eye. The question is how much are we willing to see? What is the city trying to tell us, indeed, what are we telling ourselves? Cairo is a veritable message in a bottle, a 1,400-year old experiment in living together under extreme conditions – shortages of land, water, finance and freedom – the conditions, incidentally, with which an increasing number of humans are obliged to contend. But nowhere on earth are the limits to growth so glaring. The line between life and death is clearly drawn in Egypt's desert sands.

Only 5% of the country is habitable. A population of over seventy million occupies a space the size of Holland. Half the population lives within a 100 kilometre radius of Cairo. The entire nation relies on a river that passes through nine other countries first. The need to manage a limited resource arguably gave rise to Egypt's highly-centralized state. But autocracies are less concerned with management than control. Wielding martial law (so-called Emergency Laws, in effect for nearly a century) Egypt's government attempts to act as the sole arbiter of people's fate, prohibiting individual and group initiatives. Consequently Cairo bears the scars of logistic as well as climatic meltdowns.

Poet Wallace Stevens wrote that 'a violent order is disorder, and a great disorder is order'. This paradox comes alive in Cairo, where a defensive bureaucracy manufactures obstacles and people's lives are spent circumventing them. Through the struggle between given circumstances and the need to survive, an equilibrium of sorts is achieved, a marriage of chaos and harmony that allows the city to endure, despite having outlived so much of its usefulness to its inhabitants.

As one of the one world's oldest continuously-inhabited cities, Cairo has seen it all – plague, famine, earthquake, drought and flood – and stood firm in the wake of shifting caliphates, sultanates, dynasties and empires, including the Roman, Byzantine, Ottoman, French and British. With some 500 historic sites, Cairo offers a rare cross-section of epochs: the pyramids and sphinx, Roman bastions, ancient Coptic churches, medieval Mamluk mosques, the palaces of the nineteenth-century *grande bourgeoisie*, and a belle époque downtown punctuated with the Soviet utilitarianism of Egypt's socialist 1960s and the glass towers of today's *nouveaux riches*.

Yet, this diversity characterizes but a portion of Cairo's 350 square kilometres. Approximately 60% of the city's population lives in unlicensed, makeshift housing, the bulk of it built in recent decades on precious agricultural land. Cairo hasn't gotten old, so much as new.

To redirect urban growth, the government fostered the development of several 'satellite cities' in Cairo's desert outskirts. They've garnered mixed results, partly because they cater to the rich, boasting gated residential communities with names like Dream Land, Royal City and Beverly Hills. Despite heavy promotion starting in 1976, by 1996 the total population of the new towns was less than Greater Cairo's growth in just six months. Although the satellite towns have since gained some ground, Cairenes, a gregarious, Nilo-centric people, prefer the inner city.

The only problem is that an Egyptian is born every twenty seconds. The demand for low-to-middle income housing has long since outdone the State's efforts to provide it.

Those who wish, to build for themselves, who can afford a plot of land and, building permit, must suffer years of bureaucracy to get them. With obstructive legalities, in the absence of city planning and uniformly-enforced building codes, people build where and how they can. They make bricks from irreplaceable topsoil, so the city reaps a harvest of ramshackle housing instead of food. The houses are little more than stacked compartments where people live several to a room.

Although Cairo is warm year round, summers can last six months, adversarial heat, sandstorms and off-the-charts pollution conspiring against health and productivity. In a place where the frontiers of well-being are under constant assault, survival demands flexibility, resourcefulness, sociability and above all, a sense of humour, qualities that Cairenes possess in spades.

There's a joke about living so closely together. A farmer comes to Cairo with a toothache. Tapping the offending

Al Azhar, Koranic University district.
PHOTO BY DARIO ZANNIER.

molar he tells the dentist angrily, 'take out all the other teeth and leave this son of a dog by himself!' For the average citizen, solitude is punishment and privacy an obscure concept; in colloquial Egyptian it doesn't even have a word.

At night, Cairenes take to the streets in throngs. They're out breathing or trying to do so, amidst ear-splitting, noxious traffic. Families picnic on the Nile bridges, their backs to the stream of cars. Cairenes dispose of around 1m^2 of green space each, a figure that may well include patches of grass between highways. For this reason alone, the Al Azhar Park, developed by the Aga Khan Foundation's Historic Cities Support Programme, was a tremendous boon.

Situated at an elevation adjacent to medieval Cairo, the 30-hectare park provides stirring panoramas of centuries of Islamic grandeur, including the dense geometries and domed mausoleums of the City of the Dead. This sprawling cemetery features funerary buildings of the millennial well-to-do, which for generations have been occupied by the poor. The cemetery was therefore considered a source of shame

and an eyesore. But with the park as a vantage point, the City of the Dead is revealed in all its poignant beauty, a vast and living *memento mori* skirting the city's heartland.

The Al Azhar Park and its several constructions embodies Islamic building and landscaping traditions to great effect. By virtue of its presence, the surrounding neighbourhoods have reacquired their prestige as generational communities and guardians of a rich architectural legacy.

Cairenes, however, are unaccustomed to the niceties of parks and public space. As far as they're concerned, all space is public – hence the government's wish to dominate it by imposing an authoritarian presence. When high officials circulate, streets are cordoned off by thousands of soldiers who stand in human chains, glumly holding hands. People are imprisoned in their cars for hours until the great head's entourage speeds past. Likewise, small peaceful demonstrations draw tens of thousands of riot police, paralysing entire quarters.

Cairo overview taken from Al Azhar Park.
© MARIA GOLIA.

Political, economic and physical pressures vie for the average Cairene's attention but poverty is foremost in their minds, alongside the absence of means to escape it. Unemployment is officially 17%, but considering that the informal sector's workforce (unlicensed businesses, street vendors etc.) is larger than either the government's or private sector's, it is certainly far higher.

Despite gruelling conditions and widespread want, people are remarkably unconcerned with crime. Cairo is one of the world's safest cities because of the absence of guns and overwhelming presence of witnesses. But there are cultural factors at work, a value for equanimity not least of them. Cairo is relatively crime-free thanks to the character of its people, not its police. Egyptians favour forbearance, conviviality and wit as weapons in their daily fight. But to confront the gratuitous injustice owed to systemically corrupt mismanagement, forbearance is no longer enough.

Perhaps the greatest task this city faces is to see itself for what it is: a battleground between urban and rural ways of life. Although rural migration appears to be slowing, Cairo's overcrowding is an index of Egypt's long-standing provincial neglect. With power, attention and resources concentrated in the capital – Egypt's massive, muddled head – the body has been left to wither. Irrigation water shortages are already a source of mortal contention in the countryside. Farmers, who comprise 35% of Egypt's workforce, have been reduced to serfdom. Since the onset of economic reform in the early 1990s, a million have been evicted, either by state institutions or landowners, the land often sold as haphazardly developed real estate.

Cairo's capital-intensive industries further illustrate an ill-conceived commitment to modernity, where workers are poorly paid and denied the right to strike. An infatuation with 'modernity' has paradoxically ensured that the higher quality of life the term once embodied is denied to millions.

Urban historian Lewis Mumford might have been describing Cairo when he wrote in 1938:

A world city, in order to function as such requires a world order. A world in disorder can find no use for such

a city except to make it a center of political aggression and financial aggrandizement, incapable of performing the essential functions of a city even for its own teeming population[1].

Dysfunction, as registered in cities like Cairo, has a profound utility, since it may be understood as the equivalent of pain.

Cairo's dysfunction is symptomatic of an exploitative capitalism coupled with a dearth of vital resources. The city's plight mirrors that of the planet – but writ large – because life-or-death choices are etched in its topography. For this very reason, denial is rife. Only a cathartic reassessment of Cairo's situation coupled with a conscious, consensual effort can produce a counter-movement of the magnitude required to reverse the current trends.

Cairo is in many ways a city of the future, offering a glimpse of how other places might look given the pressures that are so exaggerated here. Yet the city remains resplendent in its humanity. Its longevity provides an exceptional record of human endurance and artistry, and equal evidence of our talent for repeating mistakes. The so-called 'mother of the world' is a city rich in untapped, fragmented knowledge awaiting recognition and integration.

'In the realm of greater understanding,' goes a Sufi saying, 'when the work is finished the workshop is dismantled.' Cairo, it would seem, still has work to do. For this is the city's job: to illuminate a world not only of our concretized choices – be they triumphs or errors – but also the invisible yet imposing realm of potential actions, alternative means of using our energies with greater clarity, mastery and remembrance.

[1] Lewis Mumford, *The Culture of Cities*, New York 1938, p. 295, italics in the original.

Residential density

The Nile Valley frames the overall metropolitan development of Cairo. The densest urban areas can be found along a corridor that stretches out from the river to the north east and in parts of Giza, on the western side of the Nile.

SOURCE: CENTRE D'ETUDES ET DE DOCUMENTATION ECONOMIQUE, JURIDIQUE ET SOCIALE (CEDEJ)

People with university degrees

University-educated Cairenes tend to live in suburban developments beyond the valley and in select areas of the central city. Informal settlements, with a far less well-educated population, have filled in the space between these two zones.

SOURCE: CENTRE D'ETUDES ET DE DOCUMENTATION ECONOMIQUE, JURIDIQUE ET SOCIALE (CEDEJ)

Density [people/km²]

- 2,000
- < 4,000
- 4,000 - 10,000
- 10,000 - 20,000
- 20,000 - 30,000
- 30,000 - 3,902,477

20 km

Illiteracy

- 9.9% or lower
- 10.0% - 20.8%
- 20.9% - 29.9%
- 30.0% - 38.5%
- 38.6% or higher

20 km

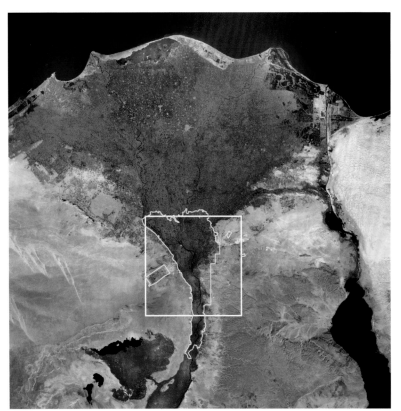

SOURCE: NASA.

90 km

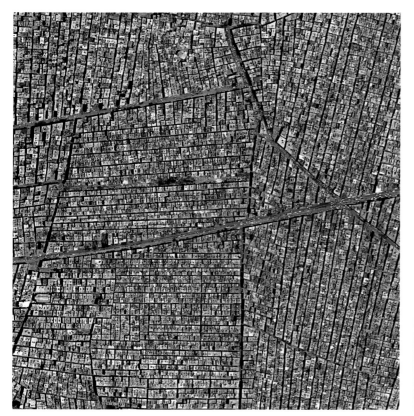
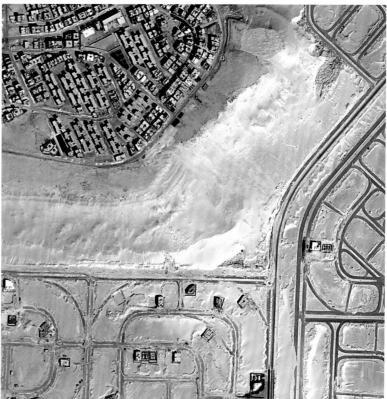

Images from the
QuickBird satellite of
Cairo.
©DIGITALGLOBE EXCLUSIVE
DISTRIBUTED FOR EUROPE BY
TELESPAZIO.

Original settlements on the site of the modern metropolis of Cairo date back roughly 2,000 years. Today, its population totals 7.8 million, but this figure grows to almost 15 million when including the greater Metropolitan Area, and non-official figures are closer to 18 million. Indeed half the population of Egypt lives within a 100-kilometre radius of Cairo. Cairo's population has increased significantly in the past century, recording a growth of about 890%, which is explained in part by an exodus of peasants from the farmlands, to the industries and commerce of the city. The current population continues to grow, albeit at a calmer rate; in the past decade it increased by 15%. Cairo's present population is extremely young: a massive 42% are under 20 years old and only 4% are older than 65.

The city of Cairo fans out from between the desert escarpments into the valley of the Nile delta, covering approximately 214 square kilometres. It has a high gross residential density of about 36,584 residents per square kilometre, roughly nine times that of greater London. Open public space is scarce: one square metre per person.

Cairo's inner city experiences a substantial urban burden from the persistent lack of low-income housing. In the past few years, soaring housing demands have resulted in an urban strategy of satellite towns, in the surrounding desert. Their success has been average; not only do they cater fairly selectively to the wealthy, but they must also compete with Egyptians' love of the inner city. This unanswered need for low-cost housing has therefore resulted in informal residential settlements in the city. In fact these settlements now constitute almost half of Cairo's total residential area and house 56.4% of Cairo's inhabitants. Over a third of Cairo's investment in real estate is in 'informal' residential real estate, totalling around € 29 billion.

The city's Gross City Product is approximately € 1,225 per capita. The Gross City Product of Cairo is equivalent to a fifth of Egypt's national economy, which is equal to only 1% of Italy's GDP.

Cairo supports a service-based economy with 67% of residents employed in the service sector. Industry is still a significant part of Cairo's economy; it employs one third of inhabitants. Cairo's economy, however, is particularly dependent on a thriving informal sector that provides more jobs than either the government or the private sectors. Unemployment is extensive; officially set at 17%, although realistically even higher, if one accounts for those employed in the informal sector. For women this figure is nearly a quarter. Indeed women account for only a fifth of the formal labour force in Cairo. Given the levels of unemployment, poverty is one of the prime concerns of Cairo's residents. Over 40% of the population of Egypt live on under €1.6 a day.

Of daily journeys in Cairo, 41% are conducted by public transport, while 13% are by car, and 36% on foot. Given these statistics, it's perhaps not surprising that the city only has 114 vehicles per 1,000 residents. Of these cars however, a large percentage are outdated, lacking modern emission-reducing features. This adds substantially to an already vast pollution problem in the city.

Cairo and its surrounding areas, constitutes one of the 26 governorates (muhafazah) into which Egypt is divided. Each governorate is headed by a governor and an executive council appointed by the president. Cairo itself is further divided into 28 districts. People's councils are elected at both the governorate and district levels, but these bodies have very limited power in relation to the executive councils.

Johannesburg
Republic of South Africa

Lindsay Bremner

Lindsay Bremner is an architect and urbanist, living in Johannesburg. She is currently an honorary research professor at the Wits School of Arts at the University of the Witwatersrand. She has published widely and lectured extensively on the city, including her series of essays, *Johannesburg One City Colliding Worlds* (STE 2004). In 2005, she was a visiting professor of architecture at the Massachussetts Institute of Technology and curated an exhibition at the second Rotterdam Architecture Biennale, entitled 'Liquid Durban'. She will shortly be relocating to the United States, to take up the position of Chair of Architecture at Temple University in Philadelphia.

High above the bustle of downtown Johannesburg's central bus terminus, Ghandi Square, tower (as in 20 storeys high) the gigantic images of two young black men. One stands next to a couch covered in a zebra pattered fabric, the other in a ceramic tiled bathroom. Both are naked from the waist up, in low cut jeans, their belts undone. Both look confidently, almost defiantly, at a spot above their heads, having 'sprayed it their way', with Axe deodorant for men.

Switch to a small, recently completed luxury hotel in the Cradle of Humanity World Heritage Site, just north of Johannesburg. Barely visible, discretely buried under roofs of swaying indigenous grass, its exquisitely designed, exquisitely priced suites open onto a timber deck fronting a reed studded dam. Here, giveaway Z 3s, Audis and BMWs in the parking lot, Johannesburg's new perfectly sculpted, designer fashioned black elite while away a Sunday afternoon, blowing vast sums of money on fat cigars and expensive brandy, served, unobtrusively, by young white staff.

In the intense experimentation with identity underway in contemporary Johannesburg, a highly charged landscape of shifting signifiers and floating signifieds, constantly adjusting to fit increasingly complex post-apartheid realities has emerged. The fixity of apartheid boundaries and identities has been dislodged and given way to a milieu of multiple, haphazard, overlapping codes, whose meanings are often unclear and constantly changing. This has transformed the uptight, affluent, racially divided, colonial city that was apartheid Johannesburg into a teeming, hybrid cosmopolis in a period of little more than a decade.

Johannesburg came into existence as the epicentre of the Witwatersrand goldfields, the world's richest gold deposits, discovered in 1886 in seams of rock deposits just below its surface. From its early incarnation as a tented mining camp, to its consolidation as a colonial town in the image of the metropolitan centre, to its working over by the instruments of apartheid (segregation, removal, restriction, resistance), to its current transformation into Africa's pre-eminent metropolis, Johannesburg has, since its inception, been a site of intense experimentation with modernity.

It began as a disruption that burst across the landscape of an already established agricultural community, rapidly disposing of its meanings and investing it with others. Its early inhabitants were *uitlanders* – foreigners, gamblers, people who came from nowhere, from elsewhere, from everywhere, in search of gold. Johannesburg was built on the logic of the lure, the dream, the anticipation of fabulous fortunes to be made overnight.[1] Its founding mythology, the mythology of gold and what it represents – spectacular wealth, luxury and good fortune – but more importantly, the appearance of it, has driven its existential history. Life in the city is about wealth, luxury and exhibition. It is a city of saturated images and surface appearances, of spectacular displays, wishful fantasies, casual encounters and shifting centres.

It is a city that has been transformed beyond recognition five times in its history. The first of these was in 1895 when a share boom on the Johannesburg Stock Exchange transformed it from a tented mining camp into a sprawling Victorian city. In the 1930s, when soaring gold prices resulted in foreign capital flooding the city, it became known as 'Little New York', boasting five skyscrapers, the highest of these, Escom House, at 21 storeys, the tallest in Africa. After the second world war, the high density residential neighbourhood of Hillbrow, much lauded for its gritty, speculative modernity by architectural critic, Nicolas Pevsner, mushroomed, serving as a point of entry for European immigrants. Then followed the great apartheid building boom of the 1960s, in which a frenzy of building – tall buildings, motorways, broadcasting towers, hospitals, universities – projected the city's image as a wealthy, modern one against growing condemnation of the racist policies of the apartheid state. Its latest transformation, in the early 1990s, saw the hollowing out of this modernist cantre as it was all but abandoned by its corporate sector and white residents, fleeing its greying streets as apartheid's boundaries collapsed.[2] Many of these relocated to Sandton, clustering around a former suburban shopping mall in the north of the city, and rapidly transformed its shapeless ersatz landscape into the heart of the city's financial and corporate life.

Lindela Repatriation Centre, Krugersdorp, 2004.
PHOTO ADAM BROOMBERG AND OLIVER CHANARIN.

The city's economy is no longer based on mining, but rather on financial, wholesale and retail services.[3] It produces 16% of South Africa's wealth, in a province, Gauteng, that produces 33% of it, and that grew 4.2% between 1996 and 2004. Its average income is 25% higher than in the country's nine other major cities combined.[4] In Johannesburg, 64% of the citizens own their own homes and 57% their own cars.[5] These levels of affluence fuel a dizzying consumer economy, centred on, but by no means limited to, the northern suburbs. Here shopping malls, elite housing estates, luxury car showrooms and, at its most extreme, the MonteCasino shoppertainment complex, sport an Italianate, or rather a Tuscan aesthetic, which acts as a fundamental compositional process (theatrical, dissonant and spectacular), providing images of the 'authentically urban', of history, civilization and urbaneness in an otherwise fragmented *polis*.

Living in Johannesburg today is a vast experiment in how to inhabit apartheid's ruins, how to live in a borderless world. What characterizes the city is, in fact, its merging of different worlds that intertwine in multiple ways. Hawkers rub shoulders with Aston Martins, informal trading shelters with Armani and Louis Vuitton. Prostitutes ply their trade on snug suburban streets. Many of the newly 'economically empowered'[6] black middle class move between worlds with remarkable ease, living their working weeks in a gated enclave in the north, but returning to their family home in Soweto over weekends, to participate in the communal street culture they still see as their own. Their children probably attend an exclusive private school, but return, on their coming of age, to their rural homeland to undergo traditional initiation rites, living as hunter-gathers in the bush before returning to the city.

At the same time as becoming more mobile, the city has battened itself down against the viral geographies of crime and fear that have permeated its post apartheid world. Fences, palisades, walls, gates, private security guards, cameras and other highly sophisticated security technologies have transformed the city's once leafy suburbs into bristling electromagnetic fields. New residential development takes place at a pace and almost without exception, in gated, walled compounds, fracturing the urban landscape into a monotony of mono-functional fragments linked by increasingly over-burdened highways. HIV Aids is taking its toll, with the current figure for those living with HIV standing at 17.5%,[7] and unemployment increased from 29% to 37% between 1996 and 2001.[8] Living in the city is like living in a state of permanent, if low level, emergency.

Despite such realities, Johannesburg's population has been growing since 1994. Between 1996 and 2001 it grew by 22%, from 2.6 to 3.2 million.[9] People still flock to 'Egoli', the city of gold, as it is known, in search of a better life. People like the Ethiopian radio announcer who told me that he 'walks the streets of Johannesburg with camels in his head'

Ponte swimming pool, Gauteng, 2004.
PHOTO ADAM BROOMBERG AND OLIVER CHANARIN.

Following pages.
Ponte, Gauteng, 2004.
PHOTO ADAM BROOMBERG AND OLIVER CHANARIN.

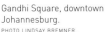

Gandhi Square, downtown
Johannesburg.
PHOTO LINDSAY BREMNER.

Johannesburg.
PHOTO LOANNA HOFFMANN,
THE MARKET PHOTO WORKSHOP,
COURTESY URBAN AGE PROJECT.

or the Nigerian barber/cellphone/spaza shop[10] owner who
rents Nollywood DVDs to Hillbrow residents.

Their origins are all over Africa and beyond – Ethiopia,
Congo, Nigeria, Senegal, Pakistan and China. In the
popular imagination the inner city is divided into Little
Lagos, Kinshasa, Mogadishu, Karachi and Beijing. The
city is constantly on the move, as transcontinental traders
and cross border shoppers circulate in migratory cycles of
various durations between the city and their countries of
origin, trading commodities or cash for fridges, televisions,
computers or clothing.[11] At the other end of the economic
spectrum, multinational executives, managers and
entrepreneurs increasingly use the city as a springboard
for their operations in Africa. In Fourways Gardens, an up-
market, gated residential enclave in the northern reaches
of the city, one could be fooled into thinking one was in any
edge city USA on Halloween or the 4th of July.

Thus the categorizations upon which apartheid rested
have been refuted and the city has been transformed into a
fluid, dynamic, rhizomic space, a particularly African form
of the modern that western urban management practices,
town planning codes and administrative systems seem at
a loss to make sense of. For what has emerged is a form
of urbanity where entanglements, hybridities, incessant
mobility and constant adaptation overlap with fragmentation,

ghettoization and homogenization, not as obstacles to
modern life, but the very modalities through which it is lived.
The challenge for the city is to figure out how to capitalize
on its increasing diversity and incessant mobility, on its
prominence in the continental imagination (and economy), on
how to make these work for it, to make the city a better place
for all its citizens.

For architecture and urban design, this means reclaiming
them from practices of separation, sanitation and fantasy,
for those that respond to mobility, intensify interaction (of
different activities, ages, ethnicities etc.) and welcome the
stranger. So, for instance, when a transportation interchange
overlaps with the dispensing and distributing of traditional
medicine, or a shopping mall becomes a radio station and
a Bollywood movie mecca, or an information centre is set
up for cross border shoppers, one can only applaud. For
what matters most in Johannesburg today is an architecture
that fosters economic, social and spatial entanglements,
that juxtaposes difference and intensifies cross-cultural
stylizations and conversations. The city needs to develop
attitudes, policies, practices and spaces that encourage
interaction, make strangers feel welcome and engender
responsibility to the urban poor. Only in doing so will it
make good on its claim of being the continent's premier
metropolis.

Plein Street, Down Town,
Gauteng, 2004.
PHOTO ADAM BROOMBERG AND
OLIVER CHANARIN.

[1] This is not surprising, given that the Witwatersrand goldfields are by far the world's largest source of gold – they have produced 40% of all the gold ever produced, and still produce 2/3 of its supply.

[2] Between 1982 and 1994, 17 of the 65 top 100 national public companies located in Johannesburg moved from downtown to decentralized locations. Similarly, of a total of 104 top national business enterprises located in Johannesburg, in 1994, only 27% were located in the city centre. Of the top ten retail companies with their head offices in Johannesburg,

only two remain in the city centre today. While these relocations can be attributed to many factors (infrastructure requirements, convenience, corporate restructuring, prestige etc.), a clear picture emerges of capital flight from the inner city. While the Johannesburg area has maintained its national head office function, the central city has weakened for nearly all sectors. Remaining are the major financial institutions that sank considerable investment into property over the preceding decades – life insurance companies, banking institutions and mining houses –

and provincial and local government departments (Tomlinson, R. *et al.* (1995). *Johannesburg Inner City Strategic Development framework: Economic Analysis.* Johannesburg: Greater Johannesburg Transitional Metropolitan Council City Planning Department).

[3] Its largest employment sectors are Retail and Wholesale (18%), Financial Services (17%) and Government Services (17%). Manufacturing accounts for 12%. (South African Cities Network. (2004). State of the Cities Report).

[4] South African Cities Network. (2004). State of the Cities Report.

[5] Based on the 2004 All Media Products Survey (AMPS) (http://www.joburg.org.za).

[6] A term referring to the beneficiaries of post apartheid Black Economic Empowerment (BEE) legislation aimed at the transfer of economic power to the black majority.

[7] HIV/AIDS figures are notoriously unreliable in South Africa. This figure for the total percentage of the population living with HIV in Gauteng Province comes from http://www.hst.org.za.

[8] http://www.joburg.org.za.

[9] http://www.joburg.org.za.

[10] A *spaza shop* is a small convenience store, usually operating from a room in a person's home, a converted garage or a shipping container opening onto the street.

[11] An estimated 1,000,000 cross border shoppers pass through the city each year. A study to be completed at the end of May 2006 will verify this figure (conversation with Tammy Lieberman, consultant for Urban Inc., May 2006).

Soweto, Gauteng, 2004.
PHOTO ADAM BROOMBERG AND
OLIVER CHANARIN.

Alexandra Township,
Gauteng, 2004.
PHOTO ADAM BROOMBERG AND
OLIVER CHANARIN.

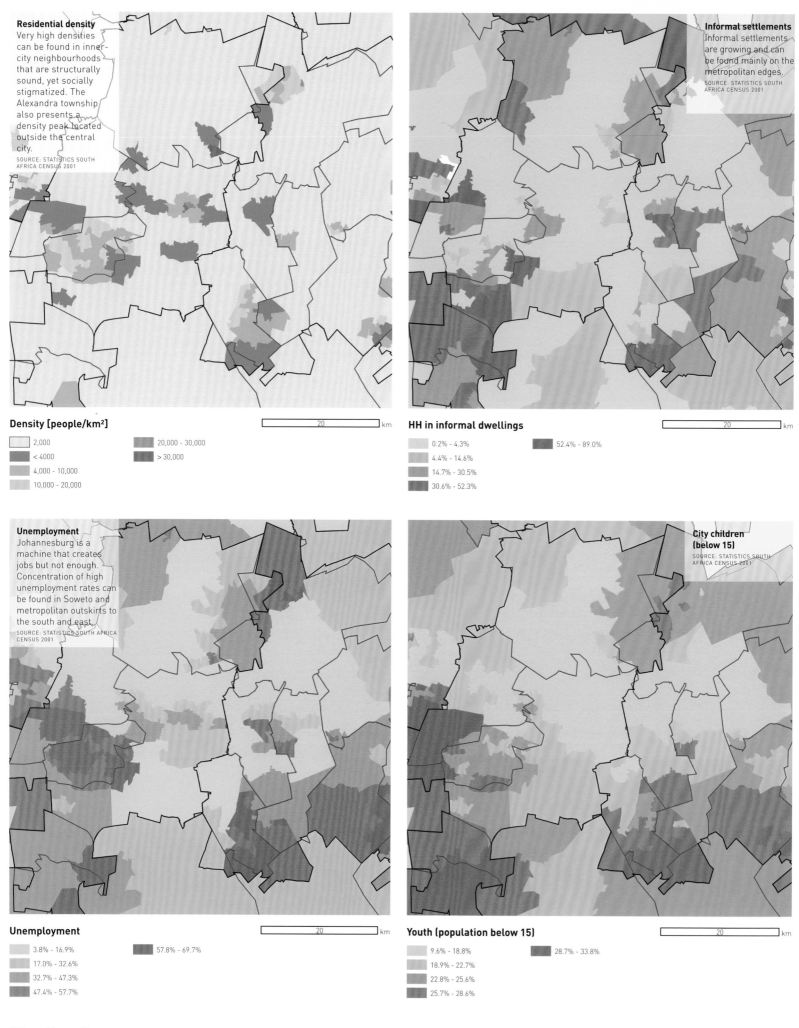

Residential density
Very high densities can be found in inner-city neighbourhoods that are structurally sound, yet socially stigmatized. The Alexandra township also presents a density peak located outside the central city.

SOURCE: STATISTICS SOUTH AFRICA CENSUS 2001

Informal settlements
Informal settlements are growing and can be found mainly on the metropolitan edges.

SOURCE: STATISTICS SOUTH AFRICA CENSUS 2001

Density [people/km²]
20 km

2,000	20,000 - 30,000
< 4000	> 30,000
4,000 - 10,000	
10,000 - 20,000	

HH in informal dwellings
20 km

0.2% - 4.3%	52.4% - 89.0%
4.4% - 14.6%	
14.7% - 30.5%	
30.6% - 52.3%	

Unemployment
Johannesburg is a machine that creates jobs but not enough. Concentration of high unemployment rates can be found in Soweto and metropolitan outskirts to the south and east.

SOURCE: STATISTICS SOUTH AFRICA CENSUS 2001

City children (below 15)

SOURCE: STATISTICS SOUTH AFRICA CENSUS 2001

Unemployment
20 km

3.8% - 16.9%	57.8% - 69.7%
17.0% - 32.6%	
32.7% - 47.3%	
47.4% - 57.7%	

Youth (population below 15)
20 km

9.6% - 18.8%	28.7% - 33.8%
18.9% - 22.7%	
22.8% - 25.6%	
25.7% - 28.6%	

Images from the QuickBird satellite of Johannesbug.
©DIGITALGLOBE EXCLUSIVE DISTRIBUTED FOR EUROPE BY TELESPAZIO.

The current population in the City of Johannesburg is approximately 3.2 million. It is estimated that the city grew 4% per year on average in the late 1990s and some projections present a growth scenario in which metropolitan Johannesburg will reach close to 15 million people by 2015. Therefore, this urban core of Gauteng province is expected to become the world's twelfth largest city-region, behind Lagos and slightly larger than Los Angeles.

With Johannesburg's new boundaries, the city now stretches over 1,600 square kilometres, reaching an average gross residential density of about 1,900 residents per square kilometre. This is a low urban density by international standards, yet the highest for all urban areas in South Africa. Densities vary widely across the metropolis, reaching peaks in both disadvantaged inner-city neighbourhoods and the peripheral township of Alexandra that does not even count upon the structural density of the former to support such residential agglomeration.

Johannesburg is a multi-racial city – 73% of the population is Black African, 16% are White, 6% are Coloured, and 4% are Indian or Asian. In recent years, there has been an increase in immigration from the rest of the continent to South Africa, and particularly to Johannesburg. This increased diversity has visible effects on many dimensions of city life, including its economy, housing and infrastructure demands, and social integration. Life expectancy in the city is notably low – especially when considering its dynamic economy and solid

infrastructure: only 4% of its residents have reached the age of 65. On the other hand, almost one out of three is younger than 20. Creating sustainable livelihoods will be a cornerstone in improving social conditions in Johannesburg. Currently, one household in five reports having no income and the number of unemployed hovers above 600,000 people.

Johannesburg is considered the economic engine of South Africa and its urban economy has a growing continental and global reach. In 2003, its share of South Africa's total economic output was about 17% or the equivalent of between 1 and 2% of Italy's GDP. Johannesburg is a service-oriented economy; 74% of people working in the city are employed by services, businesses or the real estate sector.

Of all daily journeys in Johannesburg, 33% are conducted by private car and 46% rely on various forms of public transport, both formally and informally provided. The lack of mobility among disadvantaged groups has been apparent in the city since the apartheid era. A number of transport and land-use initiatives are now addressing this issue.

The City of Johannesburg Metropolitan Municipality is an entity formed in the year 2000 that is divided into 11 regional administrations, utilities, agencies and corporate entities dedicated to the provision of urban and social services. The executive mayor, elected to the position by the council, plays the most important decision-making role in the City of Johannesburg.

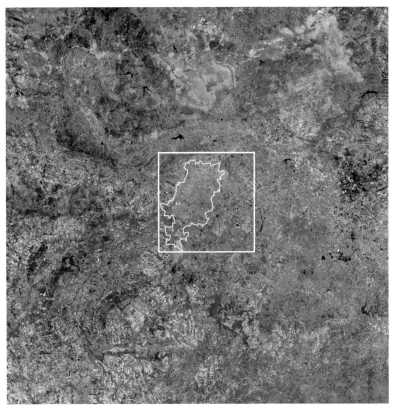

90 km

SOURCE: NASA.

Istanbul
Turkey

Korhan Gümüs and Elsa Mekki-Berrada

Korhan Gümüs is an architect and urban planner focusing on citizen-led approaches to urban planning. In Turkey he has founded several local groups for urban environmental preservation. In 2000 he founded the Human Settlements Association; as a director of the association he forms city watch groups that guide urban planning in Turkish cities.

Elsa Mekki-Berrada works in the French City Observatory of Istanbul (OUI/IFEA) and the Human Settlement Association (HSA). She is presently designing a botanic park for Alibeyky (Istanbul).

Francesco Jodice.
Istanbul.-R31-2005.

In search of modernity

The recent initiation of discussions, in October 2005, concerning the integration of Turkey within Europe, inspired the people of both Turkey and the EU to become more interested in their neighbours. The occasion also provoked debates and speculations, often based on half-truths and biased by pecuniary interests, about the possibilities for investment in Turkey and for the employment of Turks in Europe.

Istanbul, the country's commercial and cultural capital for nearly three millennia, anchors a region of 5,100 square kilometres, within which the city proper stretches over 1,800 square kilometres, 95% of this urbanized land. This territory poses undeniably large challenges to which the private sector currently responds in the practical absence, we argue, of public policies capable of initiating and managing change.

With an official population of 14 million inhabitants, Istanbul represents more than 15% of the population of Turkey (an increase from 5.7 % in 1945), with a strong annual growth rate of 3.3% (4.5% between 1895 and 1990, compared with 3.8% between 1990 and 1997). About 300,000 new inhabitants settle in Istanbul each year, most coming from small or medium-sized towns. When surveyed in 1997, 67% of the inhabitants of Istanbul had been born outside the city. However, while the city's contemporary condition derives from 40 years of unremitting population growth, we believe that the current response to that growth is the result of 40 years of political laxity.

Initially, in the absence of public policy to address housing needs, the city's newly-arrived inhabitants made do with basic shelter in squatter settlements or *gecekondu* (meaning 'to land by night'). Later they consolidated their shacks, elevating them to form *appartkondu*. The authorities exercised no restriction over these appropriations of public land, either in terms of quantity or quality. It was therefore in these urban margins – spaces without infrastructure, public spaces or property lines – that these happenstance buildings grew. Lacking any legal status, their inhabitants were easily manipulated during electoral periods. This was clearly illustrated by the laws for the legalization of the *gecekondu* in the 1980s – passed on the eve of the 1983 and 1985 municipal elections – which did nothing but further encourage the illegal occupation of public land.

The 1990s, conversely, were characterized by a political will to erase from the map, by any means possible, all of Istanbul's illegal neighbourhoods. Today, only 10% of the original *gecekondu* remain. However, it is worth noting that 60% of the constructions built over the last 25 years have nevertheless been illegal.

The use of illegal means solved, in part, the colossal need for housing that urban politicians proved incapable of addressing. Between 1984 and 1995 only 8,954 social housing units were constructed – most of these intended for earthquake victims – while in reality the city needed 100,000 units per year to respond to the needs of a population that had increased tenfold in 50 years. The decentralization law of 1984 disappointed hopes for social housing provision. In the case of Ikiteli, of the 200,000 units promised, only 7,540 were built, and only a quarter of these were distributed to those in need. Lending policy achieved little more, despite the foundation of the construction loan bank TRECB in the 1950s, and the 1981 law for mass housing that assigned 5% of public spending to social housing using Emlak Bankasi, but which in the end financed only 50,000 units.

Under these conditions, the private sector *had* to develop. It evolved slowly but surely from the model of middle-class workers' cooperatives in the 1930s, down through present-day holding companies that delegate market research to urban management services, and are privatised, as are the planning and management functions of the state. People are thus obliged to call on the services of private companies belonging to a large, influential financial group.

Today inter-urban migration is apparent: Istanbul's central neighbourhoods are emptied of their middle classes, who have fled the city in preference for the suburbs. Initially unplanned and sometimes illegal, gated communities such as Esenkent, Alkent and Buyuksehir are retroactively supported as 'externalization' projects in the discourse of the authorities (as was the case for the new town of Silivri). The peripheral neighbourhoods of Büyükçekmece, Gaziosmanpasa and Silivri grew in population by 14.5%, 9.2% and 5.4% respectively between 1990 and 1997, while in the same period the old city centre of Eminönü decreased by 4.8%.

Istanbul.
© GABRIELE BASILICO.

Based on American-style aspirations, these gated communities sell the ideas of happiness, satisfaction, elitism and security, providing single-family houses with manicured gardens, swimming pools, golf courses, private schools, privatised urban services, security cameras and the like. As such, they are the opposite of Istanbul's traditional neighbourhoods, where rich and poor live together, where 'private' space is open to all and 'public' space used as an extension of the interior. This new segregation is the spatial expression of the social differentiation between long-time citizens and underprivileged in-migrants, the latter group's integration into the city having been unsatisfactorily accomplished.

Concern about the spontaneous expansion towards the periphery has inspired public policies to reclaim the inner city and to counterbalance urban sprawl, through the construction of urban transport infrastructure such as new east-west routes and the trans-Bosphorus Bridge. Planned for 2010, 'Marmarail', the railway tunnel under the

Bosphorus, will finally link the train networks of Asia and Europe. It will also offer a practical alternative to the private car, allowing middle class inhabitants of the Asian waterfront or other private communities to access the business districts of Levent or Maslak. At present, the disjointed public transport system discourages daily commuters, who prefer to travel by car. 17 public authorities control public transport and there is no unified transport strategy; Istanbul's underground and tram routes remain poorly linked, for example.

Following the abandonment of the central historic districts, public policy has encouraged the renovation of historically-important buildings within these areas with the aim of attracting tourism. The city relies significantly on the tourism industry, which centres on the museums and monuments of the historic peninsula. The city intends to develop historic restoration projects, which will have the effect of Disneyfying entire neighbourhoods such as Sullemaniye and Sullukule. Until now, heritage in Istanbul

Istanbul.
© GABRIELE BASILICO

has only been valued if it offers the potential for tourist income. As a result, a number of minor buildings have been left untouched, in particular those not pertaining to Ottoman history, not to mention the great wall of Theodose that literally collapsed, eaten away by mismanaged urbanism. The recent support given to Sullukule's minority against their expulsion (in June 2006), has opened a new challenge for civil society; demanding that the municipality respect human rights and acknowledge the value of cultural heritage. Poor ethnic minorities, craftsmen and small industries settle in modest dwellings or occupy abandoned houses and buildings without the capacity to maintain and restore them. Nevertheless these Roma or east-European minorities are preserving another living heritage in the form of their own culture.

Istanbul's urban policy has turned radically towards the pursuit of a modern identity, in the process exiling undesirable populations or activities to the invisible margins of the city. Until recently the light and crafts-based industries

of the Ikiteli formed an integral part of the urban fabric, but these have now been pushed out of the urban core due to the city's self-conscious desire to cultivate its image as an investment-friendly cosmopolis. Relocated to the second-largest industrial zone of the near-east, situated along the Trans-European Motorway at the city's fringe, Ikiteli is now unable to manage either its image or the ground pollution it produces, as it did in its original site.

Concurrent with the relocation of these functions outside of the central city, and echoing tendencies toward nostalgia found elsewhere in Europe, the principal spatial legacies of 19th century industry are being radically transformed. The waterfronts of the Bosphorus and the Golden Horn are being made-over in both image and function. This redevelopment is turning vast industrial areas into zones of leisure, commerce and consumption, such as the anticipated *grands projects* for the Galata Port, Haydarpaşa, Sirkeçi and Tophane. The districts of the Levent and nearby Maslak have been settled as mono-functional business zones since the 1990s. In light

Following pages
Francesco Jodice.
Istanbul.-T31-2005.

of these internal movements and transformations, it appears that Istanbul is becoming a city of specialized quarters for business, culture, tourism and housing.

In order to reinforce the legal and political framework of these European-focused urban transformations, central and local governments are now giving themselves powerful legislative tools that challenge previous policies on decentralized governance, public participation and political transparency, and constitute, for the most part, a step backwards by reviving practices such as compulsory eviction.

In pursuit of its twin dreams of modernity and European inclusion, Istanbul has become embroiled in a struggle against its own true nature. Its efforts to make

itself attractive with cosmetic surgery risk inflicting disfigurements that may instead scare off the foreign experts currently working towards European co-operation and integration.

As in most cases of lost identity, certain violent reactionary movements have emerged with a desire to recover the paradise lost. To preclude such misunderstandings, and to move forward together, it is essential to deepen the exchanges between different spheres. Istanbul's recent selection as European Capital of Culture for 2010 presents one unprecedented opportunity to draw upon existing local initiatives and resources in order to envisage the Istanbul of the future.
Translated from the French by Sarah Ichioka

Istanbul 2005.
© PAOLO ROSSELLI.

Istanbul.
© GABRIELE BASILICO.

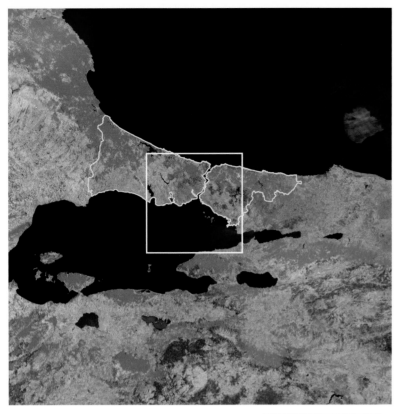

SOURCE: NASA.

90 km

Residential density
Istanbul presents higher levels of density
on its European side. Densely developed
neighbourhoods adjacent to the city's
economic and cultural nuclei house
the wealthier residents and the middle
classes. However, density can also be
found in the outlying informal settlements,
locally known as *gecekondu*, or "built
overnight."

SOURCE: CENSUS OF 2000, SUPPLIED BY MURAT GUVENÇ,
ISTANBUL BILGI UNIVERSITY.

20 km

Density [people/km²]

2,000	10,000 - 20,000
< 4,000	20,000 - 30,000
4,000 - 10,000	> 30,000

With a population of 9.8 million, Istanbul is the largest city in Turkey (although it is not the political capital, and its mayor is appointed by Ankara). It is the largest city in the Balkan region; an ancient city within a young, secular Muslim state. Istanbul spans 1,839 km2, straddling the Asian and European continents, and defined by its extensive waterfront. A full 95% of the city proper is urbanised, and gross residential density averages 4,803 residents per km2. In recent years, large-scale suburban expansions (many of them gated), have overtaken informal *gecekondu* settlements as the major form of housing provision. Istanbul is poised between a beleaguered Middle East and a European Union it may join; between its deep history and the recent infusion of global capital and culture. The many-layered city must negotiate other balances: between the dense urban centre and the sprawling outskirts; between the needs of its Turkic majority and those of minority ethnic and religious groups.

2,000 years as the capital of the successive Roman, Byzantine and Ottoman empires have bequeathed the city with an invaluable built legacy. Although most of the major monuments have now been conserved as world heritage sites, much of the city's vernacular architectural heritage, particularly along the banks of the Bosphorus, remains under threat. The city underwent a phenomenal growth of around 900% in the past 50 years, and of 27% in the last decade. A further population growth of 1.5 million is projected in the next ten years.

In-migration is driven by economic opportunity. Due to its position at an international sea and land crossroads, Istanbul has always played a key role in Turkey's economy. This holds true today; the gross city product of Istanbul is equivalent to a fifth of the national economy (equivalent to about 3% of Italy's GDP). Istanbul's Gross City Product is approximately €1,928 per capita. The service sector—spanning from banking to tourism—employs half of all people working in the Istanbul Province. Industry, while no longer the principal cog in the economy, nevertheless still employs a third of the city's population, and a significant one third of Turkey's manufacturing plants are still located in Istanbul. The combined trends of the relocation of industry to the outskirts of the city, and an increasing interest in philanthropy amongst Istanbul's elite individuals and institutions have produced plans for the refurbishment of the

city's redundant industrial sites to house cultural facilities. These brownfield sites (many of them along Istanbul's iconic and extensive waterfronts) have been targeted as locations through which to more evenly disperse cultural institutions/facilities throughout the city (particularly on its Asian side); until recently, such resources have been concentrated in the historic western peninsula.

Istanbul's population is very young, with over a third of its residents under 20 years old and only 4.7% above 65 years. While only a tiny fraction of Istanbul's population is born abroad, a significant two-thirds of its inhabitants were born outside Istanbul. The rates of social mobility for rural in-migrants to the city are perceived as high. The city has managed a troubled, but functional coexistence of minority ethnic and religious groups (Kurds, Albanians, Greeks and Jews, to name a few) with the majority Muslim Turkic culture.

Istanbul's metropolitan government has acknowledged the need for more comprehensive planning to meet the challenges of retrofitting an old city to accommodate growth, and recently established a hundreds-strong urban planning department. Desired outcomes are a structured process of project negotiation that involves community groups, academic experts and planners and more efficient administration of public works projects.

Coordinating transport is a key challenge. At the moment, over two-thirds of daily journeys in Istanbul are conducted on public transport, while under a third are conducted by private car. Despite the city's obvious dependency on public transport, the infrastructure struggles under the weight of an ever-expanding population, and a lack of coordination between the different components. Nevertheless public policy has been somewhat successful in encouraging car-free travel alternatives and planning is underway to improve the effectiveness of the current transport system, such as the new sub-Bosporus tunnel to link the train networks on both continents

Images from the
QuickBird satellite of
Istanbul.
© DIGITALGLOBE EXCLUSIVE
DISTRIBUITED FOR EUROPE BY
TELESPAZIO.

MILAN and TURIN
Italy

Guido Martinotti

Guido Martinotti is professor of urban sociology and pro-rector at the University of Milano-Bicocca. He has previously taught architecture, political science and sociology at various institutions, including the University of Milan, EPHE (Paris), the University of California (Santa Barbara) and NYU. His publications include *La città difficile*, *Informazione e sapere*, *Metropoli*, *La dimensione metropolitana* and *e-learning* with F. Del Fiore.

Turin from Piazza Statuto, 2002.

Milan, Piazza Sempione, 2002.

Cousins and strangers

As much as they stand apart, Milan and Turin belong to the same loosely urbanized area, the vast Po Valley megalopolis that stretches along the north-west of Italy reaching a population in excess of 7 million people. The growth patterns of the last two decades reveal that MITO (Milano-Torino) – the metacity dreamt up by the mayors of these two cities in the early 1980s – does not actually exist as a continuous urban form, but suggest that there are strong economic and functional interdependencies at play that may be further affected by the high-speed rail line now under construction in this part of Europe. It is not clear what level of political cooperation, if any, may exist between these two urban hubs of the north west of Italy, but there is little doubt that this area is becoming an even larger yet more dispersed urban entity, perhaps reaching up to 10 million inhabitants in the coming years.

Milan and Turin have the typical relationship that in the Anglo-Saxon world defines British and Americans, that of 'cousins and strangers'. They are 'cousins' because they are both industrial towns in a country that has elsewhere industrialized belatedly and sporadically; 'strangers' because of their differing histories, lifestyles, and urban aspects.

Perhaps in the mapping of their railways stations lies one of the major contrasts and tensions between the 'aristocratic' and the 'plutocratic' capitals of the industrialized Italian northwest. The great Porta Nuova railway station in Turin is oriented to the south and directed toward the rest of the Italian Peninsula, as befits a city that was once capital of a kingdom that unified the Italian mosaic of states and colonies. It is not directed toward the east, where at close range (120 odd kilometres, one hour by car) lies Milan, the central city of the Po Valley megalopolis of about 7 million inhabitants. On the other end the Stazione Centrale di Milano is directed to the north, toward Europe (there are also important central railway stations to the west, like Porta Garibaldi), but most notably the traditional highway node is dominated by the westbound Autostrada Milano-Torino.

To make the rail link between Turin and Milan more efficient, new tracks have recently been laid in the city of Turin, creating a large gash in the city fabric around Porta Susa, Turin's secondary but nevertheless important railway station. The Italian railway authority, Trenitalia, significantly advertizes its new high speed link between the cities with the shorter time to Porta Susa, almost ten minute less than the one to Porta Nuova, which is right at the heart of the city's fabric.

Turin is a noble city, its history inextricably embedded in the process of national unification and *Risorgimento*. The aristocratic nature of Turin is visible in many of its palaces and monuments, but moreover in the lifestyle characterized by a touch of *cortesia* or mannerism that to foreign critics borders on hypocrisy.

Yet Turin is a city of many not easily detected layers, even though each has its own architectural counterpart. The centre of the town still has its very visible Roman plan and, contrary to many other Italian cities, has been until lately under-gentrified, with a lower-class population and fairly high degree of building decay. Probably this is the counterpart of another feature unique to the city: *La Collina*, which provides a high-level amenity and favours the suburbanization of the middle and upper classes. Few Italian cities have this American-type morphology with a segregated inner city surrounded by upscale suburbia.

The medieval imprint is visible in the imposing *Palazzo Madama*, the central castle, which is almost unavoidable if you drive in Turin. But the most important heritage in the city is probably the baroque one largely dominated by Juvarra. The idea that the city must be designed from the optical point of view of the king in his central palace created some of the major axes on which the urban texture is still built: toward Stupinigi on the south west, Rivoli on the north, Superga on the east. The development of contemporary Turin followed the grid suggested by these great axes, and by the original Roman texture. Even from this point of view Turin has an American flair, with its extended grid and large avenues perfectly fit for the development of a Fordist culture and economy. There is no doubt that Turin is a modern industrial town.

Yet there is another layer to the city: an esoteric persuasion. Turin is considered part of the magical triangle of Europe with Prague and Lyon, a belief manifest in the strong concentration of mystery and carnival games (Carnival: another hugely important moment in the life of the city) and in the sympathies of even Turin's highly-sophisticated intelligentsia for esoteric practices and rites, well depicted in the novels of Fruttero and Lucentini. Furthermore, Turin has many surprising architectural symbols, none more bizarre than the huge *Mole Antonelliana*. This is a sign of the conviction of Turin's Jewish community and is exceptional in making Turin perhaps the only city in the world with a synagogue as its key landmark.

Thus Turin operates within a set of visibly-articulated opposing forces. It is an aristocratic city where the early development of the motor industry has created a large and

Turin, Piazza Statuto,
2002.
COURTESY ILEANA GUGLIELMI,
TORINO. © VINCENZO CASTELLA.

active proletariat, which still makes an unmistakable imprint on its image and politics. Unlike Milan, it is not a bourgeois city but its style in every station of life is mannered self-restraint, in opposition to the brazen Milanese striving. Turin's aristocratic style is not simply of the upper classes, but rather a way of life. This is tangible in the quieter pace of activity, and above all in an intellectual climate - one of the best in Italy – that is simultaneously literary but inclined to favour science and technology; in no other city could a writer like Primo Levi have dedicated a book to a wrench (*La chiave a stella*). Many commentators have attributed the disciplined and rational traits of the Turin character to FIAT and its Fordist organization. I am convinced that the opposite is true: FIAT could not have developed anywhere *but* Turin.

Turin is a democratic and generally tolerant city, but a tough one. During the wave of industrialization and immigration from southern Italy, Turin imported a great number of young people, mostly single males, mostly from the same areas, most going to work in the same Fordist plants, and moving into the same hastily-built neighbourhoods. At the end of this process, Turin was 50% working class compared to Milan's 30.7%. And whereas the two cities had more or less the same percentage of old immigrants (around 17%) only 23% of Turin's population was locally born (compared to 40%

in Milan) and almost 60% was recent immigrants (compared to 42% in Milan). Perhaps it's no wonder that tensions erupted in bloody clashes between workers and police on more than one occasion, and that – despicable as this might be – the quiet, conformist local population refused to rent to *meridionali* and *terroni* (southern Italians).

Today these tensions and repulsions have shifted from the *meridionali* to newcomers from outside the EU, but the impression is that they are localized, and that xenophobic policies have not proven popular, as documented by the landslide victory of the incumbent leftwing mayors in May 2006. There is no doubt that the city seems to have overcome the deep crisis of deindustrialization in an astonishing way. Turin has been able to elaborate and implement a master plan by the Milanese firm Gregotti and Cagnardi, which will revolutionize a large part of the city, and was able to host the Winter Olympics of 2005 with remarkable success.

In his book *Torino*, the sociologist Arnaldo Bagnasco traces the transformations of the city from a market economy to an organization-led, Fordist economy and finally to a less austere and more negotiation-prone style of 'political exchange'. On balance, Turin remains a city proud of itself and of its achievements, a city subtly yet significantly different from

Following pages
Milan 2002/2006.

the rest of Italy, and one that has adeptly reinvented itself in response to economic and political change.

Its 'cousin' Milan has changed in its own ways. In the more-or-less half century of which I have direct memories, Milan has transformed from a fairly austere inner-directed city to an other-directed metropolis with some, but not too much, cosmopolitan flair. That is, just enough cosmopolitanism to awe the average Italian, but not enough to compete with truly international capitals. Milanese – or at least the middle and more-than-middle class ones that I chance to talk to – are well-to-do but not very happy. The Milanese mood has gone from boisterous – as in the famous parochial song *Oh mia bela Madunina* (My beautiful little Madonna: the gold statue perched atop the Duomo) to plaintive – as in the banner of a candidate running for city council: 'Kiss the toad: the impossible mission to love Milan'.
Milan is undoubtedly rich, it lies in the middle of one of the richest areas of Europe, hence of the world. Why should it not produce happy people? Out of the many available I see two possible explanations: one based on *la longue durée*, and one based on recent changes.
If we look at the past, Milan has always been characterized by a contrast between wealth and happiness, or at least satisfaction. In 1288 a Milanese monk wrote what is probably

one of the first exercises of 'city marketing' in urban history, *De Magnalibus Mediolani* (Milan's marvels or Marvellous Milan). After having listed all its marvels, Fra' Bonvesin de la Ripa admits that the city is rife with conflicts and cruel oppression. At the end of the 19th century Milan was fully industrialized and had grown from the delightful and enlightened provincial town of the Austro-Hungarian Empire celebrated by Stendhal, to the smoke blackened sweltering city that the Milanese are now accustomed to seeing. The swelling working class paid the cost of this growth and on 8 June, 1898 General Bava-Beccaris trained the army's cannons at point blank range against protesting strikers, killing 350 and maiming hundreds more. Despite this, after a few years, the socialist party and the industrial capitalists cooperated, under the umbrella of a stern, but socially progressive Catholicism, to create a number of municipal institutions, which ran the city until very recently. Then came the First World War, more growth, more unrest, and Fascism, which had its national headquarters in Milan; followed by the Second, during which Milan was 40% destroyed and suffered two years of chilly and bloody occupation by Nazi Germans and Italian Fascists, against which a well-organized resistance mobilized insurgency and achieved liberation on 25 April 1945. Then came the reconstruction, a long season of workers' unrest, students' movements, Fascist terrorist bombings and

Red Brigades killing. And now the Berlusconian era, which has polarized anew the political arena. Maybe history teaches that wealth cannot be disembedded from conflicts; where there are riches, there is greed and strife.

Recently, deep changes have affected Milan and its image. After the first transition from agriculture to industry at the end of the 19th century, Italy experienced a long period of continuous industrial growth after the Second World War. During the so-called 'Italian Miracle', Milan was the major locomotive of this dynamic expansion of the economy. The reconstruction of huge parts of the city was not all architecturally notable, but there were a few remarkable signposts, like the 106 metre high *Torre Velasca* built by BBPR (Banfi, Belgiojoso, Peressutti and Rogers) between 1956 and 1958 and the 127 metres *Grattacielo Pirelli* built by Giò Ponti and Luigi Nervi, which along with a handful of other high-rises gave Milan an up-to-date skyline. The completion of the first real modern metro line in the country (the Red line) in 1964 and the successive Green line (1969), both built without central state capital, completed the image of a unique, self-supporting polity.

The expansion boosted demand not only of industrial workers but also of the more educated ones. Cultural industry and institutions, schools and universities, research centres, advertisement and marketing firms, all grew in Milan. There was a magic moment when all this came together in a way that would have pleased Richard Florida, mingling the artistic talent of designers with industrial technology and the progressivism and enlightenment of the political culture. But the magic of this moment was due to the presence of a large, educated middle class that shared values and perspectives with both the progressive part of the industrial bourgeoisie and the reformist and well-established part of the working class. In this period, from the mid-1950s to the oil crisis of the '70s the presence of large scale organizations and techno-structures was crucial. Among these, the city council was the largest employer, but there were also technicians and scientists working in industrial research centres, as well as intellectuals working in publishing houses, all connected by a strong, almost Protestant, common work ethic.

The crucial thing, however, was that at the time, Milan was still a 'city', growing to its peak of more than 1.7 million in 1973, but still very compact, and with a modern urban identity that stood out among other Italian cities. Milan was the 'economic' and even the 'moral' capital of Italy, in the sense that it was noted not only for its economic dynamism, but also for the pragmatic efficiency of its administrative style. Unfortunately, Milan did not cope well with the second transition from an industrial to a service economy. This began in the mid 70s, when the process of deindustrialization started to weaken the major industrial assets of the city and of its manufacturing suburbs, particularly in the northern areas.

The fact that Milan had experimented with the inclusion in the city government of traditional working class parties like the socialists and the communists well ahead of other cities has somewhat backfired. In the last decade of the century, its political elite were wiped out by scandals, in the so-called 'Tangentopoli' or 'Mani pulite' series of trials. This was particularly true for the socialist party that had been the protagonist of the particular institutional compromise that ran the city more or less since the beginning of the 20th century. Neo-liberal approaches kicked in, on the populist 'anti-political' appeal of the *Lega Nord* and of Berlusconi's *Forza Italia*, while the city radically changed its social and cultural foundations, with the development of an economy increasingly based on flexible jobs and the ensuing 'corrosion of character' so well described by Richard Sennett.

In 2001 Milan had a population of 1,256,211, more-or-less what it would have had in 1941 had a census been taken (just a bit more than 1936 and less than 1951). But the social composition is today vastly different. In 1941, despite the beginning of the war, Milan was still a thriving industrial town; today the same population could not solely support any type of sustainable economy or society. The second transition to a service economy has filtered out in the vast and expanding peri-urban area a growing number of the middle classes; of the active population, in general, and of young couples with children in particular. Milan's city centre has become increasingly a place for the elderly, the rich, and sometimes those who are both. The largest part of the ageing population is trapped in the central city in the sense that only there it finds the conditions, particularly in public housing, for a minimum level of survival. But this happens at the cost of mobility, as indicated by the increase in senior citizen mortality during heat waves.

New international immigrants filter in, finding niches in the labour market, especially in personal care and catering, and within the urban texture. So far this has occurred without creating suburban enclaves, but it has clearly influenced the Chinese district – one of the largest in Europe - which formed around a small Chinatown nucleus dating from the early 20th century, as well as Muslim areas in north-eastern Milan. In this process, Milan has become other-directed or at least outward-looking. It has lost its self-assured identity of being special and forward-looking.

The neo-liberalist rhetoric cannot hide the fact that no strategic decision has been taken to run a new breed of metropolis. It is still good to work there, but not equally good to live. Milan still has some of the proper Ts in the right place – Talent, Technology and Tolerance – but it lacks most of the Ss – Satisfaction, Solidarity and Soul – which imparted it its special status as the most advanced city of the nation. Public life is not particularly visible. Occasions of citywide collective mobilization are few, although there are spots of dynamism. The urban development at Bicocca, on the premises of the former Pirelli Factory, the smaller one in Bovisa and the planned upscale developments at Santa Giulia and the old Fiera di Milan grounds, all seem like islands in a fairly drab city where most the public life is very private and not very visible.

Following pages
Turin 2002/2006.
COURTESY GALLERIA LE CASE
D'ARTE, MILANO. © VINCENZO
CASTELLA.

Milan, 1998.
COURTESY GALLERIA LE CASE
D'ARTE, MILANO. © VINCENZO
CASTELLA.

Turin and Milan, with less than 150 kilometres separating them, are the two principal northern cities of Italy. To this day, Milan remains slightly bigger than Turin, both in terms of population and area. The current population of Milan stands at approximately 1.3 million, following a growth of 140% in the past century. In the last decade however, Milan has witnessed a population decline of about 1%, and projections for the future confirm that this trend looks set to continue. Indeed the population of the Milan Urban Agglomeration is expected to decrease by a further 22,000 in the next ten years. Turin, on the other hand, has tripled its population in the last century, an expansion rate greater than Milan. Today its population stands at 902,255, only about three-quarters that of Milan. However Turin's wider metropolitan region is closer to two million. As is the case in Milan, Turin's population is set to decrease slightly in the next decade.

The city of Milan stretches across the Lombardy plains covering approximately 182.4 square kilometres. The city of Turin, situated predominantly on the west bank of the Po River, spans approximately 130 square kilometres, or an area just over two-thirds the size of Milan. In both cities, parks and recreational space account for roughly 10% of their total areas. The gross residential density of Milan is about 7,123 residents per square kilometre, or just higher than Turin's density of 6,940 per square kilometre.

Milan, home to almost 3,000,000 foreign residents, is unquestionably cosmopolitan. Almost a quarter of its population comes from abroad, either from other European nations, the Philippines, Egypt, Peru or Africa. In contrast, Turin's population is far less international. Despite doubling since 2000, the foreign population still accounts for fewer than 10% of residents. In both Milan and Turin, over half their current population was born outside the city itself.

Milan and Turin's demographic profile is somewhat similar; 14% and 16.4% of their populations respectively are under 14 years of age. Moreover, they both host an ageing population, where the proportion of those over retirement age is considerable. In Turin almost one in five are over retirement age, while in Milan almost 23% are 65 years or older.

Milan's Gross City Product, is approximately €32,800 per capita. Milan still maintains its reputation as a critical player in the Italian economy; the Gross City Product of Milan is equivalent to 10.5% of its nation's economy.

Milan to this day remains one of the major financial and business centres of Europe. A world leader in the fashion and design industries, Milan is also home to the Italian Stock Exchange, *Borsa Valori.* Today the service sector employs over three-quarters of the population, while its industrial sector now only accounts for about 22% of jobs. Despite this, Milan continues to lead Italian cities in the manufacture of chemicals and textiles.

Historically, at least, Turin was a major industrial centre focusing mainly on cars and aerospace. Today the industrial sector in the city remains a larger source of employment than its Milanese counter-part; it provides a third of employment. Yet despite the fact that Turin was once the birth place of many of Italy's key industries, such as communications, television and cinema, many of these have now relocated to other parts of Italy. The service sector, as in Milan, is now the principal sector, employing two-thirds of the population.

Milan, the main city of northern Italy, is capital of the Milan Province and of the Lombardy region. The city is divided into nine zones, each with its own elected council. The city is governed by a mayor and a city council. Turin, although smaller than Milan, is still the capital of the Italian province of Piedmont – one of the most populous and largest regions. Not unlike Milan, Turin is divided into ten zones, each with its own elected council. The city is governed by an elected mayor and city council.

Milan is one of the richest cities in the European Union. Annual public expenditure is approximately €3,176 per capita. When compared with the average per capita income, residents in Milan earn roughly 35% more than their national counterparts.

Under half of the residents of inner city Milan rely on public transport, and just over a third of the neighbouring towns depend on this mode to access the city. This usage is low considering the fact that Milan is served by an extensive public transport infrastructure. The metro system extends for about 80 kilometres, while the tramway system serving Greater Milan is one of the most extensive in the world, with over 286 kilometres of tracks and 20 lines. Despite the quantity of transport infrastructure, the city has a very high car ownership rate: 739 private cars per 1,000 residents. In comparison, Turin's transport system is not as well established. However due to the Winter Olympics recently hosted in Turin, the city has experienced a wave of development that has changed the quantity and quality of the public transport infrastructure. The most notable development has been the installation of phase one of a metro system.

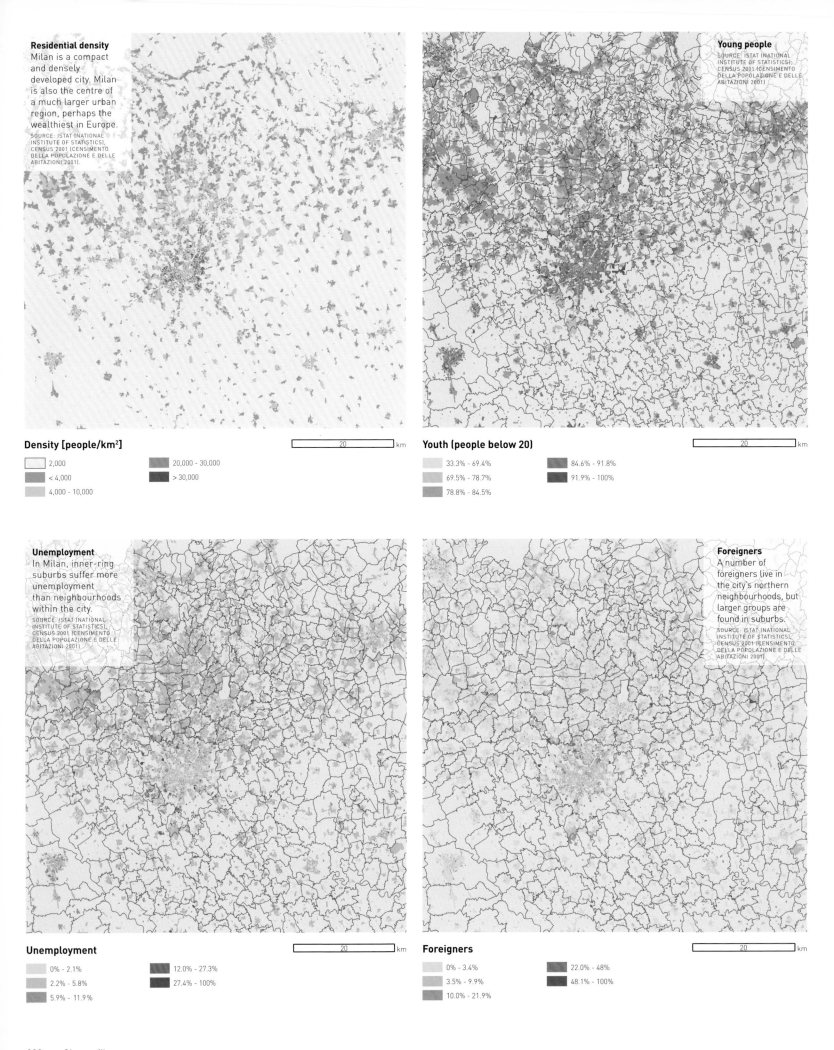

Residential density
Milan is a compact and densely developed city. Milan is also the centre of a much larger urban region, perhaps the wealthiest in Europe.

SOURCE: ISTAT (NATIONAL INSTITUTE OF STATISTICS), CENSUS 2001 (CENSIMENTO DELLA POPOLAZIONE E DELLE ABITAZIONI 2001).

Young people

SOURCE: ISTAT (NATIONAL INSTITUTE OF STATISTICS), CENSUS 2001 (CENSIMENTO DELLA POPOLAZIONE E DELLE ABITAZIONI 2001)

Density [people/km²]

2,000	20,000 - 30,000
< 4,000	> 30,000
4,000 - 10,000	

20 km

Youth (people below 20)

33.3% - 69.4%	84.6% - 91.8%
69.5% - 78.7%	91.9% - 100%
78.8% - 84.5%	

20 km

Unemployment
In Milan, inner-ring suburbs suffer more unemployment than neighbourhoods within the city.

SOURCE: ISTAT (NATIONAL INSTITUTE OF STATISTICS), CENSUS 2001 (CENSIMENTO DELLA POPOLAZIONE E DELLE ABITAZIONI 2001)

Foreigners
A number of foreigners live in the city's northern neighbourhoods, but larger groups are found in suburbs.

SOURCE: ISTAT (NATIONAL INSTITUTE OF STATISTICS), CENSUS 2001 (CENSIMENTO DELLA POPOLAZIONE E DELLE ABITAZIONI 2001)

Unemployment

0% - 2.1%	12.0% - 27.3%
2.2% - 5.8%	27.4% - 100%
5.9% - 11.9%	

20 km

Foreigners

0% - 3.4%	22.0% - 48%
3.5% - 9.9%	48.1% - 100%
10.0% - 21.9%	

20 km

Images from the
QuickBird satellite of
Milan.
© DIGITALGLOBE EXCLUSIVE
DISTRIBUTED FOR EUROPE BY
TELESPAZIO.

SOURCE: NASA.

**Incremento nel decennio 1991-2001 osservato nelle regioni
Piemonte e Lombardia nei comuni non metropolitani**

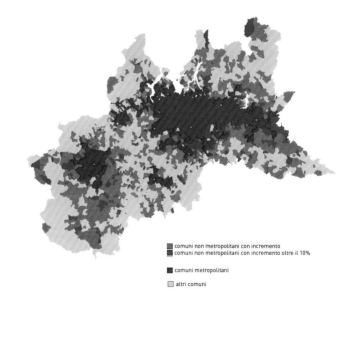

■ comuni non metropolitani con incremento
■ comuni non metropolitani con incremento oltre il 10%

■ comuni metropolitani

□ altri comuni

The North-West metropolis
Blue areas: the 1981 metropolis. Red areas: growth
in previously non metropolitan communes, 1991-2001
(Maps: amelis@unica.it).

Berlin
Germany

Jens Binsky

Jens Binsky writes for the *Berliner Zeitung*. He is also Editor of the supplement for the *Süddeutshe Zeitung*. His book *Geboren am 13. August. Der Sozialismus und Ich*, was published in 2004.
PHOTO BY STEPHAN KOAL.

Berlin: a profile

Stepping out from underneath the glass arches of Berlin's brand new main railway station, the Hauptbahnhof, one is greeted by a plethora of grandiose architectural gestures set against the backdrop of a vast expanse of undeveloped ground. The gaze may come to rest on the Federal Chancellery, designed by Axel Schultes, or on the "Band des Bundes", the "Federal Belt" of newly constructed government buildings; one may take in Norman Foster's Reichstag cupola or the completely redeveloped Postdamer Platz and recall that, a mere fifteen years ago, none of these structures existed. What is even more striking from this vantage point is that the city as people's living-space does not seem to intersect with the Berlin that is the new representative centre of Germany. City-dwellers and citizens evidently inhabit two decidedly distinct spheres. Unlike many other European cities, Berlin has no clearly defined city-centre complete with market-square, city hall and cathedral. Such central space simply does not exist here. More than ever, Berlin is a conglomeration of parallel worlds, a hotchpotch of stages on which long-established residents, newcomers and tourists make their respective entrances.

The Berlin Wall saved the Western part of the city from the fate that, after the War, had typically befallen so many other West German cities with their emptying town-centres and fraying edges, their population slowly spilling over into the surrounding countryside. Yet there was a price to pay for this in Berlin, namely the destruction of a coherent urban structure. The bombings of World War II and the subsequent partition had carved up Berlin's infrastructure, its canalization, its network of roads and its railway system. Vast areas of derelict land soon became a hallmark of this fragmented city.

When the Berlin Wall fell and Berlin became, albeit by a narrow parliamentary majority, the capital of the newly unified German, expectations ran high and grand visions abounded. Surely, the city would soon be home to six million people, and all manner of fanciful plans were drawn up for his new metropolis: Berlin was to become the powerhouse of the new Republic, the focal point for an entire "Generation Berlin", the "hub" that would connect East and West, a veritable "laboratory of unification". Such promises were directly rooted in the rhetoric and practises of the Cold War, when, thanks to huge subsidies provided by the two respective German states, West Berlin had been established as a "Window on Freedom", while East Berlin stood proud as the "capital of the first Workers' and Peasants' State on German soil". On either side of the Wall, Berliners themselves tended to view such labels – which bore precious little relation to the realities of their everyday lives – with a healthy amount of irony. While others were certainly welcome to entertain illusions of grandeur, Berliners' first loyalties lay with their neighbourhoods and their lovingly tended urban allotments.

Since the early 1990s, Berlin has, above all, been a huge building site, and architecture often had to grapple with paradoxical expectations: on the one hand, the "Planwerk Innenstadt", a decidedly anti-modern reurbanization and city-centre revitalization directive, decreed that the "historical city" should be recovered; on the other hand, politicians and residents alike expected the architectural fraternity to create a metropolis of the future. As a result, a lot of sound yet middling designs but few masterpieces were realized. Bold and innovative architectural statements are indeed very few and far between in this city. Today's general sense of disappointment with this state of affairs has less to do with the buildings themselves than with the hopes and expectations of the 1990s. People had once more been prepared to put their faith in the redemptive power of good architecture, only to discover yet again that redemption is the one thing architecture cannot offer. Most importantly, however, the new government buildings or the redeveloped Potsdamer Platz failed to project an image that Berliners could recognise. The city remained as fragmented as ever.

In the midst of this unparalleled building activity, and while ever more grand expectations were projected onto Berlin, the city's economy collapsed: the eastern part of the city as well as its Brandenburg hinterland were labouring under the consequences of deindustrialization, while the Western part of the city grappled with the effects of the

Potsdamer Platz Project in Berlin, 2006.
© PHILIPP MEUSER, BERLIN.

end of subsidization. Since 1994, population figures have been steadily declining, and today, an entire suburban belt is economically dependent on Berlin. Meanwhile, in the city itself, more than 100,000 apartments stand empty. For years, both commercial and residential properties have been in plentiful supply and remarkably cheap to get hold of. Compared to Paris, Warsaw or London, this seems an anomaly.

Maladministration and wastefulness have left the city[1] crippled with debt and effectively bankrupt since 2002. The state of Berlin has withdrawn from all major building projects, which are now exclusively in Federal hands. The attempts at regenerating the city's urban infrastructure have largely been successful and, for the most part, the effects of war and partition have been overcome, but there is a painful lack of resources when it comes to maintaining the city's libraries, schools, theatres and universities. Berlin is a poor, economically weak city that is terrifically cheap to live in.

Contrary to initial expectations, no new urban elite has emerged post unification. A bourgeoisie, in whatever shape or form, that would set the tone, function as a social barometer, speak out on behalf of the wider public and take the lead on issues of common concern simply does not exist in Berlin. Berlin is a city of ordinary people, students, newcomers fleeing the provincial backwaters of their childhoods, and a fast-living and mercurial bohemian crowd made up of artists, intellectuals, journalists, free-lancers and plain drifters. This latter set shapes the mood and lifestyle that dominates Berlin's inner-city districts. Most

of these people lead rather precarious and uncertain lives, but they have certainly made Berlin the only German city in which a carefully chosen witticism, a surprising gesture or an ingenious performance count for more than status and income. Indeed, money plays an astonishingly minor role in the social life of the city. And Berliners like to take things slowly – a fact that surprises even Swiss visitors to the city.

This bohemian scene has found a perfect form of expression in the "intermediate utilization" of disused buildings. There are many such empty structures all over Berlin, and squatters are swift to move in and put them to creative use – dissolving traditional boundaries between art and entertainment, aesthetic ambition and nightlife fun. The first such project was the "Tacheles" on Oranienburger Straße, and eventually even the "Palace of the Republic", the former cultural centre cum seat of the East German parliament now in the process of being demolished, was turned into a temporary arts venue. Three old armchairs and a hastily cobbled together installation usually suffice to transform the fleeting moment into a memorable one. This culture of the transitory, a legacy of our love-affair with everything crumbling, seems uniquely suited to the character of the city, and Berlin owes much of its attractiveness for tourists to precisely this idiosyncrasy. It has put Berlin firmly on the map of the European imagination and proves that, here at least, everything is possible and anything goes, no matter how limited your resources. A spirit of freedom is indeed key to people's life in this city.

Berlin.
© BARBARA HOIDN.

Berlin.
© SENATSVERWALTUNG
FÜR VERKEHR, BAU-UND-
WOHNUNGSWESEN, BERLIN.

Tiergarten Dreieck
project in Berlin, 2006.
© PHILIPP MEUSER, BERLIN.

Berlin's economic plight, its poverty, its lack of an effective elite, its fragmentation and abundance of disused spaces, the weakness of its administration and the continuing East-West divide – all these are the very conditions of Berlin's intellectual as well as real-life character. Three factors will determine the city's fate over the coming years: immigration from Eastern Europe, a brain drain among the young, and the continuing lack of a city centre in the good old European sense of the word.

For most of its history, Berlin has been a rather dismal one-horse town. It became the capital of Germany because it had been the capital of Prussia. Since the dissolution of Prussia, it has become apparent that the city is barely able to survive by its own efforts, surrounded as it is by an impoverished region that is gradually being abandoned by its inhabitants. The political task of countering this state of affairs with strong and effective institutions is currently tackled only hesitantly and without much energy or conviction.

What Berlin teaches architects and urban planners is, above all, humility. The building and planning frenzy of the 1990s showed that architecture cannot be expected to counteract the provisional and temporary nature of this city, nor relieve its social frailty. What it can do, however, is to continue to create stages and project images. Good metropolitan architecture has much in common with good stage design – a fact more apparent in Berlin than anywhere else in the world.

Translated from the German by Alexa Alfer

[1] Like, for example, Bavaria or Hesse, Berlin is a federal state in its own right.

Berlin Skyline.
PHOTO BY ANJA SCHLAMANN.

Following pages
Berlin 2002.
© PAOLO ROSSELLI.

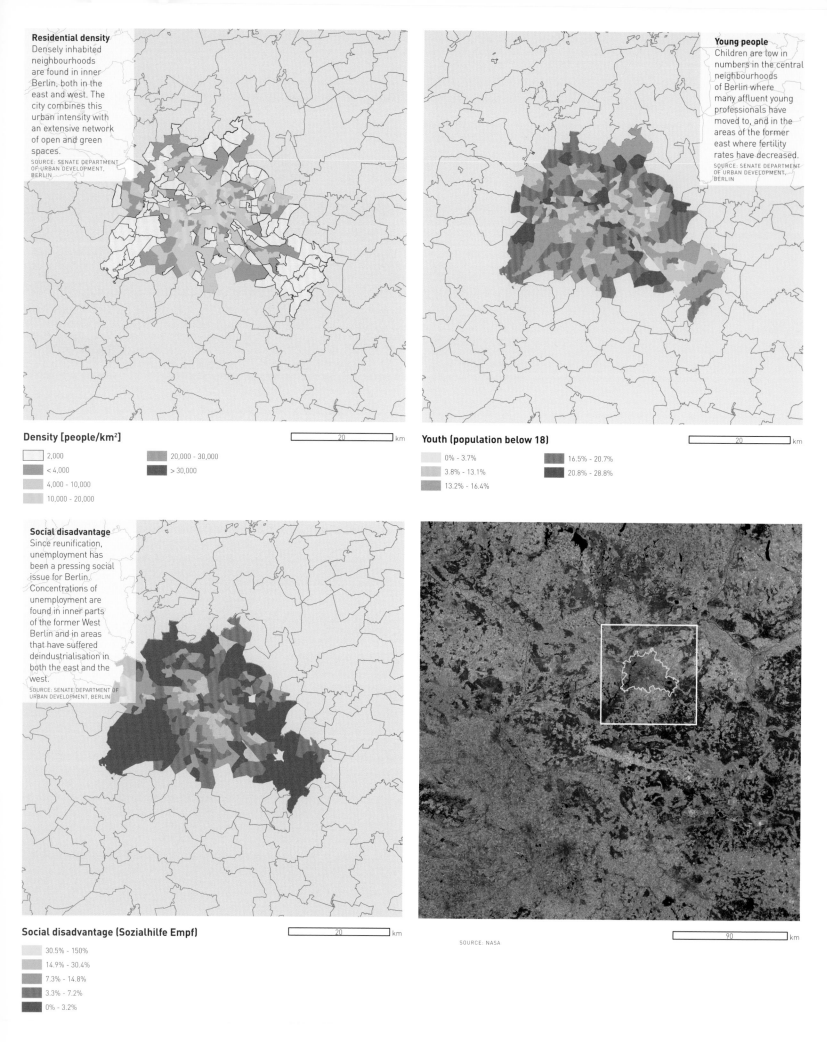

Residential density
Densely inhabited neighbourhoods are found in inner Berlin, both in the east and west. The city combines this urban intensity with an extensive network of open and green spaces.
SOURCE: SENATE DEPARTMENT OF URBAN DEVELOPMENT, BERLIN

Young people
Children are low in numbers in the central neighbourhoods of Berlin where many affluent young professionals have moved to, and in the areas of the former east where fertility rates have decreased.
SOURCE: SENATE DEPARTMENT OF URBAN DEVELOPMENT, BERLIN

Social disadvantage
Since reunification, unemployment has been a pressing social issue for Berlin. Concentrations of unemployment are found in inner parts of the former West Berlin and in areas that have suffered deindustrialisation in both the east and the west.
SOURCE: SENATE DEPARTMENT OF URBAN DEVELOPMENT, BERLIN

Density [people/km²]

2,000	20,000 - 30,000
< 4,000	> 30,000
4,000 - 10,000	
10,000 - 20,000	

20 km

Youth (population below 18)

0% - 3.7%	16.5% - 20.7%
3.8% - 13.1%	20.8% - 28.8%
13.2% - 16.4%	

20 km

Social disadvantage (Sozialhilfe Empf)

- 30.5% - 150%
- 14.9% - 30.4%
- 7.3% - 14.8%
- 3.3% - 7.2%
- 0% - 3.2%

20 km

SOURCE: NASA

90 km

The population of Berlin stands today at approximately 3.4 million. During the last century, Berlin's growth relative to other large European cities like London, has been fairly slow. In fact Berlin presents an anomaly in a world of cities that are rapidly expanding. Since 1900, the population has grown by a mere 72% and perhaps more startling, in the last decade Berlin recorded a population decline of 1.5%. Instead of housing shortages, Berlin is grappling with a housing surplus whereby literally thousands of apartments are vacant. Moreover, the population is projected to remain almost unchanged within the administrative city during the next decade, and even the growth projected within the metropolitan region is expected to be fairly minimal; 25,000 in the next ten years. So while other cities are facing issues brought on by ever-increasing populations, Berlin's future will no doubt throw up some quite different challenges.

Berlin covers approximately 892 square kilometres, stretching out along the Spree River and its plateaus. In Berlin, open space has not been an after-thought to city planning; open and recreational space accounts for 45% of Berlin. The gross residential density of Berlin is about 3,800 residents per square kilometre.

Berlin's population is aged: almost a quarter of the population is over 65, while only 15% are under 20 years old. Situated at a European transportation crossroads, it is perhaps unsurprising that Berlin's population now includes a multitude of nationalities; around 4% of Berlin's population are Turkish, 2% are citizens of former Yugoslavia and around 1.5% are from member states of the European Union. Even more revealing is the fact that 14% of the current population were born outside Germany. Indeed, culture and cultural diversity are a trademark of Berlin – after all, this is the city that attracts creative individuals with its vibrant and liberal outlook and with its multitude of galleries, museums and theatres.

Berlin has been largely successful at overcoming the effects of war and partition through the regeneration of urban infrastructure. This, however, has come at a cost; maladministration and carelessness have helped laden the city with debt; rendering it effectively bankrupt since 2002. Maintaining the city's libraries, schools, theatres and universities is difficult faced with such a severe lack of resources. For the time being, the state of Berlin has withdrawn from all major building projects, which are now exclusively in Federal hands. These economic conditions combined with stagnant population growth have, however, helped to maintain a low cost of living in Berlin; one that is somewhat at odds with rising costs in neighbouring European cities. Despite this, 8% of Berlin's population receive ongoing government subsistence, and this figure continues to rise.

Berlin's Gross City Product is substantial, at €23,354 per capita. Yet while Berlin is the largest city in Germany, its Gross City Product is only worth 3.5% of the Germany's national GDP. This, however, still equates to 9% of Italy's total GDP.

The percentage of people employed in the construction and manufacturing sector has continually decreased over time and now accounts for only a fifth of Berlin's workers. Today, over a third of the Berlin workforce are involved in federal, state and local government – including nurses, teachers and bureaucrats. Indeed the number of people employed in the service sector is substantial at 78%. Sectors such as communications, life-sciences, information technology, media and advertising are continuing to prosper. Berlin continues to maintain its position as one of the main centres for higher education in Germany, and as home to a high concentration of research institutions and think-tanks. Despite this, Berlin's unemployment rates are high at almost 20%, and certainly much higher than national unemployment rates of around 12%.

Berlin, divided into 12 boroughs (*Bezirke*), constitutes one of Germany's 16 federal states. The state of Berlin, however, is governed slightly differently from the other federal states. The executive branch is the senate, consisting of eight senators, each of whom is responsible for a certain department, such as the Senate Department of Urban Development. Conversely, the House of Representative has approximately 170 MPs elected for a term of four years. The House of Representatives is charged with electing the mayor (*Regierender Bürgermeister*), who then appoints a cabinet to run the city's agencies and carry out the executive duties of its government. The City's budget is controlled by the House of Representatives. Annual public expenditure was €6,433 (per capita) in 2005; the highest of all German federal states.

Under a third of residents in Berlin rely on public transport for their daily commute. A larger 40% use cars, although in comparison with other German cities, car ownership in Berlin is by far the lowest, with only 322 private cars per 1000 inhabitants.

London
United Kingdom

Deyan Sudjic

Deyan Sudjic is the incoming director of London's Design Museum. He is architecture critic for *The Observer* (UK) and co-founded *Blueprint* magazine. He has been an editor of *Domus*, a jury member for the Mies van der Rohe Prize for Architecture and Director of the 2002 Venice Architecture Biennale. Sudjic also directed the 1999 Glasgow UK City of Architecture and Design programme and has curated numerous exhibitions. His publications include *100-Mile City* and monographs on John Pawson, Ron Arad and Richard Rogers.
PHOTO BY STEPHEN HELLER.

An accent is an essential part of anybody's identity. Mine is the product of growing up in London in the 1950s and 1960s with two parents who didn't speak English to each other at home. I sound like the product of a constant diet of the BBC Home Service between the ages of one and five. Back before it was called Radio 4, the Home Service relayed the authentic sound of Received Pronunciation in the incarnation of Daphne Oxenford booming out of a beige plastic wireless set to invite me to *Listen with Mother* every afternoon. 'Are you sitting comfortably', Daphne would ask. 'Then I'll begin'.

I didn't, so I was told afterwards, say anything much until I was three or so, but when I did begin to speak it all came in a rush. I was fluent in the English of the BBC, as well as my parent's native Serbo Croat. Heaven knows how they must have felt at producing a son whose ever so slightly snotty version of English would have made them feel how acutely foreign they were becoming to me every time I opened my mouth.

The tools that you have at your disposal to decode and understand identity are partly those of language. But they are also based on the impact of the city in which you grow up. My mental city map is that of London. It's the template I can't help but use as a starting point to try to make sense of every city I go to. Is there a river, and if so which side is south of the river. Is there an east end? And of course that is another thing that put a barrier between me and my parents. London for them could never be the comfortable skin it is for me. Cities too could be said to have accents. They have particular ways of doing things that mark them out as distinctively different, one from another. It's the accents that give them their identity. Not necessarily the picture post card urban logos but the less obvious, and more pervasive issues that become embedded, even invisible, and yet which go on generating form. It's the turning circle of the taxis, and the density controls, it's the early history of the metro lines, and the intricacies of land tenure and the leasehold system.

Property ownership in London for example still bears the traces of the Stuart and Hanoverian monarchies, and their land grants to their courtiers. Large parts of London's most valuable pieces of real estate remain in the hands of aristocratic estates, handed to royal favourites by the crown, and are managed according to policies that evolved from

their days as agricultural estates. It's these patterns that created the urban squares of London, and the regularity of its street patterns. It's they that created the various categories of the typical terraced London house.

I used my English accent to blend as much as I could into a suburban London that still had milk bottles delivered every morning on a horse drawn float steered by a man in a peaked cap. It was a London in which the red trolley bus that ran past the end of my street disappeared one day to be replaced by a new kind of bus that didn't have sticks protruding from its roof. Inevitably there are now plans to run a new tram line along the old trolley bus routes. We lived in a modest semi on a quiet suburban street where coal was delivered every autumn by a muscled man in flat cap who poured it one sack at a time into the cellar through a cast iron hole in the pavement. For a minute or two, the whole street filled with the acrid sweet tang of anthracite.

The most exotic sight in Acton was Green's delicatessen on the Vale that offered high class English and continental foods, where melancholy Polish refugees would stock up on pickled cucumbers from a pine barrel by the door. I was more interested in the local drapery store, which had an amazing contraption to whiz my mother's change to her by way of an overhead system of electrically driven containers that shot back and forth from a central till.

35 years later, Acton is an utterly different place. The cottage hospital has been demolished, the school has been rebuilt, and what was a cautious lower middle class suburb smelling of cabbage has been transformed; it's not gentrified exactly, but different. A couple of ethnic waves have come and gone, leaving the suburb mainly in the hands of the fashionable Guardian-reading classes, the English middle class Londoners, attracted by houses more spacious than anything that they could afford closer into town. The old ways of doing things have gone: no more fishmongers, and greengrocers and toy shops on the high street; their customers have gone to IKEA, and the other giant sheds that have gravitated toward the orbital motorways that now define London's geography. And the old Art Deco cinema has been flattened, replaced by a multiplex in a mall a couple of miles away. Although the internet has brought about a second coming of the delivery van; once it was the preserve of posh

grocers, now Tesco and Waitrose do door-to-door. And in one range of ways, London too is an utterly different place. It is in the midst of a once-in-a-century spasm of growth that would have been all but unimaginable back then. There have been previous property booms of course. Notably at the end of the 1960s when stumpy office towers began to sprout, and brave plans for motorway boxes were mooted, and street after street of nineteenth-century terraced houses were demolished.

I found myself experiencing a sense of the kind of disorientation that overtook some of those communities at the end of the 1960s, the disorientation that triggered what might be called the Jane Jacobs revolution of perception. There are whole areas of London that have lost any sense of what they once were. Wander west of Norman Foster's riverside offices in Battersea, along what were once scruffy wharves and bus garages. Now it's a sleek glassy world of art galleries and penthouses. It's a city that seems to have tipped from one world – or one accent – into another. London is more of a global city than it has ever been. Its house prices are now set by rootless high-earning bankers who can afford a £3 million house from earned income, a fact that has an impact on every aspect of the city. It is boosting property values everywhere; the eastern fringe of London is benefiting from this refocus, reversing to some extent 200 years of emphasis on the westward expansion of the city.

It's the same feeling you get all along the Thames, where a decade of construction has seen the river, which the city used to turn its back on, turned into a kind of front lawn for the continuous wall of apartment blocks that now line both banks. Their occupants were attracted by the view, but there are now so many of them that the river has virtually been turned into a culvert. And there are the clusters of really tall towers coming. Mayor Livingstone has helped to push through five 1,000 feet plus ultra high towers. And to ensure that at least one of them gets built, he plans to move his transport department into 300,000 square feet of offices in the so-called glass shard, Renzo Piano's design for Europe's tallest tower situated atop London Bridge station, a move that will give the developer the confidence to begin construction.

London Skyline.
© RICHARD BRYANT/ARCAID.
CO.UK.

Following pages
London.
© JOHN TRAN. COURTESY URBAN AGE.

The transformation of post-industrial London is all but complete. The redundant banana warehouse that I remember at Canary Wharf, caught in the midst of acre after acre of dereliction, has been obliterated by a fully-fledged financial district. The abandoned power station at Bankside is the world's most popular museum of modern art. The underpinning of the economy is no longer the port or the factory; it's the financial and creative industries.

Even more striking, a London that was turning into a hollowed-out doughnut, bleeding population across the southeast, has started to grow again. This phenomenon is having dramatic effects in some unexpected areas.

The white working class eastern suburb of Barking for example is experiencing something like what happened to Notting Hill in the 1950s when London Transport started recruiting Jamaican bus drivers, and the new migrants faced a colour bar when they looked for places to live. It is a social transformation that has brought electoral gains to the political far right, just as it did in the 1950s. And yet on another level, London still has the energy and the sense of possibilities that brought my parents here. The mental map of the city I carried in my head from childhood describes a place that looks utterly different, and yet is one in which the same processes are still at work.

London Skyline looking past the Swiss rebuilding to Canary Wharf.
© RICHARD BRYANT/ARCAID. CO.UK.

After a decade and a half of significant population growth, Greater London currently has about 7.5 million residents; projections indicate that this figure will reach 8 million within the next decade. Greater London covers approximately 1,600 square kilometres of land area at a gross residential density of about 4,700 residents per square kilometre. However, almost half of this surface is comprised of open and recreational space. The city has decided to accommodate the expected population growth within its extant urbanised area through structural densification.

London is a diverse and multicultural city, with 29% of its population from ethnic minority communities: 12% is Asian or Asian British, 11% Black or Black British, 11% is Chinese, and an additional 5% is from other groups. Approximately 27% of the city's current population was born outside the United Kingdom. The additional high volume of international visitors and flows of people that pass through London has led pundits to call it the world's first post-national city.

In recent times London, a service-led urban economy with a global orientation, has experienced what is perhaps an unprecedented economic bonanza. Currently, its Gross City Product is estimated at €34,500 per capita, amounting to almost 20% of the UK's national economy. Greater London alone produces the equivalent of more than a fifth of Italy's GDP. Yet a hard core of poverty lingers in Inner London, particularly in its eastern and southern areas, where more than half of all children live in poverty when the high housing costs of the city are included in the estimation of their disposable household incomes. These high costs also have an impact on working-age people; 23% of this group throughout Greater London fall under the poverty line when their incomes are estimated according to this formula.

Of all daily journeys in London, 43% are conducted by private cars and 34% by public transport. Strengthening the capacity of the public transport system and improving the quality of its services has been a recent public policy priority in London. At the same time the abatement of congestion has been undertaken through road charging.

Greater London is divided into 33 boroughs that provide most local services and dispose of ample planning powers. Since the year 2000, Londoners have been able to directly elect their mayor and a 25-member assembly to discuss issues of citywide relevance. The Greater London Authority improves the coordination between boroughs, with a focus on economic growth, social inclusion and physical upgrading of the city's urban and natural environments.

London 2005.
© PAOLO ROSSELLI.

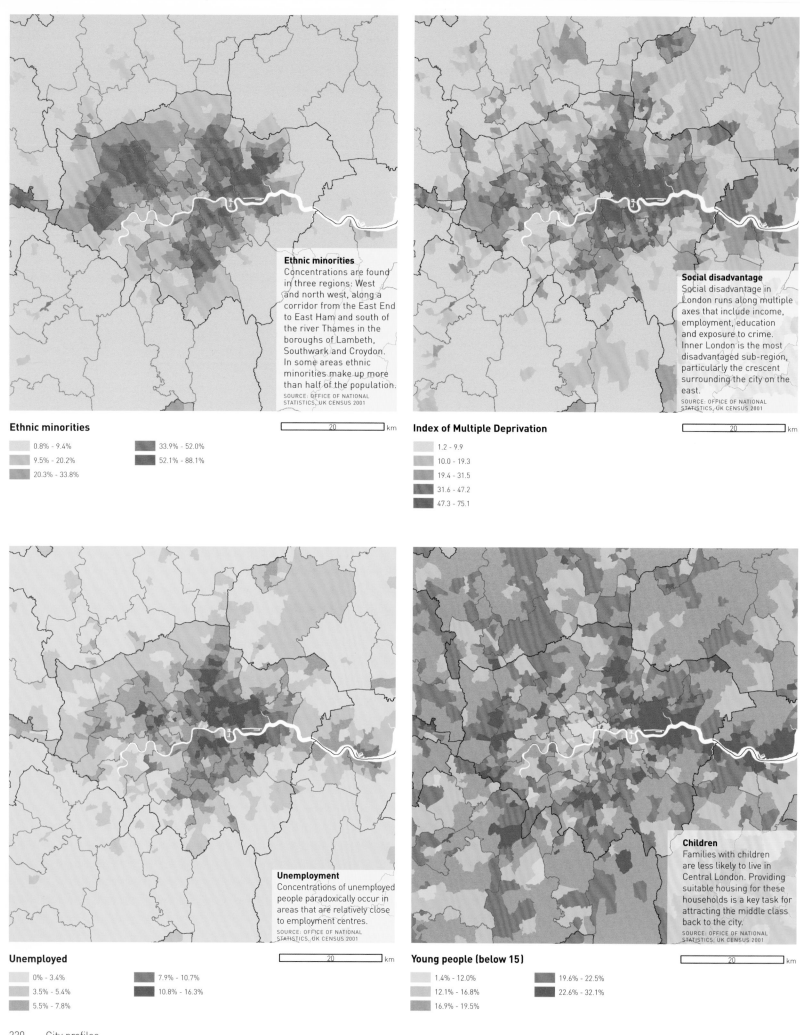

Ethnic minorities
Concentrations are found in three regions: West and north west, along a corridor from the East End to East Ham and south of the river Thames in the boroughs of Lambeth, Southwark and Croydon. In some areas ethnic minorities make up more than half of the population.
SOURCE: OFFICE OF NATIONAL STATISTICS, UK CENSUS 2001

Social disadvantage
Social disadvantage in London runs along multiple axes that include income, employment, education and exposure to crime. Inner London is the most disadvantaged sub-region, particularly the crescent surrounding the city on the east.
SOURCE: OFFICE OF NATIONAL STATISTICS, UK CENSUS 2001

Ethnic minorities

0.8% - 9.4%		33.9% - 52.0%
9.5% - 20.2%		52.1% - 88.1%
20.3% - 33.8%		

20   km

Index of Multiple Deprivation

- 1.2 - 9.9
- 10.0 - 19.3
- 19.4 - 31.5
- 31.6 - 47.2
- 47.3 - 75.1

20   km

Unemployment
Concentrations of unemployed people paradoxically occur in areas that are relatively close to employment centres.
SOURCE: OFFICE OF NATIONAL STATISTICS, UK CENSUS 2001

Children
Families with children are less likely to live in Central London. Providing suitable housing for these households is a key task for attracting the middle class back to the city.
SOURCE: OFFICE OF NATIONAL STATISTICS, UK CENSUS 2001

Unemployed

0% - 3.4%		7.9% - 10.7%
3.5% - 5.4%		10.8% - 16.3%
5.5% - 7.8%		

20   km

Young people (below 15)

1.4% - 12.0%		19.6% - 22.5%
12.1% - 16.8%		22.6% - 32.1%
16.9% - 19.5%		

20   km

Images from the
QuickBird satellite of
London.
© DIGITALGLOBE EXCLUSIVE
DISTRIBUTED FOR EUROPE BY
TELESPAZIO.

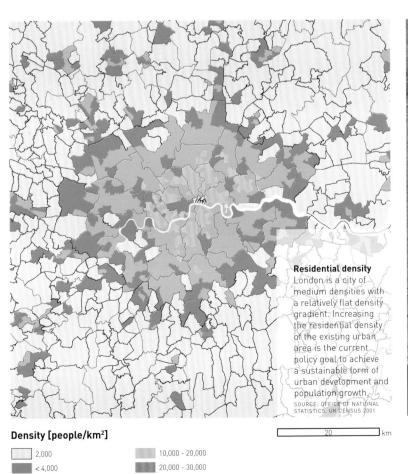

Residential density
London is a city of medium densities with a relatively flat density gradient. Increasing the residential density of the existing urban area is the current policy goal to achieve a sustainable form of urban development and population growth.
SOURCE: OFFICE OF NATIONAL STATISTICS, UK CENSUS 2001

20 km

Density [people/km²]

2,000	10,000 - 20,000
< 4,000	20,000 - 30,000
4,000 - 10,000	> 30,000

SOURCE: NASA

90 km

London 221

Barcelona
Spain

Beth Galí

Beth Galí founded the studio BB & GG, which works in industrial and furniture design, architecture, urbanism and landscape architecture. Galí worked for Barcelona City Council's Urban Projects Workshop. Her built projects include Fossar de la Pedrera and the Joan Miró Library. Galí is the author of *Architecture and Design* and is a professor at the Escola Superior de Arquitectura de Barcelona.
PHOTO BY ANTONI BERNARD.

Barcelona Googlegram

Seen from an orbiting satellite, all cities are beautiful. Textured cities, 'die-cast' cities, bombed cities or abandoned cities: they are like ink blots, like tattoos on the terrain. These are spaces without conflicts, in which all that can be perceived are the geological traces that the different levels of historical events have successively imprinted.

The zoom function on Google Earth is the ideal tool for exploring in detail different ways of looking at and planning the city. This is a tool that suggests a certain interpretation of the sequence of Barcelona's urban events: from the distant overview of the kind that appeals to military strategists, to the tightly focused close-up of the recent sociological and – above all – anthropological visions of the city. Four quick zooms in the programme can thus show us four fundamental stages of Barcelona's urban history, with the accent firmly on the present moment.

The first aerial photos of Barcelona were taken from a height of 10,000 feet, on the military reconnaissance flights that preceded the bombing of the city during the Spanish Civil War; aerial views whose purpose was not to help reconstruct the city but instead to pave the way for its destruction. In other words, the city as planned to be destroyed and rebuilt, in effect without allowing any time for the creation of memory, so that the destruction might appear not the horrific climax of a collective aberration, but rather the first stage in the more or less efficient reconstruction of the city.

With one click on Google Earth we jump to the scale that was most liked by the men who governed the city during the 40 years following the Civil War. This is the city seen from above, in the low-definition panorama of the bird's-eye view, because in the aerial perspective individuals and their sense of place are distanced to the point of becoming invisible. This distance obliterates the details: the people, their comings and goings and their desires. Whereas photographs taken at ground level countered what the politicians of those years wanted to sell to the population: the Great Barcelona born out of nothing. Such ground-level photographs would have shown only a landscape devoid of all urban value, incapable of generating any sense of place.

With the wave of inward migration of the 1950s, the city grew as a spate of isolated estates, swallowing up the great reserves of omission and absence and forming a diffuse periphery of neglected suburbs segregated from the city proper. In this context, 'The city is the perfect artefact to have appeared on the *tabula rasa*: it has only had to be ordered to emerge, by decree, new and finished, identical to itself, adult and ready-assembled, great crystalline idea'.[1]

With another click on the zoom the image is magnified to ten times the size, taking us to a moment ten years after the first restoration of democracy in Spain, with a Socialist City Council in Barcelona poised to fight and win the battle to reconstruct a city that until recently had been in the hands of unscrupulous mayors.

The screen shows streets, squares, avenues and parks, the remodelling of which gave shape to what, in the 1980s, was almost universally referred to as the Barcelona Model: an exemplar of the use of design and reconstruction of the public spaces instead of the urban plan as the sole instrument of the city's growth and improvement.

Finally, in order to examine the contemporary Barcelona, heir to the Universal Forum of Cultures 2004, we click once more and the image pans out again, taking us back to ground level. The image expands and the form of the city blurs. The urban spaces of the 1980s vanish and the great urban planning operations of the 1990s and 2000s disappear from the screen to make way for that which gives the city its intangible quality; all that is fortuitous in the completed city, in which the citizens are the principal players, the protagonists.

Beyond the more-or-less well-resolved public spaces of the spectacular architectures and the museological culture the city is a compact mass, which we move around in and inhabit as we please: 'With everything that the architects and planners design, people do what they do best: what they feel like doing.' Because in spite of everything the city is chaos: it is vandalism, pollution, rave, revolt.

Barcelona.
© GABRIELE BASILICO.

Mercat la Boqueria, Barcelona.

The relationship between 'urban culture' – everything that happens in the city – and the 'urbanistic culture' – that which politically plans and structures the urban territory – has been in bad shape for a long time now. It is precisely this mutual ignorance that occasions most social disruption in cities of a certain size and density.

Urbanistic processes today have become a kind of dictatorial fiat, the principal operators of which come from the private sector. The space of the global city is, first and foremost, a strictly economic space, with the city itself being transformed into a space on the scale of the international market. This is a context into which the city of Barcelona has been fully absorbed in the last few years: one of the chief challenges facing those who govern it today is, necessarily, how to derive local benefits from the presence of this kind of fly-by-night nomadic capital, which alights with very little warning and without the slightest concern for the city as such.

High-profile urbanistic operations and big pieces of architecture by big international names are moved around the empty board, as if in a game of chess, without a second thought for what is local, intangible, unexpected and changing in Barcelona. And it is precisely in the random turn

of events that politicians, planners and architects are most aware of not knowing how to calibrate the dialogue between the strictly urbanistic discourse and the rules and misrule of contemporary urban culture – an urban culture that, as I said above, is signified 'by the sum of different ways of living the urbanized spaces'.[2]

Over and above the inescapable sense of the exhaustion of the model, a city that has gone from having nothing to having everything cannot go on thinking exclusively in terms of planning and architecture. Barcelona today is part of one of the great corridors of European migration, and at the same time is one of the world's principal tourist destinations. Thus, 'tourism and emigration constitute two different forms of political displacement in space'.[3] At the intersection of these two very unequal flows there is the city as a space of encounters, continually changing and always unpredictable. On the one hand, an ever more opulent form of tourism, and on the other, an immigration becoming poorer all the time; the two together are inevitably and temporally bound up with this great phenomenon that we call the city.

Barcelona's Plaça Reial, a space reconstructed in the 1980s, is the microcosm that best illustrates this intersection. 'The most elegant of all the city's squares,

Barcelona.
© GABRIELE BASILICO.

Barcelona.
© GABRIELE BASILICO.

twinned with the Plaza Garibaldi in Mexico City', Xavier Mas de Xaxàs said in «La Vanguardia», 'it is a pit of humanity, a sunken eye, *lumpen* and grotesque, nailed there where Barcelona is, above all, people yearning for other realities.' In the middle of the afternoon, outside the Tarantos and the Jamboree club, toothless, drunken men used to sleeping where they can find a bed, in the street if need be, clap their hands and croak out snatches of song with a dishevelled, dark-skinned woman who doesn't so much sing as laugh and let herself go. They drink beer, polish off a bottle of Ballantines and pass round a plastic bottle refilled with wine in place of mineral water. They occupy a supermarket trolley draped with blankets and several seats of the street furniture. The National Police keep watch a few steps away; a couple of patrol cars are parked under the arches on the south side of the square. Right there, between the police officers and the flamenco group, three young Central European punks sitting on the ground exude drunkenness and accumulate the grime of the sticky summer. A girl is sleeping on her side on some pieces of cardboard in front of one of the metal shutters of *Nadal. Segells de Goma*. Another shutter announces that 'faith moves mountains and, for money, they disappear'.

After the succession of urbanistic episodes it has accomplished in the last quarter of a century, is Barcelona ready to address and embrace migratory density and plurality? This is clearly one of the many major challenges to which the government of the city will have to rise in the next few years.

[1] Juan José Lahuerta, *Badia des de l'aire i altres vols*, «L'Avenç» n. 310, February 2006.
[2] Manuel Delgado, *De la ciudad concebida a la ciudad practicada*, «Archipiélago» n. 62, 2004.
[3] Santiago Alba Rico, *Las reglas del caos*, Barcelona, 1995.

Previous pages
The changing City.
Barcelona, Poble Nou
2004.
© IÑIGO BUJEDO AGUIRRE.

Barcelona.
© JORDI TODÓ/TAVISA.

Residential density
SOURCE: INSTITUT CARTOGRÀFIC DE CATALUNYA

20 km

Density [people/km²]

- 2000
- < 4,000
- 4,000 - 9,999
- 10,000 - 19,999
- 20,000 - 29,999
- > 30,000

Unemployment
Concentrations of unemployed people in Barcelona appear in formerly industrial coastal areas, in some older neighbourhoods and in peripheral districts.
SOURCE: INSTITUT CARTOGRÀFIC DE CATALUNYA

20 km

Unemployment

- 2.3% - 8.5%
- 8.6% -11.3%
- 11.4% - 14.8 %
- 14.9% - 21.3%
- 21.4% - 35.8%

Children
Children are not well represented in the city centre. They make up larger shares of the population in some suburbs and the outskirts of the metropolitan area.
SOURCE: INSTITUT CARTOGRÀFIC DE CATALUNYA

20 km

Youth (under 15)

- 1.5% - 10.2%
- 10.3% - 12.6%
- 12.7% - 15.1%
- 15.2% - 18.6%
- 18.7% - 35.4%

Foreigners
The foreign-born population of Barcelona has increased steadily in recent years.
A high concentration of foreigners is found in the historical centre and adjacent neighbourhoods.
SOURCE: INSTITUT CARTOGRÀFIC DE CATALUNYA

20 km

Foreigners

- 0% - 3.2%
- 3.3% - 6.3%
- 6.4% - 10.9%
- 11.0% - 20.0%
- 20.1% - 40.7%

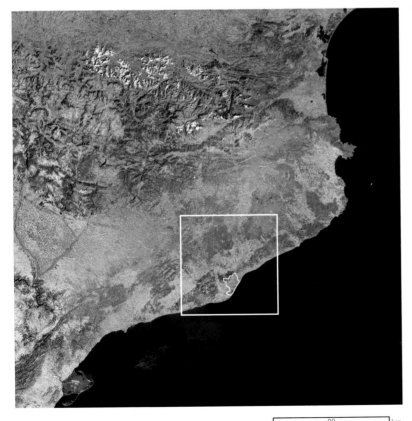

SOURCE: NASA.

90 ⊢——————————⊣ km

The current population of the City of Barcelona is approximately 1.6 million. Barcelona has grown by about 183% in the past century; and by about 6% in the last decade alone. Barcelona is expected to add another 100,000 residents over the next ten years.

The City of Barcelona covers approximately 101 square kilometres, of which 44% is open and recreational space. The gross residential density of Barcelona is about 15,365 residents per square kilometre, a much higher average than in other regions of Europe or the British Isles. Barcelona is considered a model of how cities can provide liveable high densities supported by a comprehensive system of public spaces.

At least two language groups – Catalonian and Spanish – coexist in Barcelona and approximately 16% of the current population of this increasingly multicultural city was born abroad. The city's location on the Mediterranean, Spain's historical connections to Latin America, and its dynamic urban economy are all factors that make Barcelona a magnet for immigration.

With a product per capita of approximately € 22,600, Barcelona is a wealthy city. Its Gross City Product makes up 5% of Spain's economy and is equivalent to 3% of Italy's GDP. Yet several thousand households depend on minimum income benefits and the number of those in need of food and shelter is on the rise. As is the case in many other developed cities, Barcelona is also in a process of greying. While the city still retains a youthful population – 15.6% of residents are 20 years old or younger, more than one in five *Barceloneses* is over the age of 64.

Barcelona has a service-oriented economy; the services and business sector employs 82% of the city's labour force. The fact that 13% of workers are employed in the manufacturing sector indicates that some industry still remains in the city.

Consistent with the high-density profile of the city, Barcelona moves mainly with public transport; 84.4% of all journeys are conducted by this mode. There are 385 private cars and 7 licensed taxis per 1,000 residents registered in Barcelona.

The City of Barcelona is part of the *Generalitat* of Catalonia, an autonomous government within Spain. The city is divided into 10 districts, designed for the provision of services. The mayor of Barcelona oversees the executive committee and the chief municipal executive office. The local annual public expenditure is approximately € 1,150 per capita.

Tokyo
Japan

Momoyo Kaijima and Yoshiharu Tsukamoto
(Atelier Bow-Wow)

Atelier Bow-Wow was founded in 1992 by Yoshiharu Tsukamoto and Momoyo Kaijima. Their buildings include Mini House, which won the Gold Prize for House Architecture; Moca House; Pet Architecture Museum; and Kotatsu Pavilion. They have participated in various exhibitions, including *Towards Totalscape; Japanese Avant-Garde/ Reality Projection; 2nd* Fukuoka Asian Art Triennale; and *Zone of Urgency*, 50th Venice Biennale. Publications include *Les Plus Petites Maisons; Made in Tokyo; Broken Paris*; and *Contemporary House Studies*. Yoshiharu Tsukamoto is Associate Professor at Tokyo Institute of Technology and Momoyo Kaijima is Assistant Professor at the University of Tsukuba.

Tokyo Flux. One city, nine flows

In Tokyo, the debate on public space never gets us anywhere. Perhaps that is because, in the Japanese tradition, the kind of spaces that performed this function were not necessarily public but rather communitarian... the grounds of temples and shrines, the paths within residential compounds, the places that communities dedicated for collective use and which, at the same time, contributed to the self-managed existence of these communities. Urbanization implied and continues to cause the loss of such small spaces, while the European-inspired grand squares built since the postwar period do not fit the shy character of the Japanese and their limited social experience in how to make the best use of such monumental grounds. Therefore, rather than through the public/private social binary, the urbanity of Tokyo is much better captured by displacing the debate to the manifold natural phenomena that pose a constant threat to the city – earthquakes, typhoons and several other calamities.

In addition to these disasters, there is the second nature that the city has produced with its problematic flows of cars, population change and increase in waste. All of these elements, natural and artificial, flow through and seethe in Tokyo; in fact the character of the city has arguably emerged out of successive attempts to manage their flux. Our hypothesis is that urban space in contemporary Tokyo can be read as a causal chain of responses to flux: urban planning is not based on a holistic vision of the city, but rather on determining the role for each individual building (intervention guidelines) without a clear notion of how the built ensemble should work. The role of master plans for Tokyo is limited; rather each project that responds to a given state of the city's flux modifies the flow and thus engenders the need for the next project.

Water

Japan experiences an average of 27 typhoons per year. From this statistic, it is clear why rivers and waterfronts in Tokyo are managed from a disaster-prevention perspective, rather than as recreational spaces. The larger rivers usually demarcate the limits of localities, and they are managed by the central national government and its rigid policies.

The Ministry of Land, Infrastructure and Transport foresees the contingency, particularly along the most sensitive riverfront segments, of floods with a risk of occurring once every 200 years. The ministry is currently planning a number of super dikes for these areas that, unlike the previous generation of razor-thin levees, will not collapse in the event of a flood that would rapidly inundate the entire vicinity of the area. The new model provides for much thicker dikes that are to include the elevation of adjacent ground in a gradient of 1/30. The plans to build these more substantial dams include the construction of parks, housing, agricultural and other land uses, such as waste treatment facilities, on these surfaces. Additionally, an aqueduct was constructed below the peripheral Road 7 to discharge overflows from the Kanda river at times of flooding. These improvements open possibilities for architects to engage in projects that will make riverfronts enjoyable urban spaces at various scales.

Fire

Fires often occur in the aftermath of natural disasters. Soon after the Great Kanto Earthquake hit the streets of Tokyo 82 years ago, the city turned into a sea of fire. Tokyo is prone to suffer large-magnitude earthquakes; it is estimated that one will occur in a period between 60 and 100 years. Fire drills and other earthquake-prevention measures are taken regularly. However, it would be desirable for many of the city's residential areas dotted with wooden houses to improve their fire prevention capacities. Traditionally, these areas are built at high densities and leave only thin pedestrian paths, approximately one metre wide, between rows of houses that residents decorate with plants and transform into collective gardens. Urban planning guidelines in Tokyo have led to the creation of intense-use and high-rise commercial zones along the arterial roads that surround these traditional housing districts. High-rise buildings made out of concrete act as firewalls that buffer the areas. In the parts of Tokyo where ten-metre high, densely-built traditional wooden houses are surrounded by 20-metre high concrete buildings, the urban landscape emulates the shape of crusty cream puffs.

Heat (and wind)

Tokyo faces another impending crisis: the city is becoming a heat island. Over the past 100 years, Tokyo's annual average temperature has risen by 3.0°C, in comparison to 2.4°C in other large cities and 1°C in medium- and small-scale cities. According to the Tokyo Metropolitan Government, the heat island phenomenon implies an increase in summer days with a temperature above 30°, tropical nights and concentrated

Cereulean.
PHOTO BY JOHN PARBURY.

rain. Increased energy consumption and the overheating of interstitial areas between buildings are additional problems. Cars, air conditioners, concrete and the coastal wall of high-rises that stops the cooling breeze from Tokyo Bay have all been pointed out as factors contributing to the heat island. Therefore the phenomenon is a man-made problem of flux that brings to the fore the problematic nature of the city itself. Campaigns to curb CO_2 emissions are expected to reduce car use and air conditioning and there are subsidies in place to promote the greening of the asphalt jungle. Among a number of other initiatives, universities and civil society organizations are promoting the return to a traditional Japanese custom: *uchimizu*, the watering of roads.

Earth (and waste)

Waste is another urban problem of flux. Tokyo has reclaimed land from the sea at least since the grading of mountainsides began in the Edo Period. After the Great Kanto Earthquake and the World War II air raids on Tokyo, many investments were made to reclaim land, and now Tokyo has 25,000 hectares of reclaimed land, or the equivalent of more than 40% of the surface occupied by the city's 23 central boroughs. Much of this land has been used as waste landfills. Currently, the central anti-tsunami barrier of Tokyo Bay is built with 1.2 million tons of solid waste a year. Other uses of this land include parks, one of Haneda Airport's runways, super dikes, etc.

Sky

The rise in demand for air travel has created the need for additional runways at Tokyo's airports. Given Narita's lack of capacity to expand, it was decided that the coastal Haneda Airport would be enlarged by reclaiming land from the sea. The expected effects are manifold. Residents of Chiba Prefecture have already raised complaints about noise-pollution related to air routes. And on the other hand, the projected expansion has brought Haneda closer to Yokohama and other cities in Kanagawa where airfreight companies are investing to develop new operation bases. Connectivity with the flux of the sky is dependent on both physical possibilities and political will. The effects on surrounding areas are large; airports also become a source for the flux of goods.

Electro-magnetic waves

This is the flux of information. In 1955 the 333 metre-tall Tokyo Tower was built with the purpose of television and radio transmission. In recent years, due to the mushrooming of high-rises in its vicinity, many problems have emerged and the continuous use of the tower became impossible. A number of sites bid for the construction of an even higher tower, and finally, in March 2006, it was decided that the 610 metre-tall Sumida Tower would be built by 2011. The tower will feature state-of-the-art digital broadcast capabilities, while the large shopping mall planned at its base is expected to become an important centre for the eastern side of Tokyo. However, with construction rapidly advancing, the debate on how this huge symbolic structure will affect Tokyo's cityscape has yet to materialize.

PHOTO BY NORBERT SHOERNER.

Following pages
PHOTO BY FRANCESCO JODICE.

Cars

Many projects are addressing the problem of traffic congestion. Of all the major roads planned since before the war, only one has been built, mainly due to problems with land acquisition from private owners. Local resistance to expected air pollution was another problem, even plans for underground roads faced the issue of where to place their ventilation turrets and their effects on the urban landscape. Given the impossibility of securing other suitable land, many of the city's water streams were paved over – even the landmark of Nihonbashi was buried beneath an elevated highway. Supported by Prime Minister Koizumi, a project is in place to restore the original landscape of this area. Removing a highway to restore Cheonggyecheon in the Korean capital of Seoul had a price tag of approximately 4.25 billion yen. Costs of the Nihonbashi project are expected to reach between ¥ 30 and 65 billion and three alternatives are still being evaluated as to where to trace the new highway route.

People

Greater Tokyo's population is 12.6 million. Numerous transport infrastructure and housing problems emerged from the model of urban growth adopted after World War II whereby radial commuter lines connected residential suburbs to the urban core – most Tokyo residents still face commutes longer than an hour each way into a centre where few people actually live. Investments are still being made to improve the network of underground and privately-owned surface railways. One example is the construction of bridges along the Tozai Line to remedy traffic congestion during peak hours. However, the case of Shimokitazawa indicates that these projects find enormous difficulties to be implemented when they face a strong local opposition. Also, what is promised to be the last of Tokyo's suburban commuter railways, the Tsukuba Express was completed two years ago. Departing from Akihabara, the line reaches not only this garden city but also a promised life-style, while central boroughs of Chiyoda, Chuo and Minato continue to suffer problematic population losses that are not abated by the construction of luxurious high-rise condominiums in the bay. New housing projects that follow these highly polarized urban-suburban typologies are being marketed to the generation of Japanese baby-boomers facing retirement.

Money

After the lost decade that ensued from the bursting of Japan's bubble economy, the national government under the prime minister initiated an 'urban regeneration' programme in 2001. This initiative attempts to make Tokyo more internationally competitive through the promotion of special districts where densities are to be increased, maximum height regulations removed and the planning permission process streamlined. Additional financial incentives are expected to stimulate private investment. Large-scale developers have responded in various ways. In the Marunouchi office district, a number of projects have a hybrid structure that incorporates both elements from protected historical structures and spaces, and, on the other side, high-intensity use. A case in point is the redevelopment

of Tokyo Station financed through the selling of its air rights. In a different district, it took 12 years to assemble the plots of land needed to redevelop Roppongi Hills, a high-rise structure that is able to offer ample green and open space due to the lifting of volumetric restrictions in the area.

Conclusion

The sheer size of Tokyo and the fact that it does not maintain a historical city centre preclude the possibility of an urban discourse along European lines of public versus private and political versus personal spaces. The city should rather be understood as an overlay of different flows, a composite flux. Beneath Tokyo's chaotic appearance lies a complex yet consistent assemblage of urban systems whose interactions cannot be fully regulated. The numerous urban *grands projects* currently proposed would also seem to follow a systemic rather than a spatial logic. However, the various forms of opposition manifested against the localized spatial effects of these projects will determine the form in which they will be incorporated within the urban environment. The production of urban space in Tokyo can be read as a creative tension between the flux management system set in place and the sum of individual spatial practices through which Tokyoites give shape to their city.

Translated from the Japanese by Miguel Kanai

Tokyo.
PHOTO BY FRANCESCO JODICE.

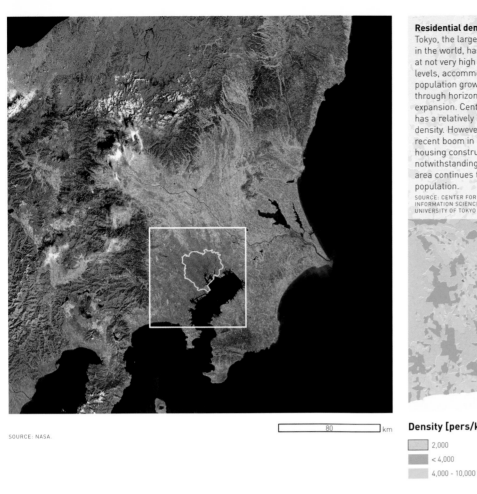

SOURCE: NASA.

80 km

Residential density

Tokyo, the largest city in the world, has grown at not very high density levels, accommodating population growth through horizontal expansion. Central Tokyo has a relatively higher density. However, the recent boom in luxury housing construction notwithstanding, this area continues to lose population.

SOURCE: CENTER FOR SPATIAL INFORMATION SCIENCE, THE UNIVERSITY OF TOKYO (CSIS)

20 km

Density [pers/km²]

2,000	10,000 - 20,000
< 4,000	20,000 - 30,000
4,000 - 10,000	> 30,000

Foreigners

Tokyo is the most cosmopolitan city in Japan. Yet, relatively few foreigners live there. Some concentrations can be found in central neighbourhoods and in areas close to the port.

SOURCE: CENTER FOR SPATIAL INFORMATION SCIENCE, THE UNIVERSITY OF TOKYO (CSIS)

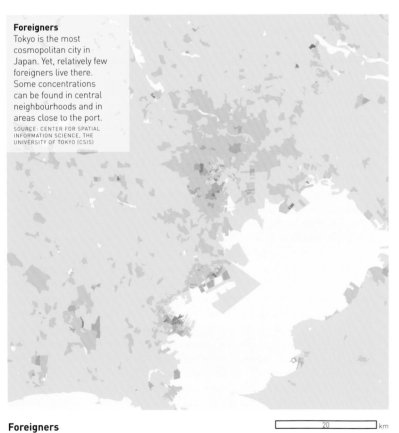

Foreigners

0% - 1.6%	14.8% - 46.2%
1.7% - 5.2%	46.3% - 100%
5.3% - 14.7%	

20 km

Unemployment

Unemployment grew during the economic recession. Concentrated unemployment is however not a pressing issue in Tokyo the way it is in western metropolitan areas that have experienced processes of deindustrialisation and economic reconversion.

SOURCE: CENTER FOR SPATIAL INFORMATION SCIENCE, THE UNIVERSITY OF TOKYO (CSIS)

Unemployment

0% - 2.8%	8.4% - 29.7%
2.9% - 5.0%	29.8% - 100%
5.1% - 8.3%	

20 km

Images from the
QuickBird satellite of
Tokio.
© DIGITALGLOBE EXCLUSIVE
DISTRIBUTED FOR EUROPE BY
TELESPAZIO.

The current population of Greater Tokyo is approximately 12.6 million. Tokyo is also part of the Kanto Region, which with approximately 35 million inhabitants is perhaps the largest and most integrated urban region in the world today. While suffering major natural disasters and man-made catastrophes, Tokyo's population grew dramatically in the 20th century. After World War II, the urbanized area multiplied its extent, and newcomers flocking into the thriving capital were accommodated in medium-density suburbs connected to employment and commercial centres by railway.

Currently, Greater Tokyo has a surface of approximately 2,187 square kilometres that covers a long, narrow stretch of land, running about 90 kilometres east to west and 25 kilometres north and south. Tokyo has a gross residential density of about 5,660 residents per square kilometre; the city does not have a significant high-density residential inner core and hence has a relatively flat density gradient curve. Less than 5% of Tokyo's total surface is dedicated to parks and green space. Given Japan's low demographic dynamism and the policies set in place to curb Tokyo's growth, the city is not expected to gain a significant number of residents in the near future. However, the city faces the challenge of producing a more balanced urban structure and a more sustainable and liveable environment for its millions of current residents.

Japan perceives itself as a highly homogeneous and cohesive country. This island-nation social narrative would seem to be confirmed by the very few registered foreign residents – currently less than half a million and most of them from other East Asian countries – living in Tokyo, the country's most internationalized city and in fact one of the world's centres of economic activity and investment. On the other hand, Tokyo is also a socially and culturally multi-faceted city where diversity assumes highly visual manifestations. Social inequality is also on the increase in the country as a whole, and Tokyo in particular. The fact that less than 2% of city residents depend on some form of public assistance masks the widening income inequality, rise in long-term unemployment and lack of economic prospects for many young people. Another challenge for Tokyo relates to the existing and future social needs of its ageing population – 16.2% of residents are 65 years of age or older, a proportion that almost equals that of young people under 20.

Tokyo has a large and diversified urban economy, with a gross city product equivalent to €562, it contributes 18% of the Japanese economy or the equivalent to about 60% of Italy's GDP. The city's business and services sector employs 64.9% of the labour force and, unlike other global cities, Tokyo has a solid manufacturing base that employs 14.8% of the labour force.

Tokyo has a comprehensive public transport infrastructure. Almost four out of five daily journeys in the city are conducted by this mode. However, commutes can take over an hour each way and often occur in highly crowded conditions.

The Greater Tokyo Government is divided into a 'central' region comprising 23 special wards, and the western Tama Area comprising 26 cities, 3 towns and one village. The Governor of Tokyo is one of the most powerful figures in Japanese politics and Tokyo receives more national fiscal resources than it contributes.

Mumbai
India

Suketu Mehta

Suketu Mehta is a fiction writer and journalist based in New York. His first book, *Maximum City: Mumbai Lost and Found*, won the Kiriyama Prize and was a finalist for the 2005 Pulitzer Prize. He has won the Whiting Writers Award, the O. Henry Prize and a New York Foundation for the Arts Fellowship for his fiction. Mehta's work has been published in the «New York Times Magazine», «National Geographic», «Granta», «Harper's magazine», «Time», among others. Mehta was born in Calcutta and raised in Mumbai and New York. He is currently writing an original screenplay for *The Goddess*, a Merchant-Ivory film and co-wrote *Mission Kashmir*, a Bollywood movie.
PHOTO BY JERRY BAUER.

On 27 July, 2005, Mumbai experienced the highest recorded rainfall in its history - 37 inches of rain in one day. The torrent showed up the worst and the best about the city. Hundreds of people drowned. But unlike the situation after Katrina hit New Orleans, there was no widespread breakdown of civic order; even though the police were absent, the crime rate did not go up. That was because Mumbaiites were busy helping each other. Slum dwellers went to the highway and took stranded motorists into their homes and made room for one more person in shacks where the average occupancy is seven adults to a room. Volunteers waded through waist-deep water to bring food to the 150,000 people stranded in train stations. Human chains were formed to get people out of the floods. Most of the government machinery was absent, but nobody expected otherwise. Mumbaiites helped each other, because they had lost faith in the government helping them. On a planet of city dwellers, this is how most human beings are going to live and cope in the twenty-first century.

At 15 million people within its municipal limits, Mumbai is the biggest, fastest, richest city in India, a city simultaneously experiencing a boom and a civic emergency; an island-state of hope in a very old country. Because of the reach of Bollywood movies, Mumbai is also a mass dream for the peoples of India. If you take a walk around Mumbai you'll see that everything – sex, death, trade, religion – are lived out on the sidewalk. It is a maximum city, maximum in its exigencies, maximum in its heart.

Why do people still live in Mumbai? Every day is an assault on the individual's senses, from the time you get up, to the transport you take to go to work, to the offices you work in, to the forms of entertainment you are subjected to. The exhaust is so thick the air boils like a soup. There are too many people touching you, in the trains, in the elevators, when you go home to sleep. You live in a seaside city, but the only time most people get anywhere near the sea is for an hour on Sunday evening on a filthy beach. It doesn't stop when you're asleep either, for the night brings the mosquitoes out of the malarial swamps, the thugs of the underworld to your door and the booming loudspeakers

of the parties of the rich and the festivals of the poor. Why would you want to leave your brick house in the village with its two mango trees and its view of small hills in the east to come here?

So that someday your eldest son can buy two rooms in Mira Road, at the northern edges of the city. And the younger one can move beyond that, to New Jersey. Your discomfort is an investment. Like ant colonies, people here will easily sacrifice their temporary pleasures for the greater progress of the family. One brother will work and support all the others, and he will gain a deep satisfaction from the fact that his nephew is taking an interest in computers and will probably go on to America. Mumbai functions on such invisible networks of assistance. In a Mumbai slum, there is no individual, there is only the organism. There are circles of fealty and duty within the organism, but the smallest circle is the family. There is no circle around the self.

India frustrates description because everything you can say about it is true and false simultaneously. Yes, it could soon have the world's largest middle class. But it now has the world's largest underclass. And so with Mumbai. Everything is expanding exponentially: the call centres, the global reach of its film industry, its status as the financial gateway to India; as well as the slums, the numbers of absolutely destitute, the degradation of its infrastructure. The city's planners have their eyes set firmly on Shanghai, as a model for Mumbai. The government has approved a McKinsey-drafted document titled *Vision Mumbai*, which aims to turn Mumbai into 'a world-class city by 2013'. As the architect Charles Correa noted of the plan, 'There's very little vision. They're more like hallucinations'.

Mumbai needs to dramatically upgrade essential civic services: roads, sewers, transport, health, security. But, as one planner said to me, 'The nicer we make the city, the more the number of people that will come to live there.' The greatest numbers of migrants to Mumbai now come from the impoverished North Indian states of Uttar Pradesh and Bihar. Mumbai's problems cannot be solved until Bihar's problems are. You have to keep them down on the farm. And that

Taxi near Victoria Station.
PHOTO BY DARIO ZANNIER

Following pages.
Chowpatty beach during the Ganesh Festival.
PHOTO BY JEHANGIR SORABJEE.
COURTESY URBAN DESIGN
RESEARCH INSTITUTE.

means that agriculture has to become viable again for the small farmer. Abolishing trade-distorting subsidies in the US and the EU would go a long way towards making, say, Indian cotton competitive with American cotton. Mumbai is at the mercy of national and international factors beyond its control.

Then there are the steps that the Indian government could take. There is no reason Mumbai should be the capital of Maharashtra state. Shifting the state government to Navi Mumbai across the harbour, as was originally intended, would free up large amounts of space in the congested office district of Nariman Point. Beyond that, there has to be legislation establishing a strong executive authority for the city, with real decision-making power. The office of the mayor is currently no more than a figurehead; the city is run at the whim of the chief minister, and the state's interests are not necessarily those of the city. There are smart and brave architects and planners who are attempting to work with the state government. But they are trying to reason with people who come from the villages, who do not have a metropolitan

sensibility. Mumbai needs a mayor with vision and political power to push through the enormous infrastructural projects that the city so badly needs. The city, which contributes 37% of all the taxes paid in India, gets only a small fraction of it back from the central government in the form of subsidies.

Land is to be opened up in the south-eastern part of the island, much of which is occupied by a naval and commercial port. There is no reason Mumbai needs a naval home base, which could be relocated further down the coast. Efficient utilization of the eastern docklands area could also alleviate the pressure; the city needs schools, parks, auditoria, public spaces. Instead, it gets luxury housing and shopping malls. The example of the mill areas, in the centre of the city, where 600 acres that were desperately needed for public use have instead been given over to developers, is a bad augury for the city.

We all – wherever we live – have a stake in helping the people of megacities like Mumbai. The desperation of slum-dwellers in cities like Mumbai directly affects the

Flooding cinema queue.
PHOTO BY RAJESH VORA.
COURTESY URBAN DESIGN
RESEARCH.

Pavement dwellers
in Monsoon.
PHOTO BY RAJESH VORA.
COURTESY URBAN DESIGN
RESEARCH INSTITUTE.

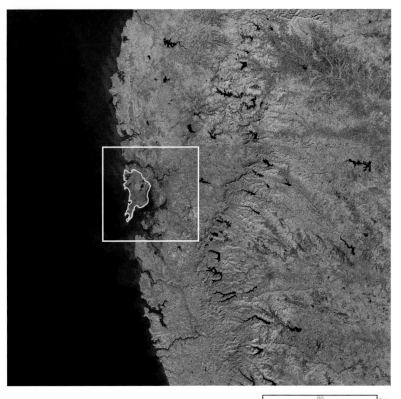

| 90 | km |

Images from the
QuickBird satellite of
Mumbay.

economic fortunes of people in New York or Los Angeles. It's as important for London to understand Mumbai as it is for Mumbai to understand London, if for no other reason than the next generation of Londoners is being born in Mumbai.

So why do people still live in Mumbai? 'Bombay is a bird of gold', a Muslim man in the Jogeshwari slum, whose brother was shot dead by the police in the riots, and who lives in a shack without running water or a toilet, told me. A Golden Songbird; try to catch it if you can. It flies quick and sly, and you'll have to work hard to catch it, but once it's in your hand, a fabulous fortune will open up for you. This is one reason why anyone would still want to come here, leaving the pleasant trees and open spaces of the village, braving the crime and the bad air and water. It is a place where your caste doesn't matter, where a woman can dine alone at a restaurant without being harassed, and where you can marry the person of your choice. For the young person in an Indian village, the call of Mumbai isn't just about money. It's also about freedom.

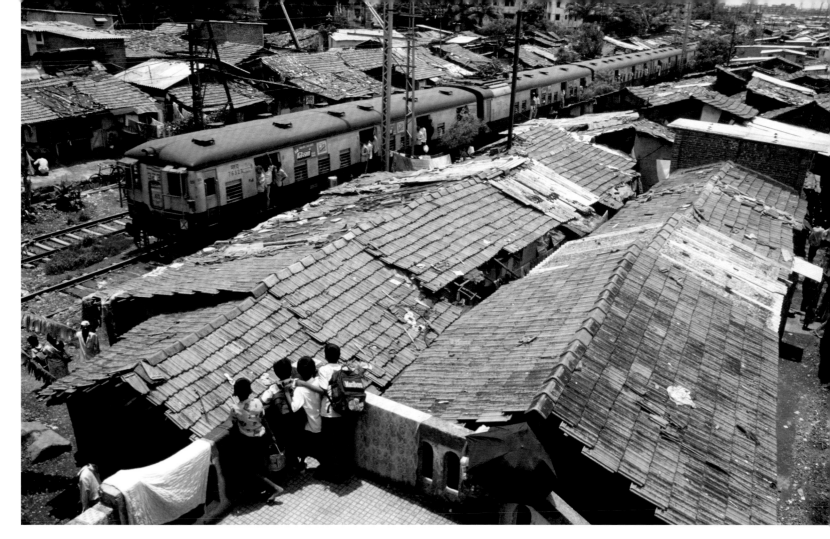

Railway across informals.
PHOTO BY RAJESH VORA.
COURTESY URBAN DESIGN
RESEARCH INSTITUTE.

Mumbai (still 'Bombay' for to many of its residents) is the most heavily populated city in India; and one of the most populous metropolitan areas in the world. Inhabited from as early as 250 BC, the municipal corporation of the city has grown to approximately 11.9 million today (excluding the additional 3 million within its municipal limits). Mumbai has experienced extraordinary growth during the past century; its population expanding by 1184%. This development is largely due to the wealth of business opportunities the city affords: from the seaport and textile mills in the first half of the 20th century to the booming IT economy today. Mumbai's population growth shows no signs of abating, with an increase of 14% recorded in the last decade, and projections for a further increase of 2.4 million in the coming decade.

Mumbai has a young population; over a third of its residents are under 20 years old and only 4% are over 65. Mumbai's population is 65% Hindu and 20% Muslim; the remainder is made up of various other religious groups. Only a minute number of Mumbai's population was born outside India.

The city of Mumbai covers 438 square kilometres of Salsette Island, although almost a fifth of this area is occupied by Borivali National Park. The urban areas are therefore condensed into 350 square kilometres supporting a high gross residential density of about 34,000 residents per square kilometre. Public open space is limited, accounting for only 1 % of this area. Indeed space of any kind is only acquired at a premium. Cramped, relatively expensive and badly located accommodation is standard. However, the harshest by-product of these spatial circumstances is the troubling reality that approximately half of the residents of Mumbai live in slum conditions.

Like many mega-cities in the developing world, Mumbai is suffering at the hands of rapid urbanization. Poverty, poor health and employment instability affect a huge proportion of the population. Unsurprisingly, low annual public expenditure (roughly €378 per capita) is not without side-effects. The lack of solid investment in urban infrastructure means that the city, increasingly crippled under the growing population's demands, is fast approaching breaking point. *Vision Mumbai*, a plan for the city in 2013 hints at an attempt to tackle some of these issues. In any case, one certainty exists; competent resolution strategies for some of these major urban issues will be fundamental to ensuring the quality of life of the millions who live in Mumbai.

Mumbai's Gross City Product remains fairly low at approximately €944 per capita. Furthermore, despite being the biggest city in India, the Gross City Product of Mumbai is only equivalent to 2.4% of India's national economy, or about 1% of Italy's GDP.

The service sector employs 80% of the people working in Mumbai. Engineering, diamond-polishing, information technology and healthcare, all rapidly expanding sectors, are injecting strength into Mumbai's economy. Due to Mumbai's position as capital of Maharashtra State, the government is also a big employer of the city's residents. The city's deep natural harbour also provides a considerable number of jobs, both directly and indirectly. A considerably smaller 18% of the population is employed in the manufacturing industry. A true representation of the economy of Mumbai, however, cannot circumvent the informal sector where an estimated 92% of Mumbai's total workers are situated.

Mumbai is divided into six administrative zones with 24 wards. It is governed by the Municipal Corporation of Greater Mumbai (MCGM). The executive authority of MCGM is vested in the municipal commissioner and the 227 elected municipal councillors who exercise authority over civic affairs through budgetary and financial controls.

A massive 10 million people, 85% of Mumbai's population, use public transport for their daily journeys between home and work. Despite commuters' high dependency on public transport, the travel conditions are far from favourable. Private car use is much less common, accounting for only 15% of daily journeys. There are just 89 vehicles per 1,000 residents. It seems, however, that this is enough to guarantee that the roads remain heavily congested, thus creating a nightmare for both commuters and the city's pollution levels.

Compact city core:
the Marine Drive Bay
and western railway arc.
PHOTO BY JEHANGIR SORABJEE.
COURTESY URBAN DESIGN
RESEARCH INSTITUTE.

The Tata Institute of
Fundamental Research
complex; Naval Housing;
Navy Nagar.
PHOTO BY JEHANGIR SORABJEE.
COURTESY URBAN DESIGN
RESEARCH INSTITUTE.

Mahalaxmi: the city
laundry.
PHOTO BY DARIO ZANNIER.

Shanghai
People's Republic of China

Qingyun Ma

In 1995, Qingyun Ma set up MADA S.P.A.M. an architecture consulting company in New York, which then moved to Shanghai in 2000. From that time, Qingyun Ma has been active in both academic and practical fields as a Chinese architect.
Born in 1965, Qingyun Ma graduated from the Architecture Department of Tsinghua University, with a bachelors degree in civil engineering. Following graduation, he attended the Graduate School of Fine Art, Department of Architecture, University of Pennsylvania in 1991.

A city of supposition

There is no doubt that Shanghai has regained its status as a global metropolis. Yet Shanghai, a city not created according to an existing urban model whose growth pattern is monitored by a known financial formula, constantly reminds us that we are still far from understanding this dense, massive and dynamic urbanism. For a city with a population twice the size of London (14 million versus 7.5 million), an urban area less than one third of Tokyo (670 square kilometres versus 2,180 square kilometres), yet with a per capita income one-twentieth of that in these two cities ($1,668/year disposable income versus $30,000/year), Shanghai might be mistakenly perceived as an unproductive, volatile city crammed with sterile buildings and suffering people. This assumption is challenged, however, by its continued GDP growth rate of 10%. Additionally, 11 new towns are planned and being constructed around the centre city. With the 2010 World Exposition on its way, Shanghai feels no fear of crisis. Instead, it aspires to grow even bigger and stronger with a confident assertion: City Makes Life Beautiful (the World Expo slogan). There is no secret to Shanghai's evolution, but there are surely aspects that are unique to that city from which we can try to extract paradigms.

Laminating density

Shanghai is made of three ideological layers softly laminated together: colonial capitalism, 1840-1949; socialism, 1949-1980; and global capitalism under Chinese circumstances, 1985-present. The first layer was created by colonial interests, distinct and sometimes antithetical parties, resulting in what one might call 'concession city'. This territory was not only segregated from the Chinese population, it was also subdivided among foreign residences. This created one of the most critical aspects of Shanghai's urbanism: multiple cores with singular boundaries, whose effect can be observed to this day. Reversing the popular post-modern urban condition, Shanghai's paradox between heterogeneity of centrality versus homogeneity in marginality, creates a pattern of energy originating from unknown creases in these centres instead of freedom at the margins. This explains a very unique Shanghai syndrome: exile in the centre.

This earlier layer was overlapped by a socialist layer modulated by 'working units': the idea of a walled (or otherwise confined) compound inherited from Russian social organization, in which working and living are placed in direct proximity. In Shanghai, this format is transformed into two tendencies: densification of residence and homogenization of population. It is typical to see a *Li-Nong* house (meaning 'hidden in the alley', a type of densely arranged urban row house with a small entry garden) that was once occupied by one family of five people now jammed full of five to ten families at once. Shanghai's leading role in China's early industrial development is arguably subject to this pattern of population/labour organization.

This organized residential density contributed to another unique urban condition of Shanghai: street life. Unlike the stereotypical socialist perception of urban streets as a source of commercialism or anti-authority protest, Shanghai's streets were never empty. Instead, they are inhabited by hyper-dense residences. Its streets have blurred the boundaries between public and private. They are populated but not public; they are communicative but not commercial. 'The Shanghai street' is something that cannot be found in other Chinese or western cities.

However, the double layers have maximized neither the edges nor the cores. Prior to the 1990s, there were still areas left-over from different generations of industrialization containing horizontal capacity and appealing to desires for verticality. In the early 1990s, a third layer was laid by a new economy, which was characterized as a 'market economy with Chinese characteristics' (Deng Xiao Ping) and quickly 'joint-ventured' by globalism in Chinese-fusion style. Unlike the previous layers, this layer is three-dimensional, with raised urban highways and super-high-rise office towers, and amorphously pervasive, with real estate projects everywhere. It is created to maximise both the cores and the edges in order to turn the whole territory into a volume of uniform density and value. This three-layered urbanism has made Shanghai a city subject to, but not under, many suppositions.

Unknown population

What is Shanghai's population? How many more people can Shanghai support? There are 13.52 million official Shanghai citizens, plus 4 million permanent residents. Additionally, there are an unknown number of unregistered people, called the floating population, including construction and other low-paid, labour-intensive workers. In tune with Shanghai's late growth, we investigate the notion of 'Shanghai's Population' not purely as a matter of census, but as a mysterious catalyst that creates fear and anxiety simultaneously. The inability to answer these questions is due to the fact that an estimated non-urban population of 60 million has been urbanized around Shanghai. But the uncertainty is systematically sustained since it fortifies the world's confidence in Shanghai's continuous capacity to attract and support more people. This confidence arouses the world's curiosity, both intellectual and speculative, to see where the condensation point of the population lies.

Rings and stars

The critical task of increasing population evenly throughout the territory is to connect points that are already high in value through points that are still low in value. This can be visualized as urban irrigation works, which spatially fertilize the whole urban field; imagery that is not unfamiliar to Shanghai considering its historical creek systems. The city's ambitious transportation scheme grows (flows) into a landscape of rings (inner and outer) and stars (satellite towns), once again overlapping with incidental offsets onto the preceding urban layers. It makes Shanghai the unparalleled leader in the advancement of automobile highways and other means of ground transportation in China, such as, subway, light-rail and maglev. It is product and cause of the phenomenon of 'Shanghai's Unknown Population'. The phenomenon is largely due to the fact that there are no physical limits to Shanghai's geographical terrain: a flat plate of slowly flowing rivers and creeks that merge and rush out to the sea. It is only convenient

to refer to the latest inner-ring road as a man-made limit that separates the 15 million known population from the still unknown 'wild' outside. But mobility is a double-edged sword, as the highway rings are expected to put the population in fixity; they increase the population even more effectively. Therefore, the goal to keep the population within the ring seems impossible. Planning officials are well-aware of the paradox of limits. What seems more reliable in the effort of limiting the population is to navigate the difference between the density of people and density of buildings. Two policies have been made to reduce FAR and increase the Green Ratio. This is transforming Shanghai with yet another layer of texture: an infra-network of urban highways and ultra-patchwork of urban parks and gardens. Will this layer absorb more people or squeeze them out? The result lies in the 11 star towns outside metropolitan Shanghai. Ostensibly, these 11 satellite towns were proposed to give Shanghai green and thematic suburbs, but in reality they are meant to balance Shanghai's increasing population.

Green or red?

Greenness is the password for a new layer of Shanghai. But is it greener to make central Shanghai 'redder', or make the star towns redder? (Density is usually shown as red in planning maps). It is hoped that the envisioned greenness, either in a dispersed or centralized formula in central Shanghai, can be guaranteed by the redness of star towns.

In the next 15 years, urbanization is estimated to result in a population growth of 500 million people in cities throughout China. Shanghai and the adjacent Yangtze River Delta (YRD) will presumably share one fifth of it, which is 100 million. The population within Shanghai's central ring road is 'fixed' at 15 million; the current star towns – each with a planned population of 500,000 to 1,000,000 – will be multiplied by ten, thereby equalling Shanghai's current population.

Two options seem to exist: one, to expand the star towns themselves according to their low standard of density

Following pages
Shanghai, 2005.
© PAOLO ROSSELLI.

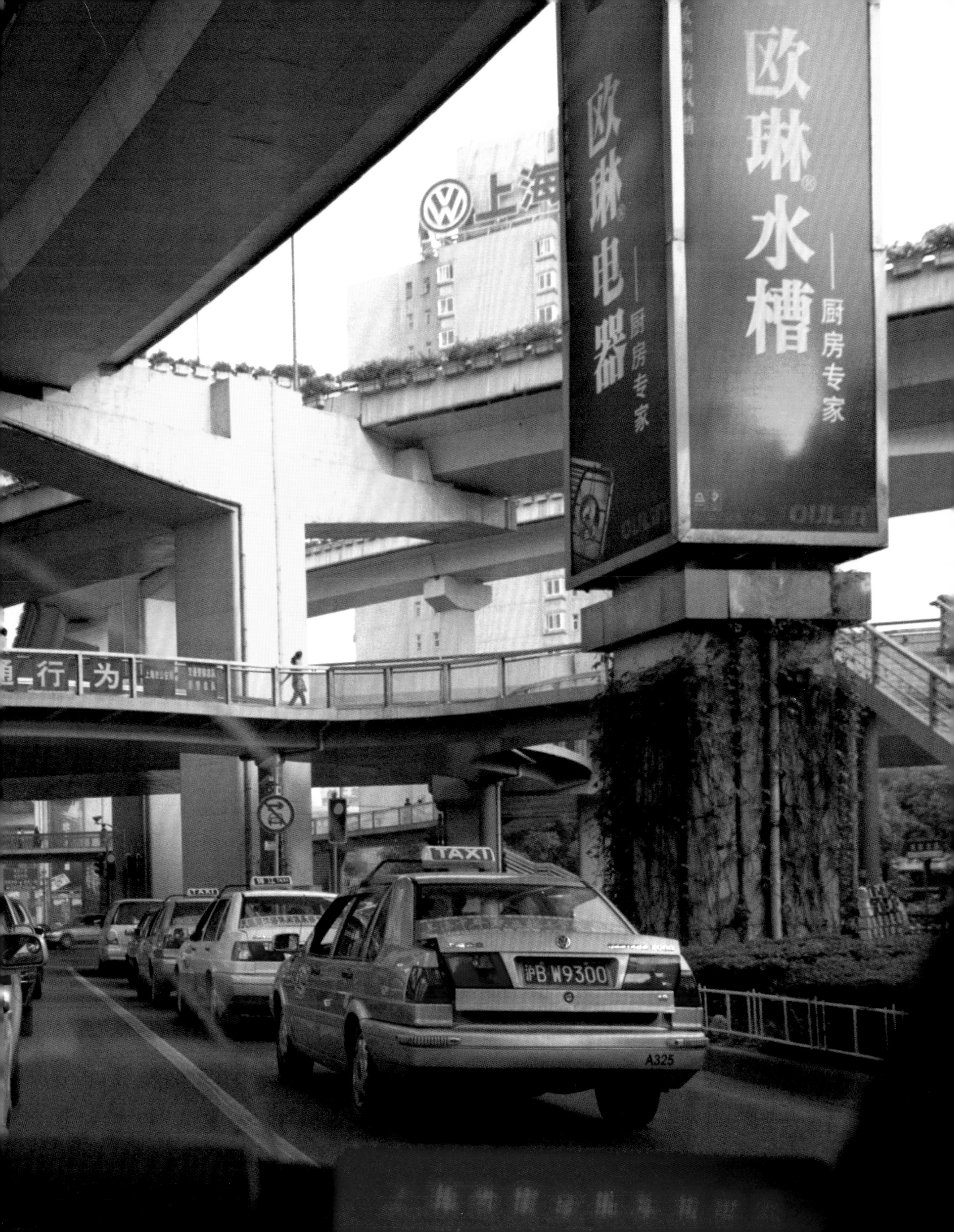
欧琳®
水槽
厨房专家
欧琳®
电器
厨房专家
上海
行
为
TAXI
沪B W9300
A325

and green characteristics; or two, to condense future construction within the assigned land limits. If the first option is followed, a carpet-like urban landscape with a gradient density pattern centred on central Shanghai will result. Not only will this eliminate agricultural lands, it will destroy the experience of changes across layers. If we follow the second option, 11 new cities with the same hyper urban density currently known in central Shanghai will be created. Obviously, neither option comforts us. Therefore, we have to rethink whether it is intelligent to freeze the population of central Shanghai and carve out green patches. Ambitious infrastructure projects in the name of improving the quality of life for a fixed population do nothing but attract more people to the city, which in turn will sacrifice the supposed 'better quality of life'. So, before the 11 new towns acquire the fundamental attributes necessary to attract and anchor population, Shanghai will become increasingly denser and redder. Speculatively, Shanghai's unlimited redness contributes to the greenness around it.

Residential density

The core of Shanghai presents extremely high residential densities. A gradual deconcentration is occurring. New urban centres are being planned at the same time that suburban sprawl is unleashed in the new China.
SOURCE: THE5ᵀᴴ CENSUS OF CHINA, 2000

Density [people/km²]

- 2,000
- ← 4,000
- 4,000 - 10,000
- 10,000 - 20,000
- 20,000 - 30,000
- → 30,000

20 km

Other provinces
SOURCE: THE5ᵀᴴ CENSUS OF CHINA, 2000

Other provinces

- 3.2% - 13.2%
- 13.3% - 23.5%
- 23.6% - 37.5%
- 37.6% - 66.0%
- 66.1% - 99.1%
- n/a

8 km

Overcrowding

Lack of living space is one of the main social problems in central Shanghai. Concentrations of overcrowded housing units appear in the central districts. However, residents are highly reluctant to trade off centrality for larger housing units in the outskirts.
SOURCE: THE5ᵀᴴ CENSUS OF CHINA, 2000

Social disadvantage (less than 12 m² hab space)

- 0.6% - 4.3%
- 4.4% - 7.7%
- 7.8% - 11.5%
- 11.6% - 17.7%
- 17.8% - 30.5%

20 km

Children

Shanghai is grewing fast. The percentages of children are very low in the urban care and higher in rural and peripherical areas.
SOURCE: THE5TH CENSUS OF CHINA, 2000

Youth (population below 15)

- 9.3% - 11.1%
- 11.2% - 12.6%
- 12.7% - 14.4%
- 14.5% - 18.5%
- 18.6% - 24.4%

20 km

Images from the
QuickBird satellite of
Shanghai.
© DIGITALGLOBE EXCLUSIVE
DISTRIBUTED FOR EUROPE BY
TELESPAZIO.

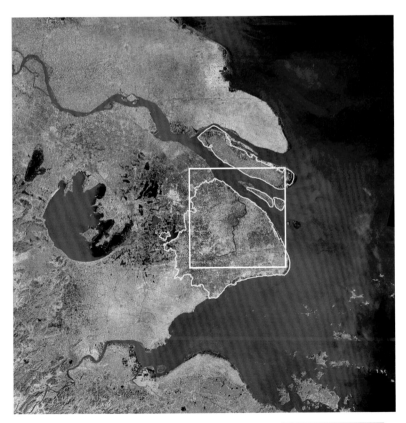

80 km

Within the China's current legal framework, Shanghai can be understood as a city-state: it extends over 6,300 square kilometres and has more than 18 million inhabitants. Whereas its traditional city boundaries demarcate an area of 289 square kilometres, in which 6.5 million people live at very high residential densities, most of Shanghai's territory is now considered urbanized and reaches an average density of 2,900 residents per square kilometre, arranged in a seemingly chaotic patchwork of agricultural, residential and industrial land uses. At the same time that sprawl pushes outwards, the urban core is experiencing a thorough and complex restructuring process. Structural densification, improvement of overcrowded conditions and expanded provision of public and green spaces are one side of the coin. Residential displacement, housing affordability problems and traffic congestion are the other.

Given its low fertility rates, the demographic dynamism of Shanghai is now driven by immigration. In the year 2000, more than 3.8 million people living in Shanghai had a registered residency in a different province. This population helps the city meet the increasing low-wage labour demand generated by its rapid economic development at the same time that it tests its capacity to be socially inclusive and integrative of cultural differences. Other social issues that Shanghai needs to tackle include the rise of long-term unemployment and the greying of its population – 17% of Shanghai's residents are now 65 years of age or older.

Since 1992, the Shanghai economy has evidenced rapid growth, and it is expected to continue expanding by more than 10% annually for at least another decade. The urban economy is also modernising: approximately half of the labour force now works in the service sector while 36% are employed in a diversified set of industries. The Yangtze River Delta – Shanghai's wider economic base reachable within a three-hour drive from the city – comprises 22% of China's productive capacity and 30% of its exports. The economic size of this region amounts to approximately 25% of Italy's GDP.

Shanghai is investing heavily in expanding its road capacity and public transport infrastructure – currently a quarter of daily trips rely on some form of public transport, including rail, metro and bus. In its modernization process, Shanghai finds itself increasingly at odds in accommodating bicycles, its traditional transport mode on which many residents still depend.

The Shanghai Municipal Government is divided into 19 districts. These local administrations have limited planning power and sometimes compete for investments. The executive is headed by the Governor of Shanghai, one of the most influential political figures in the People's Republic of China.

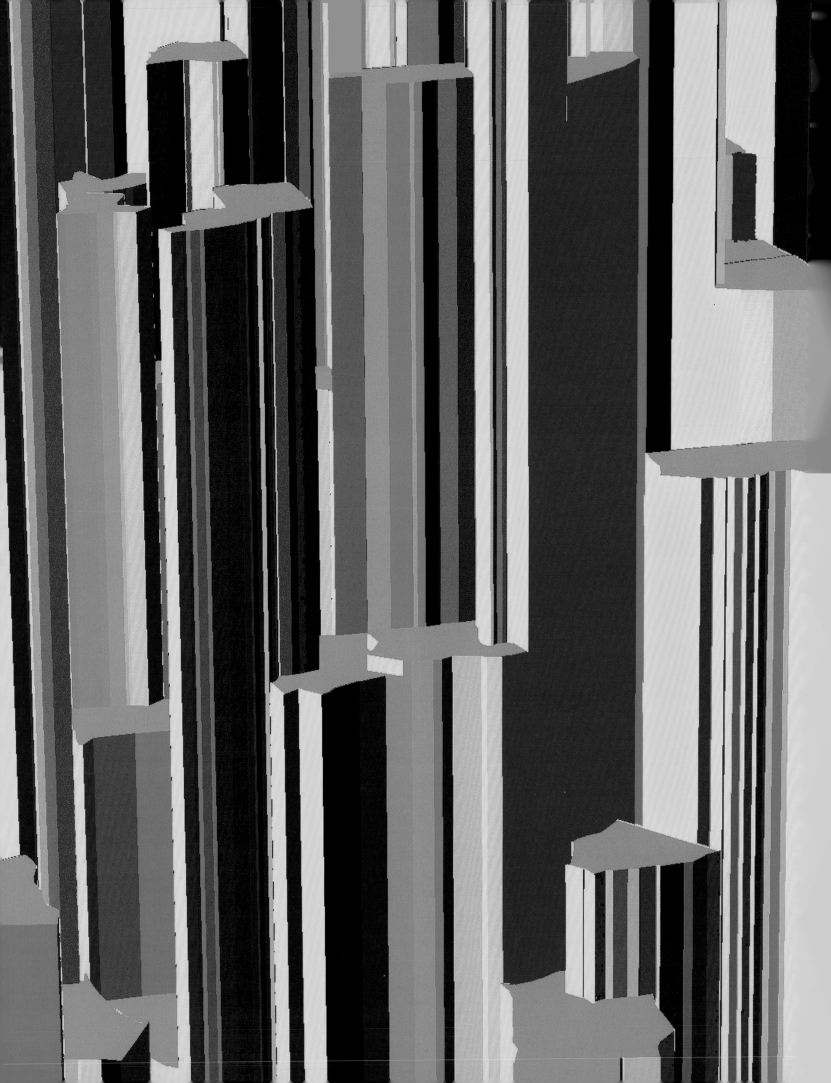

Exhibition collaborators

A street of cities

The *Cities. Architecture and Society* exhibition in the Corderie at the Arsenale and in the Padiglione Italia is being staged by the Cibic & Partners studio.

The Corderie is the most intensive and important part of the project: the aim of the Director, Richard Burdett, was to represent his narrative on the 16 cities and some important general themes through diverse media.

The first consideration was how to present such a dense account. It was decided to alternate the general themes with groups of three or four cities and to put an area for relaxation halfway down the corridor. We were then advised of the importance of maintaining attention on the contents, playing with a continuous variation of the graphics, the typography and the different available media.

At this point the staging took shape. It consists of individually designed rooms (introduction, general themes, relaxation area and conclusions) and a series of elements forming the alphabet for the story of the 16 cities that recur but are always expressed differently.

The ideal path through the Corderie begins in a big, circular, dark room, where four films on global urban change are screened on the walls with data on the cities represented graphically. This first engaging moment is followed by a square room with a strong, soft light where the 16 cities are presented for the first time and where the key tools for reading the entire exhibition are acquired.

On emerging from this room, visitors see the whole 300 metres of the corridor and the first cities begin to appear.
The staging has been designed so that the route grafts the cities onto one another.

The Corderie space is marked by big, tall, white elements perpendicular to the central corridor, with some exceptions in solid colour. These monoliths, which encompass some of the big columns in the Corderie, indicate the names of the cities and the start of the story for each.

The contents are then developed on suspended dividing walls with graphics, videos and projections.
Large, white, light shade-cylinders are arranged unevenly and emit the sound for each city.
We have tried to maintain the balance between the vertigo of the long central corridor, from which it is possible to visually take in the entire staging, with the sensation of finding oneself in a more intimate environment as soon as one moves and go into the stories of the cities, defined by dividing walls and volumes, where it is easy to focus on the contents.
Aldo Cibic and Luigi Marchetti

Installation Concept:
Cibic & Partners

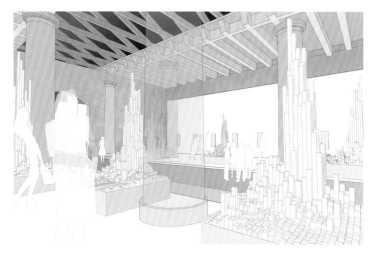

A significant amount of the International Exhibition's content builds upon the work of The Urban Age project sponsored by Alfred Herrhausen Society and housed within the Cities Programme at the London School of Economics and Political Science.

The principal aim of The Urban Age is to shape the thinking and practice of urban leaders. The two-year conference series is the first step towards the creation of an ongoing forum that will debate and influence how the city is studied, planned and managed. The six conference cities are New York, Shanghai, London, Mexico City, Johannesburg and Berlin. The series operates as a mobile laboratory, testing and sampling the urban condition using a combination of expert presentations, site visits and opportunities for informal information exchanges. These results are then analysed, in search of regional patterns and global similarities that may shape the future development of cities and the processes that sustain them.

The Urban Age is constructing the framework for a developing network of individuals that exchanges information, experiences and data, emphasising the relationships between concrete investment, design and building, and the economic, social, political and cultural processes that shape city life. A key objective of the Urban Age investigation is to identify what trends and policies are failing to respond to local needs, resulting in the continued propagation of dysfunctional urban areas across the globe.

Four core themes are the focus of the investigation. These research fields reflect the basic human activities of living, working, playing and moving or what could be summarized as 'life in the city'.

- Labour market and work place
- Public life and urban space
- Mobility and transport
- Housing and neighbourhoods

In addition, a group of broader, overarching issues representing the governance level is part of the focus of the Urban Age investigation.
- Investment and economic development
- Planning and legal structures
- Sustainability and energy consumption
- Political economy and networking cities

Urban Age brings together a wide range of professionals from a variety of different disciplines and back grounds. Sociologists, geographers, economists, political scientists and urbanists from the academic side are joining urban practitioners such as planners, architects, developers, transport experts and engineers to engage in a dialogue with the political, decision making level.

The Cities Programme at the LSE is an international centre dedicated to the understanding of contemporary urban society. Its central objective is to relate physical structure to the social structure of cities. The Programme, located in the LSE's Department of Sociology, studies the relations between the visual and social aspects of the city. We believe that design aesthetics shape social understanding, and we take as our brief Jane Jacobs' statement that 'the look of things and the way they work are inextricably bound together'. The programme offers degree courses at the MSc and PhD level. It also hosts public events with design professionals, academics, city leaders and policy

Urban Age / Alfred Herrhausen Society
(The International Forum of Deutsche Bank)

a worldwide series of conferences
investigating the future of cities

organised by the Cities Programme
at the London School of Economics and
Political Science and the Alfred Herrhausen Society,
the International Forum of Deutsche Bank

The most famous architecture review in the world
Richard Burdett asked us to transform a square kilometre of
wall space at the Corderie into an instantaneous account of that
extraordinary movement of people, things and houses that is
changing contemporary cities and what we now call architecture
and society. This task comprises the recognisability of the graphic
information even when rapidly read, but mainly the highly topical
theme of using the graphic sign architecturally.

Exhibitions like that of Burdett ask us to create and then
share a changed interdisciplinary alphabet that uses the
aesthetic aspect of the video-clip along with the scientific
density of important international observers, giving the
graphics the task – once mainly entrusted to the oral account
– of aiding recognition, memory and sedimentation. This
allows us to see the complexity instantaneously, but mainly
to share it and become authorities on it without necessarily
being an integral part of it.

This new graphic alphabet at the Corderie speaks
an accessible visual language to architecture, sociology,
economics and town planning at the same time, without
ignoring those who, outside these disciplines, simply want to
be informed.

The Fragile project relates models of density, with
statistics, films, architecture, designs and people in 16
different cities on different continents. In the end these
16 cities seem like a single planetary city, dense and
multifaceted, held together by a single narrative theme
that is each time slightly different, in order to keep shifting
attention onto the differences without ever losing sight of the
whole.
Mario and Frida Trimarchi, Fragile

Art Direction:
Fragile

Aerial Installations

Neutral's installations represent an engaging airborne experience of cities, creating physical spaces through which viewers walk, paradoxically stimulating a sense of detached reflection and intense involvement.

The chain of five installations traces urban growth across five continents using the cities of Cairo, Caracas, Los Angeles, London and Tokyo as examples of different typologies within the global phenomena of the contemporary city. Rather than adding to the information discussed within the exhibition, the installations communicate a subtle and intuitive understanding of the various topics on display. Although the aerial photography used as a base for the projections is of real places, the priority is to explore various models of urban growth expanding the specificity of the places in question.

Thus Los Angeles represents the process of suburban sprawl and Caracas stands for the spontaneous expansion of cities through illegal construction. London represents the slow and organic morphing of disparate settlements into one continuous urban fabric and Cairo illustrates the inwards densification of a city when expansion into the uninhabitable desert is impossible. The installation depicting Tokyo traces the growth of the city through land reclamation into the Pacific Ocean.

Neutral emerged out of architects Christian Grou and Tapio Snellman's fascination with urban co-habitation and mobility. The studio's aptitude for interpreting the spatial qualities of architecture on film has secured relationships with renowned architects and moving image organizations, establishing their position within a wider urban discourse.

Neutral

INSTITUTION
Neutral

DIRECTORS
Christian Grou and Tapio Snellman

STAFF
Christian Grou, Christina Liao, Jatandeep Singh, Tapio Snellman, Kate Ward, Adam Randall

SPONSOR
Digital Globe

The film installations created by Neutral provide an airborne experience of urban growth in vastly different cities across five continents.

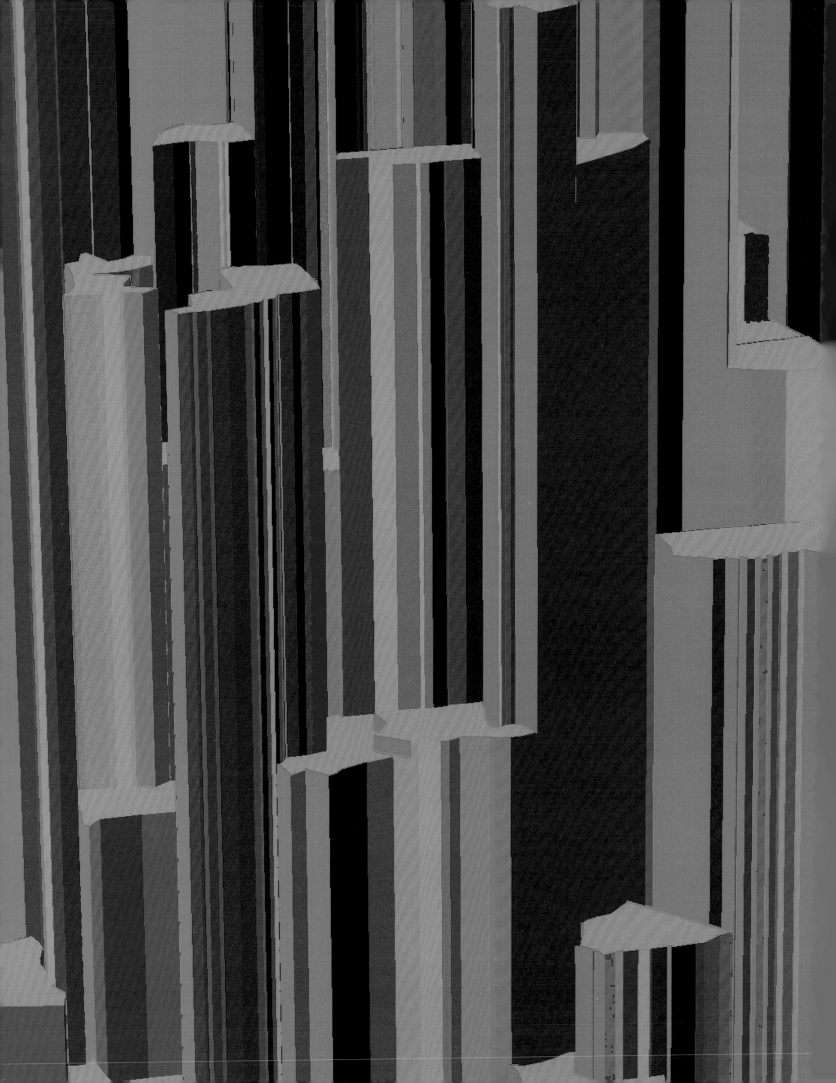

Urban Research:
invited institutions and workshops

Fields of operational knowledge

Cities nowadays are increasingly being planned and designed by everyone except architects, resulting in an endless culture of sprawl. The days of universal urban models belong to the past, but there are no new models to replace them. While contemporary urbanisation is being mapped, researched, edited, and branded by architects and the like, the way in which the discipline of architecture could prevent the city from further disintegration is being neglected. By immersing itself in the politics and systems of urban reality, the Berlage Institute – in collaboration with public and private partners – investigates which operational knowledge could project a new idea of city(ness) within the paradigmatic metropolitan areas of Europe and Asia. As a result two main positions shape the debate on the project of the city: immanence within urban systems and representation of urban ideals. This debate constitutes a constant field of tension in which the role of innovative architectural expertise and the project of the city can be evaluated. Three innovative operative fields of knowledge have been developed on either end of these ideological poles in order to address the idea of the city in our age of radical modernisation.

Economy of urban form

What kind of living, working and cultural typologies can be subtracted from the economic, the social, and the political organisation of a city? Instead of assailing reality with a formal set of a priori positions, knowledge of the economy of urban form helps architects take micro-decisions which make it possible to renew the city from within its immanent logic. In Guangzhou the local villagers owning the land play a major role in planning and managing the city. Capitalism is reinvented through Communism, embodied in the collective ownership of the villagers. Can a new strategy of 'urban script writing' be successful after the failure of the traditional master plan in Ljubljana? And how can new zones with a variety of urban functions be interlarded in mono-functional areas in Beijing?

Associative Design

Design a family of objects whereby each individual object is able to react appropriately to its urban context. The difference between each unique object is generated by a specific set of contextual rules. These rules are embedded in the institutional regimes of legislation, administration, production techniques and climate. The software driven 'associativeness' controls the body, programme and material of each urban object located in the cities of Rotterdam, Warsaw (public spaces) and Madrid (housing).

Representation

Despite the global networks of authority and governance, trade and mobility, the research on representation shows that the city cannot only be considered as an accidental field of economic forces. It requires a specific form to enhance its sustainability not only as a place to live but also as a means of central, cultural and political representation. The city must be rediscovered as a strong identifiable place with a constructible and intelligible physical form. What kind of contemporary agenda for 'Urban Design' can address the problems of the capital cities of Brussels, Tirana and Moscow?

Projecting the city
The Berlage Institute

INSTITUTION
The Berlage Institute
- postgraduate laboratory of architecture (Rotterdam, the Netherlands)

DIRECTORS
Alejandro Zaera Polo, Rob Docter, Vedran Mimica

CURATORS
Roemer van Toorn, Jennifer Sigler, Alexis Katz, Sean Mooney

STAFF
Pier Vittorio Aureli, Peter Trummer, Markus Shaefer, Yushi Uehara, Dietmar Leyk, Fernando Donis, Joachim Declerck, Elia Zenghelis, Bernard Cache, Martin Sobota, Nils Becker, Tobias Lutz.

COLLABORATORS
Visiting Experts:
Xaveer de Geyter, Freek Persijn, Kersten Geers, Edi Rama, Altin Gagani (Tirana); Frank Duffy, Kamiel Klaasse, Bernhard Kallup, Ricardo Lopez, Dorothea Scheidl, Alex Buma (Beijing); Theo Deutinger, Michelle Provoost, Sho Shigematsu (Guangzhou); Xavier Calderon, Bert Demuynck, Kersten Geers, Martine de Maeseneer, Gabriele Mastrigli, Freek Persijn (Brussels); Salvador Perez Arroyo, Mario Carpo, Kas Oosterhuis, Axel Sowa, Michael Hensel, Francisco Rubio, Stefan Waldhauser (Rotterdam, Warsaw); Kersten Geers,

Alexander Sverdlov (Moscow); Marijn Spoelstra, Miran Gajsek, Rupert Gole, Polona Filipic, Peter Senk (Ljubljana).
Berlage Institute Participants:
Bernardina Borra, Joachim Declerck, Reto Durrer, Ulrike Franzel, Katarzyna Korsak, Rodrigo Loaiza, Zhang Lu, Bart Melort, Alexa Nuernberger, Federico Rodriguez, Marc Ryan, Martin Sobota, Pier Paolo Tamburelli, Martino Tattara (Tirana); Paola Alvaro d'Alencon, Daniela Antolinc, Nana Chen, Federico Costucci, Michael Koller, Widyastuti Lioe, Weijie Liu, Tanu Veerajintsiri, Juan Bernardo Vera Rueda,

Ming-Ying Tsai, Luming Wang, Shanshan Xue (Beijing); Yuan-Sheng Chen, Tsai-Her Cheng, Joey Dulyapach, Hideyuki Ishii, Hui-Hsin Liao, Daliana Suryawinata, Taichi Tsuchihashi, Lulu Zhang, Mia Zhu (Guangzhou); Bernardina Borra, Weerapat Chokedeetaweeanan, Joachim Declerck, Cristina Garcia Fontan, Hiromi Haruki, Bart Melort, Alexa Nuernberger, Konstantinos Pantazis, Marc Ryan, Heng Shi, Pier Paolo Tamburelli, Martino Tattara, Dubravka Vranic, Niklas Veelken, Thomas Weiss,

ZhiYi Yang (Brussels); Miha Cebulj, Lovrenc Cvetko, Reto Durrer, Ulrike Franzel, Sharon Gur-Zeev, Kumiko Hayashi, Kaska Korsak, Rodrigo Loaiza, Federico Rodriguez, Daan Roosegaarde, Winter Stockwell, Martin Sobota, Marleen ter Weele, Minoru Amano, Yoon Kyung Bae, Nai-Wen Cheng, Florian Heinzelmann, Shizue Karasawa, Su Keyong Kim, Kalle Komissarov, Stephan Mehlhorn, Dusanka Popovska, Canan Saridal, Galit Shiff, Sato Takeru, Hong Yea Wu,

Teresa Nai-Tsuei Yeh (Rotterdam, Warsaw); Ross Adams, Kristijan Cebzan, Celine Jeanne, Rolf Jenni, Agata Mierzwa, Chintan Raveshia, Miguel Robles-Duran, Ivonne Santoyo (Moscow); Tina Jelenc, Jung Bin Kim, Ryuta Ohori, Yoko Sano, Changho Yeo (Ljubljana).

SPONSOR
SEDUS
Bouwfonds MAB
ARUP Amsterdam

THANKS TO
Françoise Vos (project management), Mick Morssink (graphic design).

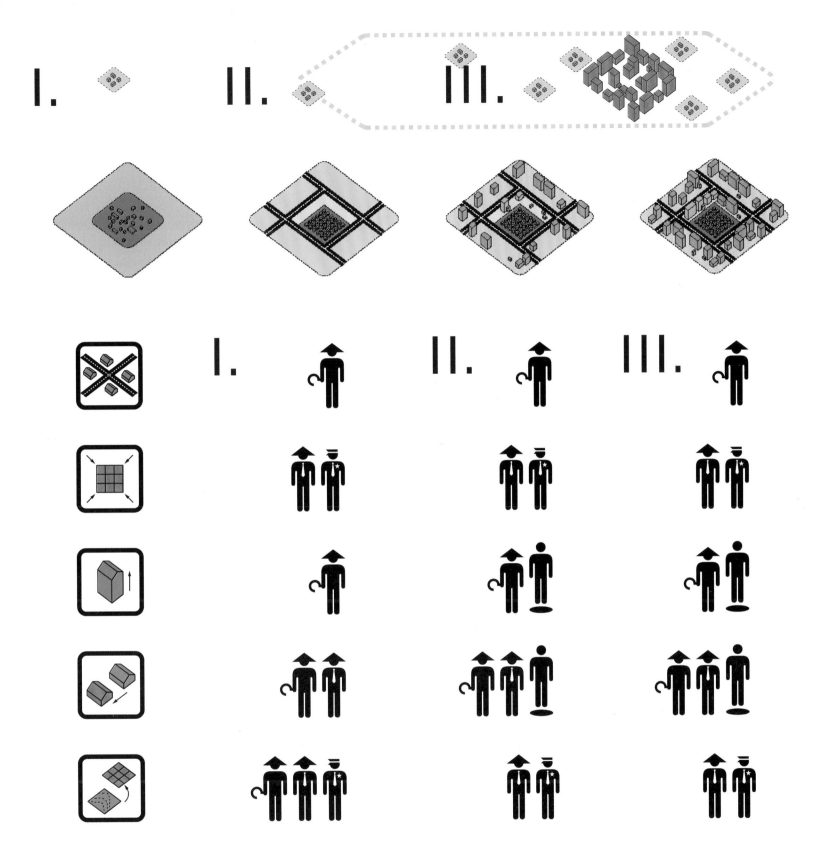

1
Development from
village to city and the
changing role of the
villagers.

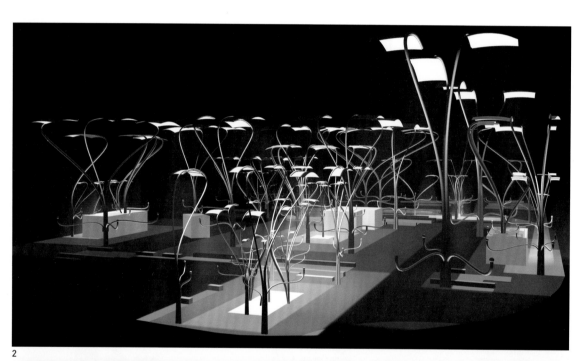

2

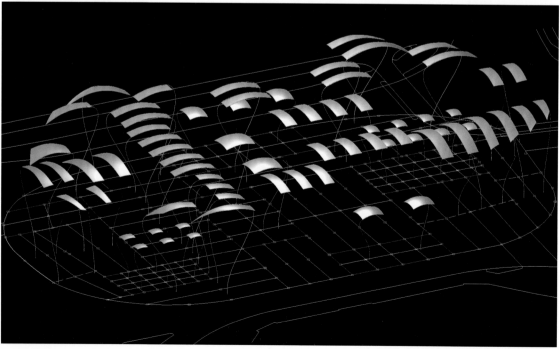

2
Warsaw, distribution of
light intensities in public
space.

3
Family of lighting objects
in Warsaw.

3

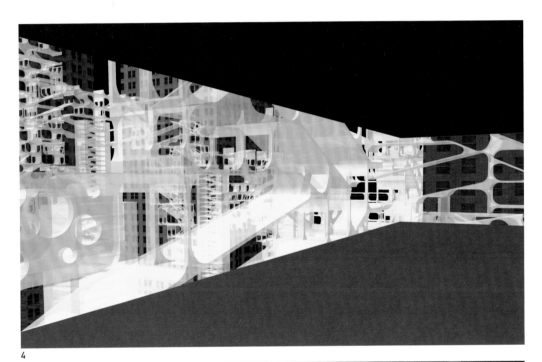

4

4
A view on the civic spider web connecting office towers in Beijing.

5
Office towers in Beijing get connected by an urban web of creative programs.

5

6

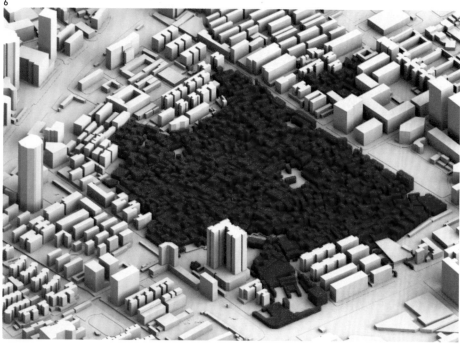

6
The 'Village in the City',
Shenzhen,
People's Republic of
China.
7-8
From village to city.

7

274   Urban Research

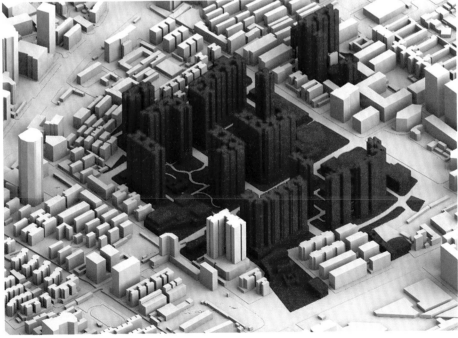

8

Since the birth of photography in 1839, this medium has enjoyed a persistent relationship with architecture and cities, both in documenting great public buildings and in reflecting the collective identity conferred by the urban setting.

*C Photo Magazine**, in collaboration with the 10th International Architecture Exhibition at *La Biennale di Venezia*, is curating a photographic exhibition entitled *C On Cities* in the halls of the Padiglione Italia. It sets out to parallel the construction and evolution of photography with the construction of cities and their gradual transformation. *C On Cities* focuses on the contemporary iconography derived from the interaction of the domestic and public realms, from the individual and the collective, and lastly from the interior and the exterior. Photographs from *C On Cities* do not simply reproduce reality; they frequently employ abstract or lateral images to depict urban lives, or they show private spaces to describe the city without obvious representations.

The reconfiguration of cities caused by migration, resulting in a new social structure, does not just affect the urban landscape; the adaptation of rural culture to these new realities has also caused rupture and feelings of uprootedness. This loss of collective identity as well as the steady dwindling of public spaces lies behind the greater isolation of individuals, who find refuge in new technologies as a substitute for direct communication. In a similar way, photographers in *C On Cities* are gradually abandoning reality as a reference point and choosing to reconstruct it digitally, shaping images according to their own vision of the world.

The need to create new maps of ideas, values and relationships is expressed in the artists' work through staged photography, the manipulation of our perceptions, mosaics or visual experiments that resemble installations. These new methodologies of representing urban and private environments have become highly significant for contemporary culture. Such developments underline the richness of photography as a means of expression, documentation and analysis in the global culture of the 21st century.

* «C Photo Magazine» is a publication created by a network of international experts. It promotes an eclectic point of view with no intention of imposing a particular model or following a specific trend. «C Photo Magazine» is published twice yearly in two editions in four languages: English/Chinese and Spanish/Japanese. To celebrate the *C On Cities exhibition*, «C Photo Magazine» has published a special issue.
www.ivorypress.com

C On Cities
C Photo Magazine

1
Andreas Feininger,
Brooklyn Bridge,
c. 1940.
COURTESY OF THE ANDREAS
FEININGER ESTATE AND BONNI
BENRUBI GALLERY, NYC.

1

INSTITUTION
C Photo Magazine

CURATOR
C Photo Magazine

CURATORE
C Photo Magazine

STAFF
C Photo Magazine

SPONSOR
Deutsche Bank
Permasteelisa SpA
Dr Pentti Kouri

EXHIBITORS
Jaime Avila

Olivo Barbieri
Edward Burtynsky
Giacomo Costa
Masaru Emoto
Nelson Garrido
Antonio Girbés
Dionisio González
Andreas Gursky
Osamu Kanemura
Mark Klett
Xiang Liqing
Maha Maamoun
Chema Madoz
Abelardo Morell
Eadweard Muybridge
Michael Najjar
Aitor Ortiz

Robert&Shana ParkeHarrison
Anders Petersen
Wang Qingsong
Miguel Rio Branco
Mitra Tabrizian
Bill Viola
Danwen Xing
Hu Yang

2
Chema Madoz,
Sin titulo, 1998.

3

4

5

3
Artist Unknown
(the Pillsbury Picture
Company), *Panorama of
San Francisco from the
Grant Building, Market
Street*, 1906.

4
Mark Klett with Michael
Lundgren,
*Panorama of San
Francisco from the Grant
Building, Market Street*,
2003.

5
Hu Yang, *Tang Zhen An
(Shanghainese, General
Manager)*, from the
series *Shanghai Living*,
2004-2005.
'Up to now, I'm satisfied
with my life, and I like
photographing and
collecting western
artware at my leisure
time. I have pressures,
mainly from competition
within the circle and
requirement from
inside. I want to do
something that I can
to promote Shanghai's
photographing industry'.

6
Hu Yang, Wei Yufang
(Shandongnese,
Vendor), from the series
Shanghai Living, 2004-
2005.
'We are leading a hard
life and eat battercakes,
pickles and a glass
of water for all three
meals. When our kids
want meat dishes, we
cook them an egg. We
work more than 15
hours a day if it doesn't
rain. We want our kids
to be educated and not
to live like us. I will risk
anything if our kids
can go to university. My
eldest son is excellent
and wins prizes every
semester. I suffer being
teased by local ruffians'.

6

7

8

7
Robert & Shana
Parkeharrison, *Turning
to Spring*, 2001. From
the series *Architect's
Brother*.

8
Olivo Barbieri,
Site Specific SHANGHAI-
04, 2004.
COURTESY BRANCOLINI GRIMALDI
ARTE CONTEMPORANEA FIRENZE,
ROMA, ITALY.

Disturbing and familiar. This is the space, the landscape, of Pyongyang, capital of North Korea.

Vast empty streets without cars, shops or bicycles. The theatrical nature of the public space of Soviet cities, though stripped of its urban crowds (apart from when there are big shows in the square). There are only straggly groups of individuals waiting in line for the scarce public transport.

Behind the enormous floral bill-boards and gardens decorated with plaster statues, are the 'giants': an enormous sphere, an enormous arch with two female figures, an enormous ring... Structures of 200, 300 metres that punctuate the city like mountains on a desert plateau. The 'giants' loom over the empty public space: the abandoned set of a cinema-city, conceived to host big crowd scenes.

And in the middle of this set, giant among giants, is the Ryungyong Hotel. A reinforced concrete pyramid 330 metres high, it was built in 1987 in preparation for the World Youth Games and never completed, a ruin-monument to the ruin of a political utopia.

The installation at the Padiglione Italia gathers three years of research and projects conducted by 'Domus' magazine on Pyongyang.

The research has been carried out by on-site reconnaissance, contacts with local researchers, maps, virtual simulations and the launch of an international competition for rebuilding the Ryungyong Hotel pyramid; a consultation that attracted more than 120 planning studies from all over the world.[1]

Thanks to this project-investigation, 'Domus' is now able to reconstruct the still mysterious story of Pyongyang.

Razed to the ground by aerial bombing in 1952, the city was rebuilt in a few years to the design of the dictator Kim Il Sung and his staff of architects, on the basis of an *ante litteram* 'Photoshop urbanism' operation. Alongside the residential settlements copied from the Soviet model, the city's reconstruction was based on reconstructions of some of the most famous monuments in the history of world architecture: from the Egyptian pyramids to Albert Speer, from Violet-le-Duc to Ludwig Hilbersheimer. Pyongyang now has archetypes of the history of architecture metabolised in the body of a quite different, spectacular, genetically anti-democratic city.

Thanks to a wraparound projection system – with new images of the city by the Italo-German photographer artist Armin Linke and by 'Domus' photographers and researchers – visitors find themselves immersed in the spaces of Pyongyang.

Alternating with the videos and photographs, data, statistics and maps show the extreme living conditions in the last prohibited city of the contemporary world.
Stefano Boeri

[1] See 'Domus', 893, June 2006 and www.domusweb.it.

Pyongyang fiction
Domus

INSTITUTION
Domus

RESPONSIBLE
Stefano Boeri, Joseph Grima, Armin Linke, Andrea Petrecca

STAFF
Laura Bossi, Elena Sommariva (editorial); Paolo Ratti, Annalisa Biliato, Nicoletta Cera, Carmen Figini (marketing & events)

ACKNOWLEDGMENTS
Zanotta

1
Ryungyong Hotel.
PHOTO BY ARMIN LINKE

2

2
Panorama of Pyongyang.

3

4

5

3
Thongil Street.
PHOTO ARMIN LINKE.
4
View from the Juche
Tower towards the
Tongdaewon District.
PHOTO ARMIN LINKE.

5
Yonggwang (Glory)
Station on the Chollima
line of Pyongyang's
underground.
PHOTO ARMIN LINKE.

What has happened is unbelievable, indeed almost inconceivable. Since we began our urbanistic studies on Switzerland in 1999, institutions and companies that seemed sacrosanct as an expression of continuity have suddenly begun to move. Developments have occurred that contradict the conventional cliché of this country's proverbial slowness and resistance to change of all kinds.

Our 'urban portrait' was motivated by the wish to examine Switzerland more closely, and from a new perspective, at the start of the 21st century-especially because all of the participants have been living and working in this country for a long time, and therefore believe they know it blind, so to speak. We were interested above all in the question of the specific urban character of Switzerland. We recognized that globalisation actually reinforces differences in patterns of urban behavior. These patterns are inevitably formed in the physical reality of cities and landscapes, in specific forms of urbanism. We wanted to explore this, with the help of our students, using the nearest object of study: Switzerland.

We wanted to proceed meticulously and take a very close look but without getting bogged down in details, like going into the Kleinbasel section of Basel to describe an urban culture marked by immigration or studying Zurich's Bahnhofstrasse to evaluate statistically its mythical discretion and exclusivity. These urban phenomena are important for everyday urban culture, but when we talk about 'specific urbanism', we mean something else, namely, how Switzerland's urban culture is different from, say, that of France, Holland, or China.

Switzerland's specific urbanism proves to be a kind of culture of refusal and prevention of density, of height, of mass, of concentration, of chance and of nearly all the other

Switzerland – an urban portrait
ETH Studio Basel – Contemporary City Institute

1

2

characteristics that are desirable in a city, and which the Swiss also love with a passion-just not in their own backyard.

We employed a variety of means in order to understand how the processes of urban transformation function in Switzerland, where the trends are going, how people move around at work or in their spare time. Frequently it was the antiquated sketch that enabled us to achieve mutual understanding most quickly and directly.

What resulted from these sketches in the end was a project, an idea for a future topography of Swiss development, based on five typologies: the metropolitan regions, the urban networks, the quiet zones, the alpine fallow lands and the resorts.

We chose a project that is radical and new because it calls for and reinforces differences and because it overcomes borders. However, the project is also simple and almost obvious, because it accepts the existing situation and reinforces present trends. The five typologies of our project are really nothing other than large-scale forms of the transformation processes that we observed. They are not imposed, invented, or superimposed by an external force; they are simply there already, and they offer an opportunity to initiate an order that is new but not alien and to change ingrained patterns of perception in a country where urban transformation is taboo and can barely be channeled.

It is largely unintentional that this 'urban portrait' has become a kind of quiet pamphlet championing different kinds of urbanism in a globalised world-based, paradoxically, on a country in which urbanism has always been suppressed.

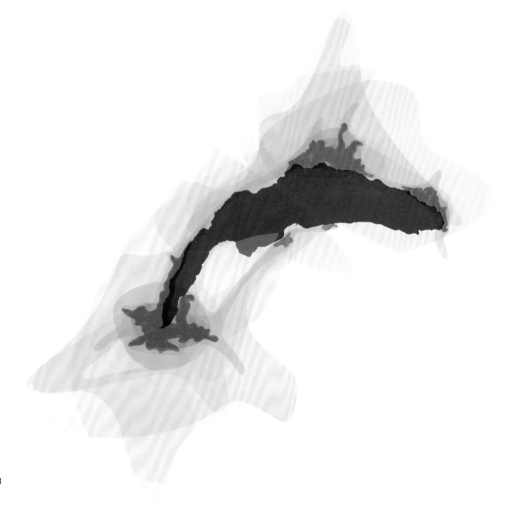

3

1
Is Switzerland a hole?
© ETH STUDIO BASEL 2005.
2
Is Switzerland an island?
© ETH STUDIO BASEL 2005.
3
Geneva.
© ETH STUDIO BASEL 2005.

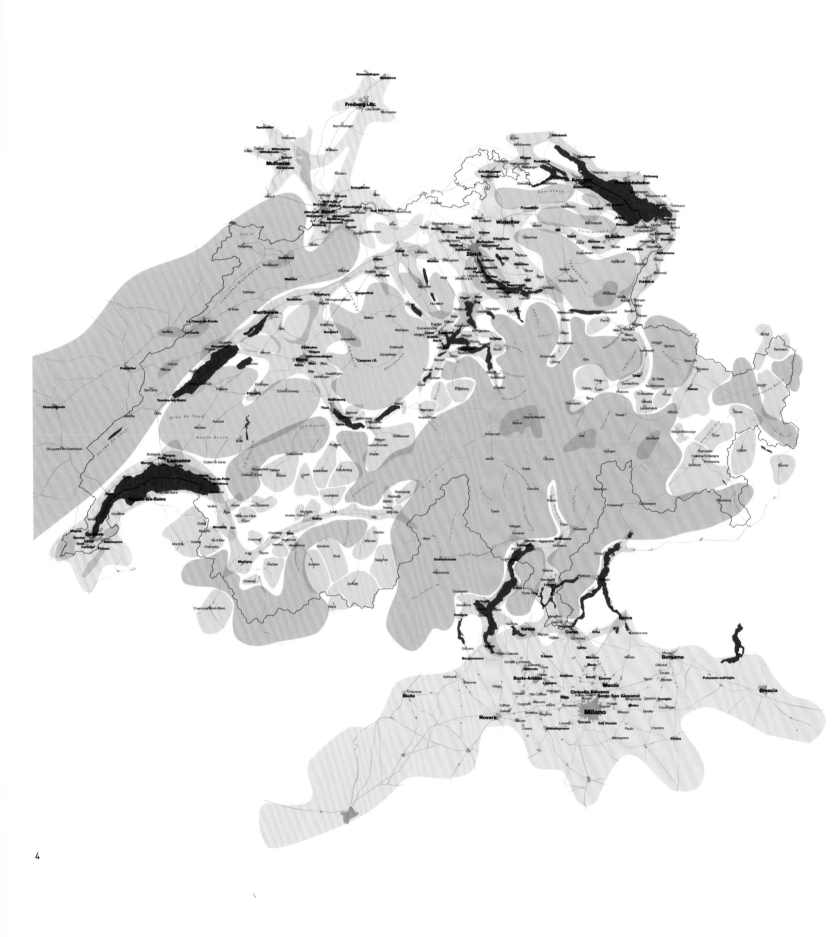

INSTITUTION
ETH Studio Basel – Contemporary City
Institute

DIRECTORS
Roger Diener, Jacques Herzog, Marcel
Meili, Pierre de Meuron

CURATORS
John Palmesino, Ann-Sofi Rönnskog.

STAFF
Christian Schmid, Emanuel Christ,
Simon Hartmann, Martin Josephy
Christina Holona, Thomas Friberg,
Jonathan Koellreuter, Stephanie
Stratmann, Lukas Kueng, Ramias
Steinemann, Ueli Degen, Jürg Keller,
Florian Tschacher, David Vaner,
Christian Müller Inderbitzin, Reto
Geiser Cornel Windlin, Manfred Perlik,
René Bossart, Orlando Eberle, Roger
Sonderegger, Markus Krause, Anna
Schindler, Thea Rauch-Schwegler,
Esther Dürrholder, Marco Corti, Miriam
Lähns, Max Schubiger.

STUDENTS
Jean-Luc von Aarburg, Barbara
Achermann, Patrick Ambrosetti,
Gabriela Arpagaus, Regula Arpagaus,
Renata Arpagaus, Franziska Bächer,
Bettina Baumberger, Thomas
Baumgartner, Matthias Baumgärtner,
Jeanette Beck, Isabelle Bentz, Denise
Betz, Julia Eva Bohler, Michael
Bösch, Michael Bosshard, Mathias
Brühlmann, Philippe Bürgler, Remo
Burkhard, Seraina Carl, Chiara
Castellan, Matthias Clivio, Ueli Degen,
Esther Deubelbeiss, Andreas Diener,
Claus Dold, Maximilian Donaubauer,
Yves Dreier, Katrin Eberhard, Samuel
Eberli, Beat Eichrodt, Francisca
Fariña, Lukas Feh r, Johannes Feld,
Jeanne-François Fischer, Andreas
Fluck, Lorenz Frauchiger, Eik Frenzel,
Andreas Friedli, David Ganzoni, Reto
Geiser, Lea Gnöpff, Rosário Gonçalves,
Florian Graf, Konrad Graser, Hans
Peter Gruber, Kornelia Gysel, Sandrine
Häberli, Pe Hadzimanovic, Raphael
Haefeli, Anja Hahn, Maiko Hahn,
Naomi Hajnos, Daniela Heimgartner,
Judith Höhener, Stefan Hörner,
Georg Hümbelin, Nadja Hutter, Kasia
Jackowska, Yves Jaquet, Regula
John, Dimitri Kaden, Eliza Karpinska,
Jürg Keller, Reto Keller, Stephanie
Koch, Markus Korrodi, Françoise
Krattinger, Raphael Kräutler, Lukas
Küng, Salome Kuratli, Andreas Landolf,
Judit Laszlo, Martin Leisi, Reto Liechti,
Gu-Sung Lim, Sven Lindner, Philipp
Lischer, Niels Lofteröd, Arthur Loretz,
Christoph Lötscher, Vanessa Mantei,
Michael Meier, Miguel Meirinhos,
Thomas Merz, Christof Messner, Anja
Meyer, Johanna Meyer-Grohbrügge,
Christoph Michels, Carolina Mojto,
Peter Moor, Charlotte von Moos, Elli
Mosayebi, Christian Müller Inderbitzin,
Christoph von Oefele, Edward Parker,
Katharina Pilz, Nicolas Pirovino,
Michael Reber, Christophe Ricq, Ann-
Sofi Rönnskog, Roland Rossmaier,
Petra Röthlisberger, Stephanie
Sandmann, Tobias Schaffrin, André
Schelker, Sara Schibler, Georg Schmid,
Patrick Schmid, Thomas Schmid,
Corina Schneider, Lukas Schnider,
Karin Schultze, Yann Sepulveda, Ines
Sigrist, Antonella Sileno, Roman
Sokalski, Ramias Steinemann, Regula
Steinmann, Claudia Suter, Samuel
Sutter, Stefan Thommen, Julia
Tobler, Ulrike Traut, Susanne Vecsey,
Christa Vogt, Philippe Volpe, Sophie
Waeber, Michael Wagner, Sibylle
Wälty, Anna-Katharina Weber, Isabelle
Weibel, Pascal Werner, Charles
Wülser, Alessandra Wüst, Jonas Wüst,
Lorenz Wüthrich, Michael Wüthrich,
Dominique Wyttenbach, Himeno Yuko,
Regula Zwicky.

SPONSOR
ETH Zurich

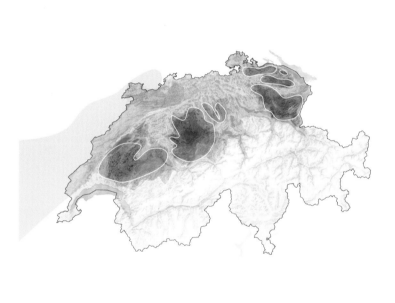

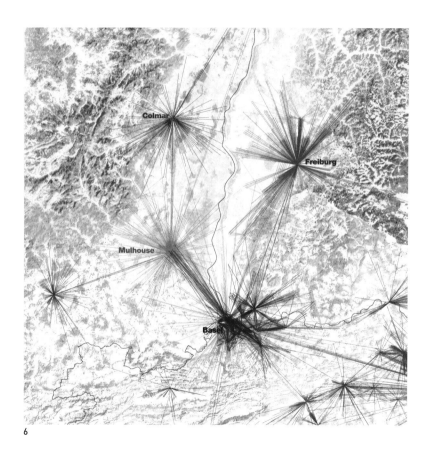

5

6

4
Urban Potential.
© ETH STUDIO BASEL 2005.

5
Quiet Zones.
© ETH STUDIO BASEL 2005.

6
Basel / Commuters.
© ETH STUDIO BASEL 2005.

Basel

Winterthur

Opfikon

Zürich

Luzern

Bern

Einsiedeln

Alt St. Johann

Flums

Glarus

Samnaun

Chur

Klosters

Sarnen
Kerns

Scuol

Thun

Engelberg

Flims
Laax

Davos

Brienz
Untersee
Interlaken
Hasliberg
Meiringen

Obersaxen

Arosa

Vaz / Obervaz

Zernez

Frutigen

Grindelwald
Lauterbrunnen

Tujetsch

Lausanne

Zweisimmen

Airolo

Celerina

Samedan

Silvaplana

Pontresina

Montreux
Saanen

Adelboden

St.Moritz

Kandersteg

Sils

Ried-Mörel

Fiesch

Poschiavo

Lenk

Bettern

Port-Valais

Randogne

Leukerbad

Leysin
Yvorne

Lens

Raron
Leuk

Brig

Avent
Montana
Chermignon

Unterbäch

Sion

Vex

Grimentz
Ayer

Grächen

Locarno
Tenero-Contra

Troistorrents
Champéry

Nendaz

Losone

Minusio

Evolène

Saas Grund
Saas Fee

Ascona

Muralto
Vira

San Nazzaro

Salvan

Bagnes

Lugano

Orsières

Zermatt

Agno

Caslano

7

292   Urban Research

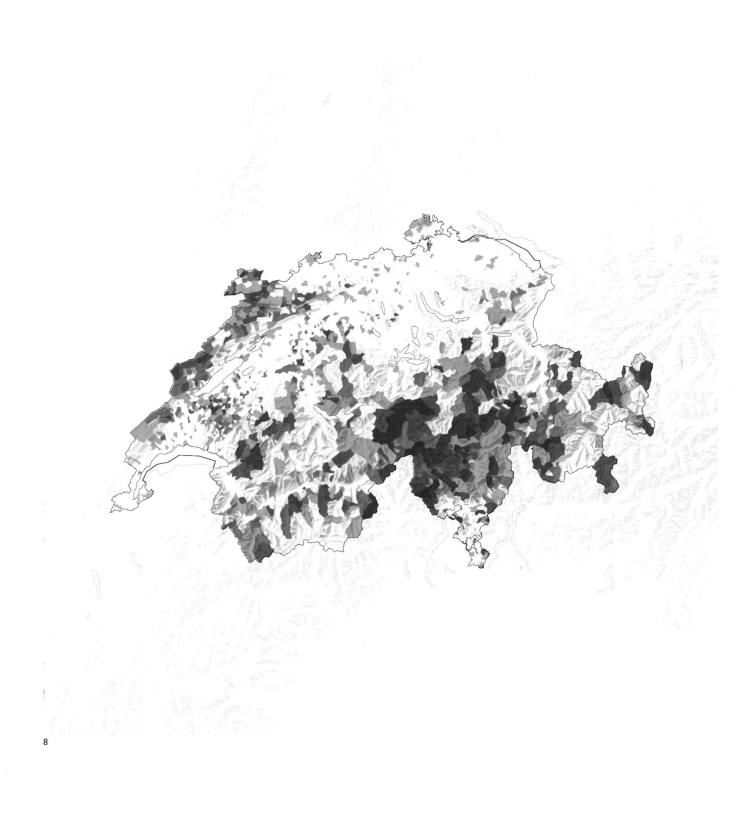

8

7
Alpine Resorts /
Temporary City.
© ETH STUDIO BASEL 2005.

8
Alpine Fallow Lands.
© ETH STUDIO BASEL 2005.

The Venice metropolis spreads over most of the provinces of Venice, Padua and Treviso. It takes in the three provincial capitals, numerous smaller towns and an extended diffuse urbanisation. This area commonly defined as 'metropolitan' is usually given the name 'Patreve', from the first syllables of the three provincial centres. In this case, however, it is given the conventional name of Venice, intended in its larger extent as Greater Venice. From a socio-economic point of view, the area is marked by extremely different phenomena: the industrial area of Marghera, once one of the biggest centres of base industries in the country, now partly closed and undergoing radical changes; a manufacturing system of small and medium businesses that are among the most dynamic in the country; an international centre of tourist-cultural attraction in the historic city of Venice; service centres for moving people and goods, such as the port and airport of Venice, both in leading positions in terms of movements.

The metropolitan dimension of Venice cannot be described in terms of 'size', of numerical quantity, for example by resident population or extent of the built-up areas in square metres. Purely quantitative indicators like these would place greater Venice on a similar scale to that of a couple of the numerous districts being built annually in Shanghai, or other big contemporary metropoli in China, India or Central America, consequently consigning this area to the realm of urban problems. What gives Venice its metropolitan dimension is rather the specific complexity and structure of the local system, resulting from the historic stratification of different, interacting systems: the historical-environmental system, the settlement system and the infrastructure system.

The historical-environmental system

The geography and the ancient settlements in the area have an important influence on the nature of the landscape and the identity of the districts, presenting considerable inertia to change. In general the overriding nature of the area in question is made up of: a strip of water courses flowing into the Adriatic Sea and the Venetian lagoon; the east-west direction that strongly influences the geometry of the parcelling of the land; a dense road network that is morphogenetic compared to the settlement; an alternate succession of densely settled strips and farming land, within which specific rural sub-spheres can be recognised, marked by different settlement and environmental systems.

The settlement system

The settlement system is marked by widespread scattering and numerous small-medium urban centres. The general phenomenon of the urban scattering has a certain internal differentiation, in which it is possible to recognise: contours similar to those of a kind of linear city making reference to roads and settlements of ancient layout; areas that are densely urbanised, adhering to the pattern of the extended city; areas of minimal infrastructure built up alongside the motorways; areas of lighter parcelling and scattered settlements.

Venice's metropolitan dimension
IUAV

INSTITUTION
IUAV University, Venice

CHANCELLOR
Marino Folin

CURATOR
Marino Folin

STAFF
Isp-Iuav Studi e Progetti, Venezia (Mario Spinelli, Michele D'Accordi)

COLLABORATORS
Water and asphalt project:
Bernardo Secchi, Paola Viganò
Mobility models: Domenico Patassini
Cartografia Gis e supporto tecnico informatico /
Technical and data information systems:
Luigi Di Prinzio
Satellite images: Circe-Iuav
Giancarlo Carnevale, Bruno Dolcetta, Carlo Magnani, Matelda Reho

SPONSORS
Gruppo Guaraldo SpA, Treviso
Gruppo Poletti SpA, Trento
Compagnia Generale Ripreseaeree SpA, Parma

ACKNOWLEDGMENTS
Comune di Venezia
Provincia di Venezia
Provincia di Padova
Provincia di Treviso
Regione Veneto
Coses, Venezia
Glocalmap.to (Maurizio Cilli, Carlo Infante, Filippo Moncelli, Stefano Ruggeri, Sandro De Francesco)
Iniziative Industriali Italiane - Progetto Sky Arrow
Planetek Italia srl, Bari

1

1
Venice metropolitan area
(Formulation) by the
Università IUAV of Venice
– CIRCE using bands
7,5 and 2 of the image
landsat 7 of 8/9/2000

2

The infrastructure system

The dense road network is part of a highly urbanised context. In general progressive stratifications seem to have resulted in a system that has superimposed a radial structure converging on Venice-Mestre over the original network structure, which remains as a basic characteristic of how the system functions. At the same time, a reference commuter gravitational environment has been defined, and a loop system of crossing that ignores the geographical-settlement system.

Greater Venice is currently undergoing vast processes of structural and infrastructural change and investment. These are related to changes in various aspects of the production system and the economic base of the city itself, and to the new international positions resulting from an expanded Europe. The problem faced by Greater Venice is recognising its own metropolitan dimension and giving it an identity capable of appreciating its different component identities.

2
Venice metropolitan area
Plan anticipations
Formulation by IUAV
Studi e Progetti Srl (ISP).
© COMPAGNIA GENERALE
RIPRESEAEREE SPA.

3

4

3-4

5

5

Real-Time-Rome

And then came the grandest idea of all! We actually made a map of the country, on the scale of a mile to the mile!' 'Have you used it much?', I enquired. 'It has never been spread out, yet,' said Mein Herr: 'the farmers objected: they said it would cover the whole country, and shut out the sunlight! So we now use the country itself, as its own map, and I assure you it does nearly as well. Lewis Carroll

In today's world, wireless mobile communication devices are creating new dimensions of interconnectedness between people, places and urban infrastructure. This ubiquitous connectivity within the urban population can be observed and interpreted in real-time, through aggregate records collected from communication networks. Real-time visualisations expose the dynamics of the contemporary city as urban systems coalesce: traces of information and communication networks, movement patterns of people and transportation systems, spatial and social usage of streets and neighbourhoods. Observing the real-time city becomes a means to understanding the present and anticipating the future of urban environments.

In the visualisations of *Real-Time-Rome* we synthesise data from various real-time networks to understand patterns of daily life in Rome. We interpolate the aggregate mobility of people according to their mobile phone usage and visualise it synchronously with the flux of public transit, pedestrians and vehicular traffic. This has been made possible by the innovative Lochness platform developed by Telecom Italia. By overlaying mobility information on geographic and socio-economic references of Rome we unveil the relationships between fixed and fluid urban elements.

Real-Time-Rome respects individual privacy and only uses aggregate data already collected by communication service providers.

The real-time city has far-reaching implications for the future. A census of people's activities as they happen can allow for the real-time management of the city's resources. Transportation systems can be optimised by an immediate awareness of traffic flows. Energy and natural resources can be efficiently allocated and priced according to their precise demand and availability. In day-to-day life, urban data can be available to individuals moving about in a city through their own communication devices like mobile phones and personal digital assistants (PDAs). The real-time city could improve the quality of life in a highly sustainable way, allocating public resources dynamically in response to the fluctuations in urban conditions.

Connections
M.I.T. SENSEable City Laboratory

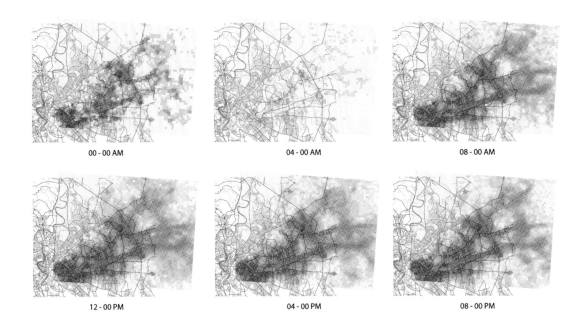

00 - 00 AM

04 - 00 AM

08 - 00 AM

12 - 00 PM

04 - 00 PM

08 - 00 PM

1

1
Cellular phone users
in north-eastern Rome
at different times of
the day.
© SENSEABLE CITY LABORATORY.

INSTITUTION
M.I.T. SENSEable City Laboratory
Department of Urban Studies and Planning
(DUSP) Massachusset Insitute of Tecnology,
Cambridge, MA, USA

DIRECTOR
Carlo Ratti

CURATOR
Andres Sevtsuk

VISUAL SOFTWARE DESIGNER
Burak Arikan

INTERACTION DESIGNER
James Patten

REAL-TIME-ROME

PRINCIPAL INVESTIGATORS
Andres Sevtsuk, Carlo Ratti

TEAM
Francesco Calabrese, Filippo Dal Fiore, Saba
Ghole, Daniel Gutierrez, Sonya Huang, Sriram
Krishnan, Justin Moe, Francisca Rojas,
Najeeb Marc Tarazi

PRINCIPAL SPONSOR
Telecom Italia

PARTNERS OF THE REAL-TIME-ROME PROJECT
City of Rome
Google
ATAC - Agenzia per la Mobilità
Taxi Samarcanda

**CONSULTANTS FOR EXHIBITION DESIGN AND
CONSTRUCTION**
carlorattiassociati – Chiara Morandini,
Walter Nicolino, Carlo Ratti, Studio Michele
Bonino

WEBSITE
www.senseable.mit.edu/realtimerome/

ZARAGOZA NEW CENTURY BUS STOP

PROJECT COORDINATOR
Assaf Biderman

TEAM
Lucie Boyce Flather, Alyson Liss, J
ames Patten, Carlo Ratti, Kenny Verbeeck

COLLABORATORS
Guy Hoffman, William J. Mitchell,
Kenneth Namkung, Scott Pobiner, James Tang

**PARTNER OF THE ZARAGOZA NEW CENTURY BUS STOP
PROJECT**
City of Zaragoza

WEBSITE
www.senseable.mit.edu/bus_stop/

ZARAGOZA DIGITAL MILE

PRINCIPAL INVESTIGATORS
Dennis Frenchman,
William J. Mitchell

FACULTY
Michael Joroff, Carlo Ratti

TEAM
Daniel Berry, Rajesh Kottamasu, Francisca
Rojas, Michal Stangel, Susanne Seitinger,
Andres Sevtsuk, Priyanka Shah, Matt Trimble,
Jake Wegmann, Albert Wei, Marlon Aranda:
exhibit designer.

WEBSITE
www.cities.media.mit.edu/

CONCEPT CAR

PRINCIPAL INVESTIGATORS
William J. Mitchell, Ryan Chin

CITY CAR TEAM
William Lark, Phil Liang, Raul-David Poblano,
Axel Kilian, Peter Schmitt, Franco Vairani,
Mitch Joachim, Ryan Chin, Susanne Seitinger,
Marcel Botha

ATHLETE CAR TEAM
Axel Kilian, Mitch Joachim, Robyn Allen, Patrik
Künzler, Raul-David Poblano, Peter Schmitt,
Franco Variani

ZERO CAR TEAM
Ryan Chin, Raul-David Poblano, Will Lark,
Phil Liang

WEBSITE
www.cities.media.mit.edu/

TANGIBLE MEDIA GROUP

DIRECTOR
Hiroshi Ishii

TEAM
Jason Alonso, Assaf Biderman, Phil Frei, Saro
Getzoyan, Rujira Hongladaromp, Seye Ojumu,
James Patten, Ben Piper, Carlo Ratti, Sandia
Ren, Yao Wang, Bo Zhu

WEBSITE
www.tangible.media.mit.edu/

SMART MOBILITY
MIT Mobile Experience Lab

PRINCIPAL INVESTIGATORS
William J. Mitchell, Federico Casalegno

TEAM
Sergio Araya, Marcel Botha, Sylvain Bruni,
Stephanie Groll, Onur Yuce Gun, William
Lark, Phillip Liang, Arnaud Pilpré, David
Raul Poblano, Susanne Seitinger, Miriam
Sorell, Tango Aaron Tang, Edgar Torres, Aaron
Zinman, and course collaborators, Ryan Chin,
David Raul Poblano, Susanne Seitinger

WEBSITE
www.mobile.mit.edu/ratp

www.mobile.mit.edu/ratp

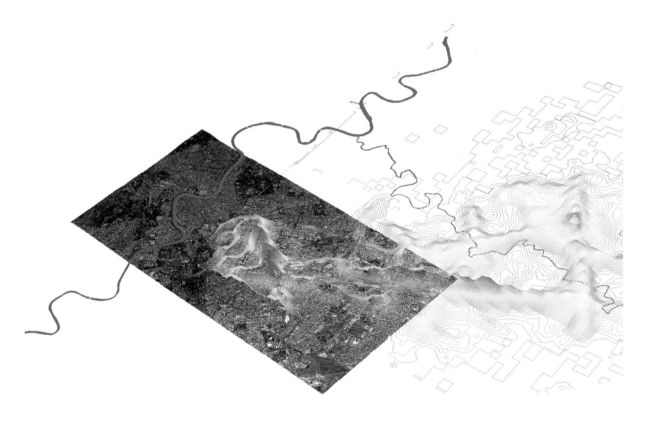

2
Real-Time-Rome
combines different
datasets in a single
interface: real-time
data, GIS data and raster
images.
© SENSEABLE CITY LABORATORY.

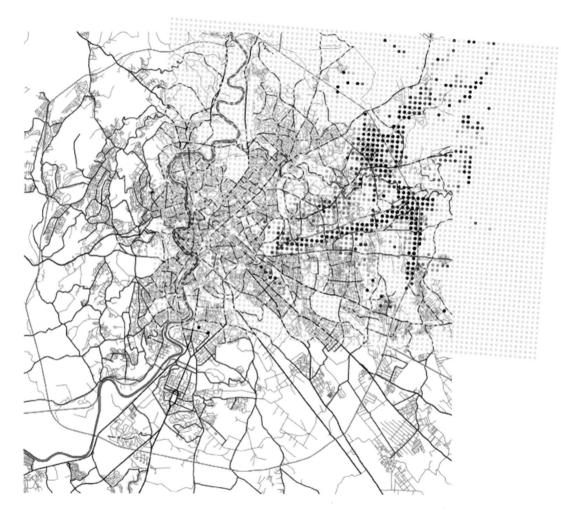

3

3
Speed of people's
movement based on
data from the cellular
network in a quadrant of
the Rome area.
© SENSEABLE CITY LABORATORY.

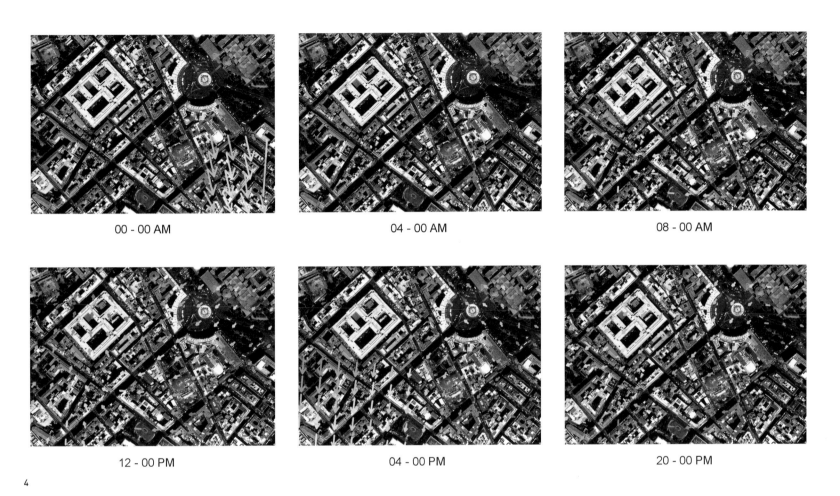

00 - 00 AM

04 - 00 AM

08 - 00 AM

12 - 00 PM

04 - 00 PM

20 - 00 PM

4

4
The movement dynamics of cellular phone users at
different times of the day in neighbourhood scale.
Area bound by San Carlo alle Quattro Fontane in the
West, the baths of Diocletian in the North, Piazza dei
Cinquecento in the East and Piazza del Viminale in
the South
© SENSEABLE CITY LABORATORY.

Maps tend to represent the eras in which they are made. These real-time visualisations of otherwise invisible networks are fundamental to our understanding of a digital culture where information and communication technologies are integral to our everyday lives.

Other projects

In addition to *Real-Time-Rome*, the SENSEable City exhibition includes additional projects developed at MIT and related to cities and technology. In particular:
- *The Zaragoza Digital Mile*. As the city is approaching the 2008 Expo, a master plan and a palette of ideas have been developed for its next strategic development, the Digital Mile. The project started during the MIT Digital Mile workshop in Fall 2005 and continued with the construction of a digitally interactive bus stop
- *Tangible Media*. A number of projects showing how the development of new tangible interfaces can highlight urban criticalities at a glance and enhance the process of design in general.
- *Concept Car and Smart Mobility*. A collaborative project which investigates the impact of vehicles on city form and redesigns them using technologically-enhanced components to satisfy the demands of the 21st century.

5

5
Cellular phone users
around the Termini
train station visualized
as a three-dimensional
interpolation.
© SENSEABLE CITY LABORATORY.

The transforming city

Both Lagos and the Arabian Coast provide examples of urban conditions that defly Western standards for urban growth. In each of these locations oil has been a vital catalyst in changing the urban landscape. Lagos rode the wave of the early 1970s oil boom, caught up in a moment of frenzied speculation by architects and engineers driven by visions of how they could change the world. Foreign architects were commissioned for large-scale projects, which generated an incredibly complex network of highways and motorways punctuated with massive pieces of modern architecture. This entire system aimed to address problems previously ignored in the rapidly expanding city. However, the oil crash and subsequent abandonment of many plans only served to worsen the conditions of a region plagued with political instability and stalling economies.

Along the Arabian Coast, AMO has identified six moment for inspection: Kuwait City, Mańama, Barahin, Doha, Qatar and Dubai; Abu Dhabi and Ra's at Kahaiman in the UAE. Each of these locations, through a mix of intra-coastal competition and self definition, has imported Western modernism and stands to re-export a new kind of urbanism through the discovery of its metropolitan ambitions.

Dubai as a significant example has managed to escape the doom of oil dependency by rapidly diversifying its economy. It has taken an independent course, investing heavily in the services industry, with aviation, finance, tourism and real estate speculation playing important roles. In a city that is constantly changing, updating itself, it has become difficult to distinguish between the various shades of newness. As the second largest construction site in the world, Dubai's buildings seem primarily designed to achieve superlatives – 'tallest', 'best', or just simply 'most'.

The populated city

With both cities representing a unique prototype of the emerging non-Western city, the interactions between the populations and their environments are crucial in understanding how these cities work.

Lagos is home to an estimated 13 million people, and is expected to be one of the world's largest cities by 2015. With its population growing by 30 people every hour, people reinvent their immediate environment, as they are forced to inhabit every available space. In the process, a spontaneous reorganization of human settlements becomes apparent, emerging within the constant friction between the formal and the informal.

The one and a half million people who live in Dubai exist in extremes - masses of low paid migrant workers from all over Asia living in sharp contrast with expatriates buying expensive timeshares. Only 1 of 6 people living in Dubai is actually from there. The concept of 'living' in Dubai takes into account a different level of commitment to one's habitation, as many who own a house in Dubai will usually have another 'home' somewhere else.

Amo's analyses of a city and a coastal region reveal new orders of regional and global competition, no longer possible to be ignored.

Lagos and the Arabian Coast
OMA-AMO

1

2

1
Dubai - potential and latency.
© OMA-AMO (FERNANDO DONIS).

2
Densification of leisure and high-rises on Dubai Beach.
© OMA-AMO (FERNANDO DONIS).

INSTITUTION
OMA-AMO

CURATOR
Rem Koolhaas

COLLABORATORS
Ademide Adelusi-Adeluyi
Samir Bantal
Tomek Bartczak
Anne-Sophie Bernard
Katrin Betschinger
Ezra Block
Reinier de Graaf
Fernando Donís

Talia Dorsey
Martin Gallovsky
Lily Jencks
Ravi Kamisetti
Julie Kaufman
Jan Knikker
Barend Koolhaas
Miho Mazereeuw
Kayoko Ota
Charles-Antoine Perreault
Daniel Rabin
William Todd Reisz
Marieke Rietbergen
Guillaume Yersin

American University of Sharjah
Natalie Al Shami
Maisa Jarjous
Sara Kasa
George Katodrytis
Banah Mustafa

Dubai Properties

WITH THE GENEROUS SUPPORT OF
The Architecture Fund (HGIS Program
from the Ministries of Foreign Affairs
and of Education, Culture and Science)
Fondazione Prada
M.H. Alshaya
RAK Promotion BoardRakeen
Development

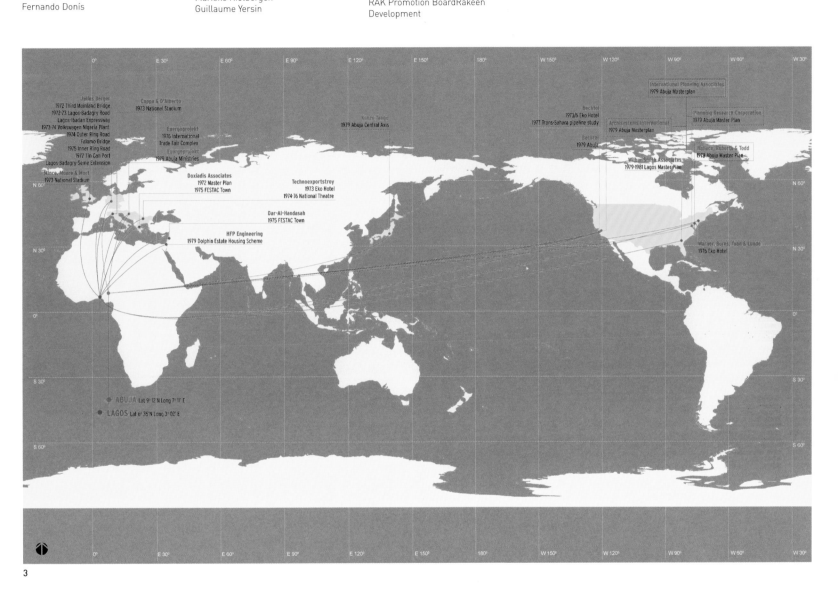

3

3
Lagos: Planning in the
1970s.
© OMA-AMO (ADEMIDE ADELUSI-
ADELUYI).

4

4
Lagos, with the
National Theatre in the
foreground.
© EDGAR CLEIJNE.

5

6

5
Lagos Island, with
the ring road under
construction.
© HARVARD UNIVERSITY/JB

6
Oshodi. A market where
even the train becomes
an accomplice in trading.
© EDGAR CLEIJNE

7

8

7
Dubai Masterplan.
© NAKHEEL LCC.

8
Lagos Island CBD.
© EDGAR CLEIJNE

Has London turned into the loft capital of Europe? Are its silly prices sustainable? Since the renaissance of the British economy that took place from the 1980s onwards, every part of London has been overhauled. Its mixed stock of historical and metropolitan buildings have been stripped of their industrial grime, refitted and adapted; new ones sparkle in a bland modernist nirvana. From the outside it looks more attractive than ever; in the foreigner's mind it's the new Manhattan. But this process is in danger of eradicating the city's inherent organic quality.

RCA/Architecture undertakes research on the architectural evolution of London. Although we're small, we are one of the most agile institutions around. Situated in the art and design environment of the Royal College, we operate within a paradigm of the creative industries that surround us. We see architecture as a key but contingent form of culture that has a dynamic relationship with everything that happens in cities. Rather than adhering to the old division between the urban and architectural scales, we consider architecture to encompass both, and its real sustenance to be the people who live in and use it. Our intention is to embrace the many languages, lifestyles and identities of the 7.5 million people who live here.

Now London is a place that belongs to the world and no longer just to Britain, and offers rewards for an infinite variety of aspirations. Although English is the official language, you can speak just about anything here, and behave as you wish. Indeed most tongues of the earth are local somewhere across London's 1,600 square kilometres. The city expects some 750,000 newcomers over the next ten years, which may not compare with the growth of Asian cities, yet London is transforming into Europe's only übercity.

RCA/A is organised into thematic areas based on specific cultural positions; together these constitute an equivalent of London's dynamic culture. The various areas of study include the ecstatic city, the city as brand environment, idiocy as modernist critique, the cross-over of underworld and overworld, sustainable futures with a selfish edge, the needs of a less stereotyped older generation, and the possibilities of the largest and most ethnically diverse city in Europe. As London expands, how do you build metropolitan intensity into those brownfield sites where none has ever existed? To get the answers to some of these questions we like to rub the city between our fingers, feel the grit and investigate how it works.

Babylon:don
Royal College of Art

1

INSTITUTION
Royal College of Art

DIRECTOR
Nigel Coates

CURATORS
Gerrard O'Carroll, Nigel Coates

STAFF
Michael Chadwick, Ruth Dillon, Clive
Sall, Fiona Scott, Payam Sharifi

COLLABORATORS
Jon Dallas, Joel Dunmore, Jordy Fu,
Andrea Goecke, Tomas Klassnik,
Nicola Koller, Marianne Kudlich, Tanya
Rainsley, Jason Scoot, Tim Simpson,
Finn Williams

SPONSORS
British Council
Concrete Centre
Slamp S.p.A.

CONTRIBUTING TUTORS
Roberto Bottazzi, Barbara Campbell-
Lange, Diana Cochrane, Fenella
Collingridge, Bobby Desai, Jeremy
Myerson, Mark Prizeman, Fiona Raby,
Domenico Raimondo

EXHIBITION PRODUCTION
Celeste Channer-Nelson, Nick Grace,
Lucy Pengilley, David Chambers, Kevin
Haley, Jake Moulson, Will Newton,
Euan Watson, Melanie Williams,
Models provided by Rapidform RCA a
partner in Exchange.

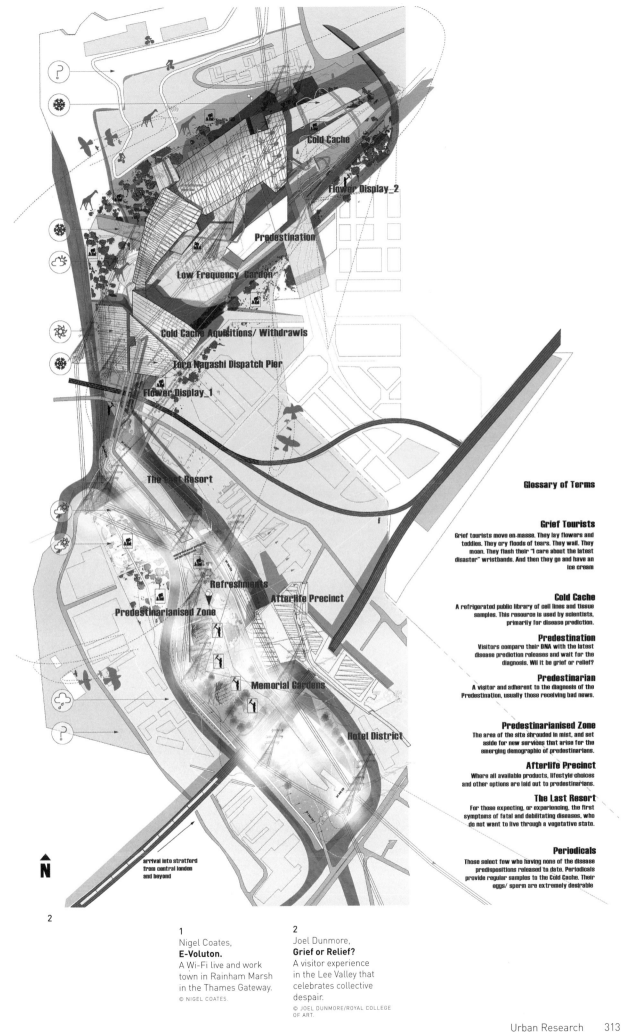

Glossary of Terms

Grief Tourists
Grief tourists move en-masse. They lay flowers and teddies. They cry floods of tears. They wail. They moan. They flash their "I care about the latest disaster" wristbands. And then they go and have an ice cream

Cold Cache
A refrigerated public library of cell lines and tissue samples. This resource is used by scientists, primarily for disease prediction.

Predestination
Visitors compare their DNA with the latest disease prediction releases and wait for the diagnosis. Will it be grief or relief?

Predestinarian
A visitor and adherent to the diagnosis of the Predestination, usually those receiving bad news.

Predestinarianised Zone
The area of the site shrouded in mist, and set aside for new services that arise for the emerging demographic of predestinarians.

Afterlife Precinct
Where all available products, lifestyle choices and other options are laid out to predestinarians.

The Last Resort
For those expecting, or experiencing, the first symptoms of fatal and debilitating diseases, who do not want to live through a vegetative state.

Periodicals
Those select few who having none of the disease predispositions released to date. Periodicals provide regular samples to the Cold Cache. Their eggs/ sperm are extremely desirable

arrival into stratford
from central london
and beyond

2

1
Nigel Coates,
E-Voluton.
A Wi-Fi live and work
town in Rainham Marsh
in the Thames Gateway.
© NIGEL COATES.

2
Joel Dunmore,
Grief or Relief?
A visitor experience
in the Lee Valley that
celebrates collective
despair.
© JOEL DUNMORE/ROYAL COLLEGE
OF ART.

3

4

3
Jordy Fu,
Family®.
Open plan living on a
neighborhood scale
in a disused quarry in
Dartford.
© JOEL DUNMORE/ROYAL COLLEGE
OF ART.

4
James Wyman,
Bargain Basement.
Regenerating a defunct
public housing scheme,
the Kings Cross Estate
in Somers Town.
© JAMES WYMAN/ROYAL COLLEGE
OF ART.

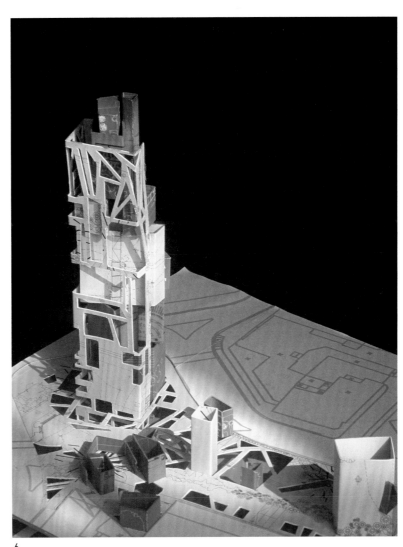

5

6

For the 10th Architecture Biennale, we have brought together recent research projects related to some of these themes. Most of these suggest ways of evolving or sustaining London, or at least correspond to what it would like to be. Yet rather than assuming that architecture adheres to a positivist role, sometimes these result in critiques intended to accentuate the identity of their users.

Projects are component parts of Babylon:don; a library of speculative projects with a high probability factor. For the most part, they use narrative design techniques and present themselves as realities that have compressed their conjecture into the present. They have the intermediary quality of what Brian Hatton called the 'mightlihood'. Visitors are asked to consider these individually as well as how they might affect one another. Even more important: how might one live in them and use them? To this end, you are asked to imagine and combine the various components of the show into your own hybrid inventions.

Nigel Coates

5
Andrea Goecke,
Cute Politics.
Local political parties
help shape the new town
hall in Lewisham.
© ANDREA GOECKE/ROYAL
COLLEGE OF ART.

6
Clive Sall,
Brand New Futures.
A multi-use tower at Old
St roundabout combines
a school, retail, offices
and penthouses.
© SCABAL.

Whether in the United States, Britain, Belgium, Finland or Italy, Russia, Kazakhstan or China, shrinking cities can be found around the globe. This situation challenges accepted notions about cities and urban development. Neighbourhoods, cities and entire regions are being drained of their population and jobs, leaving behind those who have lost out after the transition from Fordist industrial production to a society governed by globalised service industries. Dramatic changes in eastern Germany since 1989, for example, have led to the vacancy of more than one million apartments and the abandonment of innumerable industrial complexes, as well as social and cultural facilities.

While current debate is focused on the phenomenon of ever-growing megalopolises, the parallel existence of zones of shrinkage seems to have evaded public attention. Urban and regional areas have been equally affected, with the loss of millions of people and rampant unemployment. Predicted demographic trends for many countries will precipitate further polarisation in decades to come. Shrinking cities contradict the notion, well-established since the Industrial Revolution, of cities as 'boom towns' and engines of economic and demographic growth. Shrinking cities provoke us to reconsider the future of urbanism.

The epoch of modernity was characterised by comprehensive growth, and this growth lies at the heart of modern ideas, concepts, theories, laws and practices. For the past two hundred years, city planning has been almost exclusively focused on the process of growth. This historical epoch is approaching its demise. Polarisation is taking place spatially as well as socially: not everyone profits from growth and societies are increasingly divided into winners and losers. Shrinkage in one place feeds growth in another.

The process of shrinkage is not simply a reversal of growth. Rather, the growth is replaced by a sideward drift of societies, whereby the opposite trends of growth and shrinkage can run in parallel.

The shrinking of cities is an unintentional phenomenon. It is an unplanned side effect, the indirect result of political and economic decisions, circumstances and processes that lie beyond the spheres of architecture and urban planning. Previous attempts to shape the process of shrinkage have been inadequate and have often failed because the conventional means and tools of city planning and urban development are not able to tackle the problem.

This means two things. First, the factors in a given society that cause or significantly influence the process of shrinkage must be examined. The discussion thus moves away from the discourse of urban planning and toward a dialogue on values and political questions, which can lead to other ways of approaching the issues.

Secondly, urban designers are used to developing a city by undertaking construction - of infrastructures, districts, buildings. But shrinkage is a form of urban transformation that occurs in a radical manner without any initial changes in the physical space in which it occurs. This raises the questions of whether the relationship between space and utilisation should be rethought and whether the ideas of space and utilisation themselves should be rethought. The question also arises as to whether or not there may be other forms of intervention in addition to the classic mode of development-through-construction that can influence the way a city develops.
Philipp Oswalt

Shrinking Cities
Project Office Philipp Oswalt

INSTITUTION
Shrinking Cities, Project Office Philipp Oswalt

DIRECTOR
Philipp Oswalt

CURATOR
Philipp Oswalt

STAFF
Elke Beyer, Anke Hagemann, Anita Kaspar, Tim Rieniets, Füsun Türetken with the assitsance of Gabi Eisenreich and Giovanni Piovene (Researchers); Anita Kaspar and Nicole Minten-Jung (Coordination); Florian Bolenius, Peter Boragno, Nicole Minten-Jung (Management); Tanja Wesse, Hansjakob Fehr/ 1kilo (Graphic Design); stadtimbild/ Christoph Petras (Fotography); Olaf Augele (Sound); atelier 35, Jacob von Dohnanyi (Exhibition installation); 1kilo, Antje Ehmann/ Michael Baute/ Harun Farocki, Albrecht Schäfer and Sybil Kohl (Additional art work)

COLLABORATORS
Tanja Wess, Hans-Jakob Fehr / 1 kilo (graphic design); Stadtimbild/ Christoph Petras (photography); Atelier 35, Jakob von Dohnanyi (exhibition installation); Art work by Antje Ehmann/ Michael Bauten/ Harun Farocki, Albrecht Schäfer, 1 kilo.

SPONSOR
Kulturstiftung des Bundes

ACKNOWLEDGMENTS
Shrinking Cities is a project of the German Federal Cultural Foundation (Kulturstiftung des Bundes) in cooperation with Project Office Philipp Oswalt, Museum for Contemporary Art Leipzig, the Bauhaus Dessau Foundation, and the magazine archplus. Member of the curatorial team included Walter Prigge, Barbara Steiner, Nikolaus Kuhnert and Kyong Park.

1
PROJECT OFFICE BY PHILIPP OSWALT, BERLIN, PROCESSOR: TIM RIENIETS, GRAPHIK: 1KILO

Population growth of selected cities and agglomerations in %/year

Source: UN, 2002

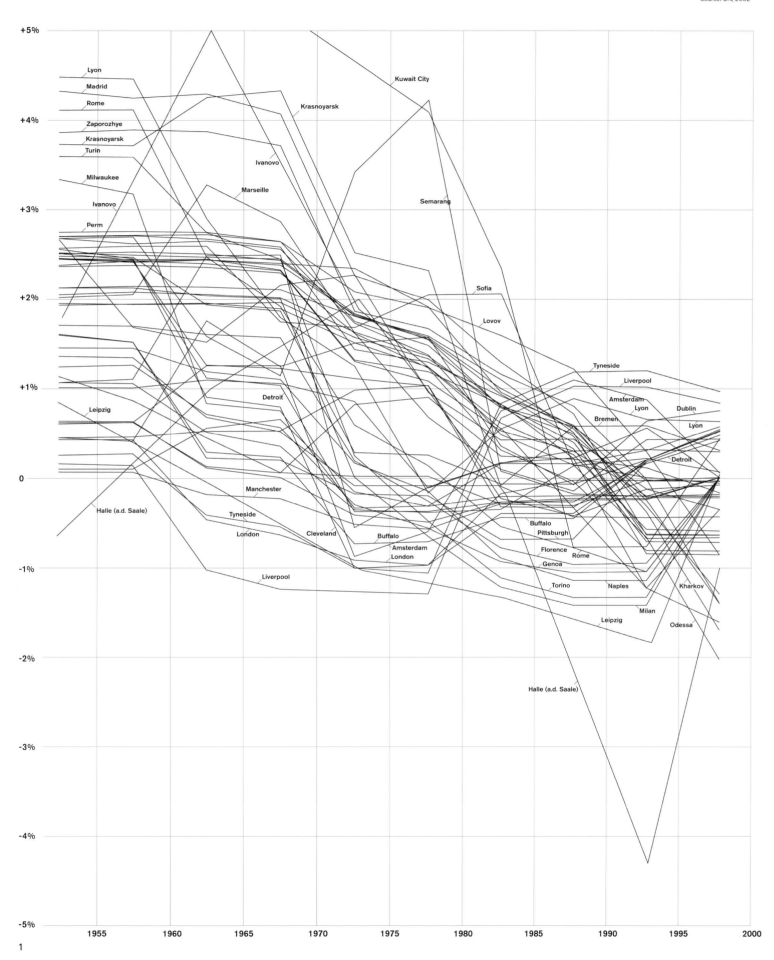

WORLD MAP OF SHRINKING CITIES

Cities with more than 100,000 inhabitants (selection)
Temporary or permanent population loss of more than 10%

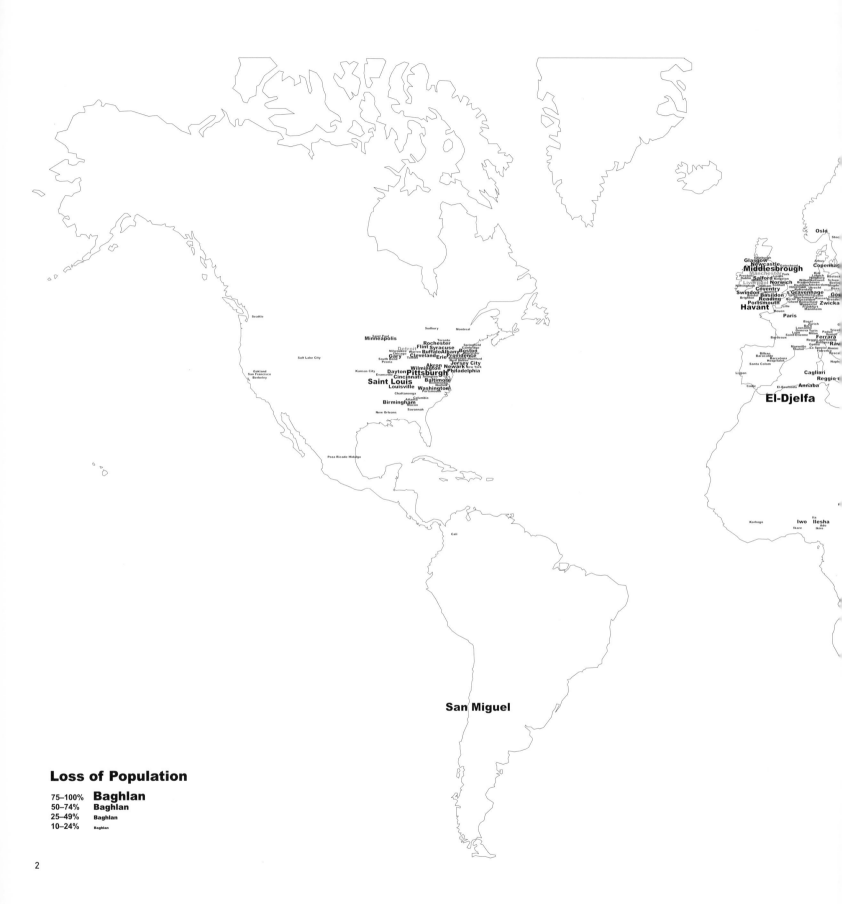

Loss of Population

75–100%	**Baghlan**
50–74%	**Baghlan**
25–49%	Baghlan
10–24%	Baghlan

Murmansk
Arkhangelsk
Vorkuta
Norilsk

Berezniki
Nizhny Tagil
Pervouralsk
Zlatoust
Kopeysk
Qizilar
Kökshetau
Rudny
Serpukhov
Krasnoturinsk
Andzhero-Sudzhensk
Leninsk-Kuznetski
Belovo
Kiselevsk
Prokopevsk
Cheremkhovo
Chita

Temirtau
Qaraghandy
Semey
Oskemen
Pavlodar
Oral
Jezqazghan

Kramatorsk
Slovyansk
Artemivsk
Yenakiyevo
Konstantynivka
Dniprorudne
Krasny Luch
Makiyivka
Horlivka
Berdyansk
Sverdlovsk
Kerch
Qiqihar

Taldykorgan
Symkent
Almaty
Tieling
Kimch'aek
Dandong
Hamhung
Wonsan
Otaru
Muroran

Sukhumi
Samarqand
Zhangjiakou
Hiroshima

Vanadzor
Kumajri
Taiyuan
Tangshan
Tanjin
Zibo
Dalian
Kaesong
Masan
Tokyo
Amagasaki
Nagasaki
Kure
Osaka

Kunduz
Baghlan
Shangqiu
Ōmuta
Yamaguchi
Miyakonojo

Tel Aviv-Yafo
Basra
Abadan
Qandahar
Amritsar
Nanchong
Chengdu
Neijiang
Yibin
Jinzhou
Yangzhou
Chao'an
Khorramshahr
Hawalli
Hufuf
Guiyang
Kunming
Guangzhou
Taizhou
Fuchou
Shantou

Narayanganj
Dum Dum
Nanning
Haikou

Asmera
Ta'izz
Kolâr Gold Fields
Huê
Đà Nẵng
Qui Nho'n
Nha Trang
Chon Buri
Phnom Penh
Manila

Pekalongan
Tegal
Cilacap

gs
an
oni
ging

don

2
The world map of
shrinking cities shows
which big cities (starting
populations more than
100,000 residents) have
shrunk in the last fifty
years.
PROJECT OFFICE BY PHILIPP
OSWALT, BERLIN. PROCESSOR: TIM
RIENIETS. GRAPHIK: 1KILO.

Periods of Shrinkage   1900–2000

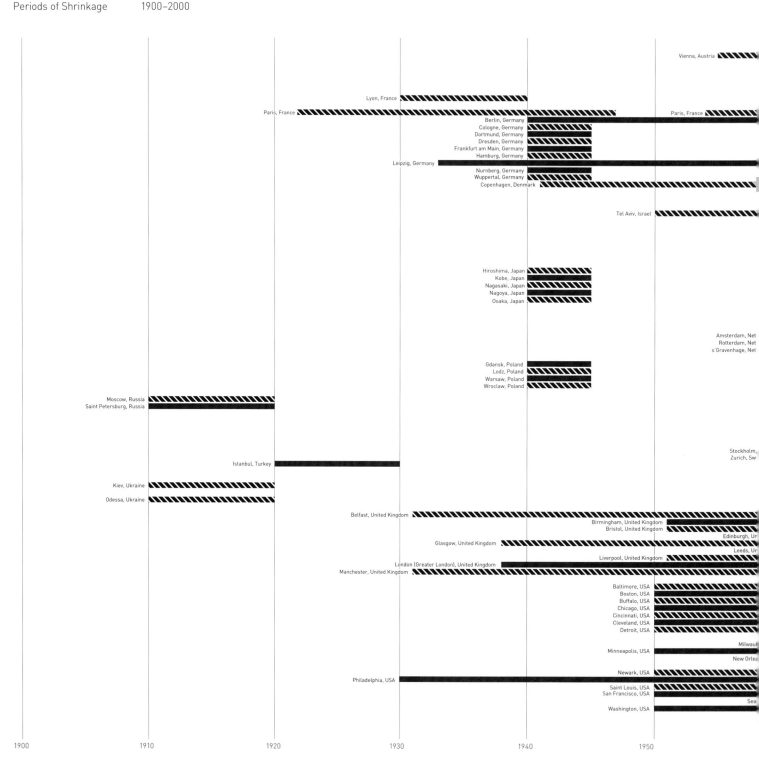

Shrinking cities of more than 400 000 inhabitants.
Short-term population losses (more than 1%/year) or ongoing population losses (more than 10%).

Source: Shrinking Cities, 2006

3

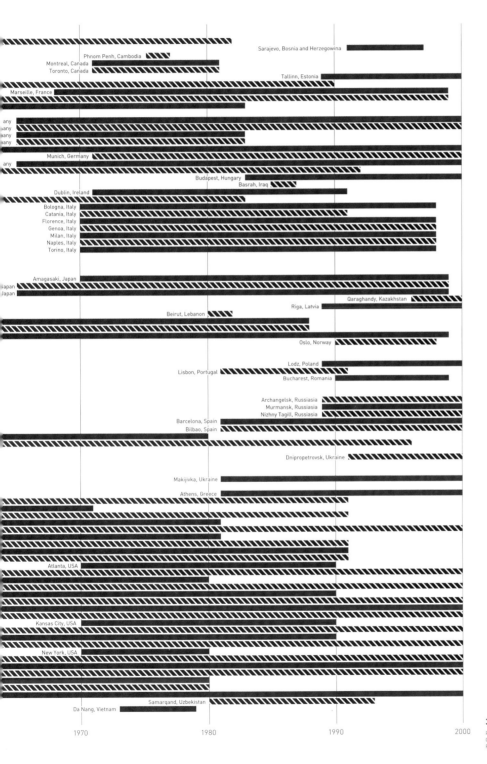

Sarajevo, Bosnia and Herzegowina

Phnom Penh, Cambodia
Montreal, Canada
Toronto, Canada
Tallinn, Estonia
Marseille, France

any
any
any
any
Munich, Germany
any
Budapest, Hungary
Basrah, Iraq
Dublin, Ireland
Bologna, Italy
Catania, Italy
Florence, Italy
Genoa, Italy
Milan, Italy
Naples, Italy
Torino, Italy

Amagasaki, Japan
Japan
Japan
Qaraghandy, Kazakhstan
Riga, Latvia
Beirut, Lebanon

Oslo, Norway

Lodz, Poland
Lisbon, Portugal
Bucharest, Romania

Archangelsk, Russiasia
Murmansk, Russiasia
Nizhny Tagill, Russiasia
Barcelona, Spain
Bilbao, Spain

Dnipropetrovsk, Ukraine

Makijivka, Ukraine
Athens, Greece

Atlanta, USA

Kansas City, USA

New York, USA

Samarqand, Uzbekistan
Da Nang, Vietnam

1970   1980   1990   2000

3
PROJECT OFFICE BY PHILIPP
OSWALT, BERLIN, PROCESSOR: TIM
RIENIETS, GRAPHIK: 1KILO

4

5

6-7 Manchester Hulme, c. 1956.

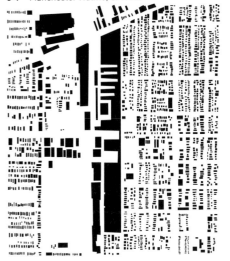

8-9 Manchester Hulme, c. 1985.

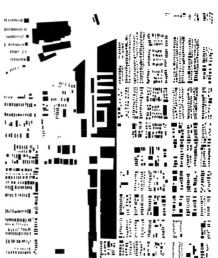

10 Manchester Hulme, c. 2000.

11 Detroit neighbourhood, c. 1950

12 Detroit neighbourhood, c. 1960.

13 Detroit neighbourhood, c. 1970.

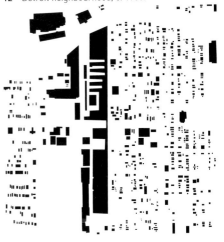

14 Detroit neighbourhood, c. 1990.

15 Detroit neighbourhood, c. 2000.

6-15
While the neighbourhood in Detroit shows the slow, but drastic deterioration of the city by abandonment (parallel to an overall growth of the metropolitan region), the case of Hulme in Manchester shows a planned shrinkage by double *tabula rasa*: the Victorian housing was demolished by a slum clearance project in the 1960s; the succeeding Crescents where themselves erased only 22 years after their construction. Today the Hulme area is partly vacant, partly covered by post-modern housing blocks built since the late 1990s.
COURTESY PROJECT OFFICE PHILIPP OSWALT.

Prospects between the archive and the map

Mexico City's specific history and geography and its condition as a metropolis *becoming*, make it a privileged site for inquiry and action for the students and faculty at the Iberoamericana University's School of Architecture (Ibero). It offers a complex intellectual and geographic terrain that affords various opportunities to engage in active discourse on the city.

The forms of urban work and research developed in design studios and urban seminars at the Ibero seem to follow the notion of *potentiality*: the contradictions, conflicts, mishaps, fragilities, shortcomings, specific geographies and conditions not only provide the raw material with which we operate in the city today, but are also its biggest asset for a renewed and effective urban practice.

These new conditions demand an adjustment in the priorities, strategies, methods, readings and inscriptions that architecture has with regards to a specific place. In short, they require from architects a whole new range of tools with which to address the issues at hand.

We maintain that the techniques, methods and forms of understanding urban phenomena in a place such as Mexico City have to be reformulated to achieve more effective instrumentality. These new tools include alternative processes of representation, new methods of registering urban phenomena, the discovery of (new and old) genealogies, and an understanding of complex temporal, social and political phenomena. Furthermore, the effectiveness of these tools necessitates the establishment of new forms of intervention, planning, strategy and action.

The present conditions, and their unavoidable acceptance, coupled with new modes of inquiry, place the architect at both ends of the professional spectrum: as an archivist, concerned with histories, and as a cartographer, concerned with geographies. It is at the intersection of these two practices that the potentiality of the urban prospect emerges; a prospect in which conditions are exploited, negotiated or subverted and spaces are transformed.

The combination of map, archive and prospect allows for material, formal, organisational, and intellectual speculations on the potentials of a city *becoming*. These speculations combine critical and pragmatic positions, but, most importantly, they recognise that the long-term and comprehensive conditions usually associated with traditional urban planning give way, in Mexico City, to the immediate, the short term, the quick-fix, the *post-de-facto*, and the fragmented. As Carlos Monsivais would put it, 'the fleeting remains'.

Mexico City: the space of potentiality
Universidad Iberoamericana, School of Architecture

INSTITUTION
Universidad Iberoamericana's School
of Architecture

DEAN
Jose Luis Cortés

ACADEMIC COORDINATION
Luis de Villafranca

EXHIBITION COORDINATION
Jose Castillo + Alejandro Hernandez

RESEARCHERS
Tatiana Bilbao, Fernanda Canales,
Enrique Martín Moreno, Armando
Oliver, Arturo Ortiz, Michel Rojkind,
Juan Carlos Tello

1

2

1
Canal de las Sales,
Ecatepec, Mexico City.
An open sewage canal
marking the limits
between informal
housing and Texcoco
Lake.
PHOTO BY JOSE CASTILLO/FDU.

2
Valle de Chalco,
Mexico City. A major
highway and an open
sewage canal on the
eastern section of
Mexico City.
PHOTO BY JOSE CASTILLO/FDU.

Urban Research   325

3

4

3
Periférico: The elevated highway.

PHOTO BY IVAN CERVANTES/
ARQUITECTURA 911SC.

4
Santa Fe district, Mexico City. The new business and high end residential district of Santa Fe, developed on former landfills and sand mines on the western section of Mexico City.

PHOTO BY PAMELA PUCHALSKI

PATTERNS AND DENSITY

Although perceptions of Mexico City as one of the most populated cities in the world prevail, the city lacks far behind other cities like New York, Hong Kong, with an overall density of 116 inhabitants per hectare. What is remarkable is on the one hand the diversity of urban patterns found in the city, and their relationship to densification. Three out of the four areas with the highest densities in the city are tight-knit patterns with low-rise/high-occupancy usually informally developed without any state approval or planning. Although population grew exponentially in the second half of the 20th century, overall density remained quite constant, even though areas such as the historic center have decreased their density considerably.

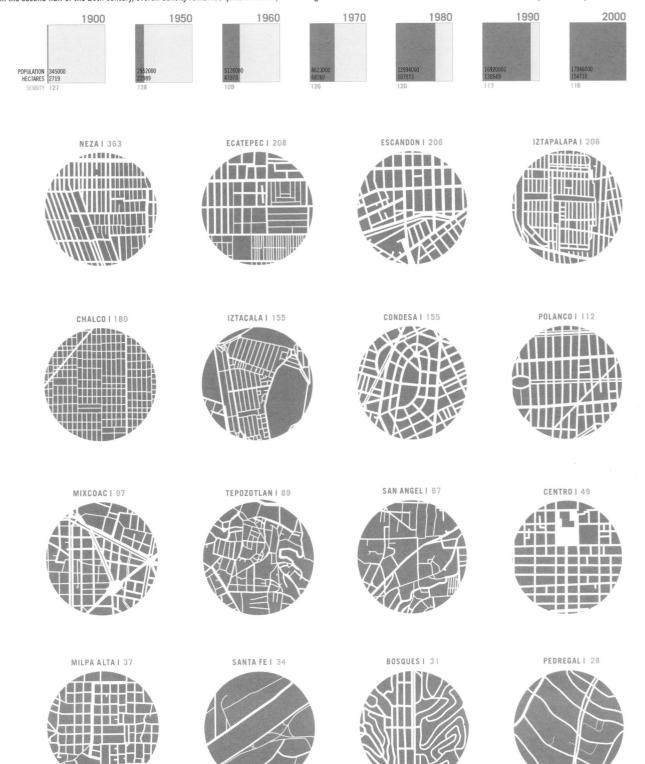

	1900	1950	1960	1970	1980	1990	2000
POPULATION	345000	2952000	5126000	8623000	12994000	16920000	17946000
HECTARES	2719	22989	47070	68260	107973	130549	154710
DENSITY	127	128	109	126	120	117	116

NEZA I 363 ECATEPEC I 208 ESCANDON I 206 IZTAPALAPA I 206

CHALCO I 180 IZTACALA I 155 CONDESA I 155 POLANCO I 112

MIXCOAC I 97 TEPOZOTLAN I 89 SAN ANGEL I 67 CENTRO I 49

MILPA ALTA I 37 SANTA FE I 34 BOSQUES I 31 PEDREGAL I 28

5
Patterns and Density.
COURTESY ARQUITECTURA
911SC+AHG.

5

6

7

6
Reforma Avenue, Mexico
City. The central busi-
ness corridor connecting
the historic center to
the western section of
Mexico City.
PHOTO BY MICHAEL CALDERWOOD.

7
Informal street vendors
in Correo Mayor Street
on the Historic Centre,
Mexico City. The endless
array of umbrellas and
shades marking the
absolute takeover of the
street by the informal
vendors in the historic
center of the city.
PHOTO BY JOSE CASTILLO.

The Gulf Coast has been battered by major hurricanes every year since 1994. In 2005 there were 26 named storms, including 14 hurricanes and 7 major hurricanes. On 29 August *Katrina* came to shore with winds of 230 km/h and a storm surge of over 10 meters, impacting more than 260,000 km[2] (the area of Italy).

This force of nature left 527,000 people homeless, resulted in 1,299 casualties, and caused over $250 billion in damages. More than 80 km[2] of marshland in Louisiana and 25% of the marshes in Mississippi were lost. For 2006, there is an 81% chance that a major hurricane will hit the Gulf Coast[1].

The Gulf Coast is one of 11 very large, rapidly growing 'megapolitan areas' in the USA. Among other characteristics, a 'megapolitan area'[2] combines at least two existing metropolitan areas, will total more than ten million residents by 2040, derives from contiguous metropolitan and micropolitan areas and constitutes an organic cultural region with a distinct history and identity.

The ability for urban areas to rebound from disaster is termed 'resilience,' a concept with growing appeal in the disciplines of ecology and planning, emphasizing equilibrium and stability. Most recently, the definition emerges from 'new ecology,' focusing on non-equilibrium and the adaptability of ecological systems. The latter is appropriate 'to urban ecosystems, because it suggests that spatial heterogeneity is an important component of the persistence of adaptable metropolitan regions'[3]. Cities are anything but stable and predictable systems. Marc Morial, former New Orleans mayor, notes that the challenge we face 'is not only about rebuilding New Orleans and the Gulf Coast, it is about rebuilding a culture, a human system.'

Curatorial efforts at The University of Texas at Austin, School of Architecture, are not so much an assembly of answers but a report on cultural, meteorological, and other natural forces that should be reckoned with in future scenarios for the Gulf Coast.

Geologists, landscape ecologists, transportation planners, urban designers, architects, landscape architects, water resource specialists, demographers and regional planners provide an examination of the megapolitan area at three scales – the building, the city and the region, during three periods – the past, the present (*Katrina* and aftermath) and the future.

The exhibition sets out the resilient foundations for the region's development. These do not represent proposals by the authorities that be, but rather are the result of independent analysis. Not everyone's expectations or needs will be satisfied, perhaps least of all those who have been most severely afflicted. Yet to reconstruct buildings and cities purely for the reestablishment of the physical fabric cannot be in anyone's long-term interest.

Ecological understanding can be advanced through mapping and design, but such generative prospects are only part of a larger concept about people's interrelation with land and water. *Katrina's* lessons will reduce the loss of life and property only if we reduce the impact of that which nature will reclaim regardless of our permission.

1 F. Steiner, B. Faga, J. Sipes and R. Yaro, *Taking a Longer View: Mapping for Sustainable Resilience*, in E.L. Birch and S. Wachter, eds,. *Rebuilding Urban Places after Disaster: Lessons from Hurricane Katrina*, Philadelphia, University of Pennsylvania Press, 2006.
2 R. Lang, *Katrina's Impact on New Orleans and the Gulf Coast Megapolitan Area*, in E.L. Birch and S.M. Wachter eds., *Rebuilding Urban Places after Disaster: Lessons from Hurricane Katrina*, Philadelphia, University of Pennsylvania Press, 2006.
3 S.T.A. Pickett and M.L. Cadenasso, *Integrating the Ecological, Socioeconomic, and Planning Realms: Insights from the Baltimore Ecosystem Study*, in L. Musacchio, J. Wu and T. Johnson, eds., *Pattern, Process, Scale, and Hierarchy: Advancing Interdisciplinary Collaboration for Creating Sustainable Urban Landscapes and Communities*, Tempe, Arizona State University, 2003.

Searching for resilient foundations: The Gulf Coast after Katrina
The University of Texas at Austin

INSTITUTION
The University of Texas at Austin
School of Architecture

DIRECTORE
Frederick Steiner

CURATORS
Kevin Alter, Larry Doll, Barbara Hoidn, Jason Sowell, Frederick Steiner, Wilfried Wang, Nichole Wiedemann

RISEARCHERS
Craig E. Colten, Barbara Faga, Reed Kroloff, James Sipes, Bob Yaro
The Resilient Foundation Team:
Jason Sowell, Nichole Wiedemann
Rachel Brown, Clayton Fry, Frank Jacobus, Brett Koenig, Jimmy Luu, Lindsey Moyer, Lynn Petermann, Agustina Rodriguez, Andrea Schelly, Lee Ulmer, Aimee Weber, Kristine Weimer

UNIVERSITY CONTRIBUTORS
Columbia University: Laurie Hawkinson, Lee Ledbetter with Lindsay Smith, Eric Cadora, David Reinfurt, Sarah Williams, Leah Meisterlin, Clare Newman
Cornell University: Jeffrey M. Chusid
Harvard University: Joan Busquets, Felipe Correa, and Ila Berman, Brad Bell of the Tulane School of Architecture
Kansas State University, Project Locus: Patrick Rhodes, Larry Brown, Melissa Coleman, Yuruani LaFontaine, Jorge Marien, Michael Rank, Deepak Tolani
Parsons The New School for Design, The Design Workshop: David J. Lewis, Terry Erickson, Joel Stoehr, Martha Murphy (client), SHoP Architects, PC (architect of record), Dunne & Markis (structural design), Compton Engineering, P.A. (civil/structural engineering), Hargrove and Associates
Princeton University University of Pennsylvania: Anthoney Fontenot with Jakob Rosenzweig, Anne Schmidt
Tulane University URBANbuild: Byron Mouton, Ila Berman, Alan Lewis of Tulane City Center, Doug Harmon of CITYbuild, Dan Etheridge of Tulane City Center, Sam Richards; Lauren Anderson, Randy Michaelson of Neighborhood Housing Services

University of Southern California, Urban Design Lab: Deborah Torres, Ferdinand Lewis, Jason Neville
University of Texas at Austin, BASIC Initiative : Art Center of Design, Design Corps, Mercy Crops/The Green Project, The Rose Fellowship Program, Tulane University, The University of Texas at Austin: James Adamson, Bryan Bell, David Mocarski, Sergio Palleroni, Peter Spruance

PROFESSIONAL CONTRIBUTORS
Fregonese Calthorpe Associates: John A. Fregonese, Glen Bolen, Scott C. Fregonese
emerymcclure architecture, l.l.c.: Ursula Emery McClure, Emery McClure, Michael A. McClure
fieldoffice: Doug Hecker, Martha Skinner, Marc Leverant; Alpine Engineering Products, Tim Takacs, Tripp Massengill, Glenn Traylor; Clemson University, David Sharpe
Wallace Roberts & Todd, l.l.c.: John Beckman for the Bring New Orleans Back Commission, Mel Lagarde, Barbara Major

SPONSORS
The University of Texas at Austin
Pelli Clarke Pelli Architects
Abbe and Michael McCall
Cindy and Howard Rachofsky
The University Co-operative Society
Apple Computers Europe
ACKNOWLEDGMENTS
Regional Plan Association; EDAW; ESRI; ASLA; The Dallas Morning News; Sarah Gamble; CITYbuild Consortium of Schools; David Gregor, and Irene Keil; Randall Charbeneau; The University of Texas at Austin: Center for Space Research, Department of Geography and the Environment, Paul Hudson; Information Technology Office, School of Architecture: Tisha Alvarado, Eric Hepburn, Kate Holiday

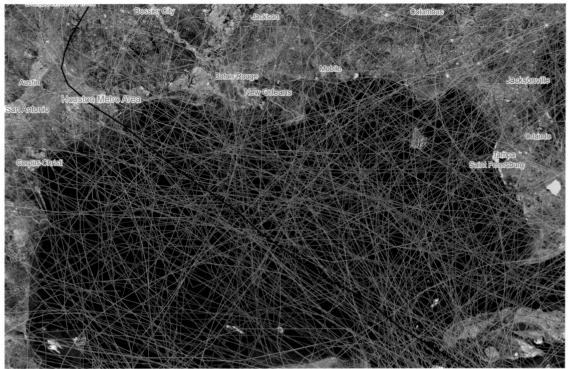

1

2

1
Severe Storms in the Gulf of Mexico, 1851 to 2000. NOAA's Historical Hurricane Tracks tool is an interactive mapping application that allows you to search and display information about hurricanes in the Gulf Coast and along the eastern seaboard. This map, showing all of the severe storms that hit the Gulf Coast from 1851 to 2000, helps illustrate the potential danger associated with living in the region. COURTESY EDAW.

2
Hurricane Katrina 14:45 UTC 29 August 2005. GOES-12 visible channel over a MODIS true-color background.
COURTESY GOES PROJECT NASA-GSFC.

3

3
08.30.05 – New Orleans, LA. A patchwork of roofs pushed through the floodwaters east of downtown, one day after Hurricane Katrina's march through the Crescent City. Flood-waters left the city a horrific mix of struggling humanity and swamped infrastructure.
PHOTO BY SMILEY N. POOL, THE DALLAS MORNING NEWS.

4
09.05.05 – New Orleans, LA. An armed search and rescue team mo-tored down North Miro Street near Interstate 10 looking for survivors. The Crescent City Connection (Highway 90 toll bridge) in top background was one of the few remaining ways into New Orleans after the storm.
PHOTO BY TOM FOX, THE DALLAS MORNING NEWS

4

5

5
Lower Ninth Ward
- truck and green
house_20051211.
PHOTO BY IRENE KEIL.

6

7

6
09.18.05 – Home Place, LA. Ms. Vogt took a breather from cleaning out her damaged house.
PHOTO BY ERICH SCHLEGEL, THE DALLAS MORNING NEWS.

7
U Loot New Orleans.
PHOTO BY DAVID GREGOR.

8

8
New Orleans - Veterans
Hospital.
PHOTO BY DAVID GREGOR.

The Urban Design Research Institute (UDRI)'s entry to the 10th Venice Architecture Biennale engages both the discrepancies between and the felicities of prescribed official land-use policy and actual practice on the scale of the personal user, developer, city planner and nation-wide Indian political concerns. Our exhibition presents the poetic, invigorating and enraging evidence of these competing agencies and the resulting silences, voids and relics in Mumbai's built environment.

The island of Mumbai is the site of a continuous and dynamic negotiation between the agencies and inhabitants of the city and their perceived rights to occupy and use the land - both built and un-built areas and the surrounding waters. Together the democratic institutions and the *demos*, the citizens, help create Mumbai's present day situation. Here land, coast and sea are not only subject to well-intentioned or arbitrary regulations, but also to the exigencies of the citizens' needs; strategies of land use and regulation are re-invented by variously cooperative and conflicting citizens

and state, from reuse to disuse, from complete abandonment to natural forces, to complete overhaul by human intention. Blurred boundaries, shifted and shifting edges, non-existent buildings, hyper and ghost developments cheek by jowl defy the logic of the plan as a prescriptive tool for land management and reveal the limitations of unilateral land-use planning.

To honour the participatory ideal of democracy, and to acknowledge the multiple oscillations of Mumbai from entopic to ectopic states, the UDRI is sponsoring two projects: a film and built-space installation and an essay and research 'catalogue' in the format of a multi-media CD and limited edition printing. Each will examine the silences, voids and relics of Mumbai from various points of view. Each will be produced as a collaborative effort of Mumbai citizenry, from architect and urban planner to artist, filmmaker, musician, journalist, archaeologist, historian and ordinary folk of Mumbai.

Mumbai's Land:
Between the relic and the void
Urban Design Research Institute (UDRI)

1

INSTITUTION
Urban Design Research Institute, Mumbai

CURATORS
Neha Choksi & Kapil Gupta (installations);
Pankaj Joshi, Rahul Mehrotra (catalogue).

STAFF
Benita Menezes, Samir Parker, Prasad Shetty,
architects of Contemporary Urban

COLLABORATORS
Ashim Ahluwalia, Shumona Goel

SPONSORS
Jindal South West Foundation
Roshni Design Foundation
Masters Project Management & SaffronArt

2

1-2
Production stills from
untitled film, 2003-2006.
PHOTO COURTESY NEHA CHOKSI.

3

4

5

3

One of many buildings in Mumbai that lies officially unoccupied due to questionable legality. This building in the Banganga neighbourhood has been partially taken over by squatters over the last two decades.

PHOTO BY NEHA CHOKSI AND KAPIL GUPTA.

4
Another building in Mumbai that lies officially unoccupied due to questionable legality. For several decades watchmen have stringently guarded this building in the Breach Candy neighbourhood after having the top eight stores demolished by the local authorities.
PHOTO BY KAPIL GUPTA.

5
A couple of sites marked as Recreation Grounds (RG) on the Mumbai Development Plan that actually has a playground on it. Most have long-standing buildings or encroachments occupying land designated as RG.
PHOTO BY NEHA CHOKSI AND SHUMONA GOEL.

6
Recreation Ground that
had trees planted on
it in 2005. By mid 2006
all were decidedly dead
save one.
PHOTO BY NEHA CHOKSI AND
SHUMONA GOEL.

7
Production stills from
untitled film, 2003-2006.
PHOTO COURTESY NEHA CHOKSI.

8

8
Pratibha Apartments.
PHOTO COURTESY KAPIL GUPTA.

Venice SuperBlog

Venice SuperBlog is a new concept for the 2006 Venice Architecture Biennale.

It is a site of debate, reaction and news in the heart of the world's largest architecture festival. It gathers, provokes and broadcasts the most exciting events and the best ideas of the greatest and smartest minds in contemporary architecture.

It is a portal between the Biennale and the world.

Curated by The Architecture Foundation in London and the Department of Architecture and Design of The Museum of Modern Art in New York, *Venice SuperBlog* has both an on-line and a physical presence. Within the Padiglione Italia is the SuperBlog Salon, a social and intellectual centre for the Biennale, where visitors are invited to contribute.

Elements of *Venice SuperBlog* include instant reviews of the Biennale pavilions and exhibits, the insights, visions and passions of architects and critics, and links to the cities featured in the Biennale.

The Venice Architecture Biennale is active from 10 September to 19 November, and *Venice SuperBlog* will act as a resource for visitors with podcasts, personal insights into the exhibitions by the main protagonists, and an online forum.

The Architecture Foundation

The Architecture Foundation promotes and encourages the best in contemporary architecture and brings it to a wide public. It runs a rich programme comprising exhibitions, talks, events, design initiatives and competitions, research, policy work and films. Established in 1991 as Britain's first independent architecture centre, The Architecture Foundation actively bridges the gap between decision-makers, design professionals and the public. The Architecture Foundation is building a new centre for architecture in Bankside, designed by Zaha Hadid and currently has a temporary experimental gallery in east London.
www.architecturefoundation.org.uk

MoMA Architecture and Design

The world's first curatorial department devoted to architecture and design was established in 1932 at The Museum of Modern Art. From its inception, the collection has been built on the recognition that architecture and design are allied and interdependent arts, so that synthesis has been a founding premise of the collection. The collection provides an extensive overview of modernism. Starting with the reform ideology established by the Arts and Crafts movement, the collection covers major movements of the twentieth century and contemporary issues. The architecture collection documents buildings through models, drawings, and photographs, and includes the Mies van der Rohe Archive.
www.moma.org

The Architecture Foundation and MoMA present
Venice SuperBlog

INSTITUTIONS
The Architecture Foundation
The Museum of Modern Art

CURATORS
Elias Redstone (Curator, The Architecture Foundation),
Paola Antonelli (Acting Chief Curator, Department of
Architecture and Design, The Museum of Modern Art)

STAFF
Rowan Moore (Director, The Architecture Foundation),
Nathalie Weadick (Deputy Director, The Architecture
Foundation), Jade Niklai (Events Co-ordinator, The
Architecture Foundation), Tina di Carlo (Assistant
Curator, Department of Architecture and Design, The
Museum of Modern Art)

COLLABORATORS
Nick Freeeman, Manha, Peter Reed (Senior Deputy
Director for curatorial Affairs, The Museum of Modern
Art)

WEBSITE
www.venicesuperblog.net

Mobility urban footprints

The contribution from the Laboratorio Macrourbanistica DPA features new research on accessibility and mobility patterns in the core cities. This section shows how the patterns of accessibility vary enormously at different times of day in each of the 16 cities. This pioneering work demonstrates how the functional edges of the city, as opposed to their political boundaries, are highly changeable and constitute a significant temporal measure that reflects the ability to carry out different urban activities (work, university, leisure,sporting events etc.). The edges of each city's 'temporal footprint' change according to the time of day and mode of transport (private, public, cycle or pedestrian). The form of the city expands or contracts, as an urban 'lung', in response to different levels of congestion, giving an indication of differing transport 'footprints' for users of the 'business city', the 'leisure city' or the 'shopping city'. The research is the result of a set of long-term studies carried out in academic and professional fields.

In addition, a global, continental vision compares the 'Europe of the regions' and the 'Europe of the cities'. Both models highlight the powerful correlation between mode of transport, network structure and cohesion of settlements.

INSTITUTION
Laboratorio Macrourbanistica DPA, Facoltà Architettura Civile, Politecnico di Milano

RESPONSIBLE
Fabio Casiroli, Transport Planning Lecturer

STAFF
Vincenzo Donato, Davide Boazzi, Elena Luoni

COLLABORATORS
Stefano Recalcati, Stilla Graf, Federico Cassani, Elisabetta Zappa, Giuseppe Pepe, Vittorio Romano, Alessandro Ridolfi

SPONSOR
Systematica spa
Citylabs

Macrourbanistica DPA,
Facoltà di Architettura Civile, Politecnico di Milano

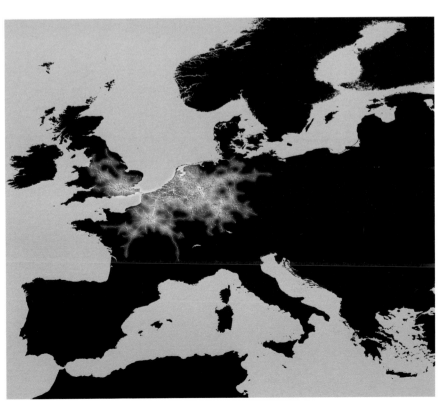

Shaping the city of the future has to do with actions, actors and tools. It has to do with politics, policies and government, or, as is nowadays commonly said, with *governance*, a quasi-universal term not entirely bereft of criticism. The first of a series of workshops that complements the *Cities. Architecture and Society* exhibition will address these key issues in a simplified way, by inviting those very actors – the mayors of major world cities – to discuss how they shape the future social and physical morphologies of their own cities, but also the ways in which urban society shapes itself through direct economic action and through mechanisms of power exchange (such as consensus and pressures) in the political realm. To this end, the workshop will invite some leading urbanists to set the individual histories of these cities in a global, geo-political and economic context, providing a platform for debate on the future of cities.

One of the major structural changes on the surface of the planet today has been defined as 'receding boundedness'. Cities, as well as other political organisations, have been traditionally defined by their boundaries – massive city walls, deep moats, masonry ramparts or imposing waterfronts - which have in turn determined the social bonds between residents and urban dwellers. The concept of a social group defined by a precise outer border is deeply embedded in social and political thinking. But since the late nineteenth century and increasingly throughout the twentieth century, boundaries have become weaker. This process is evident in many parts of the world, where the urban form has taken on the aspect of a borderless meta-city, a 'city beyond the city'. Yet boundaries still exist and produce powerful effects. Political constituencies are still based on physically defined electoral districts, while cities carefully draw up new planning regulations where new boundaries accumulate over old ones, reinforced by a new generation of walls, moats and fences. Populations composed of individuals with no need of

collective rationality doggedly wash against the fences or burrow under them, individual after dogged individual in perennial waves. But even when there are no physical barriers to signpost social and urban *limits*, their invisible counterparts are hard to trespass, like an unmarked crystal plate, or a sound barrier hardening as you try to force through. Our urban world is thickly enveloped in a complex maze of visible and invisible nets.

The other major structural mutation has to do with the changing nature, not of the fence around us, but of the human web that links individuals and groups. Cities have always been the place in which solidarity was reinforced by proximity. Size, density and heterogeneity have been the hallmarks of urbanity, yet today these links are blown away by the fast flowing 'byte'. The deepest structural change in political process has already taken place with the diffusion and intrusion of mass media, which brings information (as well as control and influence) directly to the home, like water or electricity, sucking the public agora into everybody's private den. The village becomes global but loses part of its physicality. In exactly the same way that political theory and administrative practice have gone from *Government* to *Governance* (i.e. a more interactive and less hierarchic way of governing) the new metropolis requires a shift from *eGovernment* to *eGovernance* - meaning a more interactive and less space-bound way of governing, as cities are increasingly going from spaces to flows and are fully immersed in the development of a planetary network of communications.

These issues will be debated at the *Shaping the city of the future* workshop, with presentations from the mayors and civic leaders of Barcelona, Bogotá, Caracas, London, São Paulo, Tokyo, Turin - and other world cities featured in the *Cities. Architecture and Society* exhibition - with presentations by leading international experts on global cities, including Saskia Sassen, and discussions chaired by urbanists Richard Sennett, Gerald Frug, Guido Martinotti and Enrique Peñalosa.

Workshop
Shaping the city of the future:
boundaries and connections

ORGANIZATION
La Biennale di Venezia

VENUE AND DATE
Teatro alle Tese, Venice
6 September 2006
(by invitation only)

COORDINATOR
Guido Martinotti

KEYNOTE SPEAKER
Saskia Sassen, Ralph Lewis Professor of Sociology (University of Chicago) and Centennial Visiting Professor (London School of Economics and Political Science)

WITH THE PARTICIPATION OF
Joan Clos y Matheu (Mayor ofi Barcelona)
Shintaro Ishihara (Governor of Tokio)
Sergio Chiamparino (Mayor of Torino)
Juan Barreto Cipriani (Mayor of Metropolitan District of Caracas)
Gilberto Kassab (Mayor of São Paulo)

CHAIRS
Gerald Frug, Louis D. Brandeis Professor of Law (Harvard University)
Guido Martinotti, Professor of urban sociology (Università degli Studi di Milano-Bicocca)
Enrique Peñalosa, Former mayor of Bogotá
Richard Sennett, Professor of Sociology (London School of Economics and Political Science, Massachussets Institute of Technology)

SCIENTIFIC SECRETARY
Marxiano Melotti

The *Sustainable mobility in meta-cities* workshop, organised in association with Mo.Ve International Forum, is based on the notion that mobility is embedded in urban form. Past Mo.Ve initiatives have explored urban governance, the organisation of time in the city, new technologies for monitoring and controlling mobility, transport and social exclusion, pollution and congestion in metropolitan areas. This year move will turn its attention to the key issue of sustainability in relation to patterns of mobility in large-scale metropolitan areas. In the 20th century, mobility has not only moulded the prevailing form of metropolitan areas in large conurbations - *Mega Urban Regions* (MURs) - but has also spread with astonishing speed from the established urban centres of advanced economies to cities of emerging countries. Despite some adverse effects, metropolitan development has by and large proven to be sustainable, with the parallel development of *Information Technology and Communications* (ITC), increasing, rather than reducing, overall mobility and distribution within built-up areas. Today a more conservationist mood is taking foot, particularly in older metropolitan regions, but not yet in the younger ones, although no single comprehensive structural solutions seem to be emerging to solve the problems of urban growth.

The workshop has been designed to address these issues. The first session is dedicated to 'Social justice, accessibility and the city' through the presentation of individual case studies undertaken by Mo.Ve's task force with the support of representatives from four European cities. The main outcomes will be evaluated and discussed during the debate by the experts on Mo.Ve's scientific committee. The second session will analyse these case studies and the general themes of mobility in a broader perspective under the title of 'Issues and actions toward equitable and sustainable mobility', focusing on the balance between the needs for mobility and the aspirations to social equity. The third session on the 'Mobile city: visions and strategies for the future', will include presentations by civic leaders and key decision-makers from world cities who will outline their strategies and experiences, creating the basis for a wider discussion on sustainable mobility that includes vision-making, forecasting, energy consumption, public transport, automotive innovation, and the shape of the future city – establishing a direct connection with the themes and contents of the 10th International Architecture Exhibition.

The Forum will have a total of 120 participants among whuch: representatives of European institutions (European Commission, DG for Energy and Transport, DG Environment, European Parliament, Committee on Transport and Tourism, Committee on the Environment, Public Health and Food Safety), of Transport and Environment Ministeries, of the main European cities and regions, ofn the firms and of the European associations committed to sustainable mobility.

Workshop
Sustainable mobility in meta-cities
5th edition of the Mo.Ve International Forum

ORGANIZATION
Association Mo.Ve in cooperation with
La Biennale di Venezia

VENUE AND DATE
Hotel Monaco & Grand Canal, Venice
8 and 9 November 2006
(by invitation only)

COORDINATOR
Guido Martinotti

COORDINATION
Association Mo.Ve
Franco Lucchesi, President of Association Mo.Ve
Toni Muzi Falconi, Project manager and external
relation
Marta Fiore
Karin Fischer, Project officer and scientific
coordination
Rein Van Lansberge, international relation
Guido Martinotti, professor of Urban Sociology of
the Università degli Studi di Milano Bicocca and
coordinator of the Mo.Ve Scientific Committee
Serge Wachter, coordinator of the Mo.Ve Task Force

SCIENTIFIC SECRETARY
Marxiano Melotti

WEBSITE
www.move-forum.net

The 10th International Architecture Exhibition has chosen the cities of the future as its theme for this year, with the aim of presenting a manifesto for the cities of the twenty-first century, focusing on the potential contribution of megalopoli to a more sustainable, democratic and fair world. Inarcassa, the social security fund for engineers and architects, which has more than 130,000 professionals among its members, will contribute to the discussion by developing the more specific question of 'Engineers and architects in the plan of the future city' at its own workshop. The conference will take up a full day: in the morning reports will be presented by authoritative representatives of the profession, the university, politics and associations; in the afternoon there will be an open forum chaired by the art critic Philippe Daverio.

The main theme of the conference will be the role the architect and engineer can play in governing the interaction between architecture and society in the third millennium. The big social changes and progressive urbanisation of the world population have an effect on architecture, as architecture can in its turn change the way people live in the metropoli. The architect and engineer are in this sense key figures, providing a kind of 'guide' to the social changes imposed by progress on the citizens of the megalopoli.

The conference also intends investigating the contradictions that now affect much of architecture. It is being increasingly obliged to respond to the commercial dictates of image, speed of construction and profit, at the cost of quality and the role of planning as a driving force behind all processes of developing and upgrading urban areas.

This theme is joined by that of young people as a big forgotten resource, which will be studied both in terms of the weaknesses of university education in Italy and of participation in projects.

Finally, the workshop will look into one of the problems seen as most pressing: the safeguarding, appreciation and often recovery of the environment and landscape, not in terms of mere conservation, but of sustainable development.

Inarcassa has decided to take part as a Main Partner of the 10th International Architecture Exhibition because providing assistance and support for its members means not only offering them economic assurance to cope with future necessities and moments of difficulty, but also promoting the profession at the highest levels of art and culture, of which La Biennale di Venezia is undoubtedly one of the most illustrious examples in the world.

Conference
Engineers and architects
planning the future of the city

ORGANIZATION
Inarcassa - Cassa Nazionale di Previdenza e Assistenza per gli Ingegneri ed Architetti Liberi Professionisti
www.inarcassa.it

VENUE AND DATE
Teatro Piccolo Arsenale, Venice
20 October 2006
(by invitation only)

SCIENTIFIC COMMITEE
Guido Martinotti

KEYNOTE SPEAKERS
Paola Muratorio – President Inarcassa
Mauro di Martino – Deputy President Inarcassa
Raffaele Sirica – President CNA (Consiglio Nazionale Architetti)
Ferdinando Luminoso – President CNI (Consiglio Nazionale Ingegneri)
Davide Croff – President La Biennale di Venezia
Renato Quaglia - Managing Director Sections Visual Arts and Architecture La Biennale di Venezia

COORDINATOR
Leonardo Fiori

CHAIR
Philippe Daverio

WITH THE PARTICIPATION OF
Paola Muratorio – President Inarcassa
Mario Botta - architect
Francesco Dal Co - architecture historian
Gabriele Del Mese - Peter Head - Arup group
Paolo Portoghesi - architect
Federico Oliva – President INU (Istituto Nazionale Urbanistica)
Cesare Stevan – prorector Politecnico di Milano

ORGANIZING COORDINATION AND PUBLIC RELATIONS
Teresa Pittelli and Alessandra Tolloy

Architectures for Cities

São Paulo, Brazil

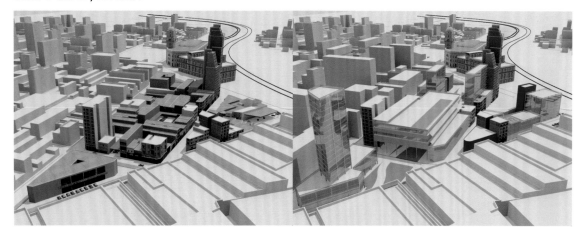

Nova Luz

The Luz neighbourhood in São Paulo contains some of São Paulo's most notorious and deprived housing estates. Despite significant public investment over the past decade, including city's new Symphony Hall, the area has not improved as anticipated. A more proactive regeneration approach has now been adopted, through the expropriation and demolition of numerous buildings (many currently used for drug dealing and prostitution), and the construction of new structures designed to house public functions which will increase the density of occupation and, it is hoped, crime. A tax reduction programme is also being implemented to attract new businesses to the area. Future phases include the reconstruction of extensive parts of the neighbourhood which should kick-start regeneration of the wider Downtown district.

Client
Prefeitura do Municipio de São Paulo
Design Team
EMURB (architect)

Itaquaquecetuba Train Station [Line F Extension]

The project of the Itaquaquecetuba metropolitan train station fits into a modernisation plan for the railway network in Greater São Paulo. It consists in revamping the today's existing large web and for use as a Metro-style mass transportation system. The project - which started in 2001 and will go up to the year 2020 - consists in transforming 270 km of railway with an investment of US$ 1 billion. The final result will be an increment of 2 million passengers per day. To cope with the demand more than 90 stations will be built or renewed. The new 152 metre-long station, on the East Side of the city is part of Line F which surrounds Tietê River marshlands and is preserved as an ecologic park. It is linked to the city by a suspended walkway over the marshland.

Client
Metropolitan Train Company of São Paulo
Design Team
Una arquitetos (Cristiane Muniz, Fabio Valentim, Fernanda Barbara, Fernando Viégas)

Costa e Silva Overpass

The Costa e Silva Overpass, locally known as the *minhocao* or big earthworm, is located in the centre of São Paulo. Every day, 80 thousand vehicles pass through this 3-kilometre thoroughfare running in the east-west direction. With two subway stations along the overpass and a bus terminal attached, the area is an important transport node. The structure is also used for recreational purposes on weekends and holidays. However, the *minhocao* has brought about major physical and environmental deterioration to its surroundings, in some sections there is only 5 meters of distance with adjacent buildings. The proposal envisions a structure that maintains the current transport functions while being transformed into an unprecedented topography which will allow for multiple urban uses, functions and links. An elevated park will cover the traffic lanes along the entire extension of the overpass. Lateral galleries for diversified uses will be located in strategic sites. Annexed and coordinated to this new scenario, infrastructure improvements will improve accessibility to the facilities and a series of public programs will secure their vibrancy.

Design Team
Jose Alves e Juliana Corradini (FRENTES)
Competition proposal

Urban Development Railway Axis (Mooca_Ipiranga)

The project claims to enhance the public investments applied on transport system and simulate an urban development possibility for the industrial settlements areas, according to prefecture plans. The urban intervention is established by starting with the project of a park alongside the railway; the construction of a new landscape where the water has a structuring roll; the preservation of the industrial memory of this neighborhood and finally the thickening of population. In the marshlands surrounding the Tamanduateí River this sector is defined by the railway stations Mooca and Ipiranga and the project itself is defined by infrastructure; division of large tracts and street planning subject to existing web; public spaces for rest and play; area for sports and local and regional drainage, connection between stations of railway and subway and crossing of railway and river and finally social housing.

Client
Secretaria Municipal de Transportes
Design team
Una arquitetos (Cristiane Muniz, Fábio Valentim, Fernanda Barbara, Fernando Viégas)

100 New Schools for São Paulo

In 2000, the school attendance rate of 11-14 year olds was roughly 20% in peripheral urban neighbourhoods of the State of São Paulo, an important reason for this low level educational achievement being the lack of school facilities in these areas. The project to erect 100 new schools is a direct response to this challenge. The same construction guidelines apply to every site: a high-quality design, simple pre-fabricated structures and durable materials. Projects have low costs and short turn-over period. Beyond its educational role, the scheme has also been successful in providing after-hours, multi-purpose spaces for the local communities. Nearly 30 projects have been completed since the scheme began in 2003. Three of these projects are showcased at La Biennale.

Client
State of São Paulo Department of Education and the Foundation for the Development of Education

Conjunto Habitacional Campinas F1 School
Design Team
MMBB arquitetos

Jardim Umuarama / Moacyr de Castro Ferraz School
Design Team
Estudio 6 arquitetos

Jardim Ataliba Leonel / Pedro de Moraes Victor School
Design Team
SPBR arquitetos

Plaza of Arts

To reinforce downtown's reputation as the cultural hub of the São Paulo metropolis, the city is proposing re-use of some of the area's prominent sites. The Anhangabau Valley is arguably the most important public space in the center of São Paulo, however it is fallen into decline in many senses. The Praça das Artes will activate the key intersection between the Anhangabau Valley and the São Joao Avenue with new cultural facilities. Among these, the new square will accommodate the city's School of Music, the city's School of Dance, and an annex of the beloved Municipal Theater. Most importantly, the project envisions the integration of these new uses with an abundant public space. This design will allow for a pleasant transition from the expansive space of the Anhangabau Valley to the intimate scale of the Plaza of Arts. The project is designed to induce a positive transformation of the dilapidated downtown, by surrounding cultural facilities with a permeable, pristine and respectful civic space.

Client
Prefeitura do Municipio de São Paulo
Design Team
Marcos Cartum (lead architect)

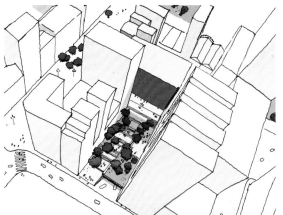

City Film

To approach the stark contrasts in his native São Paulo, Otavio Cury and his team at Mutante Filmes have composed an intricate mosaic of nine 'windows' on the city. The spatial juxtapositions highlight an underlying urban vitality common to the children of Favela Grajaú, the pedestrians on Paulista Avenue, the Japanese-Brazilian community of Liberdade, and countless other Paulistas throughout the city.

Video
Otavio Cury (director),
Rafael Antonelli,
Ana Mendonça,
Marcelle Governatori,
Everton Taccini
Sound Design
Jorge Tsunoda,
Yvo Ursini

Caracas, Venezuela

Mision Barrio Adentro
Client
Caracas Alcaldia Mayor

Gimnasio Vertical™

More than poverty, lack of security and violence are the main concerns for people in Caracas. The *barrios* suffer the most - kidnapping, the use of firearms and aggression are part of their everyday life. Initiatives to curb violence proposed the construction of sports and facilities throughout the city. However, space limitations led to the lack of such facilities in the dense informal settlements that need them the most. 'Bello Campo' was a pioneering project introducing the Gimnasio Vertical prototype. Using prefabricated construction techniques, an existing soccer field in the municipality of Chacao was transformed into a multi-level sports complex accommodating up to 200 people. This gym stands at the entrance to a *barrio*, between formal and informal areas. Free to all residents, it has brought together a wide range of the community's diverse demographics, receiving a yearly average of 180,000 visitors. Since its inception, crime has decreased by 45% in the neighbourhood, which has become one of Chacao's safest.

Client
Various

Design Team
Urban Think-Tank Architecture & Urban Design (Alfredo Brillembourg/Hubert Klumpner)

San Rafael Upgrade Project

Located in challenging mountainous terrain, San Rafael/La Vega (SR/LV) is one of the biggest spontaneous settlements of Caracas, with 95,000 inhabitants over 400 hectares. The project aims to both renovate SR/LV and to integrate it, physically and socially, with formal areas of the city. Its goal is to generate an upgraded urban space with enhanced accessibility and improved services. SR/LV is about new community areas and local facilities; transport connections between the restored area and more advantaged parts of the city; and vehicular and pedestrian networks that link the new public spaces in the settlement and also function as open sewers to channel refuse and rain water out of SR/LV. The project also contributes to the framing of an anti-sprawl growth boundary. Fueled by local participation, this intervention builds on the economic, social and cultural resources of SR/LV. Residents helped plan the project and then were trained in construction techniques to implement it with their own hands.

Client
National Program for the Upgrading of Informal Settlements of Venezuela, World Bank
Design Team
Proyectos Arqui 5

Mision Alimentacion
Client
Caracas Alcaldia Mayor

City Film

The undulating physical geography of Caracas determines its urban morphology, characterised by vast informal settlements that seem to defy gravity as they stretch outward and upward from the formal city centre. Sara Muzio has created a video diptych that urges the viewer to consider the relationship between the macro-scale of Caracas from the air and the human experience of public space in three *barrios*: La Cancha, La Quinta and La Vega.

Video
Sara Muzio
Shot in *barrio* La Cancha, La Quinta and La Vega
Aerial footage contributed by
Caracas Urban Think Tank:
Alfredo Brillembourg, David Frankfurt and Hubert Klumpner
Montage
Sara Muzio

Bogotá, Colombia

Virgilio Barco Public Library

The Virgilio Barco Public Library is one of the four regional libraries built under the Biblored scheme that has created one of the most intensely used public libraries network in Latin America. The library and adjacent complex are located in the middle of Parque Central Simón Bolívar, the largest park in central Bogotá that residents enjoy for special concerts and everyday recreational activities alike. The sinuous topography of the landscape surrounding the library elegantly blends it into the park. This area features an esplanade with restaurants, a garden, places where people can walk and ride their bikes, playgrounds and an open-air theatre. The multilayered library building is an interface between these recreational opportunities outdoors and the various possibilities that the library offers to its users inside.

Client
Bogotá City Government, County Education Office, Biblored
Design Team
Rogelio Salmona

El Tintal Public Library

The public library in the district El Tintal is one of the high-quality public facilities that the City of Bogotá has built in socially disadvantaged peripheral areas over the past decade. Originally an abandoned garbage-transfer station, the El Tintal site was retrofitted and redesigned with a theme that symbolizes creativity in the use of resources. Located on Bogotá's western fringe, El Tintal sits on the dividing line between working-class houses and the 'rough neighbourhood' of Patio Bonito. With no cinemas, shopping malls, or places where children, teenagers, or adults can spend their free time around Patio Bonito, the public library of El Tintal has become a popular place that the local population uses in multifarious ways.

Client
Bogotá City Government, County Education Office, Biblored
Design Team
Daniel Bermudez Samper (architect)

CicloRutas

A comprehensive network of cycle routes has been built in Bogotá over the past decade. Currently, the system totals 297 km and covers most parts of the city. An important characteristic of the cycle routes is that they bring the downtown areas closer to some of the most densely populated neighbourhoods, where modal choices of transport do not about. They also provide an egalitarian, inclusive and safe civic space for all Bogotanos regardless of their means and age. For a city structured along stark social and economic divides and with strong unbalances between the wealthy north and the poor south, the cycle routes contribute to the rise of living standards and social inclusion of residents in the urban peripheries. In the next 10 years, the Plan Maestro de Ciclo Rutas will feature another 301 km of new routes.

Client
City of Bogotá
Design Team
Various

TransMilenio Bus System

The TransMilenio Integrated Mass Transport System is a high-capacity bus system with dedicated lanes. Launched in 2000 with an extension of 60 kilometres, the network also reaches Bogotá's peripheries through low-capacity buses that feed into its trunk lines. It will be completed in the year 2015. This transport intervention addresses the discriminating mobility conditions aggravating residential segregation and the marginalization of the most disadvantaged in Bogotá. Before TransMilenio road space was monopolised by a minority of the population who could afford private vehicles, while 72% of citizens depended on a highly unreliable patchwork network of buses. The scheme's modest infrastructure requirements imply low costs and guarantee its the feasibility. By reducing commuting times by up to 25% it is making Bogotá more competitive. It has also spurred a wave of redevelopment and land-use intensification in the urban core.

Client
City of Bogotá
Design Team
Various (station design includes Javier Vera Lono, Fernando Leon Toro Vallejo, Gabriel Jaime Giraldo Gaviria)

City Film

Bogotá's pioneering approach to public transportation and public, open space shapes citizens' experience of a modernizing city and an inclusive society. This video is a journey through urban change and continuity in Bogotá, from *barrios* such as Pablo VI and Modelo Norte to the grand spaces of the colonial downtown.

Audio/Video contributors
Adriana Cobo Corey, Alvaro Duran (DVA Producciones), Gabriel Ossa, Ramon Villamarin
Montage
Cassim Shepard

Mexico City, Mexico

Center for Indigenous Arts

The Center for Indigenous Arts is located on one of the most important corners in downtown Mexico City, an intersection between Spanish culture and the Aztec world. The new museum will be situated across from the Metropolitan Cathedral, with the Zocalo extending beyond, flanked by the archaeological site of Templo Mayor, the Aztec's main temple. The proposal completes the evolution of the origins of the city's urban grid, introducing a visual connection between pre-Columbian culture, Colonial architecture and modern design. The project requires a negotiation between two adjacent historical structures with strict preservation demands. It will preserve the 19th century façade of one building and refurbish the entire original 18th century complex of the other, creating a contemporary glass volume in between that engages the surrounding urban context. A new public plaza will anchor the corner, providing space for street front exhibitions, concerts and theatre performances. The Museum will house Mexico's most important collection of Indigenous art and photography. The project exemplifies the regeneration of the Centro Histórico, with upgraded public plazas and new plantings creating much needed public amenities.

Client
Centro de las Artes de los Pueblos Indigenas
Design Team
TEN Arquitectos/Enrique Norten

El FARO de Oriente

La Fábrica de Artes y Oficios, FARO de Oriente, or 'lighthouse of the east' is a cultural centre anchoring the community of Ixtapalapa on the eastern edges of Mexico City. Ixtapalapa is one of the city's most populated zones, with frequent violence and inadequate amenities and urban infrastructure. Designed to evoke a ship floating on ancient Lake Texcoco, the structure sits in the now sandy basin of the drained lake, offering an architecture and program that cultivate vanguard expressions of visual and performing arts. Originally designed to serve as a government office, the building's program was altered after local officials decided to re-appropriate the building as a community arts centre with studios, galleries, library and performance space. A concrete foundation caisson creates a protective base for open and interconnected interior spaces formed by a modular light steel structure. The plan extends the public space surrounding the building's footprint to create an outdoor amphitheatre for large-scale performances, gatherings and activities, and provide a cultural oasis in this poor, industrial desert environment.

Client
El Fábrica de Artes y Oficios
Design Team
Alberto Kalach / Taller de Arquitectura X

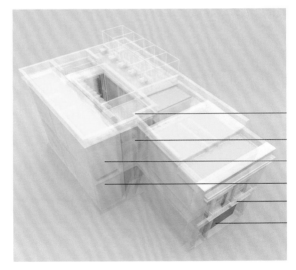

Brazil 44

Centro Historico is currently undergoing a regeneration that extends from the preservation and revitalization of existing historical structures to the creation and upgrading of infrastructure and commercial buildings. This imperative to improve the city's core brings essential public services and amenities to attract new residential growth and commercial investment. These improvements begin to resolve decades of neglect, and extend beyond the restoration of deteriorated façades. Yet this intervention strategy calls for a conscientious and coordinated development policy that accomodates constituents from various socioeconomic backgrounds and confronts the great percentage of 'shantytown' dwellings with informal and irregular ownership. A key community-based financing initiative of the federal government in partnership with the Junta de Andalucia of Spain is incrementally improving housing conditions in the Centro Histórico to create livable communities for the underserved poor. Brasil 44 offers a case study of the varying scales of this recuperation. The project encompasses five housing actions and retail space on the ground floor, deftly navigating the complex historic preservation restrictions and requirements to revitalize an existing dwelling. Most significantly, the intervention adds public space to facilitate communal living, an atypical condition among Mexico City's many inhabitants.

Client
Instituto Nacional de la Vivienda
Design Team
Javier Sanchez / Higuera + Sanchez

City Film

The sheer size of Mexico City is difficult to fathom. From a human scale, the city may be experienced as a series of different nodes of activity. Informal markets grow organically into circuits of infrastructure; *barrios* abut new commercial developments. The Mexico City video collage explores these zones of encounter through archival film and contemporary video footage. The neighbourhoods observed include Neza, Polanco, the Centro Histórico, La Condesa, La Merced, Chalco, Santa Fe and Coyoacan.

Audio/Video contributors
Francisco Laresgoiti, Enrique Martin-Moreno, Cassim Shepard
Montage
Cassim Shepard

Los Angeles, United States of America

Culver City

Culver City is covered by an immense collection of 1930s and 40s industrial and manufacturing buildings, outlined by railroad tracks, the river, long boulevards, and the power grid. The area repeated conditions typical of many contemporary ex-industrial urban districts; with cheap labour and minimum controls on the environment and working conditions it was in urgent need of revitalisation. The operational principle for the Culver City project was that the extant infrastructure should become the foundation for new building types, strategically connecting areas that had been divided. The project uses architecture as a means to identify the new social and civic opportunities in the area. The area has now become a viable option for experimental art and commerce on the west side of LA. Production buildings house associated companies in media, advertising, film, communication, music, and the performing arts, who share facilities.

Client
Samitaur Constructs, Frederick and Laurie Samitaur SmithLA
Design Team
Eric Owen Moss Architects

Grand Avenue Project

The masterplan for the Grand Avenue Project encompasses 9 acres of Downtown Los Angeles and focuses on enhancing public outdoor spaces. The plan centres on a 16 acre park that will connect landmark cultural and civic buildings with a new multi-use development. Landscaped to have several distinct areas, the park will provide space both for large-scale events and for quiet respite. Cultural events will be programmed in the west of the park, the centre will feature a garden, and the east end by the City Hall will host civic celebrations and cultural festivals. The project also includes alterations to the streetscape along Grand Avenue from Fifth Street to Cesar Chavez Avenue that will improve the environment for pedestrians. Critical to the project is the provision of affordable housing and new jobs to this area of downtown Los Angeles. The project is estimated to generate 5,300 new jobs, and $28 million in annual revenues for the city, county and state. The total development program of up to 3.8 million square feet of new development includes 400,000 square feet of retail and up to 2,600 affordable and market-rate residential units.

Client
Related Companies, Grand Avenue Committee, Los Angeles Grand Avenue Authority
Design Team
Various, includes Frank Gehry, SOM, Elkus-Manfredi Architects, Olin Partnership, Levin & Associates

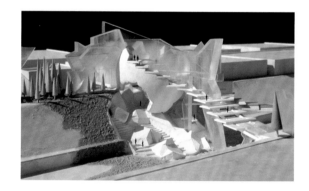

Los Angeles River Revitalisation Masterplan

The increased densification of Los Angeles has produced strong demand for more open space and parkland. In response, the City of Los Angeles Department of Public Works has instituted a plan to revitalize the Los Angeles River. Flowing for 32 miles through the city, the river is contained within a wide concrete channel that permits scant relation to the social urban environment. The plan has various aims: to improve the river environment, encourage public access to the river and increase recreational space, and improve flood control. In addition to channel improvements planned along the 32 mile corridor within the City's jurisdiction, 5 large river sites will be developed, selected for their potential to improve water quality, enhance flood protection, expand wildlife habitat and recreational space, and create economic re-investment opportunities. Pedestrian and cycle routes will be developed and connected along the river, including the construction of pedestrian bridges. The concrete channel will be invigorated through extensive tree planting, the construction of terraces and river greenways alongside the river and strengthened connections to existing local green spaces for residents. The condition of the Los Angeles River's watershed as a whole will also be tackled, with the aim of storing larger amounts of flood water and improving the water quality in the tributaries.

Client
City of Los Angeles
Design Team
Tetra Tech Inc (lead consultants), HNTB Architecture Inc, Mia Lehrer & Associates, Wenk Associates Inc, Civitas Inc

High Speed Rail HS[aRT]

In response to the overwhelming need to connect major California cities rapidly and efficiently, the California High Speed Rail Authority was created in the 1990s to implement a plan and formulate a legislative bill before 2010. The plan, based on the European system, envisioned a quicker and more sustainable means of inter-city connection, located closer to city centers with a dramatically smaller footprint than airports. Travel time is said to be comparable; the estimated travel time of 2.5 hours from Los Angeles to San Francisco equals the total combined time of airport arrival, flight and airport departure. The HS[aRT] project examines the developmental impact of such a station near the core of downtown Los Angeles at Union Station by proposing a high density multi-use complex over the rail tracks. The entire project rests on the air rights of the Los Angeles river, one of three proposed sites from the CHSRA. By cleverly re-adapting the river's much maligned industrialized concrete channel as the infrastructural track, HS[aRT] dramatically reduces the issue of land rights and eminent domain. Additionally, the infill of the Los Angeles river allows HS[aRT] to act as a bridge linking the separated East Los Angeles with the rest of downtown.

Design Team
Thom Mayne (Morphosis), UCLA School of Architecture

Speculative proposal

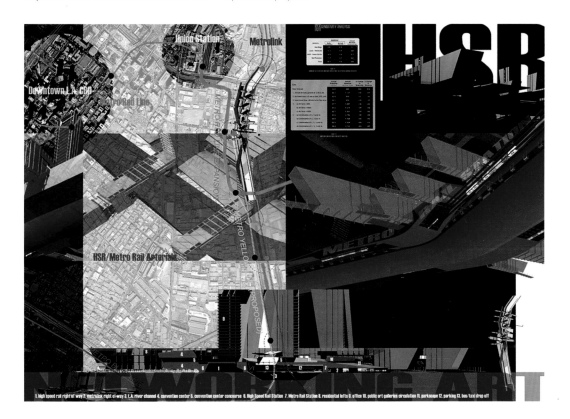

City Film

For many Angelenos, the most recurring sensory experience of the city is the vista through a moving car window. Los Angeles' expansive freeway infrastructure, however, belies a nuanced set of relationships between the citizen and the landscape. This video takes the driver's-eye-view as its point of departure to explore the human interface with the street, the sidewalk, the river, and the beach.

Audio/Video contributors
Lars Jan,
Young Sun Kim,
Jean Paul Travers
Audio contributors
Bram, Cognito Perceptu, Dobriode, Anna Holtzman, Laurent, Psaskion, Rookiee, Tsha1, Stijn
Montage
Cassim Shepard

New York City, United States of America

BAM Cultural District

The BAM Cultural District area comprises a vibrant mix of arts organizations located at a transportation and development axis in Brooklyn. The Visual and Performing Arts Library will be a catalyzing force for the new architecture defining this central zone. The library's design negotiates a narrow triangular node, simultaneously projecting out into and drawing in from Brooklyn's varied and dense streetscape. The emphasis is on contact and connectivity with the community. The library's permeable, transparent structure and v-shaped plan respond to the complexities of the site and its adjacencies, which include other cultural institutions and the third largest transportation nexus in New York City. The area represents a focal point of new development, in which private residential and commercial interests intersect with innovative visual and performing arts. The Library offers a gateway to the economic and cultural growth of the city and a new frontier of building activity in Brooklyn.

Client
BAM Local Development Corporation,
City of New York
Design Team
Various; for Visual and Performing Arts Library,
TEN Arquitectos/ Enrique Norten

East River Master Plan

Access to the East River in Lower Manhattan has been blocked for decades. The Master Plan opens up the historically vital port for recreation and provide diverse amenities for multiple users. Contributing to an open space network around Manhattan, the plan will also provide new cultural, commercial and community spaces along its 2 mile length. Six neighbourhoods, each with distinct identities and needs, engaged in the development of concept sketches to create esplanades, public amenities and open spaces. Bike and pedestrian pathways will be prioritised for the leisure activities of diverse urban populations. Through reclaiming the adjoining elevated highway as a shelter for pavilions, the project will repurpose the dense transportation infrastructure of an area designed primarily to facilitate water transport. The East River Master Plan will alleviate physical and psychological barriers to the water's edge, offering the reconstructed piers and platforms as extensions of the adjacent neighbourhoods, thereby developing significant civic space at the birthplace of New York's economy.

Client
City of New York
Design Team
SHoP Architects, Richard Rogers Partnership,
Ken Smith Landscape

High Line

The High Line chronicles New York City's manufacturing and industrial heritage, but until 2002 its future lay undetermined. Now an innovative plan will repurpose this elevated rail line as an urban playground with multiple spaces and activities, and present a new typology for parks and recreational space in New York. Topological variations and planting will create layers and distinct zones, while retaining some of the platform's uncultivated growth is another of the design's key features. Initiated by the vision of community activists, the redeveloped structure will create new urban spheres for commerce, art and culture, as well as a sweeping vista of the city and its waterfront. The 1.5 mile rail line will become a pedestrian route along Manhattan, weaving through the Meatpacking and gallery districts and up to the city's rail yards. The design proposes amenities under, on and over the rail infrastructure, responding to New York's unprecedented real estate boom. The conversion is facilitated by a zoning plan that transfers ownership from private developers to the City of New York through the allocation of air rights to adjacent buildings. The plan creates robust economic incentives to repurpose antiquated infrastructure for a 21st century urban context.

Client
City of New York, Friends of the High Line
Design Team
Field Operations, Diller Scofidio + Renfro

Main Street City Park
John Street Site
Empire-Fulton Ferry State Park
Manhattan Bridge
Brooklyn Bridge
Fulton Ferry Landing
Cadman Plaza
Pier 1
Pier 2
Pier 3
Pier 4
Pier 5
Pier 6
Pier 7

City Film

Both geographically and socially, New York City is an archipelago, defined by its relationship to water, by insularities and interdependencies. The video collage interweaves sketches of singular places with glimpses of the ferries, bridges, tunnels and trains that traverse. Through this dense network of infrastructural circuits, the city of neighbourhoods somehow manages to cohere into a dynamic, plural metropolis.

Audio/Video Contributors
Purcell Carson,
Hope Hall,
Cassim Shepard,
Sadia Shepard,
Alexander Weil
Audio contributors
Anna Holtzman,
Keith de Mendonca,
Nick Miller,
Jean-Jacques Palix,
Sal Randolph,
Jonathan Thomas
Montage
Cassim Shepard

Brooklyn Bridge Park

Brooklyn Bridge Park is designed to enhance the social functionality of landscape and open space in New York, renewing connections between the land and water's edge. The design will introduce a rugged landscape into the area's imposing infrastructure and negotiate the complex topographical profile of the 1.3 mile-long site, extending from Manhattan Bridge to the base of Atlantic Avenue. The design employs a variety of placemaking strategies and landscape materials, providing neighbourhoods in Brooklyn with a green gateway to the water and to each other. Fundamental guiding principles of the design include connectivity, sustainability, economy of space and landscape, as well as economic self-sufficiency. Water management techniques for constructed habitats and natural reservoirs also contribute to a range of structures that programmatically respond to diverse recreational activities. Strategies to diminish the noise impact of the adjacent Brooklyn Queens Expressway also provide additional space for promenades and planting.

Client
Brooklyn Bridge Park Development Corporation
Design Team
Michael Van Valkenburgh Associates (lead)

Cairo, Egypt

Al-Azhar Park

By the mid-nineties, Cairo had one of the most rations of green space per inhabitant in the world–far below the WHO raccomanded 8m² per person. Al-Azhar Park was initiated to address some of the consequences of Cairo. By the mid-nineties, Cairo had one of the lowest ratios of green space per inhabitant in the world–far below the WHO recommended 8m's rapid urban growth: its extreme population pressures, decline in housing quality and diminished living standards. The Aga Khan Trust for Culture undertook the creation of the park on a 30 hectare site that had been used as a debris dump for over 500 years. The organisation's process maintains its institutional committment to long-range historic preservation and economic development. Located in the neighbourhood of Darb al-Ahmar, one of Cairo's poorest and most populous areas, Al-Azhar Park was designed to have a catalytic effect on rehabilitation of the district. Several mosques, old palaces and historic houses are being restored in an effort to revitalise the existing architectural heritage. In conjunction with this, socio-economic initiatives have also been launched to provide residents with new opportunities, including apprenticeships, employment, micro-credit schemes, health centres and women's associations.

Client
Governorate of Cairo
Design Team
Historic Cities Support Programme (HCSP);
Sasaki Associates; Sites International

El Sawy Culturewheel

The El Sawy Culturewheel is a new cultural centre situated in the district of Zamalek in Cairo. To create the performing arts venue, Mohamed El Sawy repurposed the residual space underneath an important bridge - formerly a dark, under-utilised lot that acted as a garbage receptacle - in commemoration of his father Abdel-Monem El Sawy, a novelist and former Minister of Culture. The name Culturewheel derives from an Egyptian custom, known as a running charity, of donating to the public in commemoration of a deceased person. And the commitment to civic engagement and to maximising accessibility continues to drive the project: the Culturewheel hosts around 500,000 visitors at more than 1,000 events yearly, including free or low-cost concerts, theatre performances, art exhibitions and literary seminars.

Client and Design Team
Mohammed El Sawy (lead)

City Film

The rooftops of Cairo provide a powerful insight into a unique urban condition, where an ancient yet continuously expanding built environment accommodates uses and re-uses. The Cairo video collage maps some of the city's different urban typologies and the opportunities they provide for innovation in urban living.

Audio/Video Contributors
Magdi Habachi,
LINX productions,
Seif El-Rashidi
Neutral: Tapio Snellman and Christian Grou
Cassim Shepard
Audio contributors
Acclivity, R Humphries
Montage
Cassim Shepard

Istanbul, Turkey

Santral Istanbul/Central Istanbul

Santral Istanbul, a large-scale project for arts, science and development will regenerate the site of a 1913 thermal power plant, defunct since 1983. With 35,000 m² of building capacity located on 118,000 m² of land between the Alibeykoy and Kagithane Streams at the tip of the historic Golden Horn, the Silahtaraga Power Plant currently consists of twenty-eight buildings in various states of disrepair. While all of the primary historical elements will remain in-situ, pipes and furnaces will be removed to create 6,000 m² of space for an interactive science museum, with 3,500 m² devoted to exhibits. The 4,100 m² library, three restaurants and cafeterias, a 500-person capacity conference hall and film theater, and Bilgi University facilities will be located in new buildings distributed throughout the site.

Client
Istanbul Bilgi University
Design Team
Prof.Dr. Ihsan Bilgin
Deniz Aslan
Emre Arolat Architects
NSMH
Mimarlar Tasarim

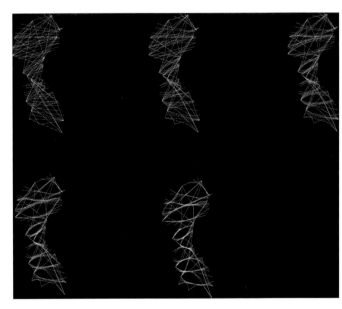

Kartal – Pendik Masterplan

The Kartal-Pendik masterplan proposes a new 555 hectare city centre on Istanbul's east bank. It is the redevelopment of an abandoned industrial site into a new sub-centre, with a central business district, residential development, cultural facilities and leisure programs. The site lies at the confluence of several important infrastructural links, including the major highway connecting Istanbul to Europe and Asia, the coastal highway, sea bus terminals, and rail links to the greater metropolitan area.
The project begins by tying together the basic infrastructural and urban context of the surrounding site. Lateral lines stitch together the major east-west road connections.

The integration of these lateral connections with the main longitudinal axis creates a soft grid that forms the project's underlying framework. In certain areas the net rises up to form a network of towers in an open landscape, while in other areas it is inverted to become a denser fabric cut through by streets, and at other times may completely fade away to generate parks and open spaces. Some areas extend out into the water, creating a matrix of floating marinas, shops, and restaurants.

Client
Greater Istanbul Municipality, Kartal Municipality
Design Team
Zaha Hadid with Patrik Schumacher

Marmaray Project

The Marmaray Project provides an upgrading of approximately 76 kilometres of Istanbul's commuter rail system, connecting Halkali on the European side with Gebze on the Asian side with a continuous, modern, high-capacity commuter rail system passing under the Istanbul Strait. 64 kilometres of 2 track systems exist but will be upgraded and renewed and 13 kilometres will be added in tunnels. The main structures and systems include the world's deepest immersed tunnel (1.3 km, approximately 58 meters under the water surface), 9.8 km of two bore TBM-tunnels, 2.4 km cut and cover tunnels, 3 new underground stations, 37 new surface stations, new operation control centres, new yards and maintenance facilities, and full renewal of existing tracks. Such an improvement in efficiency will have impact the general transportation pattern of Istanbul.

Client
Ministry of Transportation, General Directorate of Railways, Harbours and Airports Construction
Design Team
Avrasyaconsult (lead)

Istanbul Modern Art Museum

Galata Pier, has been a sea gate of Istanbul for centuries. Istanbul Modern Art Museum, situated on this pier, has accelerated the transformation of the industrial heritage along the waterfront and has been an example installing new functions to architectural heritage. Besides renovation and reinforcement of the historical buildings, various social functions have been added to these buildings; with the main objectives of rehabilitating Tophane Square and creating a modern art museum. The zone around the museum is progressively becoming a cultural quarter, integrated with its seafront environment. Istanbul Modern occupies an abandoned warehouse building, which has been adapted with minimal architectural interference; the warehouse maintained its structural essence, simplicity is preferred to highlight the artworks exhibited. Istanbul Modern is Turkey's first modern museum and received more than 500,000 visitors in its first year. Beyond its capacity of being a centre of arts and culture, Istanbul Modern has become a meeting point for citizens. Students and young people in particular are frequent guests of the facilities.

Client
Istanbul Modern Art Museum
Design Team
Tabanlioglu Architects

City Film

Istanbul's urban landscape is a palimpsest. In an attempt to probe some of the city's layers, the video collage is organized as a journey from the periphery to the centre, where the simple act of crossing the Bosphorus encompasses everything, from the quotidian realities of commuting to the urban pressures of de-industrialisation and the incomparable quality of light in this vibrant city.

Audio/Video
Contributors
Elif Akçali, Metin Çavuş,
David Rosenthal,
Andy Rice,
Cassim Shepard
Audio contributors
Anton, Laurent,
Jean-Jaques Palix,
Matthew Sansom,
Sazman, Tigersound
Montage
Cassim Shepard

Milan and Turin, Italy

Area Portello

The urban project for the Portello area refurbishes the disused areas of the former Alfa Romeo and Lancia plants, large industrial zones that have resulted in an effect of discontinuity and urban isolation, creating a new large park, fully-equipped areas and squares, services, new homes and functions compatible with the surrounding urban fabric. The masterplan sets out an urban fabric that renders the joining of the neighbouring district operational through the building of residential quarters. Moreover, the project reorganises the roads of the area through the realisation of a new itinerary and new, large half-ring able to distribute and balance incoming flows; the implementation of the rationalisation of the existing road network and improvement of the public transport. The large public park will constitute an effective environmental barrier with respect the considerable traffic flows and will be easily accessible from cycling and pedestrian paths and itineraries crossing the area.

Client
Comune di Milano
Design team
Masterplan, Gino Valle
Cino Zucchi
Guido Canali
Charles Jencks and Andreas Kipar

BEIC, Biblioteca Europea di Informazione e Cultura

The winning entry of an international competition run by the Municipality of Milan, this project for a 21st century learning and access centre is designed as the cultural centrepiece of a new neighbourhood surrounding a high-speed rail station at the heart of Milan. Designed to maximise transparency and spatial visibility, the project takes advantage of the dense urban location by opening its foyer spaces to the city with a sequence of fluid circulation spaces that duplicate the external urban condition and create a focus for readers, students and members of the public who wish to engage with BEIC's archive and collection, and expand the cultural facilities on offer – art, mixed-media and high-technology information – to Milan's growing local and international residential constituencies.

Client
Comune di Milano
Design team
Bolles Wilson

Garibaldi Repubblica

The Integrated Intervention Programme for the Garibaldi Repubblica area is part of a broader project redesigning about 35 hectares of built-up area. The principles guiding the master urban plan aim to return a unifying look to the whole, although diversified in the expressive forms of the single parts, and in the relationships between them and the surrounding area. The urban layout foresees the realisation of a large central park to be laid out in line with a design by Inside-Outside, the Dutch team that won the contest arranged by the Milan City Council with their 'Library of trees' project. The park will be overlooked by the new headquarters of the Milan City Council, the 'Other Headquarters' of the Lombardy Region and the complex of tertiary functions of the Città della Moda (Fashion City).

Client
Comune di Milano
Design teams
"Altra Sede" della Regione: Pei Cobb Freed & Partners, Caputo Partnership, Sistema Duemila, Città della Moda, Cesar Pelli.
New headquarters for the City Council
technical offices of the Comune di Milano,
consultants Cecchi & Lima

New Milan Fair Centre, Rho Pero

The Milan Fair transformation project is redesigning the boundaries, both in terms of structure and infrastructure, in the area north-west of Milan and Lombardy: they are geographical and social boundaries, but more than anything they are economic ones. The complex is divided into eight pavilions: two two-storey pavilions, four one-storey pavilions and two elevated-height ones. The sail, symbol of the entire work, came from an idea by the architect Massimiliano Fuksas; over 1300 metres long, covering 47,000 m² of surface area, it will link the East Port and the West Port of the New Centre, and comprises 9,000 tonnes of steel and glass. Due to its considerable engineering complexity, the sail has undergone numerous tests in the wind tunnel at Milan Polytechnic. The feature providing the greatest effect consists of the 7,000 m² covering the service centre, requiring constant verifications due to the stress caused by the wind and changes in temperature. At a height of over 36 metres, the one closest to the service centre is also the highest point of the entire structure.

Client
Fondazione Fiera Milano and Sviluppo Sistema Fiera
Design Team
Massimiliano Fuksas

Portello, World Jewellery Centre

WJC is a centre for work, services and initiatives aimed at showcasing the single companies and promoting Milan as one of the most important centres in the world for jewellery. WJC is home to a jewellery school, research laboratories, associations for the development of small and medium-sized companies and numerous service companies. The operation is part of the Portello urban revival project. The complex appears as a series of buildings positioned around a large central, partially-roofed unit forming an atrium. The entrance to the building is effected from a stairway flanked by four pools of water set at two distinct levels. This form of gallery creates spreading pathways leading towards the roofed area of the piazza below. As part of the "U1" project co-ordination unit, three towers will be built as residences for subsidised and other housing.

Client
WJC - World Jewellery Center - srl
TORRI STELLA srl
Promoted by
Comune di Milano
Design team
progettarecostruire; urbam; studio di architettura Mello; Andreas Kipar

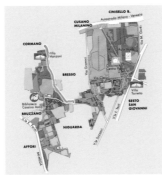

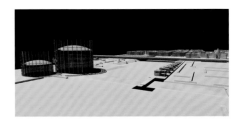

Regeneration of ex-Milan Fair Zone

With the inauguration of the Milan Fair New Pole, the famous Fair district will reduce its presence in the city leaving space for important urban regeneration work on the Milanese and Lombard panorama. The project took on the challenge of redesigning the 255,000 m² of the historic Milan Fair area and has pinpointed, among others, three characterising elements. There is the large naturalistic park, an indispensable loop for the living continuity of the large green system spreading between San Siro and Sempione Park, and a water course that links the two extremities of the park. The Tre Torri constitute the powerful symbol of transformation: they rebind the thread of a tradition that has generated examples of great efficacy and strong urban presence in Italy, such as the Pirelli skyscraper and the Velasca Tower in modern Milan. Two complexes are devoted to the most innovative and creative public functions, with the Museum and the Centre dedicated to Milanese and Italian excellence in design, whilst the spirit of educational and social initiative, aimed particularly at the younger and older groups of society, is housed in Pavilion 3. This building sees the conservation/transformation of the old Palazzo dello Sport, one of the symbols that reside in the Milanese collective memory of a recent past.

Client
Milan City Council, Fondazione Fiera di Milano
Design Team
Zaha Hadid, Arata Isozaki, Daniel Libeskind and Pier Paolo Maggiora

Santa Giulia, Montecity-Rogoredo

The 'Montecity-Rogoredo' Project will return to the city the vast area occupied since the 1970s by the Montedison plant and by the Acciaierie Redaelli works in the south-eastern part of Milan, south-east of the Rogoredo district. The area is linked to the main infrastructure connecting Milan to its hinterland and the national networks and is just one kilometre from Linate airport. The project is based around a main axis providing a point of reference, consisting of a large central part of about 333,000 square metres. This will distinguish the area as two sectors: a northern area of Santa Giulia, destined for housing, commercial structures and the Congress Centre, and a southern one, Rogoredo, for housing. The urban design and functional systems forming it are planned to be in synergy with the neighbouring districts and with other parts of the metropolitan system which are further but closely linked through strong infrastructural networks.

Client
Risanamento SpA - Gruppo Zunino
Design Team
Foster and Partners
Town project
Paolo Caputo Partnership, Raum srl

Parco Nord

The Parco Nord is one of the most successful examples of a park on the outskirts of the city, with over two million visitors a year, since it has succeeded in transforming the area in which it was founded, 'colouring' green what had been grey, and starting a project of refurbishment of the whole of the northern outskirts of Milan. Over three million m² of land have been acquired, transformed and equipped as public parkland. These operations have shown how a partial refurbishment of a river can become a realistically achievable aim even when it proves impossible to undertake a more radical cleaning up operation of the waters. After careful cleaning, removing all detritus and rendering the banks natural once more, the construction projects for sports and recreational facilities became executive: a cycleway and pedestrian itinerary, allotments for pensioners, car park and rotonda, formal garden. Through this project, the park will succeed in definitively recovering a highly important ecological corridor, available for use also by the city's inhabitants.

Client
Comune di Milano, Provincia di Milano, Comuni di Sesto San Giovanni, Cinisello Balsamo, Bresso, Cormano, Cusano Milanino
Design Team
Francesco Borella
Executive projects
Ente Parco Nord Milano

Parco delle Cave

Located between the districts of the western suburbs of Milan, the Parco delle Cave occupies a area of 135 hectares and features four lakes, the bequest of a quarrying activity for sand and gravel dating from the 1920s. It forms part of a system of public parkland realised by the council and including the Parco di Trenno and the Boscoincittà, as well as the surrounding farmland. In April 1999, the park comprised 111 hectares of public land, included within the perimeter of the Parco Agricolo Sud Milano. The entrance to the park aims to create a space providing a sense of landscape continuity between the park and the built-up area around, with a piazza at the entry as the central element of the area. The 'Cava Cabassi' project transforms the area around the lake completely. The 'Area Cascina Caldera' foresees maintaining the farm structure, with water channels, copses around drinking troughs and large open spaces. The ample parking area will be reorganised with rows of ashtrees and playing fields.

Client
Comune di Milano, Settore Parchi e Giardini
Design Team
Italia Nostra Onlus - Centro per la Forestazione Urbana

Parco Forlanini

The Forlanini is a city park linked to the suburban transportation network (ring-road, public transport) and to the pedestrian access points, thereby ensuring a functional continuity with the city. The main entrance to the park features a large *piazza* with a multifunctional centre and structures used by the railway. North of the *piazza*, there will be space for recreational activities and an area with refreshment facilities. To the south, an area has been defined for concerts and other cultural events. The project foresees the various restoration programmes for the Cascine have a cultural nature. Water represents an important element in the layout of the project, which includes the adjustment of the banks of the river Lambro, the re-opening of the artificial canals and the tidying of the existing lake. The agricultural areas area also included in the new project. Among these, the urban allotments, situated in various parts of the park, delineating the transition between the park and the area to the east of the city.

Client
Comune di Milano, Settore Parchi e Giardini
Design team
GB Arquitectos (Gonçalo byrne); PROAP; P31; Studio Silva

City Film

The artistic collective Studio dotdotdot has created a playful video piece that deftly knits together images evoking various aspects of the city through its built environment. The physicality of Milan is firmly embedded in traditions of craftsmanship and the mythic promise of urban social mobility. The fast-paced, multi-layered juxtapositions resonate with the city's incomparable energy.

Video
Studio dotdotdot, Nicolas Alvarez, Joaquin Ostrovsky
Music and Sound Design
Suite Sound Design

Milan and Turin, Italy

La Venaria Reale

The restoration work of Reggia di Venaria Reale and its area (1,000,000 m² in total), which began in 1999, comes under the investment plan of the Residenze Sabaude Circuit in Piemonte and represents one of the most important restoration sites in Europe. It is an ambitious project whose results could be decisive for the layout of the entire metropolitan area. It is an experimental site that powerfully marks the growth of Venaria as a cultural and tourist reference pole and a powerful force in the programme of urban transformation. The project, in which over 100 designers have participated, includes the Museum of Sabaud court life, the Landscape Gallery, the restoration of 80 hectares of historic gardens, which act as a contrast to the contemporary art installations, the regeneration of the historic centre, the International Centre of the Horse, the Centre for Conservation and Restoration (8,000 m²), which was created in the ex-Stables and the 18th-century riding school and which has become the third Italian centre in the sector, and a school for the university education of restorers and conservators.

Client
Comitato per la Reggia di Venaria Reale
Design Team
FIAT Engineering (Museum), Paolo Marconi (orangery and stables), Derossi Associati (Centre for Conservation and Restoration), studio Libidarch (gardens)

La Spina, Turin

The underground railway link has created a 12km-long axis along which a succession of large worksites and new areas of urban transformation with various functions have been established. The 'Spina 2' has been confirmed as the new cultural centre of Turin in which disused industries make space for new activities dedicated to culture, art and education. New works along the large, central, tree-lined avenue standing above the new tunnels include the expansion of the Politecnico, the Officine Grandi Riparazioni and, opposite, works on the area that once housed the Nebiolo works and Wastinghouse where Turin's new cultural centre will stand. The new Porta Susa Station (with a surface area of over 15,000 m²) is earmarked to become Turin's main train station. Further north is the 'Spina 3' area, covering over 1,000,000 m² of disused industries along the River Dora, with the activation of an urban regeneration programme that has involved both public and private resources to create a new mixture of urban functions. New complexes of residential buildings (Villaggio Media, Isole nel Parco), commercial enterprises (Parco Commerciale Dora in the ex Michelin plant), productive enterprises (regeneration of the disused Officine Savigliano) and research centres (Environment Park) are to be housed inside the new Parco della Dora, which acts as a connecting thread between the individual works.

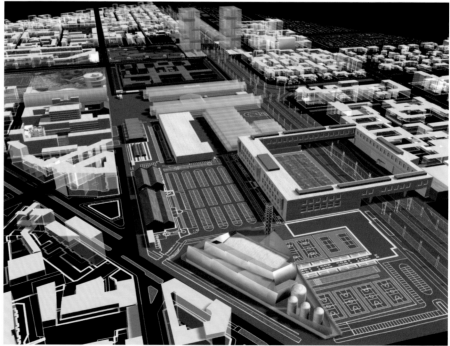

Turin Olympic Village, ex Mercati Generali area

The Olympic Village was the most important work created for the 2006 Winter Olympics and is part of a complex process of transformation and reuse of a vast urban area (approximately 170,000 m²) situated south of the city along the Lingotto railway yard. An international project team designed the three residential blocks that housed 2500 athletes and worked on the restoration and reuse of the disused structures of the famous Turin Fruit and Vegetable Wholesale Market, designed in the 1930s, to create multifunctional spaces. A 156-metre suspended pedestrian walkway powerfully marks the new urban neighbourhood and, crossing the railway, it links it to the renovated Lingotto complex. Post-Olympics, the 36 buildings containing 7-8 storeys of residences have been converted into residential and office space whilst the renovated ex Mercati Generali will house the new cultural-educational functions, confirming Turin as a city of knowledge.

Client
Agenzia Torino 2006
Design Team
Benedetto Camerana, AIA Architectes, Derossi Associati, Hugh Dutton Associés, Angela Maccianti, Inarco, Prodim, Giorgio Rosental, Steidle und Partners

Central Avenue and Railway Link
Client
Turin City, Rete Ferroviaria Italiana
Design Team
Studio Gregotti Associati, Italferr SpA

Turin Cultural Centre
Client
Turin City Council
Design Team
Mario Bellini

San Paolo IMI Skyscraper
Client
San Paolo
Design Team
Renzo Piano

New railway station Porta Susa
Client
RFI
Design Team
AREP – J.M. Duthilleul, E. Tricaud (group leader), Silvio d'Ascia, Agostino Magnaghi

Dora Commercial Park
Client
Nova Coop Scarl, Sviluppo Dora srl
Design Team
PROMO.GE.CO., Studio Granma

Environment Park, Technological Scientific Park for the Environment
Client
Environment Park SpA
Design Team
Benedetto Camerana, Giovanni Durbiano, Luca Reinerio

Società Nazionale Officine Savigliano, Regeneration ex Savigliano Workshops
Client
S.N.O.S. SpA
Design Team
Studio Granma

Le Isole del Parco: New Spina 3 residential centre, sub district south Valdocco
Client
Valdocco SpA
Design Team
1999-2000 Gabetti & Isola; 2000-2005 Isolarchitetti (Aimaro Isola, Saverio Isola, Maria Teresa La Ferla)

Parco della Dora
Client
Turin City
Design Team
Latz+Partners

City Film
To create the original video 'New Century', Turin-based filmmakers Francesca Bocca, Davide Ferrario and Enrico Verra have focused broadly on the concept of 'work'. Ranging from mass production of the FIAT factory to individuals labouring across socioeconomic strata, this video examines Turinese identity in light of its past, present and future.

Video
Francesca Bocca, Davide Ferrario and Enrico Verra
Additional support
Torino Internazionale and Paolo Verri

London, United Kingdom

100 Public Spaces Programme

In 2002 the Mayor of London, Ken Livingstone, launched a programme to create or upgrade 100 public spaces in London. The initiative was based on the Mayor's conviction that 'creating and managing high quality public spaces is essential to delivering an urban renaissance in London'. The programme seeks to enhance the value of London's existing network of public spaces and to show how new and revitalised public spaces can effect a real change on individual quality of life and community vitality. 20 projects are being developed to date.

Brixton Central Square

Brixton Central Square is formed from three separate public spaces, Tate Gardens, Windrush Square and St Matthew's Peace Garden. The spaces are loosely defined by a series of civic buildings, including the Town Hall, St Matthew's Church, Raleigh Hall and the Tate Library. However, the spaces are disconnected from each other and these civic buildings by a series of roads, two of which, Brixton Hill and Effra Road, carry heavy traffic. The project for Brixton Central Square aims to create a high quality public space that does justice to the significance of Brixton and provides a much needed open space for this pedestrian-heavy residential area.

Client
London Borough of Lambeth, Greater London Authority
Design Team
GrossMax

Victoria Embankment

Victoria Embankment is a major example of Victorian infrastructure, and is used as a setting for major events, marches and the Marathon. Yet Victoria Embankment's full potential as a riverside space for citizens remains unrealised. Currently it is primarily a key traffic route, linking the financial sphere of the City and the political sphere of Westminster, and as a consequence pedestrian access to the riverside walk is severely constrained. Proposed strategic interventions include widening the riverside walk to make pedestrian space more dominant and to enable a substantial south-facing promenade. Another row of trees could be planted to further distance pedestrians from the road. Lateral connections need to be developed between the Victoria Embankment and St. James's Park, Covent Garden and Trafalgar Square, and the new park-like environment needs to be integrated into the adjacent gardens.

Client
Greater London Authority, Transport for London, City of Westminster, City of London
Design Team
MacCormac Jamieson Prichard (lead)

Exhibition Road

London's Exhibition Road links South Kensington Underground Station to Hyde Park The area has been a centre for public education in the arts and sciences. However the predominance of car traffic on Exhibition Road, the area's main artery, precludes safe and full appreciation of the site. The project proposes London's first 'shared surface' streetscape. This traffic management idea eliminates unnecessary street furniture, traffic islands and railings, to give greater priority to pedestrians and to encourage more careful behaviour by drivers. A single surface will be marked by a yellow diagonal grid. The local authority is leading this experimental approach to urban planning and the Transport Studies unit at Imperial College will monitor the experiment. The local authority is committed to the project and the necessary adjustments that may be required as patterns of use evolve.

Client
The Royal Borough of Kensington and Chelsea
Design Team
Dixon Jones (lead)

London 2012 Olympics & Lower Lea Valley Legacy Masterplans

The Master Plans for the Olympic Games and the regeneration of the Lower Lea Valley illustrate how one of the poorest parts of the UK could stage the Olympics and Paralympics and subsequently be transformed into a new urban district for London. The area's waterways are the structuring element, with the nine new Games facilities, including an 80,000-seat Olympic Stadium, arranged along either side of the river valley and a public concourse crossing in between. Rivers and canals will undergo remediation. A 'Legacy' Master Plan will facilitate the development of new housing and community facilities around the central 500-acre Olympic Games Park. A Lower Lea Valley Regeneration Strategy will transform under-utilised industrial land into a series of new communities. New housing will be high density and 50% of the 35,000 new homes built will be affordable, served by new social infrastructure. Bridges, pedestrian and cycle routes and a new road network will re-integrate under served areas.

Client
London Development Agency
Design Team
EDAW (lead), HOK Sport, Allies & Morrison and Foreign Office Architects

City East

London's population is set to grow by a million people over the next twenty years. A quarter of this growth is expected to be housed in just three percent of its area, 32 km² known as City East. Located to the immediate east of London's existing centre, the City East area has long been integral to London's status as a world city - first as the core of London's port, and today as the focus of its rapid growth eastwards. City East is home to some of London's boldest urban visions – past and future - including Canary Wharf, the Millennium Dome, and by 2012, the Olympic park. The public sector has a key role to play in delivering these set-piece projects, and also in steering and coordinating the market-led growth generated in their wake. In City East, expanding public transport and public space infrastructure has a key role in supporting higher densities, fostering a more complex mix of uses, creating an integrated piece of city, and structuring urban change to deliver sustainable places.

Client
Greater London Authority
Design Team
Mayor of London's Architecture and Urbanism Unit, KCAP Architects

City Film

London may articulate the post-national condition of 21st century urbanism more overtly than almost anywhere else on the planet. One way to illuminate the city's baffling complexity is to explore the proximity of distinct housing typologies, the symbiotic relationship of informal markets to global financial centres, and the adjacency of iconic architecture of the 17th century to that of the 20th. The London video collage plays on these juxtapositions while exposing the importance of the elements that bind the city together. The public transit network, the parks, and the Thames bring coherence to the urban scale.

Audio/Video Contributors
Ane Larsen, Sara Muzio, Luca Paci, Hanna Shell, Cassim Shepard, Alexander Weil
Audio contributors
Jorge Alfonso, Mr Chips, Peter Bach Nicholson, Dallas Simpson, Tigersound, Matthew Twining
Montage
Cassim Shepard

White City Development

The development site hinges two polarised neighbourhoods in west London – to the east lie some of the city's wealthiest boroughs, and to the west some of the city's most notorious and deprived housing estates. This under-utilised strip of land covers 43 acres and is dissected into three parts. The site is severed from its surroundings by transport infrastructure, notably the A40 motorway and the Hammersmith & City Tube viaduct. The project's ambition is to reverse the segregated nature of the site through physical and programmatic links. The masterplan organises the site into three clusters of development interspersed with public open spaces. Drawing on existing London typologies, each cluster seeks to create a diverse range of urban environments with a unique mix of functions. Proposed functions include commercial zones, community facilities and outdoor recreational areas.

Client
The White City Partnership
Design Team
OMA

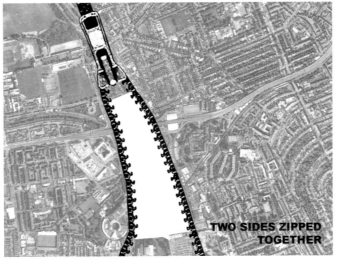

TWO SIDES ZIPPED TOGETHER

Barcelona, Spain

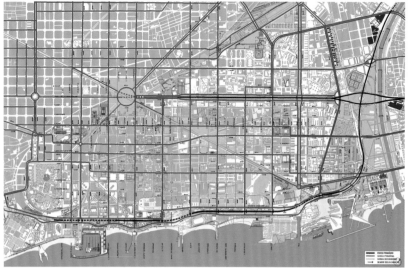

Gran Via – Zona Franca

The southwest littoral of the city, stretching between the old port and the Llobregat River, encompasses the principal industrial and logistical zone of Barcelona. In addition to the port, the proximity to the airport of this area – which will act as an intercontinental hub on completion of its expansion and the new high-speed-train link – gives it strong potential to galvanize the economy of the metropolitan region. Major urban projects are under way, including the new trade-fair site, the Ciutat Judicial (complex of legal institutions), the Plaça de Europa and the transformation of the Can Batlló site, and the development of the Marina district with over 10,000 housing units.

Client
Barcelona Regional
City of Barcelona

Sants – Montjuïc

For the past 25 years, Barcelona has gained recognition as an authentic urban design laboratory in its urban-planning efforts. Since the 80s, quality of urban space has been the touchstone for the transformation of the city, beginning with the creation of gardens, squares and streets, and continuing with projects that go far beyond the domestic scale such as the Seafront, the Ciutadella park, Diagonal Mar, the Fòrum, Montjuïc, Tres Turons, and Collserola Park. Now, the scar left by the rail lines that harshly divide the Sants district will be covered over with a park. The goal is to keep most of the rail lines while creating a high-quality urban space. Accessibility of the entire district will be improved and the arrival of the high speed train to the Sants station will make it a strong city hub.

Client
Barcelona Regional
City of Barcelona

22@ - Glòries

Barcelona has turned its development eastwards, in a clear commitment to rebalancing the city. This transformation emphasizes three key elements: Les Glòries, Sagrera and the Fòrum. Together they define a triangle which must become the metropolitan reference of the new economy. The old industrial fabric of the Poblenou district is being renovated and transformed by the 22@ Plan. Old industrial constructions are being turned into buildings geared to housing the activities of the new economy. This new technological district will encompass more then 4 million m² of economic activity and 40,000 housing units. The Plaça de les Glòries takes up a new central position that contrasts with the perception of this spot as a frontier between the consolidated Eixample and the industrial periphery of the city. Designed as a 16 hectare park, it will act as a hinge between the 22@ district and the Eixample and Ciutat Vella.

Client
Barcelona Regional
City of Barcelona

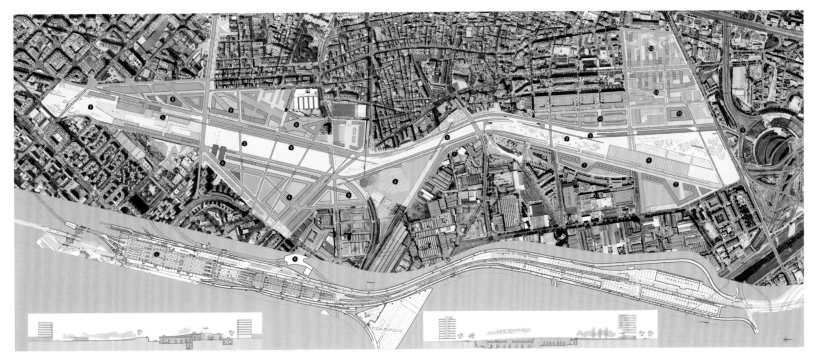

Sagrera

The Sagrera project creates a new urban centrality for Barcelona triggered by an innovative high speed train station layered on four different levels which acts as an intermodal transport node. The station will not only become an important component of the whole public transport system but will also act as a catalyst for a new urban geography. The buildings, housings, offices and hotels will constitute the largest tertiary cluster of the city. There will also be a large shopping centre (over 120,000 m^2) and offices (600,000 m^2). A linear park of over 3.5 km in length will serve as a spine for the 8,500 dwellings built on brownfield sites and will link two parts of the city which have historically been separated from each other.

Client
Barcelona Regional
City of Barcelona

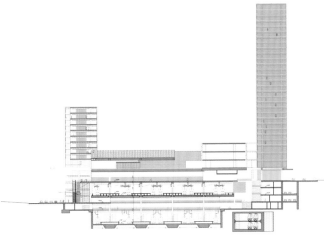

The Fòrum

On the 2.5 km of coastline running north to the Besòs River, the most important urban project of the city was developed to complete the transformation of the seafront, the first stage of which was the Villa Olímpica. Diagonal Avenue finally reaches the sea by way of a large esplanade which covers infrastructures and facilities. The Forum area, which was a major brownfield of the city is transformed, not by relocating its facilities but by updating them through state of the art technology. The new Rambla de la Mina district shapes the construction of the all-new International Convention Center, university campus, and residential complex which will contribute to the regeneration and improvement of this formerly at-risk neighbourhood. Beaches, parks and singular public spaces have thus been created.

Client
Barcelona Regional
City of Barcelona

Tokyo, Japan

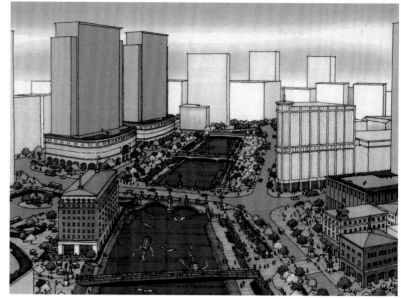

The Nihonbashi bridge project – relocating a metropolitan expressway

Originally built in 1603 as part of the national road improvements programme of the time, Nihonbashi is the starting point of the Tokaido and other historical routes. Considered a site of historical importance, the Nihonbashi has been rebuilt eighteen times. The current bridge dates back to 1911. Its two arches are made out of stone. However, not much remains from the Edo period vistas celebrated by Ukiyo-e artists. Among other issues, the Capital Expressway, built in 1964 for the occasion of the Tokyo Olympic Games, overshadows the bridge. In recent years, an initiative has been gaining ground to relocate the expressway and improve the quality of life of the area by restoring the original urban landscape. Initiated by local residents, this proposal has yet to gain consensus among all the political actors who would need to be involved.

Client
Ministry of Land, Infrastructure and Transport
Design Team
Metropolitan Expressway, Limited Company

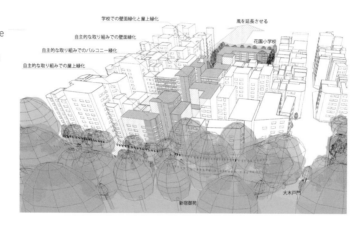

The Cool Island projects – a network of parks and green spaces

The average temperature of Tokyo is now 3 Celsius degrees higher than it was a hundred years ago. The number of summer days with a temperature over 30 degrees, sweltering nights, local downpours, and energy consumption have all increased as a result. Tokyo's heat island phenomenon is the result of ever expanding car flows, usage of air conditioners, the turning of the city into a 'concrete jungle', and the high-rise buildings on the waterfront that block the breeze from Tokyo Bay and its cooling effect. In 2004, the Ministry of the Environment initiated an evaluation of the cooling effects that green areas have on their areas of influence. Based on the experience from Shinjuku Gyoen Park and its surroundings, it was confirmed that large-scale green corridors facilitate the passage of cooling wind. The possibility of a green network linking Meiji Jingu, Akasaka Gosho, Jingu Gaien, Aoyama Cemetery and other "cool islands" is now being considered.

Client
Ministry of Environment

Expansion of Haneda Airport

Because of the increase in air traffic, many thought that the Tokyo region would need a third major airport to add to the capacity of Narita and Haneda. In September 2000, however, the Japanese government decided that additional capacity would be created by adding an extra runway to Haneda airport. The runway and other airport facilities are planned to be built on a land fill island in Tokyo Bay. However, concerns were voiced that a large number of airplanes landing may create noise pollution in adjacent neighbourhoods or spoil views from Tokyo Disneyland. In response to these issues, the angle of the runway was modified: instead of a flat surface, the runway will assume a gentle upward slope towards the North in order to help reduce the speed of arriving planes after a steep landing.

Client
Mininistry of Land, Infrastructure and Transport

The Fibre City Proposal (I) – City Gardens

The risk of fire is highest in older, densely built areas of Tokyo just outside the Yamanote belt line where the housing stock is made out of wood. Because these districts emerged in a context lacking clear urban planning guidelines, the feasibility of point interventions in specific areas is low. On the other hand, through house plants and small furniture placed on roads and other common grounds, these *mokuchin* districts present typically Japanese micro urban spaces. This intervention proposes to expand these common grounds, creating green buffers for fire protection and improving these areas' sense of place.

Design Team
Ohno Laboratory, University of Tokyo
Speculative proposal

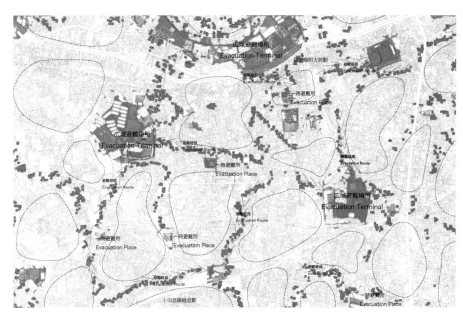

The Kanda River – the underground reservoir and canal renaissance

Because of frequently occurring heavy rains and typhoons, downstream cities in Japan tend to see the country's fast flowing rivers more as threats to be protected from than as a resource to enjoy. Local governments undertake many measures of flood control such as tracing hazard maps of easily floodable areas, erecting small barriers as well as super dykes to protect surrounding environments, and building underground water reservoirs in densely developed urban areas. The Tokyo Metropolitan Government is currently studying how to enhance the social use of its waterways and improve the quality of surrounding areas. World examples such as Venice are inspirational for this initiative towards a canal renaissance.

Client and Design Team
Tokyo Bureau of Construction

The redevelopment of Marunouchi district

A number of innovative zoning allowances are designed to encourage increased private investment and contribute to the urban regeneration of Tokyo. In 2006, a special zoning regime was set up to intensify land uses in Marunouchi, perhaps the most significant central business district in the Japanese economy. The selling of air rights above Tokyo Station is an example of how to facilitate the overall intensification of use in an area while at the same time obtaining funding for the renovation of a historically preserved building. In recent years, close to 20 high-rise buildings have been retrofitted, benefiting from new zoning provisions.

Client and Design Team
Mitsubishi Estate and others

City Film

The Tokyo video collage is a meditation on motion, on how people negotiate their paths through one of the largest urban agglomerations on Earth, on how travelling between points in a city is, in itself, a vital experience of the urban.

Audio/Video Contributors
Lars Jan, Neutral: Tapio Snellman & Christian Grou
Audio contributors
Anton, Audiblepie, Capuchin, Heigh-hoo, Jai, Ryota Kasaki, Koura, Marec, Sawako, Yuko Nexus6
Montage
Cassim Shepard

Mumbai, India

Worli Bandra Sea Link

Construction of Worli Bandra Sea Link will provide an additional connection between Salsette Island city and the western suburbs (at present there is only one). The project has earmarked almost 13 hectares of land for greenery by the Mahim Bay, reconnecting the city to its beleaguered sea and coast line. It has introduced a 1.5 kilometre promenade along the sea front and a breathing urban open space for the neighbourhood and the city. Landscaping along the approaches and waterfront promenade has enhanced the environment. The 13 ha urban park is comprised of recreational gardens intended for all sections of society. The development thus represents an example in which an infrastructure project where the alignment of the bridge has been a generator of an urban open space.

Client
Maharashtra State Road Development Corporation Limited
Design Team
M/s Ratan J.Batliboi - Architects, M/s Swati Dike, M/s Shrikande Consultants, M/s Vikas Joshi and Associates

Chikhalwadi Sanitation Project

In cities such as Mumbai, which lack sanitation facilities for more than 50% of the population, slum and pavement dwellers have little option but to squat along roads and rail tracks. This daily ritual of defecating in the open in cities and in the absence of running water and sewerage connections is degrading and potentially life threatening, with a very real risk of spread of infection and disease. For children in slums, their playgrounds are also their bathrooms. These kids can never compete in the long queues for municipal toilets and end up having to defecate outside their homes. These community toilet blocks are designed, constructed and maintained by community collectives, who are trained and supported by SPARC federation networks. They include separate spaces for men, women and children; the latter toilets include colourful open squatting platforms with handles for kids to hold on to. The capital finance for construction comes from the state or municipalities who also have to ensure that water and electricity are provided to the toilet blocks.

Client
SPARC
Design Team
Vistaar Architects and Planners

Bharat Janata

When land is scarce, especially in cities like Mumbai, communities look at multi-storey housing options. Since this type of construction is more expensive, securing subsidies is essential. The Slum Rehabilitation Authority's policy in Maharashtra allows 2.5 FSI (floor space index). While part of it can be used to rehouse the slum dwellers in-situ and the remaining part shall be sold in the open market. By taking up the Bharat Janata CHS, SPARC demonstrated that sites situated within the deepest heart of the largest slum of Asia, Dharavi, can be reconstructed with SRA provisions and decent living conditions can be enjoyed by communities. SPARC also succeeded in acquiring the financial supports in terms of bridge finance and loans from the National Housing Bank (NHB). SPARC's strategy is to set precedents for housing solutions that can be scaled up across cities and states so that very large numbers of the poor can benefit. The organisation works in partnership with various levels of local and regional authorities, financial institutions and poor communities as well as advocating for better housing policies at the city, state and national level.

Client
SPARC

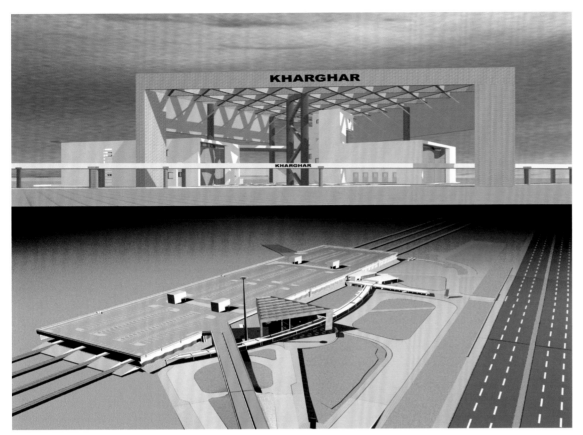

Kharghar Railway Station

Navi Mumbai, developed to decongest population and commerce from mainland Mumbai, is projected to accommodate 2 million people and 750,000 jobs in next three decades. Kharghar is one of Navi Mumbai's nodes, serving 400,000 residents. The new Kharghar Railway Station is a benchmark for a progressive railway station design in India. The station structure is adaptable to phased development in the future modernisation of the railway commuter facilities. Concepts new to Mumbai include the use of the air space above the platform level for parking to release an equivalent amount of land. 19,300 m² of parking deck area cars two wheelers released land on ground, of which 16,000 m² was sold for development and the remaining 3,300 m² developed for landscaping. The ease of direct access from car park to main railway concourse by lifts and stairways encourages private drivers to use a public facility. Various modes of traffic are segregated within the site and a definite hierarchy between the pedestrian and vehicular traffic is established within the forecourt area. Taxi and bus terminals for intra-city use could be accommodated in the 7,000 m² commercial plot on the northern side. Correspondingly the area of commercial plot for sale on the southern side could be increased to recover the overall investment costs.

Client
The City and Industrial Development Corporation of Maharashtra Limited
Design Team
M/s Ratan J. Batliboi - Architects

Turbhe Mandale Resettlement & Rehabilitation

Mumbai relies on its extensive suburban railway system to get its workforce in and out of the central city. Seven million passengers are transported each day on the five railway corridors that originate in the south of the city and branch out to the north and north-east. Trains are always overcrowded. The railway's capacity in speed and efficiency was also kept down by the illegal railway settlements that crowded each side of the tracks; by 1999, there were over 20,000 households living in shacks within 25 meter of the tracks. Most of these households have been living there for more than two decades, and many huts are built less than a meter from the passing trains. These illegal settlements, squeezed each side of the tracks, also restricted the speed of the trains. The resettlement of households living within 10 metres of the tracks was formulated by a task force appointed by the state government, which recommended that each "project-affected family" should get a temporary (or transit) accommodation measuring 120 sq.ft. and with basic amenities, who were to be moved before the permanent accommodation of a 20.9m² apartment free of cost was ready for them. The resettlement was also to be implemented with the active involvement of SPARC and the Railway Slum Dwellers Federation (RSDF) and the full participation of affected communities,

and coordinated by the MMRDA. The scheme is notable in that: it did not impoverish those who moved (as is generally the case when poor groups are moved to make way for infra-structure development); the actual move was voluntary and needed neither police nor municipal force to enforce it; and the resettled people were involved in designing, planning and implementing the resettlement programme and in managing the settlements to which they moved. These temparary transit often tend to become permanent beyond the stipulated trade line of 3 years after which they have to be demolished and the land has to be returned to his original form. Thus the temparary units were planned with a view that the layout makes community coexistence naturally possible just as in case of informal slums societies. With provision of 9m ring road as the infrastructural spine and sanitation blocks within each clusters at the rate of 1 W.C. per 20 persons and a green pocket within each cluster of about 120 tenements, the entire construction was completed within 3 months including infrastructural development. 2,500 families were resettled in Mankhurd; 891 families were resettled in Turbhe Mandale.

Client
SPARC, Railway Slum Dwellers Federation

City Film

Mumbai's overwhelming density does not allow for any space to be wasted, on trains, under bridges, between buildings. The images in this video collage focus on the innovative spatial practices that emerge from this extreme urban condition and continuously reorganize human coexistence.

Audio/Video Contributors
Amit Dutta,
Vinayan Kodoth,
Cassim Shepard,
Sadia Shepard,
Dhiren Shukla
Montage
Cassim Shepard

Shanghai, People's Republic of China

YanAn Lu Park

YanAn Lu Park is located in the heart of Shanghai, at the crossing of the two major elevated highways. As a green belt between the highways and the buildings, the park improves the air quality, reduces the density and provides public spaces for the residents in the city center. The commissioned architects divided the 210,000 m² park area into several parts, each of which will have distinct set of design guidelines. Wooded and open meadows in the parks will be punctuated by squares dedicated to particular leisure activities, including *Tai Chi* or basketball, nature walks or picnics.

Client
Shanghai Greenery Management Bureau
Design Team
Williams Asselim Askaoui

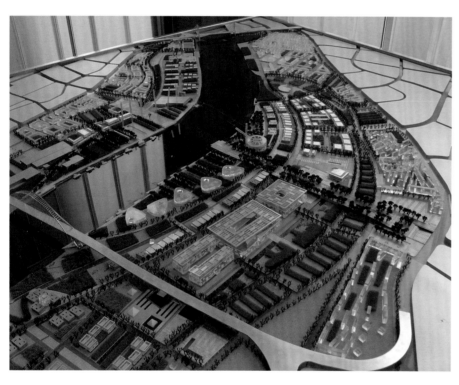

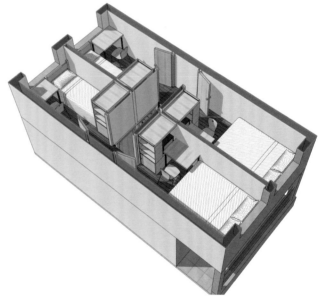

Shanghai Expo 2010
Client
Shanghai World Expo(Group) Co.,Ltd

Exhibition project "Chinascape"
Works by
Olivo Barbieri
Andrea Cavazzuti and Lu Yue
Yang Fudong
Curated by
Paola Tognon
Organisation
StART Venezia
Collaborators
Davide Quadrio, Bizart Center, Shanghai
Brancolini Grimaldi Arte Contemporanea, Italia

Low-Cost Rental Housing

Most of Shanghai's recent residential projects cater to middle or high income groups. While the real estate market is flooded with apartments of up to 250 m² floor size, the downtown area does not provide any new living spaces that are small or affordable.Only the smallest housing units are affordable, and these, increasingly, are in short supply. One of China's largest real estate companies, Vanke, initiated a project to provide affordable housing units. The buildings would accommodate the workers who support Vanke's large residential developments. Nannies, cleaners, maintenance personal and guards will be able to find affordable accommodation in the low-rent housing. These buildings which contain approximately 100 units, each unit providing a private room and shared kitchen and bathrooms for a single person or a couple. Moreover, the Low-Cost Rental Housing Project operates at a profit while increasing the efficacy and desirability of the developer's market-rate dwellings.

Client
Vanke (Shanghai)
Design Team
Peddle Thorp Architects

Dongtan Island Masterplan

Dongtan will be a holistically sustainable city of three villages. Phase one should be completed by 2010, in time for the World Expo in Shanghai, and will accommodate a population of 50,000, rising to a projected 500,000 by 2040. Dongtan will incorporate many traditional Chinese design features and is meant to feel like a 'Chinese' city. Dongtan will be self-supporting, generating all its energy needs, including transport, from renewables and will have zero emissions from the tailpipes of vehicles. In fact, the commitment to ecology, sustainability, public transport, green building and energy self-sufficiency will guide the project. For example, the delicate nature of the Dongtan wetlands and their importance to migrating birds and wildlife, has been one of the driving factors of the city's design. The plan will enhance the existing wetlands by returning agriculture land to its original wetland state to create a 'buffer-zone' between the city and the wetland - at its narrowest point, this 'buffer' will be four kilometres wide. Only 30% of the land area of the Dongtan site will be developed, protecting the adjacent wetlands from pollutants and the city's design aims to prevent pollutants reaching the adjacent wetland areas.

Client
Shanghai Industrial Investment Corporation (SIIC)
Design Team
Arup

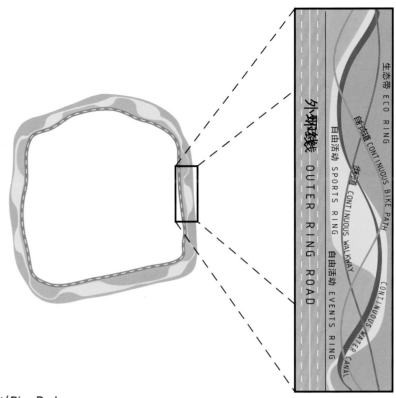

Greenbelt/ Ring Park

The Ring Park project is a large-scale urban planning intervention for a 100 km long park that will line the 3rd ring road that encircles Shanghai. The width and the functions of the green strip will vary; each segment of the park will have its own design team. The circular geometry of Ring Park will indicate to suburban residents that new developments on the outskirts are intrinsic to the new Shanghai while offering the residents a vast green zone. Especially in the low income residential zones - where large, joint families share small apartments - residents extend private life to the public areas. The residents of Shanghai engage in numerous activities in squares and gardens. Ring Park will provide an open space for such activities, thereby improving the quality of life in suburbs dramatically. Three different stripes overlap and cross each other along the ring: a sport zone will include jogging routes and fitness areas, an event zone will be used for performances and events and an ecological zone will encourage the conservation of natural resources.

Client
Shanghai Municipalità
Design Team
Shanghai Landscape Design Institute; BAU architects

Taikang Lu Development

Taikang Lu is a small scale low-rise commercial area in the southern downtown of Shanghai. Unlike most commercial areas, Taikang Lu was developed by multiple owners, although coordinated under one masterplan. The original houses were small brick-walled residential buildings and communist era office and factory buildings. The owners were seeking low budget commercial spaces and saw fit to preserve and renovate the existing buildings, sometimes adding small extensions. The pedestrian alleyways and public courtyards demonstrate innovative spatial organization: pedestrian access and good circulation encourages the use of the cafes, bars, and shops. Offices and workspaces are used by young designers and entrepreneurs. Today, Taikang Lu offers an inexpensive area, with a distinct urban character, as an alternative to the highly commercial large-scale areas in downtown.

Design Team
Various (Masterplan by SURV, Shanghai)

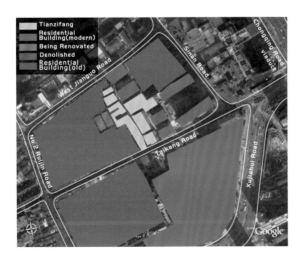

City Film

Within a small area of central Shanghai on both banks of the Huangpu, global aspirations of financial influence confront local survival strategies. This video collage examines Shanghai's image of itself in light of its rapid urban development. Recurring visual allusions to the city's past counterpose brave new visions of its future.

Audio/Video Contributors
Tomasz Gubernat, Alexander Weil
Additional footage contributed by
MADA s.p.a.m.
Audio contributors
Jmfh, Sazman, Stjson
Montage
Cassim Shepard

Johannesburg,
Republic of South Africa

City Film
Artist and urban geographer Ismail Farouk has developed a unique method of representing his city. Using his extensive research experience with Johannesburg's urban poor and a wide range of digital photographs, video and archival film, his intricate and kinetic flash animations illuminate the urban rhythms of Johannesburg in a singular way.

Sound design and original score
Ismail Farouk & Dimitri Voudouris
Video & Montage
Ismail Farouk

Berlin, Germany

City Film
This video collage takes the abundance of space in Berlin —the richness in emptiness—as its central theme. A swift visual journey through the disparate neighbourhoods of Marzahn, Neukölln, Charlottenburg and Kreuzberg reveals a public life that creatively adapts its expansive spaces to reflect the character of an increasingly diverse city of immigrants.

Audio/Video Contributors
Lena Müeller, Cassim Shepard, Wendy Taylor
Audio contributors
Giovanni Bai, Mads bech Paluszewski, Ole Rönnau
Montage
Cassim Shepard

Project image credits

São Paulo

Nova Luz
Credit EMURB/City of Sao Paulo

F Line Extension
Credit Una Arquitetos

Costa e Silva Overpass
Credit Frentes Arquitetura Ltd.

Mooca Ipiranga
Credit Una Arquitetos

100 New Schools for Sao Paulo
Credit Nelson Kon

Praca das Artes
Credit Marcos Cartum

*Special thanks to
Raul Juste Lores*

Caracas

Mision Barrio Adentro
Credit Caracas Alcaldía Mayor,
Credit Ricky Burdett

Vertical Gym
Credit Urban Think Tank

San Rafael Upgrade
© Proyectos Arqui5 C.A.

Mision Alimentacion
Credit Ricky Burdett

Bogotá

Virgilio Barco Public Library
Credit Enrique Guzmán

El Tintal Public Library
Credit Enrique Guzmán

TransMilenio Bus System
Credit Fondacion Por el Pais
que Queremos

CicloRutas
Credit Fondacion Por el Pais
que Queremos

Mexico City

Centro de las Artes de los
Pueblos Indigenas
Credit Ten Arquitectos

FARO de Oriente
Credit Alberto Kalach

Brasil 44 Housing Project
Credit Higuera Sanchez

*Special thanks to
Pamela Puchalski*

Los Angeles

Culver City
Credit Eric Owen Moss
Architects

Grand Avenue Project
© The Related Companies

HS [aRT]
Credit LA Now Project

Los Angeles River
Revitalisation Master Plan
© 2006 City of Los Angeles,
Bureau of Engineering

New York City

BAM Cultural District
Credit Ten Arquitectos

Brooklyn Bridge Park
Courtesy Michael Van
Valkenburgh Associates

East River Master Plan
Courtesy SHoP Architects

High Line
Courtesy Field Operations

*Special thanks to
Pamela Puchalski*

Cairo

Al Azhar Park
Credit Gary Otte / Aga Khan
Trust for Culture

El Sawy Culturewheel
Courtesy El Sawy Cultural
Centre

Istanbul

Santral Istanbul
Credit Emre Arolat Architects /
Bilgi University Archives

Istanbul Modern Art Museum
Photo credit Murat Germen;
Rendering credit Tabanlioglu
Architects

Urban Transformation Plan for
Kartal
Credit Zaha Hadid Architects

Marmaray Trans-Bosphorus
Crossing
Credit DLH and Avrasyaconsult
Archive

Special thanks to Sevin Yildiz

Milan

Area Portello
Courtesy Comune di Milano

Garibaldi-Repubblica
Courtesy Comune di Milano

BEIC Biblioteca
Courtesy Comune di Milano

New Milan Fair
Courtesy Fondazione Fiera
Milano

Portello World Jewellery
Centre
Courtesy Comune di Milano

Parco Forlanini
Courtesy Comune di Milano

Regeneration of old Fair Zone
Courtesy Fondazione Fiera
Milano

Parco Nord
Courtesy Comune di Milano

Parco Cave
Courtesy Comune di Milano

Montecity-Rogoredo
Courtesy Risanamento SpA
– Gruppo Zunino

Special thanks to Paolo Riganti

Turin

Olympic Village Turin 2006
© Claudio Agnese

La Spina
© Michele d'Ottavio

Venaria
© Pino dell'Aquila
© Progetto La Venaria Reale

*Special thanks to
Gaia Caramellino*

London

Brixton Square (100 Public
Places)
Credit Grossmax

Victoria Embankment Gardens
(100 Public Places)
Credit MacCormac Jamieson
Prichard

Exhibition Road (100 Public
Places)
Credit Dixon Jones

Olympics Master Plan
© EDAW consortium

White City
© OMA

City East
Courtesy Greater London
Authority

Barcelona

Gran Via—Zona Franca
Courtesy Barcelona Regional

Sants – Montjuic
Courtesy Barcelona Regional

22@ Glories
Courtesy Barcelona Regional

Sagrera
Courtesy Barcelona Regional

The Forum
Courtesy Barcelona Regional

Special thanks to Eva Serra

Tokyo

Nihonbashi bridge
© Tsukamoto Lab. Tokyo
Institute of Technology
© Nihonbashi Michi no Keikan
wo Kangaeru Kondankai

Fiber City
© Ohno Lab. University of Tokyo

Haneda Airport Extension
© Tsukamoto Lab. Tokyo
Institute of Technology

Kanda River
© Bureau of Construction of
Tokyo
© Tsukamoto Lab. Tokyo
Institute of Technology

Marunouchi redevelopment
© JR East

Cool island project
© Tokyo Ministry of the
Environment

*Special thanks to
Atelier Bow-Wow,
Akinori Hattori, Miguel Kanai*

Mumbai

Kharghar Station
Credit City and Industrial
Development Corporation of
Maharashtra Ltd.

Chikhalwadi Sanitiation
Credit Vistaar Architects and
Planners

Worli Bandra Sea Link
Courtesy UDRI

Special thanks to UDRI

Shanghai

Low-cost Workers' Housing
Courtesy Vanke

YanAn Lu Park
Courtesy Shanghai Greenery
Management Bureau

Expo 2010
Courtesy Professor Zheng
Shiling

Dongtan Island Masterplan
Credit Arup

Ring Road Park
Courtesy Shanghai Landscape
Design Institute

Taikang Lu Renovation
Courtesy SURV

*Special thanks to
Stephan Jentsch, Frank Wu,
Zheng Shiling*

Film notes and stills prepared
by Cassim Shepard

Urban project coordination
support by Giorgio Agostoni
and Emily Smith

Light on the city

It is said that light is the nervous system of contemporary civilization. A Biennale dedicated to the city and the close links between architecture and society could not but welcome its visitors with a luminous sign. The Info Light Box by Targetti was conceived for this purpose: to welcome them and guide them through the event. Images, videos and performances of chromatic and dynamic light and information relating to the main content of the 10th International Architecture Exhibition will scroll across the sides of this big cube of light, consisting of more than 80,000 leds.

The iridescent structure of the Info Light Box metaphorically takes up the central theme of this Biennale dedicated to the *City. Architecture and Society* by recognizing the indefinable nature and constant mutation of the contemporary metropolis, within which architecture and new technologies play an essential role, especially in terms of relations and communications.

Designed by Pino Brugellis as a highly distinctive architectural element and, at the same time, an innovative vector of multimedia communication, the Info Light Box is a modular structure in steel supporting a translucent external coating in alveolar polycarbonate. The technological innovation of the product lies mainly in the use of hexel™ (hexagonal pixel) technology. This ensures excellent perception of the images at considerable distances and high luminosity compared to traditional screens, despite using a smaller number of pixels. Its main design feature is that it can be connected without any visible join to a potentially unlimited number of modular panels controlled by the same software. This is compatible with all the most widely used graphic programmes and configured in self-supporting structures, highlighting new possibilities in a specifically architectural and multimedia use of light.

The Florentine company, Targetti, has become a synonym for the 'architectural culture of light' around the world thanks to its almost 80 years' experience in the field of architectural lighting. As a partner of the 10th International Architecture Exhibition, it has also installed the lighting for the Italian Pavilion, the Corderie, the Artiglierie, the Tese and the exhibitions in the Palermo section, putting its most innovative products at the disposal of the Biennale. These are the result of constant investments in research and development, for years the highest of any company in the sector.

The partnership with the Biennale di Venezia is part of a policy of investment in the promotion and appreciation of the most innovative expressions of design culture pursued by Targetti for more than a decade through the work of the Fondazione Targetti. This is expressed in a programme of advanced specialization for professionals interested in using light as an architectural building tool (the Lighting Academy) and in a cycle of meetings with the leading exponents of contemporary architectural thinking and procedures (the Osservatorio sull'architettura).

Targetti Info Light Box

PROJECT
Pino Brugellis

ENGINEERING
UT Targetti
(supervision Pio Nahum)

TECHNOLOGY
SmartsLab (design:
Tom Barker, Royal
College of Art, Londra)

VIDEO EDITING
Emiliano Morgia

CONTACTS
Stella Targetti and
Consuelo de Gara

Risanamento.
A new vision of the city.

As everyone knows it is big architectural and urban projects that make a city more modern and liveable. This is the underlying theme of the 10th International Architecture Exhibition entitled "Cities. Architecture and Society", organized by the Biennale di Venezia in conjunction with its main partner Risanamento. The partnership is by no means a coincidence. Risanamento distinguishes itself on the Italian and International real estate scene for developing excellent urban projects, whose objective is to improve the quality of life in the city thanks to architecture and design. In Venice, Risanamento will display two extraordinary projects that will contribute significantly to Milan's evolution: the refurbishment of the former Falck area, where Renzo Piano has managed to combine suggestive industrial ruins and futuristic High Houses surrounded by nature, and the ideal city of Milano Santa Giulia, an ambitious project in which Norman Foster will give life to a city within a city. Come to Venice. Discover how the work of a big Group can improve the life of a big city. **La Biennale di Venezia, from 10th September to 19th November 2006.**

Main Partner of the 10th International Architecture Exhibition

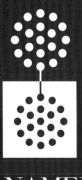

RISANAMENTO

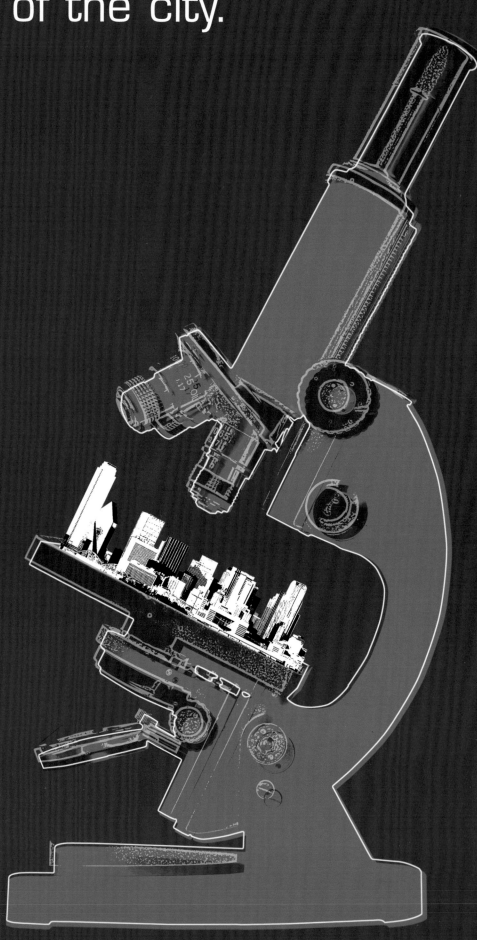

Inarcassa & La Biennale di Venezia

Inarcassa is the National Social Security and Welfare Fund for engineers and architects who work solely in a self-employed capacity.
Since 1995 it is a private association, financially and managerially autonomous, based on a statute approved by the supervising ministers.

Associates are 130,000, the number of pensions paid is 12,000.
Inarcassa pays out pensions to its members (old age, retirement, disablement, disability, revertible, indirect pensions) and guarantees assistance supplies (property mortgages, subsidies, health care policies) and further services and agreements for supporting this profession.

Board of Directors
Arch. Paola Muratorio (President)
Ing. Mauro Di Martino (Vice President)

Ing. Mario Cassano
Ing. Massimo D'Onofrio
Ing. Claudio Guanetti
Ing. Franco Gidoni
Ing. Giuliano Mazzaglia
Ing. Enrico Giuseppe Oriella
Arch. Enrico Rudella
Arch. Giuseppe Santoro
Arch. Guido Tassoni

Offices
Via Salaria 229, 00199 Roma
Tel. 06.852741
Fax 06.85274211
Call Center 06.8527330

www.inarcassa.it

*inar*CASSA
Cassa Nazionale di Previdenza ed Assistenza
per gli Ingegneri ed Architetti Liberi Professionisti

Contributing to the growth of this profession
not only through economic reforms, which are necessary, but also giving space to the culture and ideas of young people, to the role of design as a tool to improve the quality of urban life and the social wellbeing of town dwellers. This is the reason for the partecipation of Inarcassa, the architects and engineers National Insurance Fund, as main sponsor of the X International Architecture Exhibition of the Venice Biennale. Therefore, social security does not only mean safeguarding the Fund accounts in the long term in order to safeguard the young people's pensions, asking for economic reforms capable of innovating our productive sectors and modernizing the university system, demanding that architecture and town planning put design in the forefront and reform competitions so as to give young people the hope to enter the professional world permanently. It also means giving space to ideas, to culture, to the most innovative projects from Italy and Europe, so as to give professionals a wider perspective of their activity.

Progetto grafico, Giuseppe Mazzotti

Engineers and Architects in the design of the future town

20th October 2006
Teatro Piccolo Arsenale
h. 9,30

Conference
organization
Leonardo Fiori

Round table
coordination
Philippe Daverio

la Biennale di Venezia

10. Mostra Internazionale di Architettura

>> MOROSO SPA
CAVALICCO/UDINE/ITALY
T +39 0432 577111
INFO@MOROSO.IT
WWW.MOROSO.IT
>> MILANO SHOWROOM
VIA PONTACCIO 8/10
T +39 02 72016336

>> FJORD, ARMCHAIR
BY PATRICIA URQUIOLA
PHOTOGRAPHED IN THE
NORDIC COUNTRIES PAVILION
AT GIARDINI OF
LA BIENNALE DI VENEZIA

MOROSO

SPONSOR OF THE 10TH INTERNATIONAL
ARCHITECTURE EXHIBITION

PHOTO ALESSANDRO PADERNI
AD DESIGNWORK

la Biennale di Venezia
10. Mostra
Internazionale
di Architettura

Printed by
Offset Print Veneta - Verona
for Marsilio Editori® s.p.a. in Venice

edizione   anno

10 9 8 7 6 5 4 3 2 1   2006 2007 2008 2009 2010